MW00782375

Contributions to Phenomenology

In Cooperation with The Center for Advanced Research in Phenomenology

Volume 112

Scope

The purpose of the series is to serve as a vehicle for the pursuit of phenomenological research across a broad spectrum, including cross-over developments with other fields of inquiry such as the social sciences and cognitive science. Since its establishment in 1987, *Contributions to Phenomenology* has published more than 100 titles on diverse themes of phenomenological philosophy. In addition to welcoming monographs and collections of papers in established areas of scholarship,the series encourages original work in phenomenology. The breadth and depth of the Series reflects the rich and varied significance of phenomenological thinking for seminal questions of human inquiry as well as the increasingly international reach of phenomenological research.

All books to be published in this Series will be fully peer-reviewed before final acceptance.

The series is published in cooperation with The Center for Advanced Research in Phenomenology.

More information about this series at http://www.springer.com/series/5811

Rodney K. B. Parker

Editor

The Idealism-Realism Debate Among Edmund Husserl's Early Followers and Critics

 Springer

Editor
Rodney K. B. Parker (iD)
Faculty of Philosophy
Dominican University College
Ottawa, ON, Canada

ISSN 0923-9545   ISSN 2215-1915   (electronic)
Contributions to Phenomenology
ISBN 978-3-030-62158-2   ISBN 978-3-030-62159-9   (eBook)
https://doi.org/10.1007/978-3-030-62159-9

This Springer imprint is published by the registered company Springer Nature Switzerland AG
The registered company address is: Gewerbestrasse 11, 6330 Cham, Switzerland

Contents

Contributors

Michele Averchi (b. 1981) is associate professor in the School of Philosophy at the Catholic University of America. After earning his Ph.D. from the University of Milan, Michele held a post-doc at the Husserl Archives in Cologne. His research focuses on Husserlian phenomenology and early phenomenology, particularly Max Scheler and Moritz Geiger, with a strong interest in the phenomenology of the self.

Kimberly Baltzer-Jaray (b. 1977) is a sessional lecturer in both Philosophy and Social Justice and Peace Studies at King's University College, University of Western Ontario. Her main area of research is the philosophy of Adolf Reinach. She is a co-founder of the North American Society for Early Phenomenology (NASEP), a founding member of Forum Münchener Phänomenologie International (FMPI), and an associate editor for Journal of Camus Studies.

Mariano Crespo (b. 1966) is professor of philosophy at the University of Navarra, Spain. He has been professor at the International Academy of Philosophy, Liechtenstein, and the Catholic University of Chile, and visiting scholar at the Husserl Archives, KU Leuven, the Phenomenology Research Center, Southern Illinois University, and the Center for Subjectivity Research, University of Copenhagen. He is the author of *Das Verzeihen. Eine philosophische Untersuchung* (Winter 2002) and *Die Person im Kontext von Moral und Sozialität* (Bautz 2016).

Daniel O. Dahlstrom (b. 1948) is John R. Silber professor of philosophy at Boston University. He is the author of several books, collections, and articles, including *Identity, Authenticity, and Humility* (Marquette University Press 2017), *The Heidegger Dictionary* (Bloomsbury 2013), and *Heidegger's Concept of Truth* (Cambridge University Press 2001). He is also the translator of Husserl's *Ideas I* (Hackett 2014) and his latest collected edition is *Kant and His Contemporaries II* (Cambridge University Press 2018).

Daniele De Santis (b. 1983) is assistant professor of philosophy in the Department of Philosophy and Religious Studies at Charles University, Prague. His interests include Husserl and phenomenology, Kant, post-Kantian philosophy, and ancient Greek thought. His publications include *Derrida tra le fenomenologie: 1953–1967. La differenza e il trascendentale* (Mimesis 2018), as well as articles on Hermann Lotze, Jean Hering, Roman Ingarden and Maximilian Beck.

Denis Fisette (b. 1954) is professor of philosophy at the University of Quebec at Montreal. His areas of specialization are Austro-German philosophy in the nineteenth and twentieth centuries, classical phenomenology and contemporary philosophy of mind. His publications include *Lecture frégéenne de la phenomenology* (L'Eclat 1994), *Husserl's Logical Investigations reconsidered* (Springer 2003), *Themes from Brentano* (Brill 2013), *Philosophy from an Empirical Standpoint. Carl Stumpf as a Philosopher* (Brill 2015), *Franz Brentano Essais et conférences* (Vrin 2018).

Susan Gottlöber (b. 1976) is senior lecturer in philosophy at Maynooth University, Ireland. She completed her magister and Ph.D. studies at the TU Dresden with a Ph.D. on Nicholas of Cusa and interreligious toleration. She is currently vice-president of the Irish Philosophical Society. Her main research interests are philosophical anthropology with a focus on inter-subjectivity, individuality, embodiment, and human nature in relation to technology, philosophy of toleration, and value theory.

Burt C. Hopkins (b. 1954) is an associate member of the University of Lille, UMR-CNRS 8163 STL, former professor of philosophy at Seattle University, and permanent secretary of the Husserl Circle. He has been visiting professor at the University of Nanjing, The School for Advanced Studies in the Social Sciences and the Koyré Center, Paris; senior fellow at The Sidney M. Edelstein Center and The Hebrew University of Jerusalem, and researcher at The Institute of Philosophy, Czech Academy of Sciences.

Dalius Jonkus (b. 1965) is professor of philosophy at the Vytautas Magnus University, Kaunas, Lithuania. He is the president of the Lithuanian Society for Phenomenology and has published articles on Husserl, Heidegger, Ortega y Gasset, Merleau-Ponty, and Levinas. His publications include *Experience and Reflection* (Vytautas Magnus University Press 2009) and *The Philosophy of Vasily Sesemann* (Vytautas Magnus University Press 2015).

Ronny Miron (b. 1968) is professor of philosophy at Bar Ilan University. She is the author of *Karl Jaspers: From Selfhood to Being* (Brill 2012), *The Desire for Metaphysics* (Common Ground 2014), *The Angel of Jewish History* (Academic Studies 2014), *Husserl and Other Phenomenologists* (Routledge 2018) and *Hedwig Conrad-Martius: The Phenomenological Gateway to Reality* (Springer 2021). Her research focuses on existentialism, phenomenology, hermeneutics and Jewish thought.

Thomas Nemeth (b. 1950) is the author of numerous publications on Russian philosophy, Thomas has translated/edited Shpet's *Hermeneutics and Its Problems* (Springer 2019) as well as Shpet's treatise *Appearance and Sense* (Springer 1991) and Solov'ev's *Justification of the Moral Good* (Springer 2015). His book-length studies include *Kant in Imperial Russia* (Springer 2017). He has published in *Husserl Studies, Kant-Studien, Studies in East European Thought,* and elsewhere.

Rodney K. B. Parker (b. 1983) is assistant professor of philosophy at Dominican University College in Ottawa, Canada. He has been postdoctoral researcher at the Center for the History of Women Philosophers and Scientists, University of Paderborn, adjunct professor at the University of Western Ontario, and visiting scholar at the Husserl Archives, KU Leuven. His research focuses on Husserl's transcendental phenomenology and the history of the phenomenological movement.

Daniel R. Sobota (b. 1978) is associate professor at the Institute of Philosophy and Sociology, Polish Academy of Sciences. He is the author of *Źródła i inspiracje Heideggerowskiego pytania o bycie* (Yakiza 2012/13) and *Narodziny fenomenologii z ducha pytania. Johannes Daubert i fenomenologiczny rozruch* (IFiS PAN 2017). His research interests include metaphysics and nineteenth and twentieth century German philosophy, especially Heidegger and early phenomenology.

Genki Uemura (b. 1980) is associate professor at the Graduate School of Humanities and Social Sciences, Okayama University, Japan. He has been visiting researcher at the Husserl Archives, KU Leuven. His research fields include Husserl's phenomenology, the early phenomenology in Munich and Göttingen, and their opposition.

The Idealism-Realism Debate and the Great Phenomenological Schism

Rodney K. B. Parker

Abstract The following essay serves as a general introduction to the idealism-realism debate at the core of the schism between Edmund Husserl and the early adherents of his phenomenology. This debate centers around two core issues: (i) whether the "real" world exists independent from the mind, and (ii) whether epistemological idealism leads to metaphysical idealism. Husserl's early critics saw his transcendental phenomenology as a denial of the existence of mind-independent reality and as a solipsistic form of idealism. Husserl considered many of these arguments to be predicated on misinterpretations. After contextualizing the idealism-realism debate as it unfolded within the phenomenological movement, I introduce the papers that comprise the present volume. These papers revive the debate concerning Husserl's idealism among his mentors, peers, and students.

1   The Context

The present volume was inspired by the 2015 conference of the North American Society for Early Phenomenology, *The Great Phenomenological Schism: Reactions to Husserl's Transcendental Idealism*, which took place 3–6 June at the Universidad Nacional Autónoma de México in Mexico City. Some of the chapters herein are based on presentations given at that event. The aim of the conference was to better understand the reasons why many of Husserl's students and peers found his turn to idealism to be problematic. When preparing the call for papers, I chose to call that long moment around the publication of *Ideas I* in 1913 the "great phenomenological schism"[1] because it divided the phenomenological community between the

---

[1] Herbert Spiegelberg was the first to use the label "great schism" to describe the break between Husserl and the Munich phenomenologists: "Es ist schwer zu leugnen, daß auf den ersten Blick die Geschichte der deutsehen Phänomenologie das Bild hoffnungsloser Schismen darbietet. Das erste große Schisma war das zwischen Husserl in Freiburg und den sogenannten „Münchenern", das zwar oberflächlich bis zum Ende des Husserlschen Jahrbuchs im Jahr 1930 hinter dem gemeinsamen Titelblatt verborgen blieb, das aber ab 1929, als die Münchener die Mitarbeit an der Husserl-Festschrift verweigerten, unheilbar und offenkundig geworden war" (Spiegelberg 1982, p. 3).

R. K. B. Parker (✉)
Dominican University College, Ottawa, ON, Canada
e-mail: rodney.parker@dominicanu.ca

© Springer Nature Switzerland AG 2021   1
R. K. B. Parker (ed.), *The Idealism-Realism Debate Among Edmund Husserl's Early Followers and Critics*, Contributions to Phenomenology 112,
https://doi.org/10.1007/978-3-030-62159-9_1

orthodox Husserlians and the heretics,[2] or, as Husserl reportedly said to Dietrich von Hildebrand at the Vienna lecture, between the white sheep and the black sheep.[3] The conference organizers had noticed that while the *fact* of this division within the early phenomenological movement between the transcendental and the realist phenomenologists is well known, the details of the philosophical *arguments* against Husserl from the members of the movement have received scant attention in the scholarly literature. On what grounds and to what extent did the realist phenomenologists find Husserl's transcendental-phenomenological idealism to be untenable? Answering this question is not simply a matter of historical importance but of philosophical importance as well, particularly with the rise of speculative realism and its challenge to phenomenology. Today's speculative realism and object-oriented ontology is, perhaps, an unintentional revival of the early project of realist phenomenology.

Between 1905 and 1913 Husserl's phenomenology underwent an important transformation. We see this transformation reflected in documents such as his Seefeld manuscripts (Hua X; 1966, pp. 237–253, Hua XIII; 1973, pp. 1–3), the five lectures on *The idea of phenomenology* (Hua II; 1950) and the corresponding course on *Phenomenology and the critique of reason* – aka the 'Thing-lectures' (Hua XVI; 1973), the lectures on the *Basic problems of phenomenology* (Hua XIII; 1973, pp. 111–194), and *Ideas I* (Hua III/1; 1976). This was not some private affair – members of the phenomenological movement were privy to these changes in Husserl's phenomenology in personal conversation and through his lectures. With the discovery of the phenomenological reduction and after a serious reading of Kant,[4] Husserl's project moved away from the descriptive psychology of the *Logical Investigations* and the account of intentionality presented therein toward a form of transcendental idealism. This move to transcendental idealism baffled many of Husserl's students, and drew the ire of some of his contemporaries, particularly the Munich Circle and the School of Brentano. Central to the ensuing controversy among the phenomenologists was the meaning and implication of paragraph §49 of *Ideas I*, which seemed to deny the existence of reality apart from consciousness (though this must be understood in the context of the larger train of thought running from roughly §§46–62).

For many of Husserl's followers, particularly the members of the Munich Circle of phenomenologists, the turn to idealism was in stark contrast to the realism they saw in his *Logical Investigations*. It seems that they had read his refutation of psychologism in the *Prolegomena*, his talk of the intuition of essences (whether they be the essences of the objects of consciousness or the mental acts whereby we grasp such objects), and his plea to go back to the things-themselves in the Introduction to

---

[2] To borrow from Ricoeur 1967, p. 4.

[3] In his notes from an interview with Hildebrand at Fordham University in 1954, Spiegelberg writes: "Sees Husserl in 1935 (at the *Krisis* lecture): 'I divide up my students into white sheep and black sheep; you belong to the black sheep'" (Herbert Spiegelberg Papers, WUA00070/Box 2, Folder 9/070-NBK1953). The phrase "first" or "great phenomenological schism" has since become part of the common vernacular thanks to George Heffernan, whose paper from the conference in Mexico City has already been published (Heffernan 2016).

[4] See Hua XXIV; 1984, p. 449 and Kern 1964.

the *Investigations into phenomenology and the theory of knowledge*, as a move away from the primacy of the subject and a return to some variety of metaphysical realism.[5] Husserl's account of ideal objects and his attack on representationalism in the Second Logical Investigation became the sources for a Platonist interpretation of his phenomenology.[6] However, it seems that Husserl was never himself committed to realism, and that his early philosophical works trace the slow and methodical elucidation of what he came to see as the only possible consistent and rigorous philosophical position – *transcendental-phenomenological idealism*. Such a position seeks to reconcile the empirical reality of the world with the dependence of that reality on consciousness. By systematically investigating the field of transcendental subjectivity and the objects as they are constituted therein, Husserl's phenomenology attempted to argue from lived-experience to the conditions of the possibility of experience and the structures of consciousness.

Despite the backlash against *Ideas I*, Husserl did not relent or shrink from his proclamation of idealism. Instead, he doubled down on his convictions. He famously claimed in his Paris lectures that the genuine, systematic self-disclosure of the ego made possible by the phenomenological reduction "leads to a transcendental idealism, but one in a fundamentally new sense" (Hua I; 1973, p. 33), distinct from the psychologistic, subjective idealism of Berkeley (Hua XVII; 1974, p. 178) and the Kantian idealism plagued with nonsensical *things-in-themselves* (Hua I; 1973, p. 33, Hua VII; 1956, p. 235, Hua XXXVI; 2003, p. 66).[7] Large portions of Husserl's post-*Ideas* publications – such as *Formal and Transcendental Logic* (Hua XVII; 1974) and the *Cartesian Meditations* (Hua I; 1973) – attempted to clarify and defend his position against what he claimed were, for the most part, fundamental misunderstandings. In the 'Nachwort' to his *Ideas*, Husserl argues that the "scandal caused by this idealism and its alleged solipsism" impeded its reception. Yet, these objections would never have arisen given a deeper understanding and more thorough presentation of his transcendental-phenomenological idealism.

> I retract nothing whatsoever as regards transcendental-phenomenological idealism and that I still consider, as I did before, every form of the usual philosophical realism nonsensical in principle, no less so than that idealism which [realism] sets itself up against in its argumentations and which it "refutes." [...] [My transcendental-phenomenological idealism] is still anything but a party to the usual debates between idealism and realism, and so none of the objections found in their wrangling can affect it (Hua V; 1952, pp. 150–151).[8]

---

[5] Zahavi has argued that a realist reading of Husserl's account of intentionality in the *Prolegomena* is hard to square with the text (see Zahavi 2017, pp. 35–36 and Zahavi 1992).

[6] One might wonder how the students who took Husserl to be a realist understood his claims at the beginning of the Second Logical Investigation. There he writes that while he intends to defend the right of certain ideal objects "to be granted objective status alongside of individual (or real) objects," he adds that idealism alone – understood as "a theory of knowledge which recognizes the 'ideal' as a condition for the possibility of objective knowledge in general" – "represents the possibility of a self-consistent theory of knowledge" (Husserl 2001, p. 238).

[7] For more on the issue of things-in-themselves, see Luft 2007.

[8] Quoted here from Hua CW III; 1989, pp. 418–419. In his discussion of phenomenology as transcendental idealism in the *Sixth Cartesian Meditation*, Fink writes that, "Transcendental idealism is best characterized by the designation 'constitutive idealism'," and that this constitutive idealism is "beyond idealism and realism" understood in the mundane sense (Fink 1988, p. 159).

However, the aim of this volume is *not* to present Husserl's arguments or defend the thesis of transcendental idealism – that "the existence of real objects, and thus the existence of the real world, is unthinkable without reference to a consciousness that is currently experiencing them"[9] – *per se*.

This volume has two aims. The first is to sketch the interpretive framework proper to unpacking the meaning of Husserl's thesis of transcendental idealism by placing it in its historical context. The image of the philosopher as a solitary figure is misleading, and reading Husserl in isolation, removed from the active intellectual community he was engaged with, does not do his philosophical project justice. His thought was influenced by and articulated in response to the thinkers he encountered through books, letters, and conversation. As interpreters of his work, we do both Husserl and ourselves a grave disservice by neglecting these interlocutors.[10] The papers in this volume revive the dialogue between Husserl and his mentors, peers, and students; a dialogue that, in large part, took shape as a chapter in the idealism-realism debate. Assessing these criticisms helps us to better understand and evaluate Husserl's rebuttals and thus the position they were meant to explain. They might also reveal good philosophical reasons for rejecting or amending Husserl's position, or transcendental idealism more broadly. The second is to understand the positions of the other early phenomenologists with respect to the idealism-realism debate. By doing so, we can begin to assess whether their arguments are of value to contemporary philosophical discussions.

---

[9] "Sie besagt, dass die Existenz von realen Gegenständen und damit die Existenz der realen Welt nicht denkbar ist ohne Bezug auf ein aktuell erfahrendes Bewusstsein" (Hua XXXVI; 2003, p. ix). Translations from German throughout are those of the author unless otherwise indicated.

[10] That we will inevitably understand Husserl better if we read him in context is perhaps obviously true to some. But for those who are not engaged with the current historical orientation in phenomenological scholarship, the importance of a volume like the present one will need some justification. To that end, I will make a brief appeal to contemporary literature in early modern philosophy as an example. Few could claim to be a serious scholar of Locke, Leibniz, or Descartes if they were not also aware of Molyneux, Clarke, or Princess Elizabeth. Not only would the average early modern specialist recognize these names, they would also be able to concisely state their arguments vis-à-vis the "canonical" figures. Moreover, no one baulks at a paper on Suarez, Malebranche, or Bayle. Yet few phenomenologists take seriously the importance of research on Lotze, Pfänder, or Geiger. This ahistorical bias is conspicuous in phenomenology, given that the continental tradition is so steeped in contextualization. Much of the scholarly context surrounding Husserl's work remains unexplored and relatively little attention has been paid to the debates that Husserl was directly involved in. This despite evidence that Husserl openly invited criticism from his students. At least two instances of this are well known. First, there is the following note from Edith Stein to Roman Ingarden, dated 20 February 1917: "Recently, I presented to the Master, quite solemnly actually, my reservations about idealism. It was not at all an "awkward situation" (as you feared). I was seated on one end of the dear old leather sofa and then we had 2 h of heated debate, naturally without either side convincing the other. The Master said he is not at all opposed to changing his point of view if someone proves to him it is necessary. So far, I have not succeeded" (Stein 2014, p. 48). Second, in *Thing and Space*, Husserl devotes an entire lecture to responding to his student Heinrich Hofmann's objections regarding the distinction between 'things' and 'appearances' in the framework of the phenomenological reduction (Hua XVI; 1973, p. 144).

As mentioned above, the intended aim of this volume is not to defend Husserl's idealism. Nor is it to defend realist phenomenology as an alternative to transcendental phenomenology.[11] It is well-known that many of the early phenomenologists have been branded, or branded themselves, as metaphysical *realists*.[12] Zahavi and others have questioned whether realist phenomenology should be considered a form of phenomenology at all.[13] In refusing the transcendental reduction, realist phenomenology seemingly breaks with the principle of *correlationism*,[14] which is crucial to Husserlian phenomenology. This is not to say, however, that the works of the realist phenomenologists are without value or should be ignored. Not only can these writings help Husserl scholars in their attempts to interpret and defend the Master, but those figures make interesting arguments and contribute

---

[11] It is an open secret within the phenomenological community that the two most famous historians of phenomenology, Karl Schuhmann and Herbert Spiegelberg, were anti-Husserlian and preferred realist phenomenology. During his tenure at the Husserl Archives in Leuven, Schuhmann is known to have claimed that Husserl did not write anything of value after 1901. Robin Rollinger, one of Schuhmann's students, reports that he and Schuhmann shared the view that the quality of Husserl's work continually decreased after writing "Intentional Objects" (Hua XXII; 1979, pp. 303–384) in 1894. Rollinger quips: "It is an indeed ironic (the 'cunning of reason', as Schuhmann once said) that I was involved in editing Hua XXXVI" (Rollinger to Parker, 18 July 2019). It should go without saying that not all historians of the phenomenological movement share these views concerning Husserl's work, nor the hopes for realist phenomenology held by many.

[12] They are similarly branded (pejoratively) as Platonists (see Baltzer-Jaray 2009). We should be cautious here, however, not to conflate *early* phenomenology with *realist* phenomenology. While many of the early phenomenologists who studied with Theodor Lipps and Alexander Pfänder in Munich prior to studying with Husserl in Göttingen and Freiburg were realists, this is certainly not true of all the early phenomenologists. For an attempt at a genealogical definition and periodization of early phenomenology, see Moran and Parker 2015. One of the purposes of the definition given therein was to show that "early phenomenology" and "realist phenomenology" are not synonyms and, additionally, to discourage the use of the misleading term "Munich-Göttingen phenomenology" introduced by Theodor Conrad that has long been criticized (see Smid 1982, p. 112).

[13] Zahavi raised this question, directed at Hedwig Conrad-Martius' phenomenology, during his lecture on "Husserl's Transcendental Idealism" at KU Leuven, 26 April 2017.

[14] While Quentin Meillassoux did not coin the term "correlationism," his writings on speculative realism have certainly popularized it. In *After Finitude*, he defines *correlationism* as "the idea according to which we only ever have access to the correlation between thinking and being, and never to either term considered apart from the other," and claims that "every philosophy which disavows naïve realism has become a variant of correlationism" (Meillassoux 2008, p. 5). He ascribes this view to Husserl, Heidegger, and Kant (Meillassoux 2008, p. 8). Meillassoux further elaborates the notion of correlationism in his presentation at the workshop on speculative realism at Goldsmiths, University of London: "Correlationism rests on an argument as simple as it is powerful, and which can be formulated in the following way: No X without givenness of X, and no theory about X without a positing of X. If you speak about something, you speak about something that is given to you, and posited by you. Consequently, the sentence: 'X is', means: 'X is the correlate of thinking' in a Cartesian sense. That is: X is the correlate of an affection, or a perception, or a conception, or of any subjective act. To be is to be a correlate, a term of a correlation. And in particular, when you claim to think any X, you must posit this X, which cannot then be separated from this special act of positing, of conception. That is why it is impossible to conceive an absolute X, i.e., an X which would be essentially separate from a subject. We can't know what the reality of the object in itself is because we can't distinguish between properties which are supposed to belong to the object and properties belonging to the subjective access to the object" (Brassier et al. 2007, p. 409).

important philosophical insights of their own on a variety of topics.[15] Moreover, the idealism-realism debate within the early phenomenological movement anticipates the current one between phenomenology and speculative realism – a realism that positions itself in direct opposition to post-Kantian correlationism.

2   The Debate

A prominent philosophical debate at the turn of the twentieth century was the one between idealism and realism. This debate was born in the eighteenth century, primarily in response to the writings of Leibniz and Berkeley, and dominated the landscape of German philosophy following Kant's *Critique of Pure Reason*.[16] The various idealist positions that arose in the wake of Kant's Copernican turn and the attacks against them (here we can think of Schulze and Fichte, Hegel and Fries, Beneke and Herbart, Trendelenburg and Fischer, etc.) gave rise to a series of philosophical problems and disputes that serve as the backdrop against which the great phenomenological schism took place.[17]

In order to understand this debate, we must first define what we mean by philosophical idealism. Though there are as many varieties of idealism as there are idealists, broadly speaking, all such positions share in common some take on at least one of two theses:

1. Even if the possibility of the existence of something independent of the mind is conceded, we can have no knowledge of such a mind-independent reality. All we can know are the mind and its contents.
2. Consciousness is the ultimate foundation of what we call reality, or that nothing exists independently of the mind.

The first thesis is often called *epistemological* idealism, while the latter expresses what we call *metaphysical* idealism. Commenting on this distinction as it was understood in German philosophy at the turn of the twentieth century, Josiah Royce explains:

> In its "epistemological" sense idealism involves a theory of the *nature of our human knowledge*; and various decidedly different theories are called by this name in view of one common feature, namely, the stress that they lay upon the "subjectivity" of a larger of smaller portion of what pretends to be our knowledge of things. In this sense, Kant's theory of the subjectivity of space and time was called by himself a "Transcendental Idealism." But in its

---

[15] See, for example, Scheler 1973a, 1980; Pfänder 1913, 1916, 1967; Ingarden 1973; Stein 1989, 2000; Geiger 1986.

[16] Concerning whether there were any pre-Cartesian idealists, see, for example, Burnyeat 1982; Hibbs 2005, 2009; Dunham et al. 2011. For a detailed overview of the history of the use of the term "idealism" from the 18th to the early twentieth century, see Guyer and Horstmann 2018.

[17] For useful discussions of this period and its problems, see Beiser 2002, 2013, 2014.

"metaphysical" sense, idealism is a theory as to *the nature of the real world*, however we may come to know that nature (Royce 1896, pp. 12–13).

The epistemological idealist places emphasis on the undeniable role of the subject with respect to our knowledge of things, whereas the metaphysical idealist insists that the nature of all reality is fundamentally dependent upon consciousness (either individual consciousness, collective consciousness, or a Divine consciousness).

Royce's source for the distinction between epistemological (*erkenntnistheoretischer*) and metaphysical (*metaphysischer*) idealism was the German historian of philosophy Richard Falckenberg. Falckenberg had studied with Hermann Lotze, Rudolf Eucken, and Kuno Fischer.[18] Like the histories published by Fischer and Friedrich Ueberweg, Falckenberg's was a popular text on the history of philosophy.[19] His classification of the different forms of idealism reflects a general scheme we see in many writings from this time. Falckenberg further distinguishes between three forms of *metaphysical* idealism:

(i) Those who deny that there is a real difference between matter (*hyle*) and ideas (*eidos*).
(ii) Those who deny that existence of a material external world is merely an illusion but believe that it is the *product* in some sense of the mind. (Here he includes the *subjective* idealism of Fichte, the *objective* idealism of Schelling, and the *absolute* idealism of Hegel.)
(iii) Those who deny the existence of the material world and argue that there is only a world of appearance, i.e., ideas in minds. (Here he includes Berkeley and Leibniz.)[20]

Husserl's own writings seem to confirm roughly this same schema of classification for the idealist philosophers, that is, between the German idealists, Berkeley,

---

[18] See the *Lebenslauf* in Falckenberg's *Aufgabe und Wesen der Erkenntnis bei Nicolaus von Kues* (Falckenberg 1880, p. 45). For more on his relationship to Lotze's philosophy, see Woodward 2015.

[19] Fischer's *Geschichte der neuern Philosophie* (first published as Fischer 1854–77) famously formalized the empiricism/rationalism distinction. Ueberweg's *Grundriss der Geschichte der Philosophie* (first published as Ueberweg 1863–71) was a standard textbook for the history of philosophy.

[20] „Idealismus […] in *metaphysischer* Bedeutung 1. Anerkennung eines Geistigen (Ideellen), Nichtmateriellen überhaupt, Gegensatz Materialismus (es gibt kein von der Materie unterscheidenes Geistiges). 2. Überordnung des Geistes über die Materie oder die Natur, Erklärung des materiellen Daseins aus dem Geiste (des Seins aus dem Denken S. 331), Annahme eines geistigen Weltgründes, ohne daß die Existenz der Körperwelt zu bloßem Schein herabgesetzt würde; in diesem Sinne – die Materie ein Produkt des (Welt-)Geistes – faßt man Fichte, Schelling, Hegel und ihre Genossen unter den Namen der idealistischen Schule zusammen. (Gewöhnlich wird der Standpunkt Fichtes als subjectiver, der Schellings als objectiver, der Hegels als absoluter Idealismus bezeichnet. […] Jedenfalls ist der Fichtesche Idealismus ebenso absolut, wie der Hegelsche, denn das Ich ist nicht der Einzelgeist, sondern die Weltvernunft […].) 3. Leugnung der materiellen Welt = Immaterialismus, Spiritualismus, die Lehre, daß es nur Geister gebe, die Körper aber nichts seinen als Erscheinungen, Vorstellungen (Ideen) in den Geistern […]" (Falckenberg 1886, p. 476).

and Leibniz (the *metaphysical* idealists) and the Kantians (the *epistemological* idealists).[21] Part of the initial reaction to Husserl's idealism was, as a result, to determine into which of these two silos his position should be placed. Husserl was himself, to some degree, interested in identifying his idealist heritage as well.

The idealism-realism debate centers around two core issues: (i) whether the "real" world exists independent from the mind, and (ii) whether *epistemological* idealism requires or necessarily leads to *metaphysical* idealism. Opponents of metaphysical idealism claim that such a view entails the scandalous and absurd result that there is no mind-independent external world. The idealist, on the other hand, believes that realism is question-begging regarding external reality, and that only the idealist can offer an account of external reality without appealing to metaphysical speculation or dogmatism.[22] Max Scheler, in his article *Idealism and Realism* (Scheler 1927/28),[23] divides these issues into a large suite of problems: the problem of evidence, the relationship between being and knowledge, the problem of the transcendence of objects, the two-worlds problem, the problem of the relativity or contingency of being, the problem of different types of knowledge, the problem of the *a priori*, and the various problems concerning the notion of "reality." All these problems come to bear upon the position Husserl advocated in his lectures and publications from 1907 onward, which, according to Roman Ingarden, was constructed around the fundamental thesis that:

> what is real is nothing but a constituted noematic unity (individual) of a special kind of sense which in its being and quality (*Sosein*) results from a set of experiences of a special kind and is quite impossible without them. Entities of this kind exist only for the pure transcendental ego which experiences such a set of perceptions. The existence of what is

---

[21] Falckenberg's work was familiar to Husserl. In a 1901 letter to Gustav Albrecht, Husserl writes: "a number of professorships became vacant this semester: Erlangen, Basel, Vienna. Stumpf certainly thought he could place me at Erlangen because he has connections there. (Falckenberg, the well-known author of the textbook on the history of modern philosophy, owes Stumpf for his appointment to Erlangen.) Stumpf immediately wrote to Falckenberg, but did not receive a response" (Hua Dok III/9; 1994, pp. 22–23). Husserl also owned a copy of the fourth edition of Falckenberg's history, which can be found in the Husserl Archives Leuven under the signature BQ 131.

[22] In the contemporary idealism-realism debate, the realist is thought to fall prey to the "correlationist circle," that is, insofar as we never have access to the *things-in-themselves* in thought, only the *things-for-us*, the realist enters into a vicious circle with respect to claims about the supposed *things-in-themselves* (Meillassoux 2008, p. 5). As Tom Sparrow explains: "Thinking the absolute effectively renders the absolute relative to thought, and therefore undermines its absoluteness. Whenever the realist philosopher claims to have attained knowledge of the subject-independent in itself, what he or she does is engage in a viciously circular pragmatic contradiction that effectively converts the thing in itself into a concept of the thing in itself" (Sparrow 2014, p. 90). According to Meillassoux, the weak version of correlationism asserts that we cannot *know* the things-in-themselves, whereas the strong version claims that we cannot even *conceive* of things-in-themselves, i.e., things-in-themselves are meaningless and nonsensical speculative fictions. On the strong view, the things-for-us are not representations – they simply are *the things-themselves*, and hence the strong view leads to some form of idealism (see Harman 2018, pp. 142–144).

[23] For the English translation, see Scheler 1973b.

perceived (of the perceived as such) is nothing "in itself" (*an sich*) but only something "for somebody," for the experiencing ego (Ingarden 1975, p. 21).[24]

Although the controversy concerning the existence of the external world – an issue to which Ingarden himself devoted two volumes[25] – was at the core of the idealism-realism debate, Husserl's critics also took aim at his concept of the pure ego, the reductions, and the metaphysical neutrality thesis.

In addition to Scheler's essay mentioned above, we find a flourishing of publications by members of the phenomenological movement that touch upon the idealism-realism debate in the late 1920s and early 1930s. Many of them deal specifically with the place of Husserl's transcendental phenomenology in this debate. One of the earliest is Jean Hering's appendix on "The Primacy of Consciousness according to §49 of Husserl's *Ideas*" in *Phénoménologie et philosophie religieuse* (Hering 1925, pp. 83–86).[26] This was followed by Theodor Celms' *Der phänomenologische Idealismus Husserls* (Celms 1928),[27] Ingarden's contribution to the *Husserl-Festschrift*, "Bemerkungen zum Problem 'Idealismus-Realismus'" (Ingarden 1929),[28] and Geiger's *Die Wirklichkeit der Wissenschaften und die Metaphysik* (Geiger 1930),[29] to name only a few.

The essays in this edition do not cover all the works related to the idealism-realism debate in the early phenomenological movement or the related texts by Husserl's Neo-Kantian contemporaries. To survey all the writings produced on either side of the great phenomenological schism would require several volumes. Some of the early critical responses to Husserl's transcendental-phenomenological idealism are familiar in name, even if the details of the arguments are not. Husserl scholars will be aware of the critical remarks in Carl Stumpf's posthumously

---

[24] Robert Sokolowski offers a harsh critical review of Ingarden's interpretation of Husserl (Sokolowski 1977). One of the issues Sokolowski takes up is whether *constitution* amounts to *creation*.

[25] See Ingarden 2013, 2016. A third volume of this work was still in progress at the time of Ingarden's death.

[26] It would be interesting to compare what Hering writes in this appendix with Conrad-Martius' 1916 manuscript "Über Ontologie" (published in Parker 2020b), the only extant version of which comes from Hering's personal papers, as well as Hering's own 1917 manuscript "Phänomenologie als Grundlage der Metaphysik?"(Hering 2015). These manuscripts give us some of the earliest insights into the reactions of the Göttingen Circle to Husserl's idealism.

[27] Reprinted in Celms 1993. This work is famous for its argument that Husserl's idealism cannot escape solipsism. See Parker 2020a and Vēgners 2020.

[28] Unlike Scheler's similarly titled essay, Ingarden focuses on the idealism-realism problem as it emerges in Husserl's *Ideas I*. In his personal copy of the *Festschrift* (ZS 28/Festschrift), Husserl placed question marks in the margin beside the following passage by Ingarden, which references *Ideas I* §49: "Die rein intentionale Gegenständlichkeit ist in sich selbst eigentlich ein Nichts, sie hat kein *Eigen* wesen im strengen Sinne, wie E. Husserl mit vollem Rechte in seinen „Ideen" behauptet. Alle ihre existentialen, formalen und materialen Bestimmtheiten sind „bloß vermeint", sie sind ihr nicht wahrhaft immanent. Die rein intentionale Gegenständlichkeit täuscht nur ihre Immanenz dank der intentionalen Vermeinung vor: sie hat eben kein Seinsfundament in sich" (Ingarden 1929, p. 166). Husserl underlines the word "*täuscht*" as indicated here.

[29] See, for example, Geiger's discussion of Husserl's "constitutive idealism" (Geiger 1930, p. 67).

published *Erkenntnislehre* (Stumpf 1939),[30] the works of Heinrich Rickert's students, Rudolf Zocher (Zocher 1932) and Friedrich Kreis (Kreis 1930), to whom Eugen Fink famously responded on Husserl's behalf (Fink 1970), and Georg Misch's *Lebensphilosophie und Phänomenologie* (Misch 1930).[31] None of these works are discussed in the present volume. Nor are some of the less well-known criticisms, such as those found in Hans Lipps' *Untersuchungen zur Phänomenologie derErkenntnis*(Lipps 1927/28),[32] Paul F. Linke's essay "Gegenstandsphänomenologie" (Linke 1930),[33] Maximilian Beck in *Die neue Problemlage der Erkenntnistheorie* (Beck 1928),[34] or Hans Cornelius in *Transcendentale Systematik* (Cornelius 1916).[35] We have also had to leave out discussions of the more positive (though not uncritical) reception of Husserl's idealism found in the works of Dietrich Mahnke, Emmanuel Levinas, Dorion Cairns, Aron Gurwitsch, and others.[36] Husserl's defenders deserve to be acknowledged in equal measure with his detractors. Issues of space aside, one might wonder why essays dealing with some more prominent figures have been excluded from the present volume in favor of lesser known ones. One reason is that such essays can already be easily found elsewhere, as I have indicated in my notes. The second is to emphasize just how far-reaching the idealism-realism debate was. It is no exaggeration to say that the idealism

---

[30] See specifically Stumpf's "Kritik der Husserlschen Phänomenologie" (Stumpf 1939, pp. 188–200). For a discussion of Stumpf's criticisms, see Rollinger 1999, pp. 114–122.

[31] For a discussion of Husserl's confrontation with Misch, see Sandmeyer 2009.

[32] Reprinted in Lipps 1976. For a discussion of Lipps' criticism of Husserl's idealism, see Calenge 2015.

[33] See especially the section on "Gegenstandsphänomenologie gegen Aktphänomenologie" (Linke 1930, pp. 79–84). In this essay, Linke distinguishes between object-oriented phenomenology, that is, a phenomenology of the grasped object, and act-oriented phenomenology, that is, a phenomenology of the act wherein the intentional object is grasped.

[34] In the opening lines of this essay, Beck identifies Husserl as espousing "correlationism [*Korrelativismus*]," where there is no world that exists independent of consciousness *per se* and where consciousness and the world mutually dependent on one another for their existence (Beck 1928, p. 611).

[35] Cornelius was himself a member of the Munich Circle of phenomenologists, though not a particularly active one (Rollinger 1991, p. 34). His criticisms of Husserl were an influence on his student, Theodor Adorno. See Adorno 1940.

[36] It is also worth mentioning that Aron Gurwitsch's reading of Husserl influenced his student Henry E. Allison's epistemological interpretation of Kant. As Allison has stated regarding his *epistemological* interpretation of Kant's transcendental idealism: "my view of Kant's idealism was influenced by my understanding of Husserl's, though I was never what you could call a close student of Husserl. I never took a course on Husserl with Gurwitsch, but I did take a two-semester course on Husserl's theory of intentionality with Cairns [...]." (Allison to Parker, 21 January 2015) This will perhaps come to the surprise of Kant scholars unfamiliar with Allison's early paper "The Critique of Pure Reason as Transcendental Phenomenology" (Allison 1974). The first edition of Allison's monumental work *Kant's Transcendental Idealism* (Allison 1983) is dedicated to "the memory of Aron Gurwitsch, with whom I began my study of Kant," though he is critical of some aspects of Gurwitch's interpretation of Kant. See Allison 1992. Nevertheless, Husserl scholars would benefit from applying Allison's analysis of Kant's transcendental idealism to Husserl's.

controversy was one of the central issues in phenomenology during Husserl's lifetime, and it was not limited to the members of the Munich and Göttingen Circles.

Husserl's contributions to the debate seem to focus more on what we can legiti-
mately mean by terms like "external," "real" and "world." For him, the various definitions of idealism and realism, and the resulting debate, are based on equivocations
and philosophically unjustified (and sometimes utterly nonsensical) concepts.[37] His
transcendental phenomenological idealism aims to go beyond the old dispute
between idealism and realism. However, there is no consensus as to what Husserl's
transcendental idealism amounts to. When presenting his "proof" of transcendental
idealism circa 1908, Husserl begins by denying that the being of things – which we
understand to be what they are whether or not someone perceives, represents, or
thinks them – would be conceivable if there were no consciousness to conceive
them.[38] He goes on to explain that:

> Each being depends on consciousness in such a way that only the mode of consciousness
> proper to it – if it is a truly justifying one – can justify its being. If consciousness were
> something totally separate or separable, then this relation would be impossible. *What is
> totally separate, and is only connected accidentally, is an independent variable.* So: con-
> sciousness and being are necessarily connected in one way or another.
>
> *But how is the connection between the two to be understood*, and in such a way that this
> functional dependency becomes understandable? Furthermore: the world as independent
> from consciousness is said to exist in-itself. How would a consciousness reach such a world
> or any particular thing in it? A consciousness perceives, has consciousness of givenness.
> But in this consciousness of givenness the real content is merely that which belongs to
> consciousness itself, not, however, the transcendent thing (Hua XXXVI; 2003, p. 55–56).

This relationship of mutual dependence between consciousness and things,
which Husserl maintains some version of throughout his works from 1905 onward,
still needs careful interpretation and defense.[39] In order to give such an interpretation

---

[37] See Overgaard 2004, pp. 64–65.

[38] "Ist Sein von Dingen, Sein einer Natur, die doch ist, was sie ist, ob irgendjemand sie wahrnimmt,
vorstellt, denkt oder nicht, denkbar, wenn es schlechthin kein Bewusstsein gibt? Ich sage:
„Nein!"[…]" (Hua XXXVI; 2003, p. 53).

[39] One might understand this as Husserl claiming that consciousness is always consciousness of
some *thing* on the one hand, and that every *thing* receives its being-sense by virtue of sense-
bestowing or constitutive acts of consciousness on the other. But this would need to be interpreted
in light of the fact that Husserl further claims that there are no things-in-themselves, and that the
transcendental ego exists absolutely. Readers will of course be familiar with Husserl's attempt to
explain his position in the *Cartesian Meditations*, where he claims that phenomenology, properly
understood, simply *is* transcendental idealism. He argues that his transcendental idealism "is nothing more than a consequentially executed self-explication in the form of a systematic egological
science, an explication of my ego as subject of every possible cognition, and indeed with respect
to every sense of what exists, wherewith the latter might be able to *have* a sense for me, the ego.
This idealism is not a product of sportive argumentations, a prize to be won in the dialectical contest with 'realisms.' It is *sense-explication* achieved *by actual work*, an explication carried out as
regards every type of existent ever conceivable by me, the ego, and specifically as regards the
transcendency actually given to me beforehand through experience: nature, culture, the world as a
whole. But that signifies: systematic uncovering of the constituting intentionality itself. *The proof*

and defense, one needs to contextualize Husserl's work – placing it within the contours of the debates in which it was embroiled. This volume represents a step in that direction.

Did some of Husserl's critics misunderstand his writings? This seems to be true in at least some cases, as I suspect some readers of this volume will argue in response to the essay included herein. In these cases, the questions then are (i) whether the misunderstandings are forgivable given the source material Husserl's critics had access to (including access to the Master himself), and (ii) in spite of these misunderstandings, do the versions of phenomenology they advanced in response to Husserl have philosophical value in their own right. Still in other cases, it is either uncharitable or entirely misleading to say that the critical reception of Husserl was based on misinterpretations. We should also note that Husserl himself issued a word of caution for those who would use the work of his students and fellow phenomenologists as a guide to understanding his thought:

> The fact that someone was my academic student or that under the influence of my writings became a philosopher does not therefore mean – far from it – that they have penetrated to a real understanding of the inner meaning of *my*, the original, phenomenology and its method, and that they are researching into the new horizon of problems which I have opened up [...]. This is true of almost all the students from the Göttingen and early Freiburg period [...] (Hua Dok III/6; 1994, p. 457).

Even if, as Husserl here remarks, being one of his students or being inspired to do philosophy as a result of reading his work is not a sufficient condition for understanding Husserlian phenomenology or for practicing it, it does not follow that we should dismiss the works of his students and followers. If Husserl's critics misunderstood his position, particularly with respect to idealism, then it is incumbent on Husserl scholars to clearly articulate how.

3   The Contributions

The present volume is divided into four parts. The papers in Part I deal with the realist interpretation of the 1900/01 edition of the *Logical Investigations* by looking at the issue of Platonism and Husserl's account of ideal objects therein. In "**Hermann Lotze and the genesis of Husserl's early philosophy (1886–1901)**," Denis Fisette explores the influence of Lotze's interpretation of the Platonic theory of Ideas and the theory of knowledge on Husserl.[40] Central to Fisette's analysis is Husserl's unpublished manuscript "Mikrokosmos" (K I 9), which was intended for inclusion

---

[Erweis] of this idealism is therefore phenomenology itself. Only someone who misunderstands either the deepest sense of intentional method, or that of transcendental reduction, or perhaps both, can attempt to separate phenomenology from transcendental idealism" (Hua I; 1973, pp. 118–119, quoted here from Husserl 1960, p. 86).

[40] The main source for these ideas is Lotze's *Logik*, which was the focus of a seminar Husserl taught in SS 1912. The Lotze-seminar was attended by many prominent members of the Göttingen

as an appendix to the *Logical Investigations*.[41] Fisette begins by situating Lotze and Stumpf as sources for Husserl's early discussions of the objective status of logical laws. Husserl's critical engagement with Lotze thus becomes crucial to understanding why some of Husserl's followers read the *Logical Investigations* as representing a return to metaphysical realism. That said, as Fisette notes, one should not confuse metaphysical discussions of the existence of external reality with those concerning the ontological status of logical laws. Husserl argues for objective, universal logical forms, but resists their hypostatization.[42] While the debt to Lotze in the *Logical Investigations* is palpable, in K I 9, as Fisette reveals, Husserl is critical of Lotze's apparent subjectivism and logical psychologism. Husserl ultimately diagnoses the shortcoming of Lotze's philosophy as resulting from the lack of a theory of intentionality – a conclusion he reiterates in *Ideas III* (Hua V; 1952, p. 58).

Mariano Crespo's contribution, "**A realist misunderstanding of Husserl's account of ideal objects in the *Logical Investigations*,**" challenges the notion that the *Logical Investigations* can be consistently read in a way that is compatible with metaphysical realism. To help identify how a realist misreading of the *Logical Investigations* arose among Husserl's early students, Crespo turns to the work of Spanish philosopher Antonio Millán-Puelles. Millán-Puelles' addresses the notions of ideal objects and ideal being in Husserl. Like some of Husserl's early students, Millán-Puelles first read the *Logical Investigations* as marking a return to metaphysical realism. However, on closer inspection, as Crespo explains, one finds that the discussion of ideal objects remains metaphysically neutral with respect to the being-in-themselves of such objects.[43] As Crespo explains, the theory of ideal *objects* in the *Logical Investigations* is not a theory of ideal *being*. In short, Husserl resists the move to "classical realism." While there may be a certain Platonism at play in the *Logical Investigations* with respect to ideal objects and ideal logical laws, Husserl does not endorse metaphysical realism in any ordinary sense.

Part II looks at the reception of Husserl's idealism by philosophers associated with the University of Marburg, particularly Paul Natorp and his students. The fact that Natorp – one of the leading representatives of the Marburg School of

---

Circle, such as Winthrop Bell, Jean Hering, Alexandre Koyré, and Hans Lipps (Hua Dok I; Schuhmann 1977, p. 169).

[41] In the 1900 edition of the *Prolegomena*, Husserl adds a note to the end of §59 stating that in the next volume, "we will take the opportunity to critically address Lotze's epistemological teachings, especially his chapter on the real and formal content of logical laws [*von der realen und formalen Bedeutung des Logischen*]" (Hua XVIII; 1975, pp. 221–222). However, this appendix was not included in the 1913 edition due to a lack of space. For more on this, see Varga 2013.

[42] This position is similar to that of Lotze. As Nicholas Stang writes: "Lotze distinguishes between the mistaken hypostatic reading of Plato, on which the Forms (concepts, constituents of truths) are treated as entities in their own right, existing in some kind of platonic heaven, and the "true" Platonism, in which the doctrine of Forms is only intended to make the distinction between what exists (mental and physical objects and events) and what is valid (propositions/contents of acts of judgement, and, derivatively, the Forms/concepts composing them)" (Stang 2019, p. 139). See also Rollinger 2004.

[43] One might compare this analysis to Fink 1970, pp. 84–85.

Neo-Kantianism – was an influence on Husserl's mature philosophy is well known. Yet there is work to be done in terms of unpacking the extent of this influence. In the second edition of the *Logical Investigations* (published the same year as *Ideas I*), a note is added following §8 of the Fifth Logical Investigation explaining that, thanks to Natorp, Husserl had managed to find the pure ego. This debt is reiterated in a note at §57 of *Ideas I* as well.[44] However, the new turn in Husserl's thought was not met uncritically by Natorp. In **"The 'offence of any and all ready-made givenness,'"** Burt Hopkins presents a systematic account of Natorp's critique of Husserl's notion of the givenness of this ego's flowing stream of consciousness in phenomenological reflection, and a Husserlian response. For all that Natorp gets right, Hopkins argues that Husserl does offer an account of how reflection can access the streaming stream of lived-experience without stilling the waters. This is a valuable addition to the recent literature bringing phenomenology and Neo-Kantianism into dialogue with each other. It also brings into relief two important themes in the idealism-realism debate in the early phenomenological movement: 1) the absolute existence and nature of the pure, transcendental ego, and 2) the possibility of phenomenological reflection.

Dalius Jonkus' paper **"Critical ontology and critical realism,"** looks at the reactions of two of Natorp's students to Husserl's idealism. Nicolai Hartmann and Vasily Sesemann were both influenced by Neo-Kantianism and phenomenology and carved out their own philosophical positions – sometimes labelled "critical realism" and other times "gnoseological idealism"[45] – in part as a response to the idealism-realism debate. Hartmann's criticism of Husserl's phenomenology has two prongs. First, by focusing on the *acts* of consciousness, phenomenology loses sight of the true objects of consciousness – the real, transcendent things. Second, phenomenological idealism brings with it the problem of givenness, i.e., that all knowledge is determined by the manner in which objects are given to us in experience, which in turn is structured by consciousness. As Jonkus explains, the emphasis on *knowing* and *grasping* objects, overlooks the fact that in, for instance, emotional experience and practical engagement, the objects initially *grasp us*, and it is only after our encounter with the objects of the world that problems of *knowing* reality arise. Similarly, Sesemann interprets phenomenology as a form of immanentism where all that is discussed is the relationship between consciousness and its intentional object. In his criticisms of phenomenology, Sesemann follows a Heideggerian path by emphasizing concrete being-in-the-world, and the relationship between things and their practical meaning for subjects.

The papers in Part III tackle the reception of Husserl's idealism by members of the Munich Circle of phenomenologists. The section opens with Susan Gottlöber's contribution, **"The problem of reality."** Gottlöber's paper takes up the problem of reality (*Realitätsprobleme*) discussed in Scheler's essay *Idealism and Realism*. In

---

[44] See Luft 2011, pp. 240–243. See also Natorp's review of Husserl's *Prolegomena* (Natorp 1901, 1977) as well as their philosophically rich correspondence in Hua Dok III/5; 1994, pp. 39–165.

[45] See Röck 2016, p. 157 and Botz-Bornstein 2006, p. 24.

response to Husserl's idealism, which he labels a form of "idealism of consciousness [*Bewusstseinsidealismus*]," Scheler elaborates a notion of reality as *resistance* (*Widerstand*). As Gottlöber explains, according to Scheler we experience that which is real as a pure meaningless resisting that conditions every perception. Our confrontation with reality is foundational for Scheler: it is not consciousness that constitutes reality, but reality that constitutes the content of consciousness through forms of resistance.[46] The views of Scheler are important to bear in mind when reading many of the other realist phenomenologists. Not only was Scheler an important figure in Munich during his tenure there, his so-called "secret seminars" that he gave in Göttingen from 1910 to 1914 were influential on the members of the Göttingen Circle as well. Scheler's discussions of reality as resistance, which form part of his argument in *Idealism and Realism*, predates the appearance of Husserl's *Ideas I*,[47] and are useful in understanding why the Munich phenomenologists resisted the idealist turn.

The essay on Scheler is followed by one that explores the thought of Johannes Daubert – another important member of the Munich Circle. Daubert's visit to Husserl in Göttingen in the summer of 1902 is a crucial moment in the history of the phenomenological movement. It resulted in Husserl's lectures to the Munich Circle in May 1904[48] and the subsequent "Munich invasion" of Göttingen that began in the summer of 1905.[49] Daubert also visited Husserl in Seefeld in the summer 1905, at a decisive period in Husserl's turn to transcendental idealism.[50] However, in large part due to the fact that almost none of his writings have ever been published, Daubert's thought has received scant attention. Building upon the ground-breaking research of Karl Schuhmann and Barry Smith, Daniel Sobota's essay, "**The question of reality**," argues that the phenomenology of questioning and the question of being (*Seinsfrage*) are fundamental to Daubert's philosophy. This overarching theme in Daubert's writings unites his concerns about real reality (*wirkliche Wirklichkeit*), our consciousness of reality (*Wirklichkeitsbewusstsein*), the phenomenology of evidence, and speech acts. Sobota is therefore able to show that responding to Husserl and the idealism-realism debate more broadly takes on a special role in the development of Daubert's various lines of thought. Sobota also explains that Daubert

---

[46] See also Davis 2017, p. 168.

[47] While it is more fully elaborated in his *Formalism* (Scheler 1973a), which was first published in the same volume of the *Jahrbuch* as *Ideas I*, we find a discussion of resistance already in the essay "Über Selbsttäuschungen" (Scheler 1912).

[48] The manuscript *Phantasie und bildliche Vorstellung* (Hua XXIII; 1980, pp. 108–136) served as the basis for this lecture (see Hua XXIII; 1980, pp. xxxiv–xxxv). For an English translation of the manuscript, see Hua CW XI; 2005, pp. 117–151.

[49] In November 1904, Husserl wrote to Daubert that it was a pity no one from the Munich Circle had yet come to Göttingen, as he had announced his WS 1904/05 lectures on the *Phenomenology and Theory of Knowledge* primarily for them (Hua Dok III/2; 1994, p. 49). The first two parts of these lectures are published in Hua XXXVIII; 2004, pp. 3–123, the third in Hua XXIII; 1980, pp. 1–108, and the fourth in part in Hua X; 1966, pp. 3–98. This letter no doubt played a decisive role in initiating the Munich invasion by Adolf Reinach and others.

[50] See Schuhmann and Smith 2004, p. 58.

rejected the absolute existence of the ego. For Daubert, the transcendental ego is that which is constituted by consciousness, not the world.[51]

In "**Bogged down in ontologism and realism**," Kimberly Baltzer-Jaray discusses Adolf Reinach's realist response to Husserl. Given that Reinach joined the German army shortly after the outbreak of WWI in 1914 and died on the battlefield in 1917, he was not able to produce a protracted response to *Ideas I*. However, Husserl was aware of Reinach's critical stance with respect to his turn to idealism.[52] We find hints of a direct, but perhaps not fully developed, critique of *Ideas I* in Reinach's Marburg lecture *Concerning Phenomenology* from January 1914. Additionally, as Baltzer-Jaray argues, much of Reinach's writings form an alternative to Husserl's idealist phenomenology. Reinach's reaction to Husserl's phenomenological idealism is especially important since many of the members of the Göttingen Circle considered Reinach, not Husserl, to be their real teacher in phenomenology.[53] Moreover, Husserl considered Reinach one of the first to fully understand the meaning of his "new" phenomenological method and its philosophical scope, and praised Reinach's original philosophical insights (Hua XXV; 1987, p. 301). Reinach's realist phenomenology subscribes to two theses that have their roots in the school of Brentano: (1) there is a real world that exists independently of consciousness and (2) the real world is made up of various types of being. On Baltzer-Jaray's reading, insofar as Husserl abandons these theses, Reinach views Husserl's position as a type of *reductionism*. Though Husserl rejects the idea that all intuitions and laws of thought can be reduced to physiological brain activity, Husserl endorses a form of idealism where all being is reduced *via* the transcendental reduction to nothing more than being for consciousness.

Like Daubert and Reinach, Moritz Geiger was a key, yet often overlooked, figure in the early phenomenological movement. He is often known for his contributions to phenomenological aesthetics, but, as Michele Averchi shows in "**Evidence-based phenomenology and certainty-based phenomenology**," this is only one facet of Geiger's thought. Geiger understood phenomenology as a change in *stance* rather than *attitude*, and one that focuses on the given as such beyond the subjective/objective divide. While he also views phenomenology as metaphysically neutral, Geiger argues that it is always embedded in the broader context of realism. It is a variation of stance, not an alternative metaphysical theory. In this sense, unlike

---

[51] The rejection of the absolute existence of the ego is a position held by a number of Theodor Lipps' students. Here we might take note of the influence of Hume on the members of the Munich Circle. It is well know that, for Hume, when we reflect on the self, we are never intimately conscious of anything but a particular perception, and that the self is "nothing but a bundle or collection of different perceptions, which succeed each other with an inconceivable rapidity, and are in perpetual flux and movement" (Hume 2007, p. 165 [I, IV, vi]). The German translations of Hume's *Treatise* where edited by Lipps (Hume 1895, 1906). The 1895 translation of Book I was by Else Köttgen and the 1906 translation of Books II and III by Agnes Reimer, the wife of Lipps' former professor at Bonn, Jürgen Bona Meyer.

[52] See, for instance, the excerpts from Husserl's letters to Winthrop Bell and Daniel Feuling at Hua XXXVI; 2003, p. x.

[53] See Spiegelberg 1994, pp. 191–192.

some of the other Munich phenomenologists, Geiger appears much more sympathetic to Husserl. However, as Averchi argues, this does not mean that Geiger was uncritical of Husserl's phenomenology. Husserl's argument for idealism in *Ideas I* results from a misunderstanding of what Geiger calls the "givenness stance". Husserl gives a radical interpretation of this stance in articulating his *principle of all principles*, and thereby falls into idealism. In response to Husserl, as the title of the paper suggests, Geiger advocates a certainty-based phenomenology rather than an evidence-based phenomenology. Unlike Husserl's evidence-based phenomenology, which takes the problems posed by Cartesian skepticism too seriously, Geiger's certainty-based phenomenology dismisses these worries and preserves our everyday belief in the reality of the external world.

Rounding out Part III is Ronny Miron's essay "**The metaphysical absolutizing of the ideal**," which looks at the writings of Hedwig Conrad-Martius – one of the most outspoken representatives of the Munich realist phenomenology. Drawing primarily on essays written during the 1930s, Miron situates Conrad-Martius' criticisms of Husserl's phenomenological idealism within her broader concerns about idealism. The work is a pastiche that weaves together Conrad-Martius' scattered critical comments in order to give the reader a more complete portrait of her thoughts on idealism as well as an entry point into Conrad-Martius' own philosophical position. Many of these arguments appear in Conrad-Martius' earliest writings and persist through to her attack on Husserl in "Die transzendentale und die ontologische Phänomenologie" (Conrad-Martius 1959). For Conrad-Martius, by restricting philosophy to discussing only unities of meaning or things as they appear to us, we forget or disregard what accounts for the origin of the ideas in us, what lies behind the appearances. She insists that philosophy must be able to talk intelligibly (if only speculatively) about such things as they are in-themselves. The external world cannot be disregarded as Husserl's transcendental phenomenological idealism would have it even if the reality of the world cannot be known evidently. Her criticism of Husserl focuses on (i) his insistence that the ego has absolute existence and that everything else only exists for consciousness, and (ii) the distinction between appearances and things-in-themselves at the heart of all forms of idealism.

The essays comprising Part IV, the final division of the volume, look at some how some of Husserl' Göttingen and Freiburg students critically appropriated some aspects of phenomenological idealism and sought to amend others. In "**Gustav Shpet's implicit phenomenological idealism**," Thomas Nemeth looks at Shpet's understanding of Husserl's phenomenological idealism, focusing primarily on his remarks in *Appearance and Sense* (Shpet 1991) and "Consciousness and Its Owner" (Shpet 2019, pp. 153–205). Nemeth argues that there is a sense in which it would be correct to label Shpet a phenomenological idealist, but not without some caveats. Shpet understood phenomenology as a fundamental science of essences and hence of *ideal* being, and readily accepted the phenomenological reduction. However, Shpet was critical of Husserl's concept of the ego, and was uneasy about Husserl's references to *hyle*. On the one hand, he worried that Husserl's talk of sense-bestowal in *Ideas I* meant that the pure ego *creates* the sense of things in such a way that senses are merely subjective or arbitrary. Shpet is also one of the first to publish a criticism of Husserl's (diachronic) unity of consciousness argument. On the other hand, Shpet appears to regard the *hyle*, which are the bearers of sense, as *things-in-themselves*. The inclusion of Shpet in this volume speaks to the larger reception of Husserl's philosophy in Russia and the Baltics. Shpet's reading of Husserl had an impact on others in Russia, although this impact was limited owing to the political situation at that time.

Following this we have Daniele De Santis' paper "**Edith Stein on a different motive that led Husserl to transcendental idealism**." A challenge for readers of Edith Stein, who is typically read as a realist phenomenologist, is to reconcile what she says about Husserl's idealism in her letters to Ingarden and in her Habilitationschrift *Potency and Act* – specifically, that she seems to have capitulated to Husserl's idealism in some sense – with her other writings. Stein is often lumped in with the realist phenomenologists of the Munich school, though this is misleading given that she never studied with Lipps, Pfänder, or Geiger (though she did attend Scheler's secret lectures in Göttingen and took courses with Reinach from 1913 to 1914). Because of her distance from Munich, her reading of Husserl was not infected, one might say, with the Munich realism. De Santis' paper aims to clarify an argument that Stein presents in a long footnote in *Finite and Eternal Being*, where she fleshes out the "motive" that led Husserl to an idealist conception of reality. In order to achieve this task, De Santis turns to her "Excursus on Transcendental Idealism." According to Stein, Husserl disregards the twofold essence of essence and extracts the contents from experience without positing the real matter of fact that occasions their experience. She argues that Husserl misunderstands the peculiar ontological structure of individual essences and, in particular, the specific *connection with reality* that they carry within themselves.

While many of the papers in this volume deal with the first phenomenological schism, Daniel Dahlstrom's "**Senses of being and implications of idealism**" turns to the second, that is, the split between Husserl's transcendental phenomenology and Heidegger's existential, ontological phenomenology.[54] Heidegger was carving out a new path for phenomenology by the mid-1920s, parting ways with the Master but also appropriating a number of his insights. Heidegger first attacks Husserl for failing to raise the question of the meaning of being and failing to elaborate on the being-here characteristic of our embodied, human existence. Second, Heidegger criticizes Husserl's preoccupation with securing knowledge, that is, with the foundationalist search for an Archimedean point. For Heidegger, phenomenology ought not begin and end with such strictly epistemological concerns. At the same time, Heidegger adopts the phenomenological reduction and, along with it, Husserl's theory of intentionality and account of categorial intuition. While Heidegger believes that his interpretation of the world should not be construed in idealist terms, one might wonder if this confidence is justified. For instance, in *Being and Time*, Heidegger states that, "It [the world] *is*, along with the outside-itself character of the ecstasies, *here*. If no being-here [*Dasein*] exists, there is also no world *here*"

---

[54] For more on the second phenomenological schism, see Crowell 1997 and Heffernan 2016.

(Heidegger 1927, p. 365).[55] This passage invites idealist interpretations, but, as Dahlstrom argues, the case is not so straightforward.

The final paper in the volume, Genki Uemura's "**Not idealist enough**" explores the reactions of two of Husserl's Japanese students, Satomi Takahashi and Tomoo Otaka, to Husserl's idealism. As the title suggests, rather than attacking Husserl for turning to idealism, these students claim that Husserl's transcendental phenomenology does not go far enough. Takahashi argues that Husserl's idealism is not idealist enough insofar as his views on the intersubjective constitution of the world are incompatible with subjective idealism. According to Takahashi, Husserl's idealism fails to be subjective idealism because it fails to immanentize transcendent objects. Rather, he claims, what Husserl could achieve is only a substitution of transcendent objects with noemata as their copies. Otaka argues that Husserl's idealism is no idealism at all. According to Otaka, Husserl's position is compatible with realism concerning a mind-independent material reality. His arguments concerning the objective world further confirm a form of realism. For Otaka, the cultural world of meaning is a creation of our experiential activity (this amounts to idealism) and its objectivity is exhausted by its intersubjective shareability or commonality (this amounts to realism). However, Otaka's distinction between the material world and the world of meaning is not without its problems vis-à-vis the idealism-realism debate.

Acknowledgements I would like to thank Sebastian Luft, Dan Zahavi, Frederik Beiser, and Genki Uemura for their feedback on earlier versions of this introductory essay, and Henry Allison and Robin Rollinger for permitting me to quote from our personal correspondence. I would also like to thank the two reviewers of the manuscript for their thoughtful comments on the individual contributions as well as their suggestions for improving the volume as a whole. Finally, my deepest thanks are owed to the authors who contributed to this collection.

References

Adorno, Theodore (1940): Husserl and the Problem of Idealism. In *The Journal of Philosophy* 37 (1), pp. 5–18.

Allison, Henry (1974): The Critique of Pure Reason as Transcendental Phenomenology. In Don Ihde, Richard Zaner (Eds.): Dialogues in Phenomenology. The Hague: Nijhoff, pp. 135–155.

Allison, Henry (1983): Kant's Transcendental Idealism. An Interpretation and Defense. New Haven: Yale University Press.

Allison, Henry (1992): Gurwitch's interpretation of Kant. Reflections of a former student. In *Kant-Studien* 83 (2), pp. 208–221.

Baltzer-Jaray, Kimberly (2009): Adolf Reinach is not a Platonist. In *Symposium* 13 (1), pp. 100–112.

Beck, Maximilian (1928): Die neue Problemlage der Erkenntnistheorie. In *Deutsche Vierteljahrsschrift für Literaturwissenschaft und Geistesgeschichte* 6 (4), pp. 611–639.

Beiser, Frederik (2002): German Idealism. The Struggle Against Subjectivism, 1781–1801. Cambridge, Mass.: Harvard University Press.

---

[55] This passage could easily be rendered consistent with De Warren's interpretation of Husserl, where "Transcendental subjectivity is thus neither outside nor inside the world; it carries, or better, is the world in its constitutional unfolding" (DeWarren 2009, p. 29).

Beiser, Frederik (2013): Late German Idealism. Trendelenburg and Lotze. Oxford: Oxford University Press.

Beiser, Frederik (2014): The Genesis of Neo-Kantianism, 1796–1880. Oxford: Oxford University Press.

Botz-Bornstein, Thorsten (2006): Vasily Sesemann. Experience, Formalism, and the Question of Being. Amsterdam: Rodopi.

Brassier, Ray; Grant, Iain Hamilton; Harman, Graham; Meillassoux, Quentin (2007): Speculative Realism. In Robin Mackay (Ed.): Collapse III. Falmouth: Urbanomic, pp. 307–450.

Burnyeat, Myles (1982): Idealism and Greek Philosophy: What Descartes Saw and Berkeley Missed. In *The Philosophical Review* 91 (1), pp. 3–40.

Calenge, Simon (2015): Hans Lipps critique de l'idéalisme de Husserl. In *Studia Phaenomenologica* 15, pp. 181–205.

Celms, Theodor (1928): Der phänomenologische Idealismus Husserls. Riga: Walters and Rapa.

Celms, Theodor (1993): Der phänomenologische Idealismus Husserls und andere Schriften 1928–1943. Frankfurt am Main: Peter Lang.

Conrad-Martius, Hedwig (1959): Die transzendentale und die ontologische Phänomenologie. In Herman van Breda, Jacques Taminiaux (Eds.): Edmund Husserl, 1859–1959. Recueil commémoratif publié a l'occasion du centenaire de la naissance du philosophe. The Hague: Nijhoff (Phaenomenologica, 4), pp. 175–184.

Cornelius, Hans (1916): Transcendentale Systematik. Untersuchungen zur Begründung der Erkenntnistheorie. Munich: Reinhardt.

Crowell, Steven (1997): Ontology and Transcendental Phenomenology Between Husserl and Heidegger. In Burt Hopkins (Ed.): Husserl in Contemporary Context. Prospects and Projects for Phenomenology. Dordrecht: Kluwer (Contributions to Phenomenology, 26), pp. 13–36.

Davis, Zachary (2017): Max Scheler and Pragmatism. In Ondřej Švec, Jakub Čapek (Eds.): Pragmatic Perspectives in Phenomenology. New York: Routledge, pp. 158–172.

DeWarren, Nicolas (2009): Husserl and the Promise of Time. Subjectivity in transcendental phenomenology. Cambridge: Cambridge University Press.

Dunham, Jeremy; Hamilton Grant, Iain; Watson, Sean (2011): Idealism. THe History of a Philosophy. New York: Routledge.

Falckenberg, Richard (1880): Aufgabe und Wesen der Erkenntnis bei Nicolaus von Kues. Breslau: Koebner.

Falckenberg, Richard (1886): Geschichte der neueren Philosophie von Nikolaus von Kues bis zur gegenwart. Leipzig: Veit.

Fink, Eugen (1970): The phenomenological philosophy of Edmund Husserl and contemporary criticism. In Roy Owen Elveton (Ed.): The phenomenology of Husserl. Selected critical readings. Chicago: Quadrangle Books, pp. 73–147.

Fink, Eugen (1988): Sixth Cartesian Meditation. The Idea of a Transcendental Theory of Method. Translated by R. Bruzina. Indianapolis: Indiana University Press.

Fischer, Kuno (1854–77): Geschichte der neuern Philosophie. Mannheim-Stuttgart-Heidelberg: Bassermann.

Geiger, Moritz (1930): Die Wirklichkeit der Wissenschaften und die Metaphysik. Bonn: Cohen.

Geiger, Moritz (1986): The Significance of Art. A Phenomenological Approach to Aesthetics. Translated by K. Berger. Lanham: University Press of America.

Guyer, Paul; Horstmann, Rolf-Peter (2018): Idealism. In *The Stanford Encyclopedia of Philosophy*, 2018. Available online at https://plato.stanford.edu/archives/win2018/entries/idealism/.

Harman, Graham (2018): Speculative Realism. An Introduction. Cambridge: Polity.

Heffernan, George (2016): A Tale of Two Schisms: Heidegger's Critique of Husserl's Move into Transcendental Idealism. In *The European Legacy* 21 (5/6), pp. 556–575.

Heidegger, Martin (1927): Sein und Zeit. Halle: Niemeyer.

Hering, Jean (1925): Phénoménologie et philosophie religieuse. Étude sur la théorie de la connaissance religieuse. Strasbourg: Imprimerie Alsacienne.

Hering, Jean (2015): Phänomenologie als Grundlage der Metaphysik?/Phenomenology as the Foundation of Metaphysics? Edited and translated by S. Camilleri and A. Iyer. In *Studia Phaenomenologica* 15, pp. 35–50.

Hibbs, Darren (2005): Who's an "Idealist"? In *The Review of Metaphysics* 58 (3), pp. 561–570.

Hibbs, Darren (2009): On the Possibility of Pre-Cartesian Idealism. In *Dialogue* 48, pp. 643–653.

Hume, David (1895): Traktat über die menschliche Natur, I. Teil. Über den Verstand. Th. Lipps (Ed.), translated by E. Köttgen. Hamburg and Leipzig: Voss.

Hume, David (1906): Traktat über die menschliche Natur, II. Teil. Ober die Affekte Buch II. Über die Affekte, Buch III. Über Moral. Th. Lipps (Ed.), translated by Frau J. Bona Meyer (A. Reimer). Hamburg and Leipzig: Voss.

Hume, David (2007): A Treatise of Human Nature. Volume 1. Texts. With assistance of D. Norton, M. Norton (Eds.). Oxford: Clarendon Press.

Husserl, Edmund (Hua II; 1950): Die Idee der Phänomenologie. Fünf Vorlesungen. Edited by W. Biemel. The Hague: Nijhoff (Husserliana, II).

Husserl, Edmund (Hua V; 1952): Ideen zu einer reinen Phänomenologie und phänomenologischen Philosophie. Drittes Buch. Die Phänomenologie und die Fundamente der Wissenschaft. Edited by M. Biemel. The Hague: Nijhoff (Husserliana, V).

Husserl, Edmund (Hua VII; 1956): Erste Philosophie (1923/24). Erster Teil. Kritische Ideengeschichte. Edited by R. Boehm. The Hague: Nijhoff (Husserliana, VII).

Husserl, Edmund (1960): Cartesian Meditations. An Introduction to Phenomenology. Translated by D. Cairns. The Hague: Nijhoff.

Husserl, Edmund (Hua X; 1966): Zur Phänomenologie des inneren Zeitbewusstseins (1893–1917). Edited by R. Boehm. The Hague: Nijhoff (Husserliana, X).

Husserl, Edmund (Hua I; 1973): Cartesianische Meditationen und Pariser Vorträge. Edited by S. Strasser. 2nd ed. The Hague: Nijhoff (Husserliana, I).

Husserl, Edmund (Hua XVI; 1973): Ding und Raum. Vorlesungen 1907. Edited by U. Claesges. The Hague: Nijhoff (Husserliana, XVI).

Husserl, Edmund (Hua XIII; 1973): Zur Phänomenologie der Intersubjektivität. Erster Teil: 1905–1920. Edited by I. Kern. The Hague: Nijhoff (Husserliana, XIII).

Husserl, Edmund (Hua XVII; 1974): Formale und Transzendentale Logik. Versuch einer Kritik der logischen Vernunft. Edited by P. Janssen. The Hague: Nijhoff (Husserliana, XVII).

Husserl, Edmund (Hua XVIII; 1975): Logische Untersuchungen. Erster Band. Prolegomena zur reinen Logik. Edited by E. Holenstein. The Hague: Nijhoff (Husserliana, XVIII).

Husserl, Edmund (Hua III/1; 1976): Ideen zu einer reinen Phänomenologie und phänomenologischen Philosophie, Erstes Buch. Allgemeine Einführung in die reine Phänomenologie. Edited by K. Schuhmann. 2nd ed. The Hague: Nijhoff (Husserliana, III/1).

Husserl, Edmund (Hua XXII; 1979): Aufsätze und Rezensionen (1890–1910). Edited by R. Rang. The Hague: Nijhoff (Husserliana, XXII).

Husserl, Edmund (Hua XXIII; 1980): Phantasie, Bildbewusstsein, Erinnerung. Zur Phänomenologie der anschaulichen Vergegenwärtigungen. Edited by E. Marbach. The Hague: Nijhoff (Husserliana, XXIII).

Husserl, Edmund (Hua XXIV; 1984): Einleitung in die Logik und Erkenntnistheorie. Vorlesungen 1906/07. Edited by U. Melle. The Hague: Nijhoff (Husserliana, XXIV).

Husserl, Edmund (Hua XXV; 1987): Aufsätze und Vorträge (1911–1921). Edited by T. Nenon and H.R. Sepp. Dordrecht: Kluwer (Husserliana, XXV).

Husserl, Edmund (Hua CW III; 1989): Ideas Pertaining to a Pure Phenomenology and to a Phenomenological Philosophy, Second Book. Studies in the Phenomenology of Constitution. Translated by R. Rojcewicz and A. Schuwer. Dordrecht: Kluwer (Edmund Husserl Collected Works, III).

Husserl, Edmund (Hua Dok III/2; 1994): Briefwechsel II. Die Münchener Phänomenelogen. Dordrecht: Kluwer (Husserliana Dokumente, III/2).

Husserl, Edmund (Hua Dok III/9; 1994): Briefwechsel IX. Familienbriefe. Dordrecht: Kluwer (Husserliana Dokumente, III/9).

Husserl, Edmund (Hua Dok III/5; 1994): Briefwechsel V. Die Neukantianer. Dordrecht: Kluwer (Husserliana Dokumente, III/5).

Husserl, Edmund (Hua Dok III/6; 1994): Briefwechsel VI. Philosophenbriefe. Dordrecht: Kluwer (Husserliana Dokumente, III/6).

Husserl, Edmund (2001): Logical Investigations, Volume 1. Translated by J.N. Findlay. New York: Routledge.

Husserl, Edmund (Hua XXXVI; 2003): Transzendentaler Idealismus. Texte aus dem Nachlass (1908–1921). Edited by R. Rollinger and R. Sowa. Dordrecht: Kluwer (Husserliana, XXXVI).

Husserl, Edmund (Hua XXXVIII; 2004): Wahrnehmung und Aufmerksamkeit. Texte aus dem Nachlass (1893–1912). Edited by T. Vongehr and R. Giuliani. Dordrecht: Springer (Husserliana, XXXVIII).

Husserl, Edmund (Hua CW XI; 2005): Phantasy, Image Consciousness, and Memory (1898–1925). Translated by J. Brough. Dordrecht: Springer (Edmund Husserl Collected Works, XI).

Ingarden, Roman (1929): Bemerkungen zum Problem "Idealismus-Realismus". In *Jahrbuch für Philosophie und phänomenologische Forschung* Festschrift. E. Husserl zum 70. Geburtstag gewidmet, pp. 159–190.

Ingarden, Roman (1973): The Literary Work of Art. An investigation on the borderlines of ontology, logic, and theory of literature. Translated by G. Grabowicz. Evanston: Northwestern University Press.

Ingarden, Roman (1975): On the Motives which led Edmund Husserl to Transcendental Idealism. Translated by A. Hannibalsson. The Hague: Nijhoff (Phaenomenologica, 64).

Ingarden, Roman (2013): Controversy over the existence of the world, vol. 1. Translated by A. Szylewicz. Frankfurt am Main: Peter Lang.

Ingarden, Roman (2016): Controversy over the existence of the world, vol. 2. Translated by A. Szylewicz. Frankfurt am Main: Peter Lang.

Kern, Iso (1964): Husserl und Kant. Eine Untersuchung über Husserls Verhältnis zu Kant und zum Neukantianismus. The Hague: Nijhoff (Phaenomenologica, 16).

Kreis, Friedrich (1930): Phänomenologie und Kritizismus. Tübingen: Mohr.

Linke, Paul F. (1930): Gegenstandsphänomenologie. In *Philosophische Hefte* 2 (2), pp. 65–90.

Lipps, Hans (1927/28): Untersuchungen zur Phänomenologie der Erkenntnis. 2 volumes. Bonn: Cohen.

Lipps, Hans (1976): Untersuchungen zur Phänomenologie der Erkenntnis. Frankfurt am Main: Klostermann.

Luft, Sebastian (2007): From Being to Givenness and Back: Some Remarks on the Meaning of Transcendental Idealism in Kant and Husserl. In *International Journal of Philosophical Studies* 15 (3), pp. 367–394.

Luft, Sebastian (2011): Subjectivity and Lifeworld in Transcendental Phenomenology. Evanston: Northwestern University Press.

Meillassoux, Quentin (2008): After Finitude. An Essay on the Necessity of Contingency. Translated by R. Brassier. New York: Continuum.

Misch, Georg (1930): Lebensphilosophie und Phänomenologie. Eine Auseinandersetzung der Diltheyschen Richtung mit Heidegger und Husserl. Bonn: Cohen.

Moran, Dermot; Parker, Rodney (2015): Resurrecting the phenomenological movement. In *Studia Phaenomenologica* 15, pp. 11–24.

Natorp, Paul (1901): Zur Frage der logischen Methode. Mit Beziehung auf Edmund Husserls "Prolegomena zur reinen Logik". In *Kant-Studien* 6, pp. 270–283.

Natorp, Paul (1977): On the Question of Logical Method in Relation to Edmund Husserl's Prolegomena to Pure Logic. Translated by J.N. Mohanty. In Jitendra Nath Mohanty (Ed.): Readings on Edmund Husserl's Logical Investigations. The Hague: Nijhoff, pp. 55–66.

Overgaard, Søren (2004): Husserl and Heidegger on Being in the World. Dordrecht: Kluwer (Phaenomenologica, 173).

Parker, Rodney (2020a): Does Husserl's Phenomenological Idealism Lead to Pluralistic Solipsism? Assessing the Criticism by Theodor Celms. In Iulian Apostolescu (Ed.): The Subject(s) of Phenomenology. Rereading Husserl. Cham: Springer (Contributions to Phenomenology, 108), pp. 155–184.

Parker, Rodney (2020b): Hedwig Conrad-Martius' unveröffentlichtes Manuskript auf Husserls Ideen I, "Über Ontologie". In Hans Rainer Sepp (Ed.): Natur und Kosmos. Entwürfe der frühen Phänomenologie. Nordhausen: Bautz, pp. 170–188.

Pfänder, Alexander (1913): Zur Psychologie der Gesinnungen, erster Artikel. In *Jahrbuch für Philosophie und phänomenologische Forschung* 1 (1), pp. 325–404.

Pfänder, Alexander (1916): Zur Psychologie der Gesinnungen, zweiter Artikel. In *Jahrbuch für Philosophie und phänomenologische Forschung* 3, pp. 1–125.

Pfänder, Alexander (1967): Phenomenology of Willing and Motivation. And other phaenomeno-logica. Translated by H. Spiegelberg. Evanston: Northwestern University Press.

Ricoeur, Paul (1967): Husserl. An Analysis of His Phenomenology. Evanston: Northwestern University Press.

Röck, Tina (2016): The Being of Becoming in Pre-socratic philosophy. In Keith Peterson, Roberto Poli (Eds.): New Research on the Philosophy of Nicolai Hartmann. Berlin: De Gruyter, pp. 153–170.

Rollinger, Robin (1991): Husserl and Cornelius. In *Husserl Studies* 8 (1), pp. 33–56.

Rollinger, Robin (1999): Husserl's Position in the School of Brentano. Dordrecht: Kluwer (Phaenomenologica, 150).

Rollinger, Robin (2004): Hermann Lotze an Abstraction and Platonic Ideas. In Francesco Coniglione, Roberto Poli, Robin Rollinger (Eds.): Idealization XI: Historical Studies on Abstraction and Idealization. Amsterdam: Rodopi (Poznań Studies in the Philosophy of the Sciences and the Humanities, 82), pp. 147–161.

Royce, Josiah (1896): The Spirit of Modern Philosophy. An essay in the form of lectures. Cambridge, Mass.: Riverside Press.

Sandmeyer, Bob (2009): Husserl's Constitutive Phenomenology. Its Problem and Promise. New York: Routledge.

Scheler, Max (1912): Über Selbsttäuschungen. In *Zeitschrift für Pathopsychologie* 1, pp. 87–163.

Scheler, Max (1927/28): Idealismus-Realismus. In *Philosophischer Anzeiger* 2 (3), pp. 255–324.

Scheler, Max (1973a): Formalism in Ethics and Non-Formal Ethics of Values. A new attempt toward the foundation of an ethical personalism. Translated by M. Frings and R. Funk. Evanston: Northwestern University Press.

Scheler, Max (1973b): Idealism and Realism. In Max Scheler: Selected Philosophical Essays. Translated by D. Lachterman. Evanston: Northwestern University Press, pp. 288–356.

Scheler, Max (1980): Problems of a Scoiology of Knowledge. Translated by M. Frings. New York: Routledge.

Schuhmann, Karl (Hua Dok I; 1977): Husserl-Chronik. Denk- und Lebensweg Edmund Husserls. The Hague: Nijhoff (Husserliana Dokumente, I).

Schuhmann, Karl; Smith, Barry (2004): Against Idealism: Johannes Daubert vs. Husserl's Ideas I. In Cees Leijenhorst, Piet Steenbakkers (Eds.): Karl Schuhmann. Selected Papers on Phenomenology. Dordrecht: Kluwer, pp. 35–59.

Shpet, Gustav (1991): Appearance and Sense. Phenomenology as the Fundamental Science and Its Problems. Translated by T. Nemeth. Dordrecht: Kluwer (Phaenomenologica, 120).

Shpet, Gustav (2019): Hermeneutics and Its Problems. With Selected Essay in Phenomenology. Translated by T. Nemeth. Cham: Springer (Contributions to Phenomenology, 98).

Smid, Reinhold Nikolaus (1982): „Münchener Phänomenologie" - Zur Frühgeschichte Des Begriffs. In Herbert Spiegelberg, Eberhard Avé-Lallemant (Eds.): Pfänder-Studien. The Hague: Nijhoff (Phaenomenologica, 84), pp. 109–153.

Sokolowski, Robert (1977): [Review] On the Motives which Led Husserl to Transcendental Idealism by Roman Ingarden. In *The Journal of Philosophy* 74 (3), pp. 176–180.

Sparrow, Tom (2014): The End of Phenomenology. Metaphysics and the New Realism. Edinburgh: Edinburgh University Press.

Spiegelberg, Herbert (1982): Epoché und Reduktion bei Pfänder und Husserl. In Herbert Spiegelberg, Eberhard Avé-Lallemant (Eds.): Pfänder-Studien. The Hague: Nijhoff (Phaenomenologica, 84), pp. 3–34.

Spiegelberg, Herbert (1994): The Phenomenological Movement. A Historical Introduction. 3rd revised and enlarged. Dordrecht: Kluwer (Phaenomenologica, 5).

Stang, Nicholas (2019): Platonism in Lotze and Frege Between Psychologism and Hypostasis. In Sandra Lapointe (Ed.): Logic from Kant to Russell. Laying the Foundations for Analytic Philosophy. New York: Routledge, pp. 138–159.

Stein, Edith (1989): On the Problem of Empathy. Translated by W. Stein. Washington: ICS Publications.

Stein, Edith (2000): Philosophy of psychology and the humanities. Translated by M. Basehart and M. Sawicki. Washington: ICS Publications.

Stein, Edith (2014): Letters to Roman Ingarden. Trans. Hugh Candler Hunt. Washington: ICS Publications (The Collected Works of Edith Stein, XII).

Stumpf, Carl (1939): Erkenntnislehre, Bd. 1. Leipzig: Barth.

Ueberweg, Friedrich (1863–71): Grundriss der Geschichte der Philosophie. Berlin: Mittler.

Varga, Peter Andras (2013): The Missing Chapter from the Logical Investigations: Husserl on Lotze's Formal and Real Significance of Logical Laws. In *Husserl Studies* 29, pp. 181–209.

Vēgners, Uldis (2020): Theodor Celms and the "Realism–Idealism" Controversy. In Witold Płotka, Patrick Eldridge (Eds.): Early phenomenology in Central and Eastern Europe. Main figures, ideas, and problems. Cham: Springer (Contributions to Phenomenology, 113), pp. 145–162.

Woodward, William R. (2015): Hermann Lotze. An Intellectual Biography. New York: Cambridge University Press.

Zahavi, Dan (1992): Intentionalität und Konstitution. Copenhagen: Museum Tusculanum Press.

Zahavi, Dan (2017): Husserl's Legacy. Phenomenology, Metaphysics, and Transcendental Philosophy. Oxford: Oxford University Press.

Zocher, Rudolf (1932): Husserls Phänomenologie und Schuppes Logik. Ein Beitrag zur Kritik des intuitionistischen Ontologismus in der Immanenzidee. Munich: Reinhardt.

Part I
Realism, Platonism, and Ideal Objects in the *Logical Investigations*

Hermann Lotze and the Genesis
of Husserl's Early Philosophy (1886–1901)

Denis Fisette

Abstract The purpose of this study is to assess Husserl's debt to Lotze's philosophy during the Halle period (1886–1901). I first track the sources of Husserl's knowledge of Lotze's philosophy during his studies with Brentano in Vienna and then with Stumpf in Halle. I then briefly comment on Husserl's references to Lotze in his early work and research manuscripts for the second volume of his *Philosophy of Arithmetic*. In the third section, I examine Lotze's influence on Husserl's antipsychologistic turn in the mid-1890s. The fourth section is a commentary on Husserl's manuscript titled "Mikrokosmos," to which he explicitly refers in his *Prolegomena*, and which he planned to publish as an appendix of his *Logical Investigations*. This work contains a detailed analysis of the third book of Lotze's 1874 *Logic*. The last section examines Husserl's arguments against logical psychologism in his *Prolegomena*, which I discuss through the lens of Stumpf's critique of psychologism in his paper "Psychology and theory of knowledge". I argue that Stumpf's early works on this topic make it possible to establish a connection between Lotze's interpretation of Plato's theory of Ideas and Husserl's antipsychologism. My hypothesis is that Stumpf's analyses represent the background of Husserl's critique of logical psychologism in his *Logical Investigations*. I conclude by showing that Husserl's position with respect to Lotze's philosophy remains basically unchanged after the publication of his *Logical Investigations*, and that Husserl's main criticism of Lotze pertains, in the final analysis, to the absence of a theory of intentionality in Lotze's philosophy.

Keywords Logical psychologism · Platonism · Objectivism · Subjectivism · Meaning · Logic · Theory of knowledge · Husserl · Lotze · Stumpf

Thanks to M. Ramstead for his stylistic remarks on an earlier version of this paper and the Husserl Archives in Leuven for the permission to use and quote the manuscript "Mikrokosmos" (K I 59). An earlier and shorter version of this paper has been published in Spanish under the title: "Hermann Lotze y la génesis de la filosofía temprana de Husserl", *Apeiron, Estudios de filosofía*, vol. 3, 2015, p. 13–35.

D. Fisette (✉)
Université du Québec à Montréal, Montreal, QC, Canada
e-mail: fisette.denis@uqam.ca

© Springer Nature Switzerland AG 2021
R. K. B. Parker (ed.), *The Idealism-Realism Debate Among Edmund Husserl's Early Followers and Critics*, Contributions to Phenomenology 112,
https://doi.org/10.1007/978-3-030-62159-9_2

1   Introduction

Husserl once said of Hermann Lotze that he was one of the greatest philosophers since Kant. (*Briefwechsel* IX, p. 154) Husserl's reverent remark about the Göttingen philosopher shows not only his respect for Lotze's philosophy, but also the central place Lotze deserves in the history of philosophy during the second half of the nineteenth century. Most commentaries on Husserl's relationship to Lotze during that period have emphasized his debt to Lotze's interpretation of the Platonic theory of Ideas in his 1874 *Logic*. Although this aspect of Husserl's relationship to Lotze is indeed decisive in the interpretation of his own Platonism, it does not itself explain why Husserl considered Lotze one of the most important researchers of his time, as he once again asserted in 1909 in his appraisal on Adolf Reinach's habilitation thesis.[1] (*Briefwechsel*, II, p. 206) The historical significance granted to Lotze's philosophy can be measured in part by the influence he has had on the history of philosophy, not only in Germany but also in Great Britain and America. The historian John Merz, a student of Lotze in the mid-1860s and the author of the monumental *History of European Thought in the XIXth Century in Great Britain*, has pointed out that Lotze's philosophy was at that time considered authoritative among the British idealists, nearly on equal footing with Hegel and Kant.

> But of the Germans who followed the classic days of Idealism none was more zealously studied, more deeply respected, and more frequently plundered (*sit venia verbo*) than Lotze. His influence was immeasurable, less only than that of Kant and Hegel. […] Many Britons even came into personal relation with Lotze; indeed, at one time it was almost a fashion to spend a period of study at Gottingen University, so as to receive philosophical wisdom from the master's own lips. (Merz 1938, p. 256)

Merz here refers to the generation of British philosophers who succeeded the idealists and who were mainly interested in Lotze's scientific work and in his

---

[1] Husserl's Platonism is not unrelated to the idealism-realism debate in which Husserl was involved with the Munich phenomenologists after the publication of *Logical Investigations*. Already in the *Prolegomena*, Husserl used the term idealism for a rare time not to designate a metaphysical doctrine, but rather "a theory of knowledge which recognizes the 'ideal' as a condition for the possibility of objective knowledge in general". (Husserl 1982a, p. 238) That said, there is nevertheless an important distinction to be made between the realism-idealism debate, which relates to a metaphysical question concerning the reality of the outside world, and that concerning Platonism in the debate on logical psychologism which relates to the ontological status of the principles and laws of logic. The metaphysical position that one takes with regard to the reality of the outside world is distinct from that which one adopts on the status of laws because one can in fact advocates a form of critical realism on metaphysical issues while adopting a form of Platonism with regard to the status of the principles of logic, for instance. This is the position that Husserl seems to have defended, if not during the Göttingen period, at least during the Halle period. As we shall see below, Husserl has always remained faithful to his Platonism, while his position towards idealism after the transcendental turn and the late influence that could have been exercised by philosophers such as Leibniz, Lotze, and Fichte in this regard is much more complicated (see Fisette 2007).

contribution to the emergence of the "new psychology".[2] In America, William James, whom Husserl held in great esteem, had also been greatly influenced by Brentano and Lotze, "the two great masters of psychological analysis and introspection." (Stumpf 1927, p. 225)[3]

In Germany, Lotze's work was a major reference in philosophy when the young Husserl began his philosophical studies shortly after Lotze's death in 1881 (Pester 1997). The influence of Lotze's philosophy in Germany is associated with three of his prestigious students in Göttingen, namely Gottlob Frege, Wilhelm Windelband and Carl Stumpf. Windelband studied under Lotze in the early 1870s and is known as the leader of the so-called Southwestern or Baden school of neo-Kantianism, whose main members were Heinrich Rickert and Bruno Bauch, the latter of which was Frege's colleague in Jena from 1911 onwards. Rickert and Bauch developed a philosophy of culture, based on an interpretation of Lotze's theory of values, which had become one of the dominant trends in German philosophy by the end of the nineteenth century (see Misch 1912; Linke 1924, 1926).

---

[2] George Croom Robertson, a student of Alexander Bain and co-founder of the famous journal *Mind*, studied with Lotze and the physicist Weber in Göttingen in 1862, and we know that he encouraged William Robertson Smith to attend Lotze's lectures. During his stay in Göttingen, Robertson Smith maintained close relationships with Carl Stumpf and the mathematician Felix Klein, and we also know that he acted as an emissary of Brentano during his trip to England in the early 1870s. (cf. Maier 2009) James Sully, the author of several influential books in psychology, studied with Lotze in the late 1860s and is known to have reviewed several of Stumpf's works for *Mind*. (Sully 1878, 1884, 1886, 1891) James Ward, who also studied with Lotze in Göttingen in the 1870s, is the author of the article "Psychology" published in the *Encyclopaedia Britannica*, which is the basis of his major 1918 work *Psychological Principles*, in which he acknowledges his debt to Lotze, Brentano and "his Austrian connections". (1918, p. IX) His student G. F. Stout, the mentor of Moore and Russell, was deeply interested in the work of Brentano and his students, and Bell has said of his book *Analytic Psychology* (1896) that it is essentially "a presentation, for an English audience, of the doctrines which have emerged some 22 years earlier in *Psychology from an Empirical Standpoint*." (Bell 1999, p. 201) That is why it has been said that Stout served as a mediator between his students Moore and Russell, on the one hand, and Brentano and his students in the field of descriptive psychology, on the other hand (see van der Schaar 1996, 2013). Bell examined the factors and forces responsible for the emergence of analytic philosophy and argued that the most important factor concerns the debates over the emergence of the new psychology: "Moore, I have suggested, is best seen as the major, though by no means the first, British participant in an existing debate whose other participants included Ward, Stout, Russell, Meinong, Stumpf, Husserl, Twardowski and Brentano. Many of the terms and goals of this debate originated in Germany, during the 1870s, in the attempts by philosophers, physiologists, theologians and others to come to terms with, and contribute to, the emergence of psychology as a discipline in its own right". (Bell 1999, p. 208) Of course, I would add the name of Lotze as the central piece of this complex puzzle.

[3] In a series of articles on James and Lotze, Krausharr nicely summarizes Lotze's major influence on James's *Psychology*: "There was so much in Lotze that coincided with and paralleled the course of James's ideas, that he became for a time very much enmeshed in Lotze's *Problemlage*. The philosophical position that is developed in the *Principles of Psychology* leans heavily upon Lotze's philosophical and psychological doctrines. He did not extricate himself therefrom fully until the final working out of his philosophy of pure experience." (1939, p. 458) Krausharr (1936, p. 245) rightly pointed out that it was under the influence of Stumpf's *Raumbuch* that James became interested in Lotze's theory of local signs.

Frege pursued his studies in mathematics in Göttingen between 1871 and 1873, and although he only attended Lotze's lecture on philosophy of religion, many of his ideas were anticipated in Lotze's logic.[4] In the context of this study, it is important to recall that Frege has long been considered the father of the two main traditions that have dominated the history of philosophy starting from the beginning of the twentieth century, namely phenomenology (see Smith 2013) and analytic philosophy (Dummett 1993). Commentators of Frege, including Hans Sluga (1980, 1984) and Gottfried Gabriel (1989, 2002, 2013), have called into question Michael Dummett's thesis about the Fregean origin of analytic philosophy and stressed the alleged influence of Lotze and the Baden neo-Kantians on the young Frege, such that Frege could plausibly be considered a *Neokantianer*. They further argue "that at least *early* analytic philosophy has its roots in the tradition of continental philosophy, especially in the philosophy of Hermann Lotze." (Gabriel 2002, p. 39) However, even if one recognizes Lotze's influence on Frege, this does not *ipso facto* make him a neo-Kantian, unless one uses the concept of neo-Kantianism in a sense broad enough to include Lotze's philosophy.[5]

Finally, the name of Carl Stumpf is of particular importance in this study because of his close relationship with Lotze during the six years he spent in Göttingen (1867–1873) and later with Husserl in Halle, where he held a chair in philosophy

---

[4] See Kreiser's biography of Frege (2001, p. 86–111). Frege himself acknowledged Lotze's influence on his thought, as evidenced by Bauch: "I heard it myself from the mouth of Frege, our great mathematician, that for his mathematical—and, if I may add what Frege modestly did not mention—epochmaking investigations, impulses from Lotze were of decisive importance". (in Schlotter 2006, p. 45) See also Gabriel (1989) who convincingly shows the influence of Lotze's logic on Frege.

[5] Gabriel's arguments, which support his construal of Frege as a neo-Kantian, are mainly based on Frege's personal acquaintance with Bauch in Jena and on the alleged affinities of Frege's epistemological positions with those of the neo-Kantian Windelband, even if Frege almost never refers to neo-Kantians. Paul F. Linke, who was Frege's colleague in Jena starting from 1907 and one of his strongest supporters in Germany, excludes any influence of his fellow neo-Kantians in Jena on Frege. (Linke 1946, p. 77) Linke was close to Husserl and to the Brentanian circles. He published in Husserl's *Jahrbuch* and he was one of the first to emphasize the influence of Frege on Husserl; (Linke 1926, p. 228–229) he is the author of "Gottlob Frege als Philosoph" and in his later writings showed great interest in Frege (see Dathe 2000). Through his conversations with Linke, Frege might have been informed of Husserl's work and that of Brentano's students in general. In any case, it is worth remembering that Brentano's students were responsible for the early reception of Frege's work in Germany. Indeed, in 1882, Stumpf received a letter from Frege, in which he described the basic ideas of his *Begriffsschrift* in great detail and asked Stumpf to publish a review of his book, which, at that time, had been ignored since its publication in 1879. Frege feared above all that the works he was preparing on the logical foundation of arithmetic would suffer the same fate as his *Begriffsschrift* and approached Stumpf for advice. Stumpf responded to Frege's letter a few weeks later by promising to review his *Begriffsschrift* and recommended that Frege first publish his research in vernacular language (*gewöhnlich*) and postpone the publication of his theory of arithmetic based on the technical language of his *Begriffsschrift*. Yet, as we know, it was not Stumpf but Anton Marty, another of Brentano's students, who in 1884 reviewed and commented Frege's theory of judgment and his *Begriffsschrift* in the second article in a series of papers on subjectless propositions. (Marty 1884) Finally, let us mention Benno Kerry, another student of Brentano. Kerry was very interested in Frege's works (see Peckhaus 1994).

from 1884 to 1889. Stumpf attended Lotze's lectures, and successfully defended a dissertation on Plato (1869) and then his habilitation thesis on mathematical axioms (1870) under his direction. At age 22, Stumpf became *Privatdozent* at the University of Göttingen, where he was Lotze's colleague. During his three years as *Privatdozent* in Göttingen, he maintained a close relationship with Lotze, and undertook extensive research on the topic of space perception, which led to the publication of his book *On the Origin of the Representation of Space* in 1873, dedicated to Lotze.[6]

Lotze's three main students in Germany find a common starting point in a theme that Lotze had already set up in his logic, organized around the epistemological issues arising from the unprecedented development of both the new psychology and logic, which in turn led to many reform projects at the time. These epistemological questions are at the heart of the early debates over psychologism, to which contributed not only Frege (1884), but also Windelband (1877) and Stumpf (1891). Although the positions advocated by these students of Lotze are slightly different, their struggle against psychologism converges towards Husserl's position in his *Prolegomena*. This line of criticism targets a research program not very different from Quine's program to naturalize epistemology in contemporary philosophy. At that time, this program was widespread among philosophers such as Wilhelm Wundt and John Stuart Mill, for example, who are the main targets of Frege, Stumpf, and Husserl in their criticism of logical psychologism. Husserl's main argument against Mill is based on the ideal or objective character of the laws of logic, which Husserl conceived of in terms of *Geltung*. But while Frege and the neo-Kantians advocated a solution to this problem that involved the outright rejection of psychology as a philosophical discipline[7], Brentano's students recognized, as Lotze had as well, the

---

[6] See Stumpf (1917, 1976, p. 18 ff) for an account of his activity in Göttingen between 1870 and 1873. The main subject of Stumpf's *Raumbuch* is the nativism-empiricism controversy; Stumpf's starting point is Lotze's theory of local signs, which represents, according to many, his main contribution to the problem of space perception. Lotze responded to Stumpf's criticism in his "Mitteilung an Stumpf," which is annexed to Stumpf's work. (1873, p. 315–324) After leaving Göttingen, Stumpf continued to consider Lotze's work. Besides his reminiscences of Lotze published in *Kantstudien* (Stumpf 1917) and the constant references to his work, Stumpf reviewed most of Lotze's posthumous works published in German between 1882 and 1892 (see Fisette 2015d). In 1893, he published an article in which he revised his position on local signs. (Stumpf 1893) In his inaugural address as Rector of the University of Berlin, delivered in 1907 under the title "The renaissance of philosophy", Stumpf associates Lotze's thought with a revival of German philosophy in the mid-nineteenth century. Stumpf distinguishes two main orientations of German philosophy in the second half of the nineteenth century, the first being neo-Kantianism, which advocated a return to Kant, and the second being the so-called *Erfahrungsphilosophie*. At the time, in Germany at least, *Erfahrungsphilosophie* was the common denominator of several schools of thought, including the school of Brentano, which sought to practice philosophy in the spirit of the natural sciences. Stumpf maintains that, through their empirical work in the field of philosophy of mind and physiological psychology, philosophers like Lotze and Fechner contributed significantly to a renaissance of philosophy in Germany.

[7] Windelband's and Rickert's positions on psychology come out clearly from their classification of sciences into idiographic and natural sciences, which was intended to replace the traditional classification based on the distinction between *Natur-* and *Geisteswissenschaften*. Windelband's and Rickert's main argument is that, methodologically, the new psychology was more akin to natural

indispensable contribution of psychology to the theory of knowledge. This theme is at the heart of the young Husserl's research during the Halle period and it is sufficient on its own to justify his judgment on the importance of Lotze's philosophy to the development of his phenomenology and pure logic during that period.

The purpose of this study is to assess Husserl's debt to Lotze's philosophy during the Halle period. I am mainly interested in the genesis of the young Husserl's thought from his arrival in Halle in 1886 to the publication of his *Hauptwerk* in 1900–1901. I shall first track the sources of Husserl's knowledge of Lotze's philosophy during his studies with Brentano in Vienna and then with Stumpf in Halle. I shall then briefly comment on Husserl's references to Lotze in his early work and research manuscripts for the second volume of his *Philosophy of Arithmetic*. In the third section, I examine Lotze's influence on Husserl's anti-psychologistic turn in the mid-1890s. The fourth section is a commentary on Husserl's manuscript titled "Mikrokosmos," to which he explicitly refers in his *Prolegomena*, and which he planned to publish as an appendix of his *Logical Investigations*. This work contains a detailed analysis of the third book of Lotze's 1874 *Logic*. The last section examines Husserl's arguments against logical psychologism in his *Prolegomena*, which I discuss through the lens of Stumpf's critique of psychologism in his paper "Psychology and theory of knowledge". I argue that Stumpf's early works on this topic make it possible to establish a connection between Lotze's interpretation of Plato's theory of Ideas and Husserl's anti-psychologism. My hypothesis is that Stumpf's analyses represent the background of Husserl's critique of logical psychologism in his *Logical Investigations*. I shall conclude this study by showing that Husserl's position with respect to Lotze's philosophy remains basically unchanged after the publication of his *Logical Investigations*, and that Husserl's main criticism of Lotze pertains, in the final analysis, to the absence of a theory of intentionality in Lotze's philosophy.

2 Husserl's Main Sources: Brentano and Stumpf

The young Husserl inherited his sympathy for the philosophy of Lotze *via* his relationship with Brentano in Vienna (1884–1886) and then with Stumpf in Halle, where he arrived in the fall of 1886 to complete his habilitation thesis. There is indeed a direct filiation between Lotze, on the one hand, and Brentano and his students, on the other, including the young Husserl. Indeed, we know that Brentano, before obtaining his chair at Würzburg in 1872, was not habilitated to supervise theses, and that is why, in 1867, he recommended to Stumpf, and later to Anton

than to moral science and therefore could not be considered an idiographic science. In his 1927 lecture *Natur und Geist*, Husserl criticizes their interpretation of Lotze's theory of values from the perspective of a philosophy of culture based on a "critical science of values" and accuses them of ruling out intentional psychology, to which Husserl assigns a central place in his Freiburg phenomenology. (Hua XXXIII, p. 80–81, 95)

Marty, that they move to Göttingen in order to study with Lotze. Although Brentano's philosophical program constitutes the main background of Stumpf's thought, one cannot underestimate the influence of Lotze's philosophy on Stumpf's philosophy during the six years he spent in Göttingen. (Stumpf 1895, p. 735)

In his correspondence with Stumpf, as well as in his *Psychology from an Empirical Standpoint*, Brentano unequivocally expressed his esteem for Lotze and indicated several aspects of his work that he considered lasting contributions to philosophy. In a passage from a letter to Stumpf dated November 3, 1867, Brentano explains why Lotze was among the best German philosophers at the time to supervise his studies:

> Because I could not name any other professor of philosophy whose doctrine in its essential aspects I do not hold to be false, and because Lotze, despite all that he lacks, is in many ways remarkable. Notably, his philosophical method, his emphasis on experience and observation, the way he uses scientific results, the caution and meticulousness with which he exposes his theses, all set him apart, and advantageously so, from most other scholars of our time. And I do not know anyone else from whom you could learn more in this regard. (Brentano 1989, p. 3; see Stumpf 1817, p. 2)

Brentano had even taken steps to facilitate Lotze's hiring at Würzburg, in order to keep his students in the same university. (Brentano 1989, p. 11) Elsewhere in his correspondence with Stumpf, Brentano criticizes Lotze for the noxious influence of Kantianism on his thinking, for his incomplete knowledge of ancient philosophy, and for his inadequate classification of mental phenomena. He nevertheless acknowledges that Lotze's writings were "superior to those of most contemporary philosophers". Brentano confirms these views in the preface to his *Psychology*. There, he acknowledges the influence of Lotze on his thought (Brentano 2008, p. 4) and repeatedly refers to two of his important works, *Medical Psychology* and *Microcosmos*, thoroughly discussing Lotze's views on emotions and feelings (Brentano 2008, p. 167 f.; p. 262 f.; 268 f.) along with his classification of acts. (Brentano 2008, p. 206 f.; p. 254 f.)

Furthermore, considering Lotze's great notoriety at the time, in Germany and abroad, and Stumpf's close relationship with the Göttingen philosopher, there is no doubt that Lotze was a key factor not only in Brentano's career, but also in Stumpf's and Marty's. Thanks to Lotze, Stumpf inherited Brentano's chair in Würzburg in 1874; the correspondence between Brentano and Stumpf also indicates that Lotze had a hand in Marty's hiring in Czernowirz in 1875 and in Prague in 1880. For, besides Brentano's and Stumpf's numerous manoeuvres to promote Marty's hiring in Czernowitz, we know that Stumpf went so far as to personally travel to Göttingen in order to gain the support of Lotze and of his student Baumann for Marty's candidature. Shortly after he resigned in Wurzburg, Brentano undertook discussions with the University of Vienna to fill the position left vacant since the departure of Franz Lott, a position he obtained thanks once again to Lotze, who spoke with the Austrian ministry in favour of his candidacy. (Stumpf 1976, p. 34; Lotze 2003, p. 595–596)

As we can see, the close relationship between Brentano, Stumpf and Lotze, both personally and philosophically, may have favourably disposed the young Husserl towards the Göttingen philosopher. However, Husserl's first significant exposure to

Lotze's philosophy occurred during his two years of study with Brentano in Vienna (1884–1886), where he attended several of the great scholar's seminars (see Rollinger 1999, p. 17), namely those on logic and psychology, in which Brentano occasionally discussed the work of Lotze.[8] As Husserl explains in his "Reminiscences of Franz Brentano," Brentano's main concern at that time was descriptive psychology. (Hua XXV, p. 307) Husserl's correspondence with Brentano confirms his interest in Brentano's research on descriptive psychology during the Halle period (*Briefwechsel* I, p. 6) The results of Brentano's research were the subject of lectures he held in 1890–1891 on descriptive psychology (which he also calls "psychognosy" or "descriptive phenomenology"), in which he subjected his earlier conception of psychology to substantial revisions. In this regard, Brentano might have been influenced by Lotze, who frequently used the notions of descriptive psychology and phenomenology in his published writings and lectures. (Misch 1912, p. L–LV; Orth 1995, 1997)

3   Lotze and Husserl's Anti-psychologistic Turn

The Halle period is one of the richest in the development of Husserl's thought, and it has been repeatedly commented on in Husserl studies. However, besides the studies that have focused on Husserl's assessment of Lotze's logic in his *Logical Investigations*,[9] the importance of Lotze in the genesis of Husserl's phenomenology during this period has not been sufficiently investigated. Yet there are many indications in Husserl's work, namely in his 1896 lectures on logic, which confirm that Lotze is not foreign to Husserl's abandonment of the research program that guided his early work, and that the reform of logic he began to carry out in the mid-1890s goes hand in hand with his anti-psychologistic turn. The other main aspect of Husserl's research during this period relates to descriptive psychology, on the basis of which he defines his own phenomenology (in the *Logical Investigations*) and his theory of intentionality, which he elaborated in several writings of this period. These include his 1894 "Psychological studies" and several research manuscripts, such as "Intentional object," where he critically examines Kazimierz Twardowski's book *On the Content and Object of Presentations* (1894). We shall see that this manuscript bears the mark of Lotze's influence and constitutes an essential complement to another important manuscript titled "Mikrokosmos" (1895–1897), in which Husserl initiates a critical examination of Lotze's theory of knowledge in his

---

[8] Although Husserl acquired a copy of Lotze's *Microcosmos* as early as 1880 (Schuhmann 1977, p. 8), nothing indicates that he was interested in Lotze's philosophy at that time; and it is unlikely that he had any direct contact with Lotze, who arrived in Berlin in April 1881 and passed away in July of the same year.

[9] There are indeed quite a few studies on Husserl's relationship to Lotze's philosophy. Let me here mention the latest: Dastur (1994); Beyer (1996); Hauser (2003); Dewalque (2012a, 2012b); Varga (2013).

"greater" *Logic*. Finally, Husserl discusses Lotze's positions on space perception in his draft of a *Raumbuch*, which belongs to the same period. We shall see that accounting for the Lotzean elements in the young Husserl's work opens new perspectives on this complicated period in the genesis of his thought.

Let me first say a few words about the project of a *Raumbuch*, which was part of Husserl's research for the second volume of his *Philosophy of Arithmetic*. Those fragments from this project that have survived evince a marked interest for the psychological question of the origin of space perception and for the nativism-empiricism debate. Husserl's position in these manuscripts, and especially in the important fragment §10, are very close to the kind of "nativism" advocated by Stumpf in his own *Raumbuch*, and there one also finds discussions on Lotze's theory of local signs. (Hua XXI, p. 269, 309) In an article published two years later titled "Psychological studies for elementary logic," Husserl describes the work of Lotze and Stumpf on space perception as "masterful research". (Hua XXII, p. 123) Although this project was never carried out, we can still distill some results, which are partly exposed in his "Psychological studies". The most important of these lies in the concept of psychological part or moment, on which is based Stumpf's main position in § 5 of his *Raumbuch*. Now, the first version of Husserl's theory of parts and wholes, which he develops in the first part of this article, is based primarily on Stumpf's ideas, as Husserl acknowledges in this article and later in the third *Investigation*. (Hua XXII, p. 92, 94)

Part-whole relations pertain to a general theory of relations, which Husserl briefly mentions in his *Philosophy of Arithmetic* and outlines in this article. In a footnote to chapter III of this book, in which he deals with collective relations (2003, p. 84), Husserl refers to Lotze's *Metaphysics* and to the first volume of Stumpf's *Psychology of Sound* (1883, p. 96), in which he introduced his famous notion of fusion in the context of a study of basic relations (*Grundverhälnisse*). Drawing on the work of Stumpf and Lotze, Husserl distinguishes two classes of relations: intentional and primary relations. The latter class of relations bear the character of primary contents (or sensory content) and they have a "peculiar phenomenal character". (Husserl 2003, p. 71)[10]

Each relation belonging to this class, for example the relation of analogy between two contents, is included non-intentionally in a presentation. (2003, p. 71) The relations belonging to the class of intentional relations pertain exclusively to the class of psychical phenomena. They are characterized by acts, which relate and unify several contents. The main difference between these two classes of relations is that, for the first class, "the relation is immediately given along with representing the terms, as a moment of the same representational content," (2003, p. 72) whereas for

---

[10] Husserl seeks to avoid Brentano's concept of physical phenomenon because it does not properly designate an analogy, gradation, etc., and he instead prefers the concept of primary or immanent content. Nevertheless, the concept of intentional inexistence, which is Brentano's criterion for the distinction between these two classes of phenomena, remains the basis for the classification of relations in this work. (Husserl 2003, p. 73)

the second, in order to represent the relation, one has to perform "a reflexive act of representing bearing upon the relating act". (2003, p. 73)[11]

As for the class of intentional relations, Husserl's conception considerably evolved from that in his first works, in which he uncritically adopted Brentano's immanent theory. This uncritical adoption lasted until 1894, as shown in his work "Intentional objects," where he critically examines Twardowski's treatment of the problem of objectless presentations. In addition to the significant contribution of this text to Husserl's theory of intentionality in the Fifth Investigation (Fisette 2003, forthcoming), the problem of intentional objects is not unrelated to the central issue in Husserl's 1895–1897 manuscript on Lotze's logic and his interpretation of Plato's Ideas in terms of *Geltung*. Indeed, Lotze himself in his greater 1874 logic (Lotze 1884, p. 504) explicitly related the problem he sought to solve with the concept of *Geltung* and that of objects of thought (*Gedankendinge*) in Medieval philosophy. This issue is related to Brentano's and Twardowski's postulation of an immanent mode of existence for intentional objects of thought. In his 1894 manuscript, Husserl repudiates this postulate and accuses Twardowski of conflating objective and subjective intention in his discussion with Bernard Bolzano. Husserl (1990, p. 168) argues that the discourse on the in-existence of intentional objects is an improper way of speaking and calls into question the view advocated by Twardowski and Brentano, according to which an existential valid affirmative judgment of the form "A exists" presupposes the in-existence of an intentional object. (Husserl, 1990, p. 145) Husserl's solution in this work, in his unpublished review of Twardowski's book (Husserl 1994, p. 391–392) and in the Appendix to §§ 11 and 20 of the Fifth Investigation, rests on the identification of intentional and valid objects.[12] This solution is very likely inspired by Lotze, as shown by the following passage, in which Husserl summarizes his solution to the problem of intentional objects following the paradigm of objects of judgment, i.e., states of affairs:

> If, for example, we impute an object to the *proposition,* as what is represented by means of its signification content and indeed its *whole* signification content (thus we have in mind not the mere object for which the subject of the proposition stands, the characteristic corresponding to the predicate, and the like)—then by that we pick out the "state of affairs," which subsists if the proposition holds true, and does not subsist if it does not hold true. If the question about the distinction between true and intentional objects in the case of nominal representations has led us to existential assertions in which those representations function as subject representations, and which, depending on the circumstances, were advanced absolutely or were understood as only conditioned, then all of that carries over analogically to the case now at hand, if only we replace the assertions of *existence* with assertions of *validity (Gültigkeitsbehauptungen) (A is valid [A gilt])*. But these assertions, too, can be

---

[11] The importance of the distinction between these two classes of relations is confirmed by several other texts belonging to the Halle period (see Fisette 2000).

[12] Husserl writes: "It need only be acknowledged *that the intentional object of a presentation is the same as its actual object, and on occasion the same as its external object, and that it is absurd to distinguish between them.* The transcendent object would not be the object of *this* presentation, if it was not *its* intentional object. This is plainly a merely analytic proposition. The object of the presentation, of the 'intention', *is* and *means* what is presented, the intentional object". (Husserl 1982b, p. 127)

meant, at one time absolutely, and at another time under hypothesis. The circumstance that with reference to each proposition an equivalent existential proposition can be found, which, however its signification content may be modified, represents the same state of affairs as the proposition originally given, in a way reduces the present case back to the earlier one, comprising merely nominal representations. And so the talk of intentional and true objects agrees in the two cases. (Husserl 1994, p. 376–377. Translation modified.)

Several other aspects of this writing are relevant in the context of this study, namely the parallel Husserl establishes between the problem of the imaginary in mathematics and that of objectless presentations in psychology. For the mathematical problem pertains to justification in mathematical calculation that employ imaginary numbers. We know that this problem was at the heart of Husserl's concerns ever since his habilitation thesis (Husserl 2003, p. 307) and constitutes one of the main factors at the origin of the abandonment of the research program of *Philosophy of Arithmetic*. Likewise, Husserl's remarks on assumptions (*Annahmen*) (Husserl 1994, p. 363–368) constitute an important step towards the final solution that he proposed to the problem of imaginary numbers through his doctrine of definite multiplicities, which in turn represents the cornerstone of his *Wissenschaftslehre*. (Husserl 2001; Fisette 2003, forthcoming)

The next step in the genesis of the *Logical Investigations* leads to the issue of Husserl's anti-psychologistic turn, which occurred between 1894 and 1896, i.e., between the definitive abandonment of the research program that guided Husserl since his habilitation thesis and the new program based on pure logic. The "cause" of this paradigm shift has long been associated with Frege's 1984 review of Husserl's *Philosophy of Arithmetic* and the so-called Fregean reading of Husserl's phenomenology, which I mentioned earlier. We have no evidence that corroborates the alleged influence Frege might have had on Husserl's "conversion," but there are good reasons to assume that Husserl could not remain indifferent to Frege's criticism. I cannot address the issue as to whether Frege's review had a triggering effect on Husserl's turn, and it is not necessarily the best way of addressing the conversion. For we know from the correspondence they exchanged in 1891 (*Briefwechsel*, VI, p. 106–118) that Husserl knew the work of Frege, which he extensively discusses in his *Philosophy of Arithmetic*. (Fisette, 2004) How could Husserl have possibly ignored the contribution of this student of Lotze to an issue that animated the entirety of his thought during this period? Moreover, we know that Frege's criticism in his correspondence and in his review of Husserl's first book is based on several distinctions that are essential to Husserl's pure logic, including the distinctions between proposition and concept, between subjective and objective presentations, between *Sinn* and *Bedeutung*, etc. (cf. Husserl 1982a, p. 201)[13]

---

[13] These distinctions are also central in Husserl's criticism of Twardowski. (Husserl 1994, p. 374–375, 388–390; 1982b, p. 125–127) In a footnote to his *Prolegomena* (1982a, p. 318), Husserl confirms Frege's influence: "G. Frege's stimulating work *Die Grundlagen der Arithmetik* (1884, p. vi) (I need hardly say that I no longer approve of my own fundamental criticisms of Frege's anti-psychologistic position set forth in my *Philosophie der Arithmetik*, I, pp. 129–32). Here, I may seize the opportunity, in relation to all of the discussions of these *Prolegomena*, to refer to the Preface of Frege's later work *Grundgesetze der Arithmetik*, vol. I (Jena, 1893)".

That being said, the two names that Husserl explicitly associates with his anti-psychologistic turn and his conversion to Platonism are those of Bolzano and Lotze, as Husserl confirms in his correspondence with Brentano: "These conceptions of Bolzano [representation and proposition in itself] have produced a major effect on me, as did Lotze's interpretation of Plato's theory of Ideas." (*Briefwechsel*, I, p. 39)[14] As early as 1896, in his lectures on logic, Husserl recognizes his debt to Bolzano's *Wissenschaftslehre* with respect to his pure logic, understood as a theory of science, and he also refers to Lotze's thesis that arithmetic is only *ein Stück* from logic, a thesis formulated at the beginning of his *Logic*. Husserl stresses the great importance of Lotze's thesis for his own reform of logic and claims that it is the most powerful tool invented by the human mind for the purposes of deduction.[15] Lotze's

---

However, this reference to the *Grundgesetze* is problematic because Frege's main argument against logical psychologism is based on the normative character of the laws of logic, an argument that Husserl dismisses in the *Prolegomena*. This is shown by the following excerpt from Frege's *Grundgesetze der Arithmetik*: "It is commonly granted that the logical laws are guidelines which thought should follow to arrive at the truth; but it is too easily forgotten. The ambiguity of the word "law" here is fatal. In one sense it says what is, in the other it prescribes what ought to be. Only in the latter sense can the logical laws be called laws of thought, in so far as they legislate how one ought to think. Every law stating what is the case can be conceived as prescriptive, one should think in accordance with it, and in that sense it is accordingly a law of thought. This holds for geometrical and physical laws no less than for the logical. The latter better deserve the title "laws of thought" only if thereby it is supposed to be said that they are the most general laws, prescribing how to think wherever there is thinking at all." (Frege 2013, p. XV)

[14] This dual influence is well documented in Husserl's work, particularly in his 1903 review of M. Palágyi, in which he once again confirms the influence of Lotze's and Bolzano's contributions: "In particular, *Lotze's* reflections about the interpretation of *Plato's* theory of forms had a profound effect on me. Only by thinking out these thoughts from *Lotze*—and in my opinion he failed to get completely clear on them—did I find the key to the curious conceptions of *Bolzano*, which in all their phenomenological naivety were at first unintelligible, and to the treasures of his *Wissenschaftslehre*." (Husserl 1994, p. 201)

[15] "And so, we will have to be content with Lotze's at first arguably strange view that arithmetic is only a relatively independent and since ancient times particularly sophisticated part of logic. In fact, in practical terms, it also represents the greatest instrument the human mind has ever devised for the purposes of deduction" ("Und so werden wir uns der zunächst wohl befremdlichen Auffassung Lotzes befreunden müssen, dass die Arithmetik nur rein relativ selbständiges und von alters her besonders hoch entwickeltes Stück der Logik sei. Tatsächlich repräsentiert sie auch in praktischer Hinsicht das großartigster Instrument, das der menschliche Geist zu Zwecken der Deduktion ersonnen hat"). (Husserl 2001b, p. 271–272) Husserl discusses several other aspects of Lotze's logic in this lecture: § 44 ("Inhaltsinterpretation dieser Form" p. 152–153; § 45 „Die negativen kategorischen Sätze und die Bedeutung der Negation", p. 155–157, 162. It is also worth recalling that, in his correspondence with Stumpf in the early 1890s as well as in a letter to Brentano published recently (Husserl 2015), Husserl emphasized the urgent need for a thorough reform of logic. He already considered the hypothesis that the *arithmetica universalis* "is a segment of formal logic." (1994, p. 17) However, logic was at that time defined as a practical science, as "a symbolic technique" and not as a purely theoretical logic or as a theory of science, as will be the case starting from his 1896 lecture on logic.

logicist thesis had a lasting effect on Husserl, as confirmed by several passages of his work, particularly in the *Prolegomena*.[16]

4   Remarks on Husserl's Manuscript K I 59 (Mikrokosmos)

The Husserl Archives in Leuven have preserved some manuscripts in which Husserl provides a critical examination of Lotze's *Logic*. Besides the annotations in the margins of his copy of Lotze's *Logic*, the manuscript K I 59—to which Husserl refers in the first edition of his *Prolegomena* as being intended for inclusion as an appendix to the second volume of his *Logical Investigations* (Hua XVIII, p. 221 f.)—provides a detailed analysis of the third book of Lotze's *Logic*, titled "*Vom Erkennen*".[17] This manuscript is dated 1895–1897 and essentially consists in a critical commentary on the third book of Lotze's *Logic*. It is divided into two parts. In the first part, which is incomplete in the transcription I am using in this study (K I 59, p. 4a–7a), Husserl briefly comments on some passages from §§ 314–316 of the second chapter of the *Logic*, titled "The world of ideas," and attributes to Lotze the merit of having stressed the decisive significance of the distinction between the subjective aspects of thought and the objective aspects of its propositional contents. Husserl also credited Lotze for having formulated the principle of the independence of *Gedanken* as the guiding principle of his logic and theory of knowledge. (K I 59, p. 5a) The second part, which occupies the major part of the manuscript, is a critical examination of §§ 316 f. of Lotze's *Logic*. Husserl tries to show that several passages

---

[16] Husserl 1982a, p. 108, 136 ff; *Briefwechsel* VII, p. 97). In his *Prolegomena* and *Formal and Transcendental Logic* (1969, p. 83), Husserl refers to the following passage of Lotze's *Logic*: "It is necessary, however, to expressly point out that all calculation is a kind of thought, that the fundamental concepts and principles of mathematics have their systematic place in logic, and that we must retain the right, at a later period, when occasion requires, to return without scruple upon the results that mathematics have been achieving, as an independently progressive branch of universal logic." (Lotze 1884, p. 26)

[17] Lotze's *Logic* belongs to the last period of his work (1869–1881), during which he began to develop a comprehensive and systematic exposition of his philosophy, which he calls his system of philosophy. His 1874 *Logic* is actually the first book of his "System of philosophy"; the second book is his *Metaphysics*, published in 1879. The third volume, which has never been published, was to contain his aesthetic, moral theories as well as his philosophy of religion. His *Logic* is divided into three parts. In the first book, titled "Pure logic," Lotze describes systematically the formation of concepts, judgments, and inferences independently of their context of application, and especially of psychology. In the second book, "Applied logic," Lotze explains how the particular contents of our representations are subject to the ideal forms of concepts, judgments, and inferences. The third book, titled "On Knowledge," addresses the question of how our thoughts can lay claim to an objective understanding of the objective correlates and causes of our representations, i.e., the real world. In the first chapter of this third book, Lotze discards the skeptical arguments by arguing, as Husserl does in his *Prolegomena*, that skeptical doubt presupposes a recognized truth and that skepticism is a contradictory doctrine. The second chapter, "The world of ideas" (§§ 313–321), contains Lotze's well-known interpretation of Plato's Ideas, which Lotze seeks to defend against the objection of hypostasis, as well as the famous notion of *Geltung*.

of the *Logic* do not always harmonize with Lotze's objectivism in his interpretation of Plato's Ideas and that Lotze does not always respect the boundary between the objective and the subjective. Husserl claims that Lotze has not succeeded in standing out decisively from what he calls subjectivism. Establishing this claim had been the main subject of the untranscribed portion of the first part of the manuscript (K I 59, p. 5a).

The manuscript begins with the conclusion of this analysis of subjectivism, a position that Husserl accuses of omitting numerous basic distinctions essential to pure logic, especially those between thought and its objective content, between objective forms and subjective acts, between concept and proposition, object and state of affairs, existence and truth. (K I 59, p. 4a) In conceiving of judgement and inference solely in terms of mental acts of judging, subjectivism does not respect the boundary between psychology and logic. On the other hand, Husserl suggests that the normative character of logic is not a decisive argument against subjectivism and in favor of the separation between logic and psychology. In this context, Husserl criticizes Johann Friedrich Herbart for conceiving of logic as merely a normative science and for thus conflating the normative use of the laws of logic with their theoretical content. Husserl's pure logic is a theoretical science and the main argument against psychologism that he elaborates during this period is not based on normativity, but rather on the ideality and objectivity of the laws of logic, which he conceives, in this manuscript, in terms of *Geltung*. Husserl credited Lotze for having introduced the main conditions that a pure logic has to meet in his 1874 *Logic*, but criticized him for his subjectivist interpretation of logical forms (as mental or subjective movements of the thinking subject), relations, *Gedanken* (as product of judgment), inferences, etc. That is why Husserl believes Lotze failed to draw all the logical and epistemological consequences from the objectivist position he attributes to Plato in his interpretation of Plato's Ideas.

Now, let us see what we can draw from Husserl's remarks on the chapter "The world of ideas." Let me begin with the cardinal distinction between proposition and concept, on which depend most of the distinctions mentioned above. In this chapter, Lotze criticizes Plato's conception of Ideas as isolated concepts and argues that a concept only has a meaning in the context of a complete sentence or statement, which expresses a *Gedanke* and the content of a propositional attitude. The same criticism holds for Kant's forms of thought, conceived as general concepts or categories. (Lotze 1884, p. 448) Plato's world of eternal truths must necessarily take a propositional form insofar as propositions are the smallest unit of meaning and the only bearers of truth. Husserl conceives of propositions in terms of Bolzano's propositions in themselves, as shown in this passage from his review of Melchior Palágyi, where they are defined as follows:

under "proposition in itself" is to be understood what is designated in ordinary discourse— which always objectifies the Ideal—as the "sense" *("Sinn")* of a statement. It is that which is explained as one and the same where, for example, different persons are said to have asserted the same thing. Or, again, it is what, in science, is simply called a theorem, e.g., the theorem about the sum of the angles in a triangle, which no one would think of taking to be someone's lived experience of judging. (Husserl 1994, p. 201)

This is actually Husserl's starting point in this manuscript, given that the objective character of propositions had been clearly established in his debate with Twardowski. His interest for Lotze in this manuscript primarily concerns the nature of propositions (in relation to Lotze's *Geltung*), the logical conditions of the objective truth (truth in itself), the logico-psychological (or noetico-noematic) conditions of judgment, and the epistemological conditions for our knowledge of the external world in connection with Lotze's theory of knowledge.

Let us first examine the famous passage from § 316 of Lotze's *Logic*, in which he introduces the concept of *Geltung* in the context of a distinction between four forms of effectivity (*Wirklichkeit*):

> For we call a thing Real (*wirklich*) which is, in contradistinction to another which is not; an event Real which occurs or has occurred, in contradistinction to that which does not occur; a relation Real which obtains, as opposed to one which does not obtain; lastly we call a proposition Really true which holds or is valid as opposed to one of which the validity is still doubtful. (Lotze 1884, p. 439)

Validity (*Geltung*) is a primitive form of effectivity and should therefore not be confused with the three other forms of effectivity. Lotze explains that the effectivity of Platonic Ideas (or propositions) should be understood in the sense of validity, which is a logical form that holds only for the truth of a proposition, and it is therefore independent of the existence of things in the outside world and of one's mental states, which are called real in an ontological sense. (Lotze 1884, p. 448) Husserl fully agrees with Lotze's interpretation (K I 59, p. 7a), and explains in his review of Palágyi that the notion of *Geltung* makes it possible to understand in a non-metaphysical way Bolzano's *Sätze an sich* and the ideality of meaning, which he conceives of in the *Logical Investigations* as species of acts:

> The proposition thus relates to those acts of judgment to which it belongs as their identical meaning *(Meinung)* in the same way, for example, as the species *redness* relates to individuals of "the same" red color. Now, with this view of things as a basis, *Bolzano's* theory, that propositions are objects which nonetheless have no "existence," comes to have the following quite intelligible signification: —They have the "Ideal" being *(Sein)* or validity *(Gelten)* of objects which are universals (*"allgemeiner Gegenstände"*)—and, thus, that being which is established, for example, in the "existence proofs" of mathematics. But they do not have the real being of things, or of dependent, thing-like *Moments*—of temporal particulars in general. (Husserl 1994, p. 201–202)

As for the notion of effectivity (*Wirklichkeit*), which Lotze associates not only with the truth of a proposition but also with the existence of things, it is conceived in terms of assent or affirmation (*Wirklichkeit als Bejahung*), as confirmed by the following passage quoted by Husserl in his manuscript:

> This use of language is intelligible; it shows that when we call anything Real, we mean always to *affirm (Bejahung)* it, though in different senses according to the different forms which it assumes, but one or another of which it must necessarily assume, and of which no one is reducible to or contained in the other. (Lotze 1884, p. 439)

In his commentary on this passage, Husserl observed that this concept of ascent is only compatible with the validity and objectivity of *Gedanken* if one understands it as a "relation" and not as an act or an operation of positing (*Operation der Setzung*) in the Kantian sense, which Lotze discards because it would amount to making a proposition (*Satz*) the product of this operation. Husserl argues that the meaning of the "relation" to reality is one and the same relation while the differences (between the forms) reside in the matter to which one assents.[18]

Husserl's important remark takes on its full significance in light of his theory of judgment. Following Brentano, Husserl conceives of ascent (and of its opposite, negation) as a judgment and distinguishes the quality and the matter of an act of judgment or, to use a better-known distinction, between the noesis and the noema of an act. The term quality refers to the type of act, such as the act of judgment as opposed to a representation, a desire, an emotion, etc., while the term matter stands for the contents of an act, and in this case, for the propositional content of judgment. In his discussion of Twardowski, Husserl already distinguished, on the one hand, the quality of an act from its content and its object, and on the other hand, the sensory content (Twardowski's depictive content or image) from the objective or logical content, which is similar, as I remarked, to Bolzano's propositions in themselves. Specific as well to the class of judgment are their objects, which Husserl calls, after Lotze and Stumpf, states of affairs. What binds all the elements that are part of an act of judgment is intentionality, which constitutes the common structure to all acts and whose main property is aboutness or directionality (*Richtung*), i.e., the property of an act of being about something or being related to an object. This property belongs to the matter of an act insofar as its main function consists in conferring to an act its relation to an object. More precisely, the function of the propositional content of a judgment is to mediate the relation of an act to its object:

> Thinking only thinks of the content, i.e., it refers to it by means of this or that thought. The content of objective thoughts (such as concepts and propositions, for example) may change, but the object they (and by means of which, and in a different way the mental acts) mean, remains identical to itself. [...] This means that thoughts, such as different propositions, refer to the same object, thereby we have the most immediate and most evident knowledge. No image can make the evident even more evident to us, can claim to clarify what we directly see. (K I 59, p. 10a)[19]

---

[18] "In any case, we could only give our consent to these misinterpretations of speech, if, contrary to the wording, the *meaning* of the 'relation' here, as in all cases, is only one, and that the differences lie only in the affirmed matter. I am far from thinking that the affirmation is an act" („Jedenfalls könnten wir dieser, Missdeutungen nicht unzugänglichen Rede unsere Zustimmung nur geben, wenn sie, dem Wortlaut entgegen, meinte, dass der *Sinn* der « Beziehung » hier wie in allen Fällen nur einer sei und dass die Unterschiede bloß in der bejahten Materie lägen. Die Bejahung als Akt liegt uns aber fern"). (K I 59, p. 8a–9a)

[19] Das Denken denkt nur den Inhalt, d.h. es bezieht sich, auf ihn mittelst dieser oder jener Gedanken. Der Gehalt an objektiven Gedanken (z.B. an Begriffen, an Sätzen) kann wechseln, aber der Gegenstand, den sie (und mittels ihrer und in anderer Weise die Denkakte) intendieren, bleibt identisch derselbe. [...] Was das heißt, es beziehen sich Gedanken, etwa verschiedene Sätze, auf denselben Gegenstand, davon haben wir das unmittelbarste und sicherste Wissen, kein Bild kann uns das Evidente noch evidenter machen, kann das, was wir direkt sehen, verdeutlichen wollen). (K I 59, p. 11a)

It follows that, from this perspective, the effectivity of a thing that exists, or that of a valid proposition, does not vary according to one's attitude or ascent as Lotze argues, but according to the matter or content, which is always variable but whose "meaning relation" to effectivity remains the same. The invariant is the intentional relation of the act of judgment to its object, while its objective correlate, the judged state of affairs, varies as a function of its propositional content. The effectivity or existence of a judged state of affairs depends neither on ascent nor on what is taken for true, but rather on the validity of its propositional content (the state of affairs exists or is effective only when the proposition is valid).

After having established the distinction between *Sein* and *Geltung,* Lotze claims that the concept of validity has lost nothing of its "wonderful character," considering the difficulties that still remain with respect to the relationship between the being of things and that of general truths (the valid laws) that govern the relation between these things. It is in this context that Lotze speaks of an *Abgrund der Wunderbarkeit* (Lotze 1884, p. 446), to which Husserl attaches considerable interest in his commentary. Husserl sees in this remark an admission of failure by Lotze to satisfactorily   explain   the   foundation   (*Grund*)   of   the   correspondence (*Übereinstimmung*) between the world of things (reality in the sense of being) and the world of thought (reality in the sense of validity). The source of this problem stems from the fact that, after having established the conditions for a pure logic in his chapter on the world of ideas, Lotze then relapsed into a form of subjectivism by creating a dependency between his *Gedanken* and the experiences of the knowing subject. This is what Husserl seeks to show in the second part of his commentary. (Husserl 1975, p. 46) On the other hand, in so doing, Lotze creates an insurmountable gap between the field of objective realities and that of subjective thoughts, as Husserl claims in this passage:

> Of course, whoever partly gets stuck in subjectivism, anyone who, on the one hand, assumes things, events, worlds as existing in themselves, and, on the other hand, absorbs everything logical in subjective thinking activities, opens up, precisely as a consequence of such unclear half-heartedness, this abyss of wonder: Here the things, there our thinking. How do they come together, how does one explain the miracle of their harmony? And from such a point of view, it remains a miracle. But does one not realize that if everything logical subjectively volatilises, there is nothing left over from the being of things and again that nothing is left of the harmony between thinking and being? (K I 59, p 10a)[20]

The answer to this last question again lies in Husserl's doctrine of intentionality, more precisely in the concept of correlation, which he uses here to demystify the *Abgrund* (strangeness) and to restore the harmony between thought and world. For,

---

[20] „Freilich, wer im Subjektivismus zu einer Hälfte stecken bleibt, wer einerseits Dinge, Ereignisse, Welten als an sich existierend annimmt, und auf der anderen Seite doch alles Logische in den subjektiven Denktätigkeiten aufgehen lässt, für den öffnet sich, eben als Konsequenz der unklaren Halbheit dieser Abgrund von Wunderbarkeit : Hier die Dinge, dort unser Denken. Wie kommen beide zusammen, wie das Wunder ihrer Harmonie erklären? Und für diesen Standpunkt bleibt es ein Wunder. Aber merkt man denn nicht, dass wenn alles Logische subjektivistisch verflüchtigt wird, auch vom Sein der Dinge nichts übrig bliebe und wieder dass auch von der Harmonie zwischen Denken und Sein nichts übrig bliebe?" (K I 59, p. 10a)

we are not dealing here with two incommensurable worlds, but rather with correlates of an intentional relation which "belong together and match each other, like
truth and true things, the one as objective as the other, and both correlatively, i.e.,
inseparably related to each other". (K I 59, p. 10a) [21]

We can see that most of the problems that Husserl attributes to Lotze's theory of
knowledge in this manuscript stem from the lack of an adequate theory of intentionality, which would have allowed Lotze to combine the psychological conditions for
an act of judgment with the logical conditions for objective truth into a coherent
structure. It would have also enabled him to develop a theory of knowledge immune
to the objection of logical psychologism. We shall see that, in his later writings,
Husserl criticizes Lotze and Bolzano for the absence of an adequate theory of
knowledge, as well as for having neglected the elucidation of the basic concepts of
logic and of the fundamental relation "between signification, signification moment,
and full act of signifying." (Husserl 1994, p. 202; see *Briefwechsel* I, p. 39; 1975,
p. 46) Hence the repeated criticism that Husserl addressed to Lotze's theory of
knowledge, which he characterized as a hermaphrodite or a contradictory hybrid of
pure and psychologistic logic.

5   Lotze and the Criticism of Logical Psychologism in the *Prolegomena*

The Halle period culminated in the publication in 1900–1901 of Husserl's
Hauptwerk, the *Logical Investigations*, whose first volume, *Prolegomena to Pure
Logic*, can be considered a plea against logical psychologism. I propose to address
this issue by following the thread that I have unravelled since the beginning of this
study, i.e., the connection to Brentano and especially to Stumpf, who published a
treatise titled "Psychologie und Erkenntnistheorie," which focuses on psychologism, the same year that Husserl published his *Philosophy of Arithmetic*. Elmar
Holenstein (Hua XVIII, p. XIX) and Dieter Münch (2002, p. 50) rightly pointed out
that Stumpf's position on psychologism in this paper is not foreign to Husserl's
criticism of logical psychologism in his *Prolegomena*. Moreover, Münch clearly
saw that this issue was also central to Stumpf's reflections in the first part of his
habilitation thesis, in which he sides against Mill and Kant on the nature of

---

[21] "… gehören zusammen und stimmen zusammen", wie Wahrheit und wahre Sache, das Eine so
objektiv wie das andere, und beide korrelativ, also untrennbar aufeinander bezogen". (K I 59,
p. 10a) Compare with what Husserl says about the mythical conception of Lotze's two worlds in
the draft of a preface to the *Logical Investigations*: "Another such presupposition in Lotze is a
mythological metaphysics: he distinguishes a representational world (*Vorstellungswelt*), which has
merely human-subjective validity, from a metaphysical world of monads in-themselves, concerning which, under the label of metaphysics, we can venture metaphysical proposals by completely
mysterious methods. Such proposals are inferior to novels, since novels have an aesthetic truth, and
hence, an essential common ground with reality that is intelligible, something which is necessarily
lacking in all such metaphysical fiction". (Husserl 1975, p. 47)

mathematical axioms. The recent publication of Stumpf's habilitation thesis raises many interesting questions, which have been the subject of several recent studies, notably by Wolfgang Ewen (2008), who emphasizes Stumpf's relation to Frege and draws several parallels between the contributions of Stumpf, Husserl, and Frege to the foundation of mathematics and to the criticism of logical psychologism (see W. Ewen 2008, 97 ff.). Ewen (2008, 13, 22) claims that Stumpf's position on psychologism is closer to Frege's anti-psychologistic position than to his student Husserl's. Ewen's argument rests on Stumpf's and Frege's relationship with Lotze during their stay in Göttingen in the early 1870s. Historical testimony shows neither whether Frege attended Stumpf's lectures on Aristotle's metaphysics, which he taught for three consecutive years in Göttingen, nor whether he attended his lecture on "inductive logic with a particular focus on the problem of natural science," which he taught during the summer semester of 1873. But since Ewen does not provide a clear definition of what is meant by "psychologism" and does not clearly expose Stumpf's, Frege's, and Husserl's respective arguments against logical psychologism, there is no way to settle this debate. Nevertheless, we shall see that Stumpf's position on psychologism is closer to Husserl's than to Frege's.

Stumpf's 1891 article allows us to establish a new connection between Lotze's interpretation of Plato's theory of Ideas and the issues underlying logical psychologism in the *Prolegomena*. Prior to the publication of this article, one can find traces of Lotze's interpretation of Plato's Ideas in Stumpf's dissertation on Plato, published in 1869, and in his 1870 habilitation on mathematical axioms.[22] Indeed, one of Stumpf's central concerns in his dissertation *The Idea of the Good in Plato* is to defend Plato's theory of Ideas against the objection of hypostasis, as Lotze already had in his *Microcosmos* and then in his 1874 *Logic*. (Stumpf 1869, II, 2, p. 46 ff.) In an article celebrating the centenary of Lotze's anniversary in the *Kant Studien*, Stumpf suggested that the discussions he had with Lotze on his interpretation of Plato's theory of Ideas were one of the motivating factors that led him to undertake his research on the nature of mathematical axioms in his habilitation thesis. (Stumpf 1918, p. 7) And indeed, Stumpf's investigation in this work is based on the cardinal distinction, which we discussed previously, between concept and proposition; this Lotzean distinction is at the heart of his criticism of psychologism in his article "Psychology and Theory of Knowledge". Moreover, Husserl explicitly refers to Stumpf's article in his *Prolegomena* (Husserl 1982a, § 18, pp. 335), and we shall see that Husserl's *Prolegomena* (1982a, p. 40–42) adopted the same theoretical framework that we find in Stumpf's 1891 article and in his *Über die Grundsätze der Mathematik*. Husserl's debt to this student of Lotze in his *Logical Investigations* involves several central aspects of his logic and phenomenology (see R. Rollinger 1999), and it is no coincidence that this book is dedicated to Stumpf.

---

[22] Although these two works by Stumpf were written before the publication of Lotze's greater *Logic* in 1874, one can find in Lotze's *Microcosmos*, first published in 1864, an outline of his interpretation of Plato's Ideas in terms of *Geltung*, as well as the distinction between concept and proposition (see Lotze 1899, Book VIII, chapter I, p. 325 ff.).

Husserl refers twice to Stumpf's 1891 article in his *Prolegomena*. The first reference is in a footnote to § 18, "The line of proof of the psychologistic thinkers," in which Husserl points out that he uses the term "psychologism" without any "evaluative colouring" (*abschätzende "Färbung"*), following Stumpf. This remark seems to suggest that, unlike the anti-psychologistic position defended by Kant, the neo-Kantians, and Frege, Husserl follows Stumpf in refusing to exclude the contribution of psychology to epistemological issues, as is confirmed by Husserl's definition of phenomenology as a descriptive psychology in Brentano's sense in his *Logical Investigations*. Husserl's second reference pertains to a passage in Stumpf's paper, where Stumpf (1891, p. 469) formulates his main argument against psychologism, i.e., that it can never lead to necessary truths. Husserl adds that even if Stumpf is mainly concerned, in this article, with the theory of knowledge and not with logic as such, this "is not an essential difference". For, as Husserl points out in his review of Palágyi, the main target of his criticism of logical psychologism in his *Prolegomena* is also a kind of theory of knowledge.[23] In this footnote, Husserl opposes Stumpf's position to that of Erdmann in his *Logic*, which he associates to an extreme form of subjectivism (Briefwechsel, III, p. 132), and to a passage from Lotze's *Logic* (Lotze 1884, p. 467–468), which Husserl already quoted in his 1895–1897 manuscript (K I 59, p. 23a) to criticize Lotze's concessions to subjectivism. These two references to Stumpf thus suggest that Husserl's criticism of logical psychologism in his *Prolegomena* follows the path blazed by Stumpf in his 1891 treatise (see Fisette 2015a).

Husserl's starting point in his criticism of logical psychologism in his *Prolegomena* is similar to Stumpf's in his habilitation thesis, namely the opposition between Mill (Husserl 1982a, p. 40) and Kant (Husserl 1982a, p. 41–42) on the relation between logic and psychology. In the controversy over logical psychologism, this opposition is expressed concretely as normative anti-psychologism, which Husserl attributes to the Kantian tradition and sometimes to Frege,[24] and logical psychologism, to which are associated the names of Mill, Wundt, Bain, and Theodor Lipps, for example. Following Husserl's diagnosis, this controversy stems from the fact that both sides conceive of logic in two different ways: the psychologistic party

---

[23] "My work shows that my struggle against Psychologism is in no way a struggle against the psychological grounding of Logic as methodology, nor against the descriptive-psychological illumination of the origin *(Ursprung)* of the logical concepts. Rather, it is only a struggle against an epistemological position, though certainly one which has had a very harmful influence upon the way in which logic is done". (Husserl 1994, p. 199)

[24] Opinions diverge as to whether Frege would share ranks with the Kantians or with the phenomenologists. Some argue that Frege's anti-psychologistic arguments are based on normativity and it is precisely on this point that he differs from the Husserl's position. Others, such as Dummett, dispute this interpretation of Frege's logic as a normative science. According to Dummett, there are no significant differences between the positions of Husserl and Frege on that issue: "a characterization of logic as a normative science is quite superficial, for logic is best regarded as the theoretical science underlying the relevant normative principles; the important question is the proper characterization of the subject-matter of this theoretical but non-prescriptive science". (Dummett 1991, p. 225)

only considers logic from the point of view of its method, i.e., as a technology dependent on psychology, while anti-psychologistic sympathizers only consider it from the point of view of its theoretical content, and therefore as a theoretical discipline entirely independent from psychology. To this difference between two conceptions of logic corresponds two different conceptions of the laws of logic: as these laws "*serve as norms* for our knowledge-activities, and laws which include normativity in their thought-content, and *assert* its universal obligatoriness". (Husserl 1982a, p. 101) This distinction corresponds concretely to that of logic understood as a normative and practical discipline (as a *Kunstlehre* of knowledge) and of logic understood as a theoretical and ideal discipline. According to Husserl, the confusion underlying the psychologism–anti-psychologism debate can be explained by the fact that the first party, when it claims to base logic on psychology, only considers the practical-normative aspect of logic, while the arguments of the opposing party rely on logic understood as a theoretical discipline. Thus, if one only considers the practical aspect of logic, the claims of psychologism to partially base logic on psychology are legitimate. However, Husserl criticizes the anti-psychologistic partisans who conceive of logic strictly in normative terms, and thus ignore the essential difference between the proper content of logical propositions and their practical application (Husserl 1982a, p. 102), i.e., between the use of a proposition for normative means and its theoretical content, which is in principle separable from the idea of normativity. To acknowledge the validity of this distinction is to acknowledge that the one and only probative argument against logical psychologism does not rest on the opposition between the normative character of logical laws and the natural laws of psychology, but rather on the ideal character of the logical laws, which, as we have seen, is understood by Husserl in terms of *Geltung*.

Kantians are thus right to emphasize the theoretical content of logic and to argue, against logical psychologism, that the propositions of logic are independent of the "properties of human nature in general". But they are wrong to conceive of this propositional content and logic in general in terms of normativity. Husserl uses two arguments against normative anti-psychologism. First, normativity is not a decisive argument against psychologism because "every normative and likewise every practical discipline rests on one or more theoretical disciplines, inasmuch as its rules must have a theoretical content separable from the notion of normativity (of the 'shall' or 'should'), whose scientific investigation is the duty of these theoretical disciplines". (Husserl 1982a, p. 33) Thus, the principles of logic are not normative propositions, for any normative proposition presupposes a certain type of evaluation that refers to non-normative propositions and disciplines. Second, logic, understood as a normative discipline, in turn requires a psychological basis. Husserl is not saying that psychology provides its essential foundation, but he nevertheless concedes to psychologism that "psychology *helps* in the foundation of logic". (Husserl 1982a, p. 45) Husserl's arguments against logical psychologism thus differ from Frege's in his *Grundgesetze*, whose critique of psychologism rests on the normative character of logic. Frege argues that the main error of psychologism is to confuse the normative character of the laws of logic—what ought to be—with the use of these laws to describe "what is". Finally, unlike Lotze, Husserl, and Stumpf, Frege's anti-psychologism amounts to entirely dismissing the field of mental phenomena, thereby creating an unbridgeable gap between this field of investigation and that of logic and philosophy as a whole.

6   Conclusion

Despite the many changes that marked the development of his phenomenology after his arrival in Göttingen in 1901, Husserl never renounced his Platonism and always recognized his debt to Lotze, as evidenced by a letter to Edward Parl Welch in 1933:

> My *Formal and Transcendental Logic* (especially in the second part) will best enlighten you as to what role my "Platonism", my vigorous defense of a universal ontology, i.e., for the elaboration of intuition of essences (for the genuine a priori) in all spheres of knowledge, played in my development, and what new meaning it gained in the matured transcendental phenomenology, although only "formal ontology" is in question in that book. For this "Platonism", I am indebted to the well-known chapter in Lotze's *Logic*, even if his epistemology and metaphysics have always very much repelled me. (*Briefwechsel* VI, p. 460–461; see Husserl 1969, p. 83, 146, 264)

We also know that Husserl's interest in Lotze's theory of knowledge retained all its power, as shown by several lectures that he gave in 1912 in Göttingen ("Lotzes Erkenntnistheorie im Anschluss an das Buch der Logik 3. Lotzes") and in 1922 in Freiburg (see Hua III/1, p. xxxiii). However, Husserl's remarks on Lotze after the publication of his *Logical Investigations* show the same ambivalence toward the philosophy of Lotze as the 1895–1897 manuscript. For, while acknowledging his debt to Lotze's logic and theory of knowledge, Husserl criticizes him in the same breath for his subjectivism and for his failure to overcome psychologism. Husserl believes that Lotze did not see all the philosophical implications of his own interpretation of Plato's theory of Ideas in his logic and was not able to draw all the right consequences for his theory of knowledge. Rather, as Husserl explains in the sketch of a preface to the *Logical Investigations*, after having established Plato's theory of Ideas in all its purity, Lotze relapsed into a form of psychologism, namely anthropologism, by asserting a dependence of his *Gedanken* on the thinking subject. Hence the criticism that Husserl repeatedly addressed to Lotze's theory of knowledge, namely of being "a product of the incompleteness that balks at ultimate consistency". (Husserl 1980, p. 50)

In his writings after the publication of the *Logical Investigations*, Husserl confirms the diagnosis of his 1895–1897 manuscript by attributing part of the failure of Lotze's theory of knowledge to the absence of a theory of intentionality, as shown by his remarks on Lotze's descriptive psychology and phenomenology. Husserl acknowledges that the starting point of his "ontological" research in the field of consciousness was Lotze's idea that "the realm of sense-data, of color- and sound-data [are understood] as a field of ideal, and thus 'ontological' cognitions". (Husserl 1975, p. 43; 1977, p. 28) However, he deplores the fact that Lotze's phenomenology "reduces itself to the reference to a few *a priori* relations in the sphere of sensuous contents". (Husserl 1980, p. 50) This amounts to saying that Lotze's phenomenology, like Stumpf's (Hua III/1, § 86; D. Fisette 2015c), in the final analysis, only accounts for what Husserl called "primary relations" in his *Philosophy of Arithmetic*, i.e., the class of relations that have the character of primary contents and that have a "special phenomenal character". But Lotze's theory does not account for intentional relations belonging to the class of mental phenomena. That is why, despite of all his merits, Lotze never succeeded in elaborating a genuine phenomenology:

> Finally, that there could be such a thing as an eidetic doctrine of consciousness at all, and further an eidetic doctrine of the relations of consciousness and noema of consciousness, a constitution of objectivities, etc., of that he never had a notion and therefore had no notion of what *we* here call phenomenology. (Husserl 1980, p. 50)

This passage sums up Husserl's main criticism of Lotze, namely that he has not succeeded in reconciling the subjective and objective aspects of lived experience, i.e., the ideal noematic content, with the noetic aspect of the subject's experience. Therefore, Lotze lacked a theory of intentionality, which represents the heart of Husserl's phenomenology.

References

Bell, D. 1999, "The Revolution of Moore and Russell: A Very British Coup?" in A. O'Hear (ed.), *German Philosophy since Kant,* Cambridge: Cambridge University Press, 137–66.

Beyer, C. (1996) *Von Bolzano zu Husserl*, Dordrecht : Kluwer.

Brentano, F. (2008) *Sämtliche veröffentlichte Schriften*, vol. 1, *Schriften zur Psychologie, Psychologie vom empirischen Standpunkte*, M. Antonelli (ed.), Frankfurt a. M.: Ontos.

———— (1995) *Psychology from an Empirical Standpoint,* trans. A. C. Rancurello, D. B. Terrell, and L. McAlister, London: Routledge.

———— (1989) *Briefe an Carl Stumpf 1867–1917*, G. Oberkofler (ed.), Graz: Akademische Druck und Verlagsanstalt.

Dathe, U. (2000) *Der „Geist" Freges in Jena—Paul Ferdinand Linke. Ein Beitrag zur Jenaer Universitätsgeschichte*, in G. Gabriel & U. Dathe (eds.) *Gottlob Frege. Werk und Wirkung.* Mentis: Paderborn p. 227–244.

Dastur, F. (1994) „Husserl, Lotze et la logique de la validité », *Kairos*, no. 5, 1994, p. 31–48.

Devaux, P. (1932) *Lotze et son influence sur la philosophie anglo-saxonne.* Bruxelles: Maurice Lamertin.

Dewalque, A. (2012a) « Idée et signification. Le legs de Lotze et les ambiguïtés du platonisme », C. Bernard & B. Leclerq (dir.), *La subjectivation de la notion d'Idée*, Louvain: Peeters, p. 187–213.

———— (2012b) « Le sens de l'idéalisme platonicien selon Lotze », in S. Delcomminette & A. Mazzu (dir.) *L'Idée platonicienne dans la philosophie contemporaine*, Paris: Vrin, p. 71–95.

Dummett, M. (1993) *Origins of Analytical Philosophy*, London: Duckworth.

———— (1991) *Frege and other Philosophers*, Oxford: Oxford University Press.

Ewen, W. (2008) *Carl Stumpf und Gottlob Frege*, Würzburg: Königshausen &. Neumann.

Fisette, D. (forthcoming) "Overcoming Psychologism. Twardowski on Actions and Products", In Arnaud Dewalque, C. Gauvry & S. Richard (eds.), *Philosophy of Language in the Brentanian Tradition*, Basingstoke: Palgrave.

——— (2015a) "Reception and Actuality of Carl Stumpf's Philosophy", in D. Fisette and R. Martinelli (eds.) *Philosophy from an Empirical Standpoint. Carl Stumpf as a philosopher*, Amsterdam: Rodopi, p. 11–53.

——— (2015b) "Introduction to Stumpf's Lectures on Metaphysics", *Philosophy from an Empirical Standpoint. Carl Stumpf as a Philosopher*, D. Fisette and R. Martinelli (eds.) Amsterdam: Rodopi, 2014, p. 433–442.

——— (2015c) "A Phenomenology without Phenomena? Stumpf's Criticism of Husserl's Ideas I", in D. Fisette and R. Martinelli (eds.) *Philosophy from an Empirical Standpoint. Carl Stumpf as a philosopher*, Amsterdam: Rodopi, p. 319–356.

——— (2015d) "Bibliography of Carl Stumpf's Publications / Bibliographie der Schriften von Carl Stumpf", *Philosophy from an Empirical Standpoint. Carl Stumpf as a Philosopher*, D. Fisette and R. Martinelli (eds.) Amsterdam: Rodopi, p. 531–543.

——— (2015e) « La théorie des signes locaux de Hermann Lotze et la controverse empirisme-nativisme au XIXe siècle », in F. Boccaccini (dir.), *Lotze et son héritage. Son influence et son impact sur la philosophie du XXème siècle*, Frankfurt a. M.: Peter Lang, p. 41–67.

——— (2010) "Descriptive Psychology and Natural Sciences. Husserl's early Criticism of Brentano », in C. Ierna et al. (dir.), *Edmund Husserl 150 Years: Philosophy, Phenomenology, Sciences*, Berlin: Springer, p. 135–167.

——— (2009) "Husserl à Halle (1886–1901)", *Philosophiques*, Vol. 36, no. 2, 277–306.

——— (2007) « Phénoménologie et/ou idéalisme? Réflexions critiques sur l'attribution d'une forme ou d'une autre d'idéalisme à la phénoménologie », M. Maesschalck et al. (dir.), *Idéalisme et phénoménologie*, Hildesheim: Olms, p. 25–55.

——— (2004) "Logical Analysis versus Phenomenological Descriptions", Richard Feist (ed.) *Husserl and the Sciences*, Ottawa: University of Ottawa Press, p. 69–98.

——— (2003) « Représentations. Husserl critique de Twardowski », in D. Fisette et al. (dir.) *Aux origines de la phénoménologie. Husserl et le contexte des Recherches logiques,* Paris: Vrin, p. 61–92.

Fisette, D. & R. Martinelli (eds.) (2015) *Philosophy from an Empirical Standpoint. Carl Stumpf as a Philosopher*, Amsterdam: Rodopi.

Fisette, D. & G. Fréchette (eds) (2013) *Themes from Brentano*, Amsterdam: Rodopi.

Frege, G. (2013) *Grundgesetze der Arithmetik, begriffsschriftlich abgeleitet*, vol. I, Jena: H. Pohle, 1893; trans. P. A. Ebert, M. Rossberg, & C. Wright, *Basic Laws of Arithmetic. Derived Using Concept-script*, Oxford: Oxford U. P.

——— (1976) *Wissenschaftlicher Briefwechsel*, Hamburg: Meiner.

——— (1894) 'Rezension von: E. Husserl, *Philosophie der Arithmetik I*, in *Zeitschrift für Philosophie und philosophische Kritik*, vol. 103, p. 313–332.

——— (1884) *Die Grundlagen der Arithmetik: Eine logisch mathematische Untersuchung über den Begriff der Zahl*, Breslau: Koebner.

Gabriel, G. (2013) « Frege and the German background to analytic philosophy », in M. Beaney, M. (ed.) *The Oxford Handbook of the History of Analytic Philosophy*, p. 280–297

——— (2002) Frege, Lotze, and the Continental Roots of Early Analytic Philosophy, in E.H. Reck (ed.) *From Frege to Wittgenstein. Perspectives on Early Analytic Philosophy*, Oxford: Oxford University Press, p. 39–51.

——— (1989) „Objektivität : Logik und Erkenntnistheorie bei Lotze und Frege", in H. Lotze, *Logik. Dtittes Buch. Vom Erkennen*, Hamburg: Meiner, p. IX-XXXVI.

——— (1986) "Frege als Neukantianer", *Kant-Studien*, vol. 77, p. 84–101.

Hauser, K. (2003) "Husserl and Lotze", *Archiv fur Geschichte der Philosophie*, vol. 85, no. 2, p. 152–178.

Husserl, E. (Hua III/1), (Hua III) *Ideen zu einer reinen Phänomenologie und phänomenologischen Philosophie*, Husserliana Bd. III/1, 2nd ed., K. Schuhmann (ed.), The Hague: Nijhoff, 1976.

——— (Hua XVIII) *Logische Untersuchungen, Erster Band. Prolegomena zur reinen Logik*, Husserliana Bd. XIII, E. Holenstein (ed.), The Hague: Nijhoff, 1975.

――― (Hua XXI) *Studien zur Arithmetik und Geometrie. Texte aus dem Nachlaß* (1886–1901), Husserliana Bd. XXI, I. Strohmeyer (ed.), The Hague: Nijhoff, 1983.
――― (Hua XXXIII) *Natur und Geist. Vorlesungen Sommersemester 1927*, Husserlian Bd. XXXIII, M. Weiler (ed.), Dordrecht: Kluwer, 2001.
――― (Briefwechsel) *Briefwechsel*, 10 vols, K. Schuhmann (eds.) Dordrecht: Kluwer Academic Publishers, 1994.
――― (2015) "A Letter from Edmund Husserl to Franz Brentano from 29 XII 1889", C. Ierna (ed.), *Husserl Studies*, Vol. 31, No. 1, p. 65–72.
――― (2003) *Philosophy of Arithmetic*, transl. D. Willard, Collected Works X, Dordrecht: Kluwer Academic Publishers.
――― (2001a) „Husserls Manuskripte zu seinem Göttinger Doppelvortrag von 1901", K. Schuhmann (ed.), *Husserl Studies*, vol. 17, p. 87–123.
――― (2001b) *Logik. Vorlesung 1896*, Husserliana, Materialien, Bd. 1, E. Schuhmann (ed.), Dordrecht: Kluwer.
――― (1997) *Psychological and Transcendental Phenomenology and the Confrontation with Heidegger (1927–1931)*, transl. T. Sheehan and E. Palmer, Collected Works VI, Dordrecht: Kluwer.
――― (1994) *Early Writings in the Philosophy of Logic and Mathematic*, trans. D. Willard, Berlin: Springer.
――― (1990–1991) „Ursprüngliche Druckfassung der Abhandlung ‚Intentionale Gegenstände' von Husserl", in Karl Schuhmann, « Husserls Abhandlung "intentionale Gegenstände". Edition der ursprünglichen Druckfassung, *Brentano Studien*, Vol. III, p. 142–176.
――― (1982a) *Logical Investigations*, vol. 1, transl. J. N. Findlay, 2nd ed., London: Routledge.
――― (1982b) *Logical Investigations*, vol. 2, 2nd ed., London: Routledge.
――― (1980) *Ideas Pertaining to a Pure Phenomenology and to a Phenomenological Philosophy, Third Book. Phenomenology and the Foundations of the Sciences*, trans. T. Klein and W. Pohl, Collected Works, vol. 1, The Hague: Nijhoff.
――― (1977) *Phenomenological Psychology. Lectures, Summer Semester 1925*, J. Scanlon (ed.), The Hague: M. Nijhoff.
――― (1976) „Reminiscences of Franz Brentano", trans. L. McAlister, in L. McAlister (ed.) *The Philosophy of Franz Brentano*, London: Duckworth, p. 47–55.
――― (1975) *Introduction to the Logical Investigations. A Draft of a Preface to the Logical Investigations*, trans. P. Bossert & C. Peters, The Hague: M. Nijhoff.
――― (1969) *Formal and Transcendental Logic*, trans. D. Cairn, The Hague: Nijhoff.
――― (K I 59) "Mikrokosmos", 1895–1897, Husserl Archive, Leuven.
Kraushaar, O. F. (1939) "Lotze as a Factor in the Development of James's Radical Empiricism and Pluralism", *Philosophical Review*, vol. 48, p. 455–471.
――― (1936) "Lotze's influence on the psychology of William James", *Psychological Review*, vol. XLIII, p. 235–257.
Kreiser, L. (2001) *Gottlob Frege: Leben, Werk, Zeit*, Hamburg: Meiner.
Linke, P. F. (1946–1947) « Gottlob Frege als Philosoph », *Zeitschrift für philosophische Forschung*, Vol. 1, p. 75–99.
――― (1926) "The Present Status of Logic and Epistemology in Germany", *The Monist*, Vol. 36, p. 222–255.
――― (1924)„Die Existentialtheorie der Wahrheit und der Psychologismus der Geltungslogik", *Kant-Studien*, Vol. 29, p. 395–415.
Lotze, H. (2003) *Briefe und Dokumente*, R. Pester (ed.), Würzburg: Königshausen & Neumann.
――― (1899) *Microcosmus: An Essay Concerning Man and His Relation to the World* (1856–58, 1858–64), 4th ed., trans. E. Hamilton and E. C. Jones, Edinburgh: T. & T. Clark.
――― (1887) *Metaphysics, in three books: Ontology, Cosmology, and Psychology* (1879), ed. and trans. B. Bosanquet, 2nd ed., Oxford: Clarendon Press.
――― (1884) *Logic, in three books: of Thought, of Investigation, and of Knowledge*, ed. and trans. B. Bosanquet, Oxford: Clarendon Press.

——— (1852) *Medicinische Psychologie oder Physiologie der Seele*, Leipzig.

Marty, A. (1884) "Über subjektlose Sätze und das Verhältnis der Grammatik zur Logik und Psychologie", *Vierteljahrschrift für wissenschaftliche Philosophie*, vol. 8, p. 161–192.

Maier, B. (2009) *William Robertson Smith. His Life, his Work and his Times*, Tübingen: Mohr Siebeck.

Merz, J. (1938) *History of European Thought in the XlXth Century*, 4 vols, London: Allen & Unwin.

Misch, G. (1912) „Einleitung", in H. Lotze, *System der Philosophie. Erster Teil: Drei Bücher der Logik*, Leipzig: Meiner, p. IX–XCI.

Münch, D. (2002–2003) „Erkenntnistheorie und Psychologie. Die wissenschaftliche Weltauffassung Carl Stumpfs", *Brentano Studien*, vol. 10, p. 11–66.

Orth, E. W. (1997) „Metaphysische Implikationen der Intentionalität. Trendelenburg, Lotze, Brentano", *Brentano Studien*, Vol. VII, p. 15–30.

——— (1995) „Brentanos und Diltheys Konzeption einer beschreibenden Psychologie in ihrer Beziehung auf Lotze", *Brentano Studien*, Vol. VI, p. 13–29.

Palágyi, M. (1902) *Der Streit der Psychologisten und Formalisten in der modernen Logik*, Leipzig: W. Engelmann.

Peckhaus, V. (1994) „Benno Kerry. Beiträge zu seiner Biographie", *History and Philosophy of Logic*, Vol. 15, p. 1–8.

Pester, R. (1997) *Hermann Lotze. Wege seines Denkens und Forschens. Ein Kapitel deutscher Philosophie- und Wissenschaftsgeschichte im 19. Jahrhundert*, Würzburg: Königshausen & Neumann.

Rollinger, R. (1999) *Husserl's Position in the School of Brentano*, Dordrecht: Kluwer.

Schaar, M. van der (2013) *G. F. Stout and the Psychological Origins of Analytic Philosophy*, Hampshire: Palgrave.

——— (1996) *"From Analytic Psychology to Analytic Philosophy; the Reception of Twardowski's Ideas in Cambridge"*, Axiomathes, Vol. 7, No. 3, p. 295–324.

Schlotter, S. (2006) "Frege's Anonymous Opponent in 'Die Verneinung'", *History and Philosophy of Logic*, vol. 27, p. 43–58.

Schuhmann, K. (1977) *Husserl-Chronik*: Denk- und Lebensweg Edmund Husserls. Den Haag: Martinus Nijhoff.

Sluga, H. (1984) "'Frege: The Early Years", in R. Rorty & Q. Skinner, (eds.), *Philosophy in History*, Cambridge, Cambridge University Press, p. 329–356.

——— (1980) *Gottlob Frege*. London: Routledge & Kegan Paul.

Smith, D. W. (2013) "The Role of phenomenology in analytic philosophy", in M. Beaney (ed.) *The Oxford Handbook of the History of Analytic Philosophy*, Oxford: Oxford University Press, p. 1495–1527.

Stout, G. F. (1896) *Analytic Psychology*, Vols. I and II, London: George Allen & Unwin.

Stumpf, C. (2015) *Metaphysik. Vorlesung*, R. Rollinger (ed.), in D. Fisette & R. Martinelli (eds), Amsterdam: Rodopi, p. 443–472.

——— (2008) *Über die Grundsätze der Mathematik*, W. Ewen, (ed.), Würzburg: Königshausen & Neumann, 2008.

——— (1999a): Syllabus for Psychology. English tr. of "Vorlesungen über Psychologie, 1886–1887" by R. Rollinger, in R. Rollinger, *Husserl's Position in the School of Brentano*, Dordrecht: Kluwer, p. 285–309.

——— (1999b): Syllabus for Logic. English tr. of C. Stumpf "Vorlesungen über Logik, 1886–1887" by R. Rollinger, in R. Rollinger, *Husserl's Position in the School of Brentano*, Dordrecht: Kluwer, 311–337.

——— (1976) „Reminiscences of Franz Brentano", trans. L. McAlister, in L. McAlister (ed.) *The Philosophy of Franz Brentano*, London: Duckworth, 1976, p. 10–46.

——— (1939–1940) *Erkenntnislehre*, vol. I–II, Leipzig: Barth.

——— (1930) "Carl Stumpf", transl. C. Murchison, in C. Murchison (ed.) *History of Psychology in Autobiography,* Vol. 1, Worcester: Clark University Press, p. 389–441.

——— (1927) *William James nach seinen Briefen*, Kant Studien, Vol. 32, No. 2–3, p. 205–241.

———— (1917) "Zum Gedächtnis Lotzes", *Kant-Studien*, vol. 22, 1–26.

———— (1895) "Antrittsrede", *Sitzungsberichte der Königlich-Preußischen Akademie der Wissenschaften*, Berlin: Reimer, 735–738.

———— (1893) „Zum Begriff der Lokalzeichen", *Zeitschrift für Psychologie und Physiologie der Sinnesorgane*, Vol. 4, p. 70–73.

———— (1891) "Psychologie und Erkenntnistheorie", *Abhandlungen der Königlich Bayerischen Akademie der Wissenschaften* 19, zweite Abt., München: Franz, 465–516.

———— (1883) *Tonpsychologie*, vol. I. Leipzig: S. Hirzel.

———— (1873) *Über den psychologischen Ursprung der Raumvorstellung*, Leipzig: S. Hirzel.

———— (1869) *Verhältnis des platonischen Gottes zur Idee des Guten*, Halle: C.E.M. Pfeffer.

Sully, J. (1891) "Review of *Tonpsychologie* [vol. II] by Carl Stumpf," *Mind*, Vol. 16, No. 62, p. 274–280.

———— (1886) "Review of 'Musikpsychologie in England' by C. Stumpf", *Mind*, Vol. 11, No. 44, p. 580–585.

———— (1884) "Review of *Tonpsychologie* [vol. I] by Carl Stumpf", *Mind*, Vol. 9, No. 36, p. 593–602.

———— (1878) "The Question of Visual Perception in Germany", *Mind*, Vol. 3, p. 167–195.

Twardowski, K. (1894) *Zur Lehre vom Inhalt und Gegenstand der Vorstellungen: Eine psychologische Untersuchung*, Wien : Hölder.

Varga, P. A. (2013) "The Missing Chapter from the Logical Investigations: Husserl on Lotze's Formal and Real Significance of Logical Laws", *Husserl Studies*, vol. 29, no. 3, p. 181–209.

Ward, J. (1918) *Psychological Principles,* Cambridge: Cambridge University Press.

———— (1886) "Psychology", *Encyclopaedia Britannica*, 9th ed., Vol. 20, Edinburgh: Black, p. 37–85.

Windelband, W. (1877) „Über die verschiedenen Phasen der Kantischen Lehre vom Ding-an-sich", *Vierteljahrsschrift für wissenschaftliche Philosophie*, Vol. 1, p. 224–266.

A Realist Misunderstanding of Husserl's Account of Ideal Objects in the *Logical Investigations*. Discussing the Arguments of Antonio Millán-Puelles

Mariano Crespo

Abstract Husserl's conception of ideal objects convinced some of his early disciples that he was presenting a new form of realism. This impression arises, in my view, from a twofold misunderstanding. First, there was a misunderstanding of the limits of the phenomenological claims of *Logical Investigations* and, second, an erroneous belief that ideal objects are interpreted in a realist fashion therein. The ultimate source of the first phenomenological schism is not, therefore, so much a reaction to an alleged sudden change in Husserl's position, but rather a misunderstanding of the concept of ideality presented in *Logical Investigations*. Further, an alleged "compatibility" between the realist conception of ideality and the Husserlian conception is to be found in one of the ways that Husserl addresses the problem of constitution. However, the Spanish philosopher Antonio Millán-Puelles has shown that the use of terms such as "constitutive activity" or "genesis"—in a realist metaphysics, to designate the arising of ideal objects—should not be interpreted in a psychologistic way, as though these objects remained absorbed by the reality of the mental processes they are made present by.

Keywords Ideal objects · Millán-Puelles · Realist phenomenology · Psychologism · Mental processes

1 Introduction

As we know, some of the disciples of Husserl perceived—in the Lectures that he had published in 1905 under the title *The Idea of Phenomenology*, but, above all, in the second edition of his *Logical Investigations* and in *Ideas I* (both from 1913)—a radical change in what the *Logical Investigations* propose. The discovery of the

M. Crespo (✉)
Universidad de Navarra, Pamplona, Spain
e-mail: mjcrespo@unav.es

© Springer Nature Switzerland AG 2021
R. K. B. Parker (ed.), *The Idealism-Realism Debate Among Edmund Husserl's Early Followers and Critics*, Contributions to Phenomenology 112,
https://doi.org/10.1007/978-3-030-62159-9_3

phenomenological reduction and a new reading of Kant, together with certain other elements, led these first disciples of Husserl to see their master making a turn towards what seemed to be transcendental idealism, giving the impression of radically distancing himself from the positions defended in the *Logical Investigations*. This provoked a division between realist phenomenologists and transcendental phenomenologists regarding the existence of a "phenomenological realism" or a "realist phenomenology."

In this paper I will not deal with the question of whether this supposed "Copernican turn" really took place in Husserl's thought, although I am inclined to think not. Hence, I share the view of Walter Biemel, who, in his well-known Royaumont paper "The decisive phases in the development of Husserl's philosophy", notes—as a common thread running through all the works of the founder of the phenomenological method—that in order to illuminate the essence of a thing one must go back to the origin of its meaning in consciousness, and to the description of that origin.[1] I am not going to critically analyze all the issues that the realist phenomenologists perceived in *The Idea of Phenomenology*, in the second edition of *Logical Investigations* and in *Ideas* I as constituting a radical change with respect to the first edition of *Investigations*, nor am I seeking to deny that these authors had the impression of a change of this sort. Nor, finally, do I wish to deny the unquestionable philosophical value of the detailed analyses of various central philosophical questions that one finds in the writings of Adolf Reinach, Alexander Pfänder, Edith Stein, Dietrich von Hildebrand, Roman Ingarden, Jean Hering, etc. While my purpose is more limited, it is also more daring. What I seek to show is that it is an error to interpret one of the central elements of the ontology of the *Logical Investigations* in a realist manner, that is, to hold that the conception of ideal objects is realist. Certainly, to the degree that Husserl explores the topic of ideality in that work, in his effort to ground an autonomous logic freed from the threat of that particular form of empiricist phenomenalism that is logical psychologism, one can understand the initial impression of realism. This becomes even more understandable in the context of the atmosphere of objectivity in which ideal objects appear, as well as a certain similarity between Husserlian ideal being and the manner in which realist Scholasticism understood universal natures.[2] On the other hand, I do not want to give the impression that the conception of ideality in the *Logical Investigations* is the only element that these authors see as susceptible to a realist interpretation. Nevertheless, to the degree that this element is decisive in the impression of realism that these authors took away after their study of the *Logical Investigations*, I suggest that the key to this—so-called—first phenomenological

---

[1] Biemel 1959, p. 190. Biemel points out that the general framework of this common thread is the question of the correlation between subject and object. In the case of ideal objects Husserl asks himself how it is possible that these objects – whose validity is independent of every psychic fulfillment – can be given to consciousness. In other words, how is the correlation between ideal objects of a purely logical realm and subjective lived-experiences possible. Cf. Biemel 1959, 199–202.

[2] Cf. Millán-Puelles 2012a, p. 289ff. Millán-Puelles discusses the motives that, at first glance, support a realist interpretation of ideal being as it is presented in the *Logical Investigations*. These have to do with certain terminological coincidences and similarities between some of the descriptions of what Husserl calls "ideal object" and what realist Scholasticism refers to as *ens rationis*.

schism[3] is an erroneous conception of the manner in which Husserl understands ideal objects. Said more succinctly, the Husserlian theory of ideality that we encounter in the *Logical Investigations* is not realist.

To carry out the task of showing that the conception of ideality that Husserl defends in the *Logical Investigations* is not realist, I turn to the work of Antonio Millán-Puelles (1921–2005). Like many of Husserl's early students before him, Millán-Puelles converted to phenomenology upon reading the *Logical Investigations* and originally had the impression of realism when reading the text.[4] Later, however, he would defend a classical realist position.[5] Here I have in mind his doctoral thesis *El problema del ente ideal. Un examen a través de Husserl y Hartmann* (1947), *Ser ideal y ente de razón* (1953) and his monumental *Teoría del objeto puro* (1990) – all three of which are of great value, but unfortunately are little known even in the Hispanic world. In this last work—and, I repeat, from the perspective of classical realism—Millán-Puelles defends a theory of the "production" of pure objects that bears—with due respect for the inevitable differences—certain similarities to the phenomenological thesis of the constitution of objects present to consciousness.

Millán-Puelles offers two main reasons why a realist interpretation of the ontology of the *Logical Investigations* would be erroneous. First, the proof of ideality given by Husserl is invalid and, second, the manner in which Husserl interprets the universal does not coincide with the manner in which classical realism interprets it. These two considerations lead to a third which, given that it has been woven in with the other two, I will not dedicate an entire section to; rather, I will refer to it over the course of my discussion of the other two. This is because the Husserlian theory of ideality that we find in the *Logical Investigations* involves transcending the limits of phenomenology's ambitions.

2   First Critique: The Proof of Ideality Is Invalid

2.1   How the Proof Works

In the first place, Millán-Puelles holds that the proof of ideality invoked by Husserl in the Second of his *Logical Investigations* is invalid. To demonstrate this invalidity, he begins with a reconstruction of the schema of the proof itself. As we know,

---

[3] Heffernan 2016, p. 556.

[4] "Allow me to include myself here among those who, from rashness or naïveté, saw in the refutation of psychologism the sunrise of a new realist current in the climate, perhaps a bit equivocal, of phenomenology" (Millán-Puelles 2012b, p. 24) Millán-Puelles was not, however, a member of either the Munich or Göttingen Circles of phenomenology. He did not begin studying philosophy until 1939, the year after Husserl's death, and was educated in Spain. Millán-Puelles was introduced to phenomenology by Manuel García Morente, one of the translators of Husserl's *Logical Investigations* into Spanish and therefore one of the philosophers who, together with Ortega y Gasset, introduced phenomenology to the Spanish speaking world.

[5] By "classical realism" I mean, above all, the Aristotelian-Thomistic philosophy.

Husserl defends—arguing against nominalism and after having criticized the funda-mental mistakes of logical psychologism—the ideal unity of the species against modern theories of abstraction. He uses two arguments. The first of these refers to the *phenomenological place* in which ideality is inscribed, while the second points to the nature of the ideal objects themselves.[6] For Husserl, universal objects present themselves, in their unity and ideal identity, in a special mode of consciousness. This mode of consciousness is irreducibly different from that in which the individ-ual being is presented to us. The "phenomenological places" of both are, therefore, radically different. Ideal being (or being as species) is irreducible to individual being, for the act in which consciousness refers to it is different from the act in which the second is grasped. The difference between the two types of objects derives, therefore, from that difference which exists among their respective modes of presenting themselves to consciousness.[7] The second argument points, as I have noted, to the very nature of ideal objects. It would be insufficient to simply demon-strate the difference between the mode in which ideal objects present themselves (being as species) versus real objects (individual being). Rather, the nature of ideal objects must be clarified. This is the proper objective of the proof of ideality.

2.2 The Two Strata of the Proof of Ideality

Millán-Puelles highlights how the proof of ideality that we encounter in the *Logical Investigations* is made up of two strata. On the one hand, a *fact*, that is, the confirming of the existence of true propositions in which one judges about universal objects[8] and, on the other hand, a *law*, i.e., that "every truth implies, by its essence, the *being* of the presupposed objective at which it aims."[9] Or, stated another way, that the "truth or validity of a proposition means that what is thought in it, is."[10] Husserl's proof would

---

[6]The expression "phenomenological place" (*lugar fenomenológico*) is used by Millán-Puelles to refer to "the place" in which ideality is given. He explains that this wording corresponds to the term "where" (*wo*) in Nicolai Hartmann's question: "*Wo also ist das Phänomen des idealen Seins fassbar?*" (Hartmann 1965, p. 22). In Husserl's terms, we are conscious of ideal objects in acts which differ from those in which we are conscious of individual objects. In any case, it is clear that it is not about "where are the ideal objects", but rather about "where are they to be grasped". Cf. Millán-Puelles 2012b, p. 43. The first of these two arguments from Husserl mentioned here is found in his theory of abstraction as eidetic intuition in the Second *Logical Investigation*. From the description of the different lived-experiences in which ideal and individual objects are respectively given to consciousness, Husserl transitions to a description of the different natures of these objects.

[7]Millán-Puelles 2012b, p. 108ff.

[8]Millán-Puelles 2012b, p. 110.

[9]Millán-Puelles 2012b, p. 110.

[10]Millán-Puelles 2012b, p. 110.

consist, therefore, in affirming—given that the universal (ideal) objects are the presupposed objects of those true propositions in which the universal objects are judged—
that universals *have being*.[11] Husserl writes:

> Ideal objects [...] exist genuinely. Evidently there is not merely a good sense in speaking of
> such objects (e.g. of the number 2, the quality of redness, of the principle of contradiction,
> etc.) and in conceiving them as sustaining predicates: we also have insight into certain cat-
> egorical truths that relate to such ideal objects. If these truths hold, everything presupposed
> as an object by their holding must have being (*Gelten diese Wahrheiten, so muß all das sein,
> was ihre Geltung objektiv voraussetzt*). If I see the truth that 4 is an even number, that the
> predicate of my assertion actually pertains to the ideal object 4, then this object cannot be a
> mere fiction, a mere *façon de parler*, a mere nothing in reality.[12]

It appears, then, that the ground of the existence of ideal objects resides, according
to Husserl, in their capacity to be subjects of categorical *judgment*s.

2.3   Millán-Puelles' Critique of Husserl's Proof of Ideality in the Logical Investigations

Millán-Puelles' critique of Husserl's proof of ideality in the *Logical Investigations*
turns on three points, (1) the invalidity of the starting point, (2) confusion between
the object and subject of judgment and (3) confusion about the scope of the objective presupposition of logical truth. According to Millán-Puelles, these three criticisms point to the fact that Husserl lacks an adequate understanding of the logical
realm. This misunderstanding would consist in a kind of "ontologizing" of this
realm. This is shown by the main argument given by Husserl to defend the being of

---

[11] In the First of his *Logical Investigations* Husserl writes: "If the meaning is identified with the
objective correlate of an expression, a name like 'golden mountain' is meaningless. Here men
generally distinguish objectlessness from meaninglessness. As opposed to this, men tend to use the
world 'senseless' of expressions infected with contradiction and obvious incompatibilities, e.g.
'round square' [...] Marty raises the following objection [...]: 'If the words are senseless, how
could we understand the question as to whether such things exist, so as to answer it negatively?
Even to reject such an existence, we must, it is plain, somehow form a presentation of such contradictory material' . . . 'If such absurdities are called senseless, this can only mean that they have no
rational sense.' These objections are clinching, in so far as these thinkers' statements suggest that
they are confusing the true meaningless [...] with another quite different meaninglessness, i.e., *the
a priori impossibility of a fulfilling sense (apriorischen Unmöglichkeit eines erfüllenden Sinnes)*.
An expression has meaning in this sense if a possible fulfillment, i.e., the possibility of a unified
intuitive illustration, corresponds to its intention" (Hua XIX/1, 60–61; Husserl 2005, p. 202). We
thus see that "absurd expressions" such as 'round square' have meaning for Husserl, they are not
senseless. The being of a round square is in our thinking it. Husserl explains the ontological character of the fictitious and the absurd: "It is naturally not our intention to put the *being of what is
ideal* on a level with the *being-thought-of* which characterizes the fictitious in contrast to the nonsensical. The latter does not exist at all, and nothing can properly be predicated of it: if we nonetheless speak of it as having its own 'merely intentional' mode of being, we see on reflection that this
is an improper way of speaking". (Hua XIX/1, 129–130; Husserl 2005, p. 250)

[12] Hua XIX/1, 130; Husserl 2005, p. 250.

ideal objects, namely, that there are truths about these objects. "If these truths hold, everything presupposed as an object by their holding must have being."[13] But, as Millán-Puelles argues, this proof of ideality would aim only to establish the presence of the ideal in consciousness, it would not be necessary to appeal to the concept of truth. True or false, those propositions whose subject is an universal concept are there, given to consciousness. But, at the same time, Husserl defends the notion that ideal being is different from the being of the fictitious. This would show that the term "being", when Husserl associates it to "ideal" overflows the simple meaning of being given to consciousness and becomes independent of it.

For Millán-Puelles, the starting point of Husserl's proof is "invalid for concluding about a being, because it is found installed on a purely noematic and negatively abstract plane."[14] Accordingly, one can say a judgment is "invalid" in two senses: either because of its material falsity or because of a teleological criterion, i.e., as determined by the function that it plays in the totality of the argument.[15] This latter type of invalidity is that which Millán-Puelles sees as applicable to the starting point of the Husserlian proof, insofar as that proof aims to draw a conclusion concerning ideal being.

> So long as we understand for "being" something so general and vague, like the meaning of the pronoun "it" or that of the expression "object," no problem arises on accepting Husserl's arguments. But nothing else is demonstrated with this; rather the ideal, ideal objects, are part of the repertoire of our unstable consciousness.[16]

It does not seem to be the case that the Husserlian proof of ideality is directed only towards establishing the presence of the ideal in thought. If that were so, it would make no sense to refer to the concept of truth and to the law that Husserl believes will spring from its meaning. As Millán-Puelles notes, those propositions—true or false—whose subject is a universal object, would be in thought, and this would mean that the ideal is exhibited in human consciousness, either as grasped by it or else as its product. This latter alternative is strenuously rejected by Husserl, insofar as he insists that the being of the ideal is different from that of the fictitious. In his effort to distinguish between absurd objects and ideal objects, Husserl may have gone too far, not having seen that ideal objects are *true objects of thought,* but not *objects that truly are.* In this way, the term 'being' when it is associated with that of 'ideal', "overflows the simple signification of the object of consciousness and

---

[13] Husserl 2005, p. 250. The original German reads: "Gelten diese Wahrheiten, so muß all das sein, was ihre Geltung objektiv voraussetzt."

[14] Millán-Puelles 2012b, p. 112.

[15] Millán-Puelles writes: "En dos sentidos, pues, cabe llamar inválido a un juicio: según una perspectiva absoluta, esto es, por su falsedad material, por la inadecuación positiva de su contenido con la estructura sobre que se juzga, o según un criterio relativo, teleológico, en orden a la especial función que se le asigna al encuadrarlo en la totalidad de un argumento. Este último tipo de invalidez es el que asigno, por lo pronto, al punto de partida de la prueba de Husserl." (Millán-Puelles 2012b, pp.111–112)

[16] Millán-Puelles 2012b, p. 112.

becomes independent of it."[17] But this is where the problem arises. "How, from a starting point that is purely noematic, can one extract a whole region of beings that are independent of consciousness?"[18] Husserl would "leap," therefore, from the plane of propositions concerning universal objects to the ontological plane of ideal being, by recourse to intellection as a springboard.[19]

This is certainly not the vision of classical realism, which, as Millán-Puelles indicates, admits the possibility of a "transit" from the noematic plane to the plane of being, when the point of departure was previously a point of arrival of another process that has its roots in the plane of being itself, i.e., abstraction.

> Without a prior doctrine of abstraction, which would anchor ideas in the domain of being, every leap from the noematic plane to the ontic plane is a jump into the void. But Husserl's doctrine only knows the final stage of abstraction: eidetic intuition, simple contemplation verified by patient understanding, liberating itself precisely of those other moments in which the conversion of the sense datum into pure idea is verified.[20]

The second point of Millán-Puelles' critique of the Husserlian proof of ideality contained in the *Logical Investigations* is closely related to the previous one, and makes reference to the confusion between the object and subject of judgment. In this ordering of things, predication is understood by Husserl "as something that falls on the subject of the judgment and concludes in it."[21] The object of the judgment is, therefore, the subject of the proposition. Taking this into account, one can better understand the meaning of the starting point for the Husserlian test, and of the entire argument: "the truth of the propositions in which one judges universal objects only has meaning [for Husserl] when supported by the being of these objects."[22] The entire weight of the argument, then, becomes dependent on the identity between object and subject of the judgment.

For its part, classical realism has rigorously delimited the role of the subject in the *judgment*. In every predication, Millán-Puelles writes, "there exists an element that acts *formally, the predicate,* and another which behaves *like matter, the subject.*"[23] The only role of the subject is to be determined by the predicate, but that does not affect at all the structure proper to the judged object. The being of that thing which is judged is indifferent to judging in itself. That which constitutes the subject of the

---

[17] Millán-Puelles 2012b, p. 112.

[18] Millán-Puelles 2012b, p. 112.

[19] "The existence of true propositions about universal objects constitutes a reality of a logical character. Can one pass from a purely noematic domain to the domain of a being, *which,* despite all of its onto-logical 'weightlessness', rules and governs our consciousness?" (Millán-Puelles 2012b, p. 113) While the expression "noematic" does not appear in the *Logical Investigations*, Millán-Puelles' use of it here indicates his familiarity with Husserl's later works.

[20] Millán-Puelles 2012b, p. 113.

[21] Millán-Puelles 2012b, p. 114. Millán-Puelles does not give a precise bibliographical reference to Husserl here. But it is clear that Husserl's argument fails to make the distinction between subject and object of the judgment which classical realism makes.

[22] Millán-Puelles 2012b, p. 114.

[23] Millán-Puelles 2012b, p. 114.

judgment is not the object, but rather its representative, a mental substitute, i.e., a concept. "The concept which acts as a subject is a sign," Millán-Puelles asserts, "and therefore something whose entire function consists in maintaining, in its own way, the presentiality of the judged object, which is incapable in itself of entering into the ideal screen of predication."[24] The concept-subject is, therefore, something *with which* one judges, but not that *about which* one judges. The error of the Husserlian logicism[25] of the *Logical Investigations* would consist, therefore, in the confusion of these two dimensions of *judgment*: the material dimension and the intentional dimension. "In terms of the School, the distinction between one and another perspective, referred to the subject, will confirm in the subject its function of *id, quo praedicatur*, and will negate, in contrast, every other role that is not that of a simple vicarious form of the intentional term of the entire *judgment*, or *id, de qua praedicatur.*"[26] In sum, the Husserlian proof of ideality would fail due to confusing the role as subject that universal concepts fulfill in certain propositions, with the objects that are pointed to in those propositions.

The third point criticized by Millán-Puelles in the Husserlian proof of ideality has to do with the way Husserl understands the relationship between truth and its objective presupposition. The Husserlian proof of ideality we find in the Second *Logical Investigation* states that if the truths on ideal objects hold, then "everything presupposed as an object by their holding must have being."[27] It looks as if Husserl conceived this relationship as an expression of the classical *adaequatio rei et intelllectus*. However, there is a difference. To understand the complete meaning of logical truth it is necessary to define exactly the correspondence between intellect and thing, between proposition and its objective presupposition. An examination of the proof of ideality can help to understand the way Husserl considered this relationship. As we pointed out, this proof concludes with the affirmation of the being of ideal objects and not just with their validity (*Gültigkeit*) before consciousness. If the objective presupposition of the truth of those propositions whose subjects are universal concepts are those ideal, universal objects, then the relation of correspondence (*adaequatio*) would be absolute and complete. Understanding truth, Millán-Puelles holds, as the absolute and complete correspondence between proposition and its objective presupposition, one could deduce – from the truth of a proposition whose subject is an universal concept – the being of this universal object.

This would show, according to Millán-Puelles, a dogmatism in the way Husserl understands the mentioned relationship between truth and its objective presupposition and would ignore the "peculiar subjective condition of judgment."[28] He did not make a fundamental distinction between the object *prout est in se* and the object as

[24] Millán-Puelles 2012b, p. 114.

[25] On the relation between logicism and psychologism, see, for instance, Wundt 1910 and Kusch 2020.

[26] Millán-Puelles 2012b, p. 115.

[27] Hua XIX/1, 130; Husserl 2005, p. 250.

[28] Millán-Puelles 2012b, p. 116.

known concept of an "objective presupposition of logical truth." Millán-Puelles refers to how exaggerated Husserl's view of its scope is. In conceiving of the objective presupposition of logical truth, there would be essential differences between the traditional realist formula and Husserl's interpretation. The ultimate root of this problem is found in the way in which Husserl understands the truth of a proposition.

> [...] Only by understanding as truth the absolute and complete fit between the proposition and the corresponding objective presupposition, can one deduce—from the truth of a proposition, whose subject is a universal concept—the *being* of the universal object which is understood to be judged in the proposition.[29]

3   Second Critique: The Husserlian Theory of Ideality in the *Logical Investigations* Is Not Realist

As is well known, in the *Logical Investigations* the phenomenological modality of ideal being is that of signification. These constitute identical intentional units, in contrast with the multiplicity of expressive experiences. This identity of the signification is nothing other than the "identity of the species." The singular beings of these species are the corresponding *moments* of the act of signifying. Returning to logic, Husserl affirms that:

> The pure logician is not primarily or properly interested in the psychological judgment, the concrete mental phenomenon, but in the logical judgment, the identical asserted meaning, which is one over against manifold, descriptively quite different, *judgment*-experiences [...] the concern of the pure logician is not with the concrete instance, but with its corresponding Idea, its *abstractly apprehended universal* [...].[30]

Here, "abstraction" appears to mean *experience of significative ideality*. In this case, as Millán-Puelles indicates, "the universal grasped in abstraction" will coincide with the ideal signification.[31] The question is whether this authorizes us to think of this signification as the universal of classical logic. Millán-Puelles believes that there are a number of reasons why the response to this question is in the negative. Let us look at some of these reasons systematically.

In the first place, if the individuals of the species that are ideal significations are also the corresponding characters or moments of the act of signifying, then what we are dealing with here – more than an *ad extra* universality that points to transubjective "inferiors" – is an *ad intra* universality, "of a repeatability of the significative identity in the abstractions that have that identity as the object of its mention."[32] So the individuals of ideal significations are, so to say, "confined" in the limits of the

---

[29] Millán-Puelles 2012b, p. 116.

[30] Hua XIX/1, 8; Husserl 2005, p. 167.

[31] Cf. Hua XIX/1, 97ff.

[32] Millán-Puelles 2012b, p. 49.

subject of the expressive lived-experiences. One cannot find in *Logical Investigations* a "reference to objectivity as such, according to the potentiality that is enclosed in the concept of the universal," as though it were to be found in the conception that classical realism has of universals.[33]

Second, and in relation to the already-mentioned specific character of ideal objects according to Husserl, Millán-Puelles makes note of numerous problems that derive from conceiving the laws of logic as one conceives the laws of arithmetic. These latter are grounded purely on the ideal essence of the genus of number. Therefore, the individualities that fall under the sphere of these laws are ideal, not real (as are, for example, the acts of counting). In this respect, Husserl affirms in section § 46 of the *Prolegomena* that: "what we have said here in regard to pure arithmetic carries over at all points to pure logic."[34] If this is so, if it is a matter of a total applicability and not of a simple analogy, then the logical laws "are conceived of as being made up of concepts that lack empirical extension."[35] Millán-Puelles cites the following passage from Husserl:

> The concepts that logical laws are composed of "cannot [...] have the character of those mere universal notions whose range is that of individual singulars; rather, they must be *truly generic notions, whose range is exclusively one of ideal singulars, genuine species.*"[36]

In this way, and from an unequivocally realist perspective, Millán-Puelles holds that the sphere of logic is, according to Husserl, enclosed in a domain in which concepts remain infinitely far away from real individuals.

> In order to escape from psychologism, Husserl has cast out from logic every *real* member of experiences. However, at the same time, he also has eliminated contact with other entities which, because they do not constitute integrating moments of the experiences, did not put objectivity in danger: on the contrary, they would have grounded and confirmed it.[37]

Finally, and as we saw before, the class of existence that—in realist Scholasticism—corresponds to formally universal natures is merely the existence of reason. The question here is whether these universal natures "exhaust their being in being affected by universality, and thus they only *are* in the understanding that thinks them."[38] The answer to this question, according to Millán-Puelles, involves distinguishing between the being of reason and *obiective* being (that being which *is* for consciousness). "The *being* of reason is not 'objective' being, but rather *that* to which only this mode of being corresponds."[39] A failure to make this distinction is what causes people to think that universal real natures are beings of reason. If we

---

[33] Millán-Puelles 2012b, p. 49.

[34] "Was wir hier in betreff der reinen Arithmetik ausgeführt haben, überträgt sich durchaus auf die reine Logik" (Hua XVIII, 172; Husserl 2005, p. 110)

[35] Millán-Puelles 2012b, p.41.

[36] Hua XVIII, 173; Husserl 2005, p. 111.

[37] Millán-Puelles 2012b, p. 41. Cf. Hua XVIII, § 46. Millán-Puelles sees the same problem in Pfänder. Cf., for example, Pfänder 2000, p. 17

[38] Millán-Puelles 2012a, p. 199.

[39] Millán-Puelles 2012a, p. 199.

remain simply with the *esse obiective*, then there would be no distinction between a chimera and the universal "human being."

> A being of reason, then, is not just that which happens to be objectively in the understanding, while it could equally be outside of it. Rather, it is that to which it alone pertains, due to an internal demand, to be objectively in the understanding. The being of reason is not only an object: it is that which is only object, *pure object.*[40]

In sum, the formally universal natures, *qua* beings of reason, are, in a certain way, "products" of thought, but *cum fundamentu in re*. In the *Theory of the Pure Object*, Millán-Puelles explains what he means with an example:

> As with any other abstract or universal number, 2 undeniably has a foundation *in re*, but neither does it exist nor could it exist as a universal or abstraction. What exists is determinate, concrete, individual. Redness likewise is no genuine entity either. There are red things, and one finds, as part and parcel thereof, corresponding individual moments of redness. 'Redness' as such, however, either in the abstract or 'disindividualized', is nowhere to be found, except as a mere mental product, as an *ens rationis* which undoubtedly has its foundation *in re* in those concrete moments of redness. For its part, the principle of contradiction is no less true for its lack of true being. As with any other *enuntiabile*, it is a mental construct, a structure devoid of effective being, which does not mean that it is an arbitrary issue, inasmuch as it has a foundation *in re*. But it is precisely because impossible or absurd objects are, in contrast, bereft of any such foundation that they are to be seen on a plane qualitatively other than that proper to ideal objects, as conceived by Husserl.[41]

The "truly existing" beings, real objects, exist *in actu*, they have a being that goes "beyond" their being thought by a consciousness. They have, hence, a "transobjectual" being, a *sistere extra cogitationem*. On the other hand, pure or irreal objects do not exist *extra cogitationem*. They are not *res obiecta*, but rather *obiectum*.[42] If we say that "there are" irreal objects, this "there are" refers to a mere objectual being. "*Cogito, ergo sum*, indeed, but not *cogitatum, ergo est*."[43] Therefore, holding that universals are beings of reason, a class of pure objects, and that therefore they *are* only qua objects of the understanding, does not mean that it is a question of pure, capricious fictions, as chimeras are, for example. "The being of reason has, in its own way, i.e., '*obiective*', an unavoidable consistency".[44] Certainly, Millán-Puelles reminds us, Husserl clearly opposed the real to the fictitious. So, when this occurs

---

[40] Millán-Puelles 2012a, p. 200.

[41] Millán-Puelles 1990, p. 212; 1996, p. 247.

[42] "[…] anything irreal has only the standing of *mere objectuality*, that is to say, a mere and simple object-givenness present to some actually conscious subjectivity. An irreal entity should in no way be constructed as a *res objecta* [an objectivated reality]; it has being only as an *objectum*, i.e., merely as that which is *before* consciousness and *for* consciousness. Apart from this, it is nothing at all, if indeed one is entitled to use the word 'is' to refer to something which is that and just that. Hence, one can understand the intrinsic opposition of the irreal to the real qua real, which is taken to be *trans-objectual*, in the sense that the being of the real is neither limited to being an object before an actually conscious subjectivity, nor does it consist in being that at all" (Millán-Puelles 1990, p. 21; 1996, p. 35)

[43] Millán-Puelles 1990, p. 277; 1996, p. 260.

[44] Millán-Puelles 2012a, p. 205.

the term "real" is taken in the strict sense of the individual, real being. This was so, not because we see that ideal beings are not, but rather insofar as they exist, they *are* not like individual, real beings. Certainly, on this point there is a coincidence between the Husserlian doctrine of ideality and the classical realist theory. The difference lies in that in classical realism, clarifications were made "in regards to what there is of extramental and mental in those objects, while Husserl [...] leaves in a situation of complete equivocity the character of 'being' that ideal beings are recognized to have."[45] For him, ideal beings truly are, but "they do not have a single ontic meaning; rather, it is purely phenomenological."[46] Hence, Husserl's defense of ideal beings would be more the affirmation of an unavoidable datum than the affirmation of a type or modality of being.

In sum, Millán-Puelles thinks that, given the failure of the Husserlian proof of ideality, failure likewise accompanies every intent of conceiving the *phenomenological* theory of the ideal "being" as an *ontological* theory of the ideal "being." That would involve weakening the ambitions of the phenomenological method itself. Realism postulates an ontological theory of the ideal being, while the phenomenological theory consists in the description of a special type of object, those we call "ideal." In this way, when Husserl deprives the concept of being of all entitative weight, when he refuses to hypostatize ideal being, he thereby "imprisons the ideal in the metaphysically neutral domain of the 'being' of the phenomenologists and distances himself from the meaning of 'being.'"[47] Seeing things in this way, Husserlian phenomenology would evade the problem of ideal being as such or, in what amounts to the same thing, it would leave unanswered the question: *"how is [ideal being] possible? and where does the indubitable objectivity of the ideal proceed from?"*[48]

In classical realism, the ideal being has been seen as "a being that is able to be any other without totally identifying itself with it. [...] *Such an entity belongs to the domain of logic and is traditionally known by the name 'concept'.*"[49] Ideal being is, therefore, concept. It is important to note that I am not talking here about Husserl, but about the realist conception of ideal objects. One of the main points in Millán-Puelles' concerns the notion that, given the fact that one can make categorical judgments about some entities, this means that these entities exist. Following Aquinas, Millán Puelles defends that there are two meaning of beings. One of them is the predicative one. So, ideal beings are – in a precise sense – concepts, *entia rationis* "created" by the human mind. But this thesis seems to conflict with the proposal of some phenomenological realists who interpret Millán-Puelles' position as being

---

[45] Millán-Puelles 2012a, p. 204.
[46] Millán-Puelles 2012a, p. 204.
[47] Millán-Puelles 2012b, p. 125.
[48] Millán-Puelles 2012b, p. 125.
[49] Millán-Puelles 2012b, p. 128.

equivalent to subjectivism.[50] For them, linking ideality to the domain of the concept is to expose it anew to the risk of a psychologistic interpretation.

In *El problema del ente ideal en Husserl y en Hartmann*, Millán-Puelles holds that in order to maintain his own thesis—which, as I have already stated, is nothing other than classical realism—nothing else is necessary than the distinction in classical logic between *formal concept* and *objective concept*. A formal concept is a psychic reality while the objective concept is, on the contrary, a non-psychological reality.

> The objective concept is the *ratio intellecta,* which is opposed to the understanding as its object; it is the *noema* that correlates to that *noesis* in which the formal concept consists. The objective concept belongs to mind not *subiective,* but rather *obiective,* that is, by confronting it. The 'identity' with which Husserl characterizes the ideality of significations—as opposed to the plurality of the acts of signifying—fully fits the objective concept, which remains itself, even though the formal concepts, by means of which it is made an object for various intellects, perhaps many.[51]

As a result, the concept is a "psychological entity," that is, simultaneously psychical and logical:

> Considered from the perspective of "exercise," we have the formal concept. Seen from the facet of "specification," we find the objective concept. But phenomenology is accustomed to working with only the psychical dimension of the concept and must access the sphere of ideality in order to fill up the emptiness of the objective concept.[52]

But where does the objectivity of the "objective concept" come from? While the ideal sphere that Husserl describes is disconnected from all psychical and physical reality, the concepts "emit a double relationship by which they appear as linked both to the mental world as well as the world of physical natures. It is on the side of the relation to these that one must seek the explanation of eidetic objectivity."[53]

The second response to which I was alluding a moment ago has to do with the meaning of the expression "mental product" applied—from a classical realist perspective such as that of Millán-Puelles—to ideal objects. Thinking of ideal objects as "mental products" is equivalent to putting them on the same plane as fictitious objects. To do so would mean we have not developed a key distinction, that is, that which exists between *real genesis* and *intentional genesis*. Certainly, we know that

---

[50] Cf., for instance, the preface of Josef Seifert to the English edition of Millán-Puelles' *Theory of the Pure Object*.

[51] Millán-Puelles 2012b, p. 128.

[52] Millán-Puelles 2012b, p. 129.

[53] "With the reduction of ideal being to the objective concept, the matter of the former remains defined as the metaphysical universal. But the metaphysical universal refers *quasi transcendentaliter* to its inferiors, and not precisely as it refers to its terminus *ad quem,* i.e., according to what happens to the logical universal, but rather to its terminus *a quo,* that is, as the point of departure of a determined process that, relying upon those inferiors, leads back to the metaphysical universal. This is the process of abstraction. The metaphysical universal is an abstract nature; hence its special relationship to the inferiors, where it had been taken from. With the doctrine of abstraction that objectivity of the ideal is therefore justified" (Millán-Puelles 2012b, p. 129.)

the being of real, transobjectual objects,[54] is not reducible, therefore, to the acts in virtue of which these objects are "object-ized" for a consciousness. This is, as is known, a fundamental affirmation of every metaphysical realism. But not just that: metaphysical realism is not reducible to the recognition of this irreducibility. The irreducibility of the irreal to every act that represents it also plays an important role. The recognition of the irreal implies, as we saw, the distinction between the "truly existing" and "merely being objectually present." To this difference there corresponds the distinction between the *real genesis* of the acts of the representation and the *mere intentional genesis* of irreal objects.[55] This merely intentional genesis does not involve a real creation of something; rather, it has to do with the appearance of determinate objectivities as present to the consciousness.

It is true that irreal objects appear to consciousness via the real production of certain acts.[56] Within classical metaphysical realism the usage of terms such as *fieri, consurgere, fabricatio*, among others, to characterize the "constitution" of irreal objects present to consciousness must not be understood, according to Millán-Puelles, in any psychologistic mode. Francisco Suárez, for example, uses these terms to designate those acts in virtue of which the *entia rationis* are present to the mind. Suárez writes as follows:

> [...] the intellect is the efficient cause of beings of reason. However, it effects them merely by producing some thought or concept of its own, by reason of which a being of reason is said to have objective being in the intellect.[57]

---

[54] "Transobjectual objects" or "real objects" are those objects whose being goes beyond their being given to consciousness.

[55] Millán-Puelles 1990, pp. 613ff.

[56] "'Intentional genesis' means the genesis of an object, no matter if what is constituted thereby is not concurrently being made present as an object. Such a genesis is merely intentional in nature, inasmuch as it does not amount to the effective or real production of something. Nevertheless, it is a genuine genesis, because it is responsible for making an object arise before consciousness. In turn, the thing in question is not the representational act itself, which physically emerges *in* consciousness (or, better yet, in the subjectivity performing it). Consistent with this fact, the very arising of the act would not amount to an intentional but to an ontic, real genesis. The merely intentional genesis of the representational act itself occurs in conjunction with the physically real genesis of the act by means of which one reflects on the representational act. It is in such a reflective act that the explicit representation of objectuality *ut sic* takes place as well" (Millán-Puelles 1990, p. 618; 1996, pp. 701–702); "Every intentional genesis makes something arise 'before' and 'for' a subjectivity that is actually conscious (and not just capable of consciousness). This is the reason why it is a genuine genesis, even though it produces nothing real, [for] a genesis that is intentional in character is genuine only by virtue of the fact that it goes hand in hand with the effective production of the reality of a representational act. If the latter were not genuinely 'produced' or 'generated', taking these two words in their strongest sense, nothing irreal would genuinely be made to arise" (Millán-Puelles 1990, p. 625; 1996, pp. 708–709)

[57] English translation in Suárez 2004, p. 66. The Latin original reads: "*Intellectus est causa efficiens entium rationis; efficit autem illa efficiendo solum aliquam cogitationem vel conceptum suum, ratione cuius dicitur ens rationis habere esse obiective in intellectu.*" (Suárez 1866, Disp. LIV, sect. 2, n.4)

Here we have a clear distinction between thought (*cogitatio*), which the intellect produces, and *ens rationis*, which is said to have objective being (*esse obiectivum*) *in intellectu*. This means that the *ens rationis* in the *intellectus* does not have an authentic *esse*. If the *ens rationis* has objective being only in *intellectus*, this means that it has *esse obiectivum* thanks to an act of the intellect. This is a matter, then, of an *efficentia* of this act, of a genesis, but *lato modo*.

Certainly, there exists a fundamental difference between Husserl's theory of the constitution and Millán-Puelles' theory of the intentional genesis of pure objects. Nevertheless, it is interesting—not to say strange—that a possible point of contact between classic realism and phenomenology is situated in a phase of the latter that has been called "transcendental idealism."

4   Conclusion

The theory of ideal objects that we find in the *Logical Investigations* is—permit me the tautology—just that, a theory of ideal *objects* and not a theory of ideal *beings*. The task, then, is to determine "the properties of this object *as ordered* to their appearance in the mind, but never their most intimate nature, their being in itself. In conclusion, phenomenological descriptions do not reveal its positive character, the character proper to specific being, i.e., to ideal being."[58] The problems arise when, as Millán-Puelles notes, this metaphysical neutrality is violated and being-present and being-*simpliciter* are confused with one another, or, as in the case we are studying here, when "the being of the ideal objects is left without having been clearly determined."[59] This implies, ultimately, transgressing the limits of the phenomenological method itself, a method that seeks to analyze what is given to consciousness, prescinding from any affirmation about the possible being of what is given beyond this correlation.[60] If this is so, and the critique of Millán-Puelles is valid—as I believe it is—the realist interpretation of phenomenology remains open to questioning on an important point.

---

[58] Millán-Puelles 2012b, p. 151.

[59] Millán-Puelles 2012a, p. 204.

[60] Sparrow defends a radical version of this thesis: "[…] phenomenology remains a poor choice for metaphysical realists precisely because its method prohibits the phenomenologist from actually committing to a reality outside human thought." (Sparrow 2014, p. 13); "What I maintain is that for a philosophical description, study, or conclusion to count as phenomenological – that is, to mark it as something other than everyday description, empirical study, or speculative metaphysics – that description must take place from within some form of methodological reduction that shifts the focus of description to the transcendental, or at least quasi-transcendental, levels." (Sparrow 2014, p. 14)

References

Biemel, W. (1959). Die entscheidenden Phasen der Entfaltung von Husserls Phänomenologie. *Zeitschrift für philosophische Forschung* 13, 187–213. Spanish translation: (1968) Las fases decisivas en el desarrollo de la filosofía de Husserl. In Maci, G. (ed.). *Husserl. Tercer Coloquio filosófico de Royaumont.* Buenos Aires: Paidós, 35–67.

Hartmann, N. (1965) *Zur Grundlegung der Ontologie.* Vierte Auflage. Berlin: Walter de Gruyter

Heffernan, G. (2016). A Tale of Two Schisms: Heidegger's Critique of Husserl's Move into Transcendental Idealism. *The European Legacy* 21:5/6, 556–575.

Husserl, E. (Hua XVIII; 1975). *Logische Untersuchungen. Erster Band: Prolegomena zur reinen Logik.* Hrsg. E. Holenstein. Nijhoff, Den Haag

Husserl, E. (Hua XIX/1; 1984). *Logische Untersuchungen. Zweiter Band, Erster Teil: Untersuchungen zur Phänomenologie und Theorie der Erkenntnis.* Hrsg. U. Panzer. Nijhoff, Den Haag.

Husserl, E. (2005). *Logical Investigations*, vol. 1, J.N. Findlay (Trans.) New York: Routledge.

Kusch, M. (2020), Psychologism. *The Stanford Encyclopedia of Philosophy* (Spring 2020 Edition), Edward N. Zalta (ed.), URL = https://plato.stanford.edu/archives/spr2020/entries/psychologism/

Millán-Puelles, A. (1990). *Teoría del objeto puro.* Madrid: Rialp.

Millán-Puelles, A. (1996). *Theory of the Pure Object*, J. García-Gómez (Trans.) Heidelberg: Carl Winter.

Millán-Puelles, A. (2012a). "Ser ideal y ente de razón." In A. Millán-Puelles, *Obras completas* (Vol. 12). Madrid: Rialp, 289–299.

Millán-Puelles, A. (2012b). "El problema del ente ideal en Husserl y Hartmann." In A. Millán-Puelles, *Obras Completas* (Vol. 1). Madrid: Rialp, 25–156.

Pfänder, A. (2000). *Logik.* 4. Auflage. Heidelberg: Winter.

Sparrow, T. (2014). *The End of Phenomenology. Metaphysics and the New Realism.* Edinburgh: Edinburgh University Press.

Suárez, F. (1866) Disputationes metaphysicae universam doctrinam duodecim librorum Aristotelis comprehendentes. In *Opera Omnia*, editio nova, edita da C. Berton. Paris: L. Vivès, 1866, vol.25 e 26.

Suárez, F. (2004) *On Beings of Reason (De Entibus .ationis),* Metaphysical Disputation LIV. Translated from the Latin with an Introduction and Notes by John P. Doyle. Marquette University Press, Milwaukee 2004

Wundt, W. (1910) Psychologismus und Logizismus. In *Kleiner Schriften I*, Leipzig 1910.

Part II
The Marburg Reception of *Ideas I*. Neo-Kantian and Critical Realist Critiques

The "Offence of any and all Ready-Made Givenness". Natorp's Critique of Husserl's *Ideas I*

Burt C. Hopkins

Absract I present the first systematic account in the literature of a Husserlian response to Natorp's critique of Husserl's account (in *Ideas I*) of the pre-givenness of both the absolute stream of lived-experience and its essences to reflection. My response is presented within the broader context of what I argue is Heidegger's misappropriation of Natorp's critique of the phenomenological limits of reflection in Husserl's transcendental phenomenology and the misguided French attempt to address Heidegger's critique by introducing the dialectical notion of "pre-reflective" consciousness to phenomenology. My Husserlian response (1) shows that Husserl's account of reflection in *Ideas I* is able to rebut Natorp's critical claims that transcendental phenomenology cannot access the streaming of the stream of lived-experience without "stilling" its flow and (2) that a gap in Husserl's account of the transformation of the natural phenomenon of reflection into transcendental reflection provides justification for Natorp's criticism of the ambiguity of Husserl's account in *Ideas I* of the givenness of the essence of lived-experience investigated by transcendental phenomenology.

Keywords Husserl · Natorp · Heidegger · Sartre · Zahavi · Reflection · Non-reflective · Pre-reflective · Absolute givenness

1 Introduction

More than a century after Husserl's publication of phenomenology's foundational works there is an impatience on the part of some who want to "do" phenomenology, as opposed to engage merely in phenomenological scholarship or worse, phenomenological "scholasticism." This impatience is understandable, on the assumption that both the method and problems presented in these works are sufficiently clear

B. C. Hopkins (✉)
Institute of Philosophy, Czech Academy of Sciences, Prague, Czech Republic
e-mail: burt-crowell.hopkins@univ-lille.fr

© Springer Nature Switzerland AG 2021
R. K. B. Parker (ed.), *The Idealism-Realism Debate Among Edmund Husserl's Early Followers and Critics*, Contributions to Phenomenology 112,
https://doi.org/10.1007/978-3-030-62159-9_4

and distinct to be appropriated by others in the service of the "doing" phenomenology rather than just talking about it. On my view, however, both this assumption and the opposition it generates are problematic. There can be an opposition between phenomenological scholarship and the doing of phenomenology provided that phenomenology's principles are not only perspicuous but also are able to stand up—on their own—to philosophical critique. The absence of either one or both of these conditions, I submit, is what is responsible for the situation Husserl's phenomenology has found itself in from the beginning: the inseparability of an essential part of the doing phenomenology from the—in many ways scholarly—task of deciphering the philosophical meaning of its basic principles; a deciphering necessarily propaedeutic to the end of testing these principles in the critical crucible that is the *sine qua non* of all genuine philosophy.

Paul Natorp's[1] 1914 review of Husserl's *Ideas for a Pure Phenomenology and Phenomenological Philosophy*[2] is noteworthy in this regard for calling attention to a number of phenomenological principles whose meanings are either less than self-evident or unable independently to stand up to rigorous philosophical criticism. Natorp's critique of one of these principles, 'reflection' [*Reflexion*], is also important for the significant role it came to play in the history of the phenomenological movement, albeit at second hand. The hand in question belonged to Heidegger. In his lecture courses leading up to *Being and Time*,[3] Heidegger appropriated Natorp's Neo-Kantian critique of Husserl's account of the *scope* of phenomenological reflection for his own hermeneutical purposes. These purposes, Heidegger's ontological critique of Husserl's transcendental phenomenology, however, fundamentally distorted Natorp's critique in a manner that has proven to this day a fateful obstacle for a proper understanding of the meaning, function, and critical problem of reflection in Husserl's transcendental phenomenology.

To anticipate, Natorp's critique of phenomenological reflection's limited capacity to gain access to the lived-moment of lived-experience as lived, the streaming of

---

[1] "Paul Gerhard Natorp was one of the most prominent philosophers in Germany at the turn of the last century… [He was a student of] Hermann Cohen and F.A. Lange, and of their interpretation of Kant … Boris Pasternak, Karl Barth, and Ernst Cassirer were among his students … In addition to Cohen, academic colleagues included the philosopher Nicolai Hartmann, the theologians Rudolf Bultmann and Rudolf Otto, and the literary scholar Ernst Robert Curtius. Late in life, Natorp directed Hans-Georg Gadamer's doctoral dissertation … and, together with his long-time philosophical interlocutor, Edmund Husserl of Freiburg, engineered Martin Heidegger's appointment as an *Extraordinarius* at Marburg in 1923. Upon Natorp's death the following summer Heidegger assumed his chair, thus bringing the department's Kantian orientation to a decisive close" (Kim, Alan, "Paul Natorp", *The Stanford Encyclopedia of Philosophy*, Summer 2016).

[2] Paul Natorp, "Husserls *Ideen zu enier reinen Phänomenologie*," *Die Geisteswissenschften* I (1914): 426–448. Republished in *Logos: International Zeitschrift für Philosophie der Kultur* 7 (1917–18): 224–246. References here, cited as "Natorp 1973" are to the reprint in Hermann Noack's volume *Husserl* (Noack 1973, 36–60). English: "Paul Natorp. Husserl's Ideas Pertaining to a Pure Phenomenology," trans. J. Veith, in *The Sources of Husserl's 'Ideas I*, eds. A. Staiti and E. Clarke (Berlin, Boston: de Gruyter, 2017), 305–324.

[3] See especially "War Emergency Semester 1919," in *Zur Bestimmung der Philosophie* (Heidegger 1987). Hereafter cited as *ZBP*.

the stream, without changing it, is appropriated by Heidegger as an indictment of the very possibility of Husserl's conception of transcendental phenomenology as radical philosophy. For Natorp, on the contrary, the limit of reflection is not presented as evidence for an argument against the possibility of transcendental phenomenology as an originary philosophical discipline but as a critical limitation of Husserl's account of transcendental consciousness; namely, Husserl's misguided account of it as something that is given absolutely in an otherwise legitimate phenomenological cognition. However, the largely positive reception of Heidegger's ontological critique of transcendental phenomenology has given rise to the pervasive belief that reflection is intrinsically "objectifying," together with the conviction that the "objectivation" it brings about is a methodical liability for phenomenology because the most original phenomena are either not objective or pre-objective. Moreover, the conclusion is drawn from these supposed states of affairs that Husserl's methodological reliance on reflection brings with it an *a priori* limitation that is at variance with its radical philosophical intentions.

An important epiphenomenon of the positive appraisal of Heidegger's critique of Husserl's transcendental phenomenology is, beginning with Sartre, the French attempt to meet halfway Heidegger's premise that reflection—which is to say, reflective consciousness—is intrinsically objectifying, by introducing the notion of a "pre-reflective" and therefore non-objectifying consciousness. Although originally introduced by Sartre within the context of the dialectical argument that "there is a pre-reflective cogito which is the condition of the Cartesian cogito,"[4] the term "pre-reflective" has entered the lexicon of Husserlian phenomenology and enjoys to this day a meaning that is seemingly severed from its dialectical origin. Thus, not only is it commonly—but falsely—assumed that Husserl himself employed the term,[5] but also, that at worse its status is descriptively neutral and at best its referent is a phenomenon with a genuine Husserlian provenance.[6]

A close look at Natorp's review will show the source of the problems already hinted at with Heidegger's appropriation of Natorp. It will also show that there are problems with Natorp's critique of Husserl's account of phenomenological reflection. Finally, a consideration of the relevant passages of the book under review will

---

[4] Sartre 1956, liii.

[5] An exhaustive digital search of *Husserliana* reveals two instances where Husserl does in fact use the term "pre-reflective," once as an adjective, "vorreflektiven Sphäre" (Husserl 1952, 252) and once as a noun: "Offenbar kann sich mein Ich erst konstituieren, nachdem sich schon das Vor-Reflektive, das Geradehin-Seiende, konstituiert hat" (Husserl 2014, 459). In both cases, however, the context is not a transcendental judgment about the eidetic relationship between reflectively and non-reflectively modified lived-experiences but a general description whose province is not rigorously transcendental. These isolated instances, therefore, on my view, do not provide evidence of Husserl's employment of the term in a rigorous terminological sense.

[6] See, for instance, Zahavi 1999, p. 54ff. Zahavi, of course, is not alone in operating uncritically on the basis of this assumption. But given his high visibility, his work is perhaps emblematic of it. In the passage referred to, Zahavi appeals to Husserl's own words to explain, "how reflection also relies on a prior prereflective self-awareness" (Zahavi 1999, 54), even though those words in the passages he cites (and everywhere else) do not include the word 'prereflective'.

show a systematic gap in the author's account of the capacity of phenomenological reflection to apprehend essences, especially the essences of unreflectively modified lived-experiences.

2   Natorp's Account of an Ambiguity in Husserl's Notion of the "Given" in Pure Intuition

Natorp's critical discussion of phenomenological reflection is situated within his assessment of Husserl's account of how the knowledge of the pure phenomena that is sought by pure phenomenology comes about. This assessment has two interrelated foci. One is Husserl's principle of "givenness," which Natorp systematically subjects to critical scrutiny. The other is the critical connection between the systematic limits Natorp finds in Husserl's account of givenness and what Natorp maintains are the historically determined limits of Husserl's account of the general *eidos*.

Natorp's systematic interrogation of the principle of givenness in Husserl finds compelling his systematic differentiation of facts and essences, the "clarification of the *sense of the a priori*" this differentiation yields, and the convincing refutation of empiricism that is its result (Natorp 1973, 38–39). Natorp therefore agrees with Husserl that "the knowledge of the essence is thus *not to be grounded through experience*" (Natorp 1973, 39).

Natorp's first critical concern emerges with respect to Husserl's appeal to pure intuition as that which provides the ground for knowledge of the essence. Significantly, Natorp's concern is *not* whether there is such a thing, in the case of essences, as "'giving intuition' ['*gebender Intuition*']" (Natorp 1973, 40), but whether Husserl is claiming that these essences, as given, are given as being "there in *advance*" of the pure intuition in which they are seen. That is, Natorp grants that "What is to be seen must be *there*, must be *before one's eyes*; and what is to be grasped must, as our language puts it so well, be '*present-at-hand*' [*vorhanden*]" (Natorp 1973, 41). But according to him, it does not follow from this that what is given there *was* there prior to its being given in a "'giving' that must have the sense of a completely peculiar 'act'—the fundamental act of knowing, the act of *positing*" (Natorp 1973, 40). In other words, when it comes to the sense of the "given" in which the knowledge of essences is given, for Natorp "there is no given in the sense of mere *receptivity*."

Natorp's concern about Husserl's account of givenness grows out of what he detects is Husserl's inconsistent expression of the manner in which essences are given in pure intuition. On the one hand, Husserl writes, "'*essences are given as objects in an originary way just as much as* individual realities are given in experiential intuition' (§21)" (Natorp 1973, 40). On the other hand, Natorp can find no mention by Husserl "of a straightforward *being*-given, but of an originally *giving act* or *consciousness* (§23), of *giving* intuition, etc." Husserl's comparison of essential intuition with individual intuition invites the analogy between essential and sensible vision. Natorp, however, then questions, "wherein [for Husserl] does the *analogy* to sensible vision or grasping lie?" (Natorp 1973, 41). Does it lie in the "obviousness that what one sees and grasps in any case *is*," and as such must be there? Or is its basis the being there in advance, in the "matter" (*Sache*), of the *given*?

Natorp's argument that the givenness of essences cannot be passive has two dimensions, both of which are united by the supposition that because *knowledge* is involved in the givenness of essences, that givenness must be capable of "'justification'." Justification, in turn, is an interrelated twofold process: the determination of the finite as the delimitation of "the infinite or trans-finite as the undetermined or *predetermined*" (Natorp 1973, 44) and "the grounding of the initially isolated single positing of thought *from* the continuity of thinking, *out of it* and *by virtue of* it" (Natorp 1973, 42). On Natorp's view, "the 'act' of giving ultimately may not—and cannot—mean anything other than" this grounding.

3   Historical Grounds of Natorp's Conviction that Mediation Is a Necessary Condition for the Givenness of Knowledge

Despite his appeal to the authority of Kant regarding the loss of "*all critique of understanding*" and the consequent being "open to every delusion" (Natorp 1973, 41) that is the result of accepting "some propositions '*without justification and proof, as directly certain*'," Natorp's conviction regarding the mediation necessary for the givenness of knowledge rests upon the foundation of Plato's thought. According to Natorp, Plato was the first to realize that the foundation of knowledge cannot be provided by resting content with the unmediated "'looking'" at the intelligible *eidê*, that is, by accepting without further ado their "looks" as passively received by looking directly at them. Rather, Plato demanded an account of "their *accomplishments* as ὑποθέσεις, 'foundations' for firm *knowledge—sciences*." For Natorp, Plato's demand was based in his "deepest discovery: that of the *kinêsis* of the *eidê*" (Natorp 1973, 44), from which it follows both that "relations" are "prior (logically) to things" and that "a rigorous logical account (λόγον διδόναι)" of the *eidê* is called for in order to ground knowledge. This account cannot be based in "mere 'seeing'" (Natorp 1973, 41), because mere seeing's *immediacy* presupposes precisely what the rational justification of knowledge demands through proof or deduction: the "*being*-determined [Bestimmt*sein*]" (Natorp 1973, 42) of the single instances of knowing. Being-determined, then, is for Natorp "the only acceptable sense of being-given." No immediate, which is to say, "mere" seeing can provide this determination, because *being*-determined presupposes "*an act of determining*" and therefore the grounding mediation of "the original *continuity* of thought."

On Natorp's view, the mediation called for here can be provided neither by Aristotelian "'*apodeixis*'" (Natorp 1973, 41) nor by Descartes' intuition of the mediating steps of deduction. The problem with both is that they cannot but remain on the plane of "mere seeing," which is an issue because the mediation called for in order to justify cognitively what is seen presupposes something more than this direct and immediate seeing. Aristotelian *apodeixis* falls short of providing this because the seeing-together it posits is "just another mere 'seeing'," which "would need to grasp the coherent whole [*Zusammenhanges*] itself as an individual 'sight' – regardless of how 'logical' the coherent whole is." So, too, does Descartes' grasping "the single steps of *mediating* deduction" (Natorp 1973, 42) presuppose that they are "grasped in *immediate* intuition, such that deduction is just a chain of intuitions whose connections are themselves a matter of intuition, albeit intuition of a second order." Both accounts exhibit the shortcoming of what "mere seeing" cannot provide, namely a "*coherent whole* of the individual thought-positings [*Denksetzungen*]." In Aristotle, "the successive ordering of the logical according to the relation of conditioning and conditioned" is supposed to provide this; in Descartes, "the simultaneous order of mutual conditioning" is appealed to in order supposedly to bring it about. Neither can pull it off, however, because each "conceals the decisive moment," viz., thinking, which is "movement not fixation; the stases can only be in passages, just as the point can only be part of the drawn line, not present for itself prior to it, and not 'determined' through itself." Precisely this, then, is what Plato's "διαλέγεσθαι, logic as dialectics, understanding as *discursus*, means: that thinking is movement, that one is to inquire about the *fieri* [what is becoming], and only on the basis of the *fieri* can one recognize the *factum*."

4   Natorp's Account of the Offence of Ready-Made Givenness

It is within the context of this account of the epistemological limits of "mere seeing" that Natorp speaks of "the offence [*Anstoß*] of any and all *ready-made* [*fertigen*] givenness, every *tout-fait* [absolute], be it called *a priori* or empirical" (Natorp 1973, 42). The offence being that "the *rigidity*, the *pointilistic* character of the 'insight'" yielded by mere seeing is "taken in isolation" from the movement of a coherent whole [*Zusammenhanges*] in which it alone can be given, and it is therefore treated as something that is given *in advance, passively*, and thus in "isolation" from this movement. To avoid this offence, "the purported 'fixed-stars' of thinking are to be recognized as 'wandering stars of a higher order'; the purported *fixed points* of thinking must be dissolved, made fluid within the continuity of the thought-process." According to Natorp, Husserl's talk about both the "*absolutely grasped* essence 'completely as it is in itself'" (Natorp 1973, 52) and the absolute presentation of pure consciousness, are indications that Husserl has not come close to the "insight" (Natorp 1973, 44) that recognizes that "to speak of a *being*-given without a giving *process*, especially a process of thought, ... is wrong." Husserl, then, in his way of talking about essences, showed that he had "advanced to Plato's *eidos*." However, "he [nevertheless] remained standing on the *first step* of Platonism, that of the rigid *eidê* that stand immobile 'in Being'; [this way of talking showed] that he did not follow the final step of Plato's that was his greatest and most properly his own: to bring the *eidê* into movement, to make them fluid within the ultimate continuity of thought."

Natorp diagnoses Husserl's proximity to Aristotelianism, specifically, that "the Aristotelian concept of substance seems to have been taken over completely in the purely analytically grounded postulate of the final, absolutely individual 'this here' (§§11, 14), as being behind Husserl's conviction that "things are *prior* to relations, instead of relations being (logically) prior to things." This conviction is what allows "the old system of genus and species" to "reappear without debate (§12)" in Husserl's eidetics. Because Aristotelianism missed Plato's discovery of the *kinêsis* of *eidê*, Natorp maintains it only "seemingly" took over Platonism's "rationalism of 'proving'" and therefore in truth it held "philosophy back for thousands of years." Natorp's suggestion that the Aristotelian "truly old-Hellenic flinching before the infinite" holds back Husserl's phenomenology as well, too, however, is tempered by his recognition that it's possible that "the error corrects itself in the development [of phenomenology in the later parts of Husserl's book]," either in whole or part" (Natorp 1973, 45).

Natorp's criticism so far of Husserl's talk of "givenness" in pure phenomenology has singled out both critical and eidetic deficiencies. Insofar as the phenomenological method seeks to ground its cognition of pure essences in "straightforward" seeing, it is Natorp's position then that rational proof or demonstration of what is putatively given in such "mere" seeing will be precluded. This is the case because such seeing is inseparable from the presupposition that the given is something passively received, and therefore is somehow in the *Sache* in advance of the cognitive act in which it is given. This presupposition rules out the connection between thinking and such cognition. Specifically, ruled out are the thought processes that are necessary conditions for what is seen in the cognition of essences and that therefore must be appealed to in that cognition's rational justification. In Natorp's words, *"The process [of thinking] itself is the 'giving' [das 'Gebende'] for the (always only relative, never absolute) principles; only in this way 'is' there ['gibt' es] a given, or in other words, only thus does the given 'give itself'"* (Natorp 1973, 43).

5   Natorp's Account of the Difference Between Plato and Aristotle, and Husserl's Error

Natorp's identification of the eidetic deficiency in Husserl's talk about pure essences with the "first step" of Platonism, wherein the *eidê* are immobile, of course begs the question about Plato's "final step." Without elaborating, Natorp reports that this step brings the *eidê* into movement, and thus into the ultimate continuity of thought. It also establishes the logical priority of relations to things, which, Natorp mentions, "recent research has discovered to be the specific difference between Plato and Aristotle" (Natorp 1973, 44). The research in question here is most likely Natorp's own *Plato's Theory of Ideas*,[7] which does indeed present a significant advance in understanding Plato's late, non-Socratic thought. Briefly, Natorp shows that in Plato's dialogue the *Sophist*, the Socratic opposition between *kînesis* and *on* must be overcome in order to account for the relation of thinking to the *eidê*. The paradigmatically greatest *eidê*, *kinêsis*, *stasis*, *on*, *touton*, *heteron*, are by nature mutually related to one another, that is, in community (*koinonia*). Thinking this community, in the sense of giving an account of the relations that hold between them, thus involves *kinêsis*, movement from one *eidos* to another. From this there follows for Natorp not only the "ontological" priority of relations over things in Plato's thought, but also the philosophical necessity of a logical investigation of this priority by thinking in order to justify the knowledge these relations make possible.[8]

Natorp's lack of scruple in not only relating Husserl's pure phenomenology to traditional metaphysics but also in relying on the supposed differences between the first and second stages of Plato's eidetics as well as the supposed difference between Plato and Aristotle to identify Husserl's "error" in understanding "givenness"', raises the legitimate question of whether the criticism behind the identification of this error is justifiably immanent. That is, it raises the question of whether Husserl's pure phenomenology is sufficiently related to traditional metaphysics to warrant Natorp's criticism on its basis. For all that, Natorp's review does not return to the explicitly metaphysical dimension of its criticism. However, the focus of the rest of his critical discussion focuses on the issue raised by this criticism, namely, the philosophically problematic status of absolute givenness. His strategy is to show that Husserl's notion of the absolute presentation of pure consciousness in cognition is

---

[7] Paul Natorp, *Platos Ideen Lehre. Eine Einführun in den Idealismus* (Hamburg: Felix Meiner, 2004a). Originally published 1902 and again in 1921 as a Second Edition. English trans. *Plato's Theory of Ideas. An Introduction to Idealism*, trans. Vasilis Politis and John Connolly (Academia Verlag, 2004b). Cited as "*PTI.*"

[8] Andrea Staiti's generally informative discussion of Natorp's review in "The *Ideen* and Neo-Kantianism" (Staiti 2013), seems to identify Natorp's reference "to bringing the *eidê* into *motion* and fluidifying them" (78) with "Plato's dialectical method as the way to grasp the essence of things," and to claim, on this basis, "Natorp here represents a longstanding tradition in philosophy according to which essences 'manifest themselves' only in cognition" (80). While Natorp does indeed refer to Plato's dialectical method, he argues in *Plato's Theory Ideas* that that method is used (in Plato's *Sophist*) to investigate not the "essence of things" but the relation to one another of the five greatest *gene* (*eidê*). The "community" of these *eidê*, however, is not established for Natorp through dialectically produced "definitions" (80) that discover "true relations in the intelligible realm." Rather, on Natorp's view, the dialectical investigation of the community or participation of the *eidê* in one another establishes that the condition of every cognitive relation *itself* involves a deeper relation, namely, the "positing [*Setzung*]" (*PTI*, 305) of the "pre-relational [*vorbezügli-chen*]" self-reference of each of the greatest *eidê* as well as the positing of each *eidos's* proper relation to the other greatest *eidê*. It is thus because *kinêsis* is involved in both what he calls "the fundamental situation of relation [*Beziehungsgrundlage*]" (303) of the pre-relational self-reference and the relation to an other, that Natorp draws the conclusion behind his critique of Husserl's Aristotelian account of the *eidê*, namely, that relations are more fundamental than things. Although I cannot go further into it here, the acceptance of this critique would not lead to Husserl's genetic phenomenology, as some have argued, but rather to a casting aside of the Aristotelian priority of the *tode ti* as an implicit "guiding clue" for phenomenology's eidetics.

not only "untenable" (Natorp 1973, 51), but also that givenness loses the character of the *absolutely* given on grounds internal to Husserl's phenomenology. These grounds are Husserl's own accounts of the infinitude of the field of absolute consciousness and the acts of reflection in which this field is supposed by him to be given.

6 Natorp's Account of the Overlap of his Position and Husserl's Regarding the Opposition Between Immanent Consciousness and Posited Objectivity

Natorp begins with Husserl's distinction between the givenness of "experienceable reality" (Natorp 1973, 45) and pure consciousness. He fully accepts Husserl's account of the fundamentally inadequate givenness of the real thing, just as he accepts Husserl's conclusion that "rational positing on the basis of the appearance can never be final or unsurpassable (§138)." Moreover, he follows Husserl in understanding the essence of this givenness "as '*idea*' in the Kantian sense (of the 'endless' process, §149)," and thus that "the field of these processes is *determined a priori*, but is a continuum of appearances that is *infinite in all directions*, with various yet determined dimensions, pervaded by *fixed essential lawfulness*—but because of its infinity can never be given in complete (determining) unity (§143)" (Natorp 1973, 47).

Natorp also accepts Husserl's claim that "an *epochê*, a refraining, an inhibition, a *setting-out-of-action* of the *thesis*, of the *judgment*, by which reality is 'posited'" (Natorp 1973, 47), is both possible and universal in its scope. Likewise, Natorp accepts that "what is reached in this manner is not the *psychological* reflection upon the *I and its lived-experiences*," but that rather "what then remains, as a 'phenomenological' *residue* (p. 59), is consciousness *in itself*, in its own being, *pure* or *transcendental consciousness* (§33)." Thus, Natorp remarks on "the extensive overlap with *my* position, especially concerning the fact that one here does not suppose a *double objectivity*, to which would correspond a *double mode of appearing and perception*, but rather just the originary, indissoluble opposition of *immanent consciousness to everything objectively posited*" (49). Therefore, on Natorp's view, Husserl not only rightly "rejects the distinction of *external* and *internal perception*," but he also agrees with Husserl "that the acts of reflection are '*acts of a second order*', directed at all of the (primary) acts, in which the positing of the object is accomplished." Natorp follows Husserl in characterizing what is at stake in these reflective acts "as an *immanently directed intention that remains in same stream of lived-experience*" (Natorp 1973, 48). Thus, in the immanently directed intention that characterizes reflection, "[t]here is [*Es gibt*] precisely not a *second kind of thing* [*Dinglichkeit*] ... but over against all transcendence, *lived-experience* itself."

7   Natorp's Critical Distinction Between Thinking's Demand for Immediacy and the Capacity of Reflection to Give it

However, Natorp ceases to follow Husserl's characterization of pure consciousness as "*given* 'absolutely'" (Natorp 1973, 49). On Natorp's view, pure consciousness is not "capable of being delimited as an unquestionable 'residue' through a simple 'reduction,' indeed through the mere *refraining* from the objectively positing act." Natorp's concern, however, is not that "lived-experiencing [*Erleben*]" is not both "immediate" and "absolute." On the contrary, for him "all *mediating* positing by thinking requires an *ultimate immediacy*." The "immediacy" and "absolute" of "pure consciousness is *necessarily thought* and inevitably *demanded*" by the way it is thought. Thus, Natorp does not appear to contest Husserl's claim that "every *immanent perception* necessarily guarantees the *existence* of its object" (Natorp 1973, 48), and that "[w]hen reflective grasping directs itself at my lived-experiencing, then I have grasped an *absolute self* whose existence [*Dasein*] is in principle not negatable." What he does contest is Husserl's claim, "my consciousness is originary and absolutely given *to me*, not merely according to its essence, but according to its existence as well." And Natorp contests this claim by appealing to Husserl's own account of the givenness of lived-experience, which "presupposes the necessity of mediation when he speaks of a 'perception', an 'apprehension', a peculiar type of 'experience', specifically acts 'of a second order', i.e., those directed at the original acts" (Natorp 1973, 50).

Before going into the specifics of Natorp's detailed and sophisticated argument that "the streaming stream" (Natorp 1973, 51) of lived-experiencing "is something other than what is grasped and retained of it in reflection," however, I think a few remarks on Heidegger's appropriation of the argument are in order. From what I've presented so far of Natorp's critique, it should be clear that he's not contesting the very possibility of transcendental phenomenology, as Heidegger reinterprets his position. Likewise clear is that Natorp is not challenging Husserl's transcendental turn and the philosophical appeal to the immanence of pure consciousness that drives it, again, as Heidegger avers. Rather, he is contesting Husserl's self-interpretation of what the method that yields transcendental consciousness is capable of yielding, namely an unmediated and therefore absolute givenness "of the infinite field" (Natorp 1973, 49) of "absolute consciousness," together with "reflective knowledge of this field that is absolute" (Natorp 1973, 51). Natorp's critique therefore has two prongs, both of which, however, are hinged together by the indispensable role of reflection in Husserl's method and its mediating function for access to and knowledge of absolute consciousness.

8   First Prong of Natorp's Critique of Phenomenological Reflection's Incapacity to Provide Unmediated Access to Absolute Consciousness: Stilling the Stream

The first prong of Natorp's critique claims that the "ultimate immediacy" of pure consciousness demanded by thought, if realized, would yield "full lived-experiencing and not merely *experience of* lived-experiencing" (Natorp 1973, 49). This is a problem for Natorp, since the fulfillment of this (impossible) demand would be tantamount to the givenness in advance of the full concretion of lived-experiencing, the immediacy of which would need neither a science nor a method for its realization. Natorp puts the point thus: "But the point is not to *experience* our lived experiencing in a lived manner ... Rather, the point is to go beyond the lived-experiencing and bring it to cognition, *to hold it fast* in cognition, to *secure* it for cognition." Natorp supports this point by arguing, "[j]ust as certainly as lived-experience is not mere experience of lived-experiencing, so must the experience of lived-experiencing be something other than lived-experiencing" (Natorp 1973, 49–50). It is the former—lived-experience without the *explicit experience* of that lived-experience—that for Natorp is "'immediate' and 'absolute';" and the latter—the *explicit experience* of lived-experiencing—that is "necessarily mediating." Natorp, like Husserl, understands this explicit experience of lived-experiencing to be 'reflection', in the precise sense of "a second lived-experience for which the first *becomes an object* (§74, p. 145)" (Natorp 1973, 53). But unlike Husserl, he is of the mind that when the first, "unreflected" lived-experience becomes the object for the second, reflecting lived-experience, that first lived-experience is changed. Natorp maintains that the change involved in the first lived-experience "goes against its nature," because its streaming stream is stopped and its concretion dissolved "in a sum of *abstractions*." Husserl is not of such a mind, and that of course is the rub of the matter.

To make his critical case Natorp appeals both to Husserl's account of "the coherent whole of lived-experience [*Erlebniszusammenhang*]" (Natorp 1973, 50) as a "streaming stream" and his account of the difference between the abstract essences investigated by exact sciences and the concrete essences investigated by transcendental phenomenology. On his view, when the second order acts of reflection make the first order acts of lived-experience "into its own objects, it is 'intentionally' directed towards them, i.e., directed in a way that is first *questionable* for knowing, to be *established*, not *standing established* in advance." Because the reflected "object" in the case of the first order acts of lived-experience is conceived by Husserl "as a continual '*stream*'," Natorp maintains, "the knowledge of the coherent whole of this lived-experience must stop the stream, as it were, must try to *hold it fast* at a determinate point." However, just this knowledge brings it about that "the streaming stream," as the "object" of reflection, "is something other than what is grasped and retained of it in reflection." Hence, Natorp concludes, in the case of the "streaming stream" of lived-experience, the indispensable condition for knowledge of it, reflection, "*changes* what is grasped *in its very character*." Natorp cautions that the difference between the streaming stream of the coherent whole of lived-experience and the reflective knowledge of it that must hold it fast is "not just one of 'complete-ness'." But rather, his point is "the 'immediate' of pure consciousness"—namely the streaming of the coherent whole composing its stream—"is not already *immedi-ately known* or knowable as such." Knowledge of it, like knowledge of the transcen-dent object, is mediated, and indeed, "the knowledge of that 'immediacy' [of the streaming stream] is even more of a 'mediated' knowledge than that of the transcen-dent object."

9   Second Prong of Natorp's Critique of Phenomenological Reflection's Incapacity to Provide Unmediated Access to Absolute Consciousness: It Dissolves *concreta* into *abstracta*

Natorp draws the same conclusion on the basis of Husserl's account of the distinc-tively concrete, "morphological" essences investigated by the descriptive eidetic science of transcendental phenomenology. In contrast to the "*abstract eidē*" (Natorp 1973, 52) investigated by mathematics, which lend themselves to "conceptual and terminological *fixities*," "phenomenology deals with 'essences of lived-experience' (§73) that are not abstract ones [*Abstrakta*] but concrete ones [*Konkreta*], *flowing* essences and indeed concrete ones that are *flowing in all their parts*."[9] Just this con-cretion of lived-experience, however, on Natorp's view, is dissolved by the second lived-experience—the act of reflection—"through which alone we *know* anything about the stream of lived-experience" (Natorp 1973, 53). Thus, he asks, "but does this not *stop up* the *streaming stream* of consciousness against its nature, dissolve its *concretion* in a sum of *abstractions* – especially if (according to Husserl) what is individually experienced in a lived way is immediately grasped in '*eidetic universality*'?"

Natorp acknowledges, "basically this is the old interjection about the 'self-observation' as such *changing* what is observed." Moreover, he acknowledges Husserl takes the objection seriously, that "in the 'process of forming a new idea'" about the first (unreflected) level of lived-experiences some "new idea" is intro-duced, making it impossible to claim that reflection has "therefore gleaned the essential components of *unreflected lived-experience*." But Natorp finds that Husserl's response to the question raised by this objection is "not answered radi-cally enough." He avers that Husserl is right to maintain that "even whoever raises doubt [about reflective knowledge of unreflected lived-experience] cannot avoid *presupposing* a knowledge, by reflection, of unreflected lived-experience – for this

---

[9] The distinction Natorp really wants here is that between "exact" and "inexact" (morphological) essences, because either kind of essence, on Husserl's view, can exhibit "abstracta" that, in turn, lend themselves to essential explication. See *Ideas for a Pure Phenomenology and a Phenomenological Philosophy*, §74.

indeed is a *requirement* of the thesis itself; for by doubting the epistemological significance of reflection one still *reflects* and for *one's own* reflection makes use of the
general epistemological significance that one denies." However, rather than *prove*
that this presupposition is correct, Husserl's answer "only confirms that the epistemological status of reflection is a *presupposition*, an *hypothesis*."

Proof of the hypothesis must occur in what Natorp calls "the process." By this he
understands "genuine induction" grounded by "reliable reflection." No "pure doctrine of consciousness and no science can dispense with this." The 'induction' at
issue for Natorp, however, is not "of such a sort that seeks magically to produce
general propositions from singular *facts* (as if those were fixed in advance)" (Natorp
1973, 54), but the "'*reconstruction*'" of the movement from possibility to actuality.
In Natorp's terms, reconstruction is the method of all "objectivation," which he
maintains Husserl's phenomenology of "*the constitution of objectivity for subjectivity*" (§80, p. 161) "comes close to." Proof of the hypothesis that phenomenological
reflection has the capacity to intuit absolutely the givenness of pure (transcendental)
consciousness, however, is, on terms internal to Husserl's own constitutional
researches, not forthcoming according to Natorp. Husserl's account of objectivation
as an infinite task, "in the strict sense of the Kantian 'idea'," (Natorp 1973, 55) must
also "apply to subjectively oriented research of consciousness," for otherwise
Husserl's account of the eidetic parallelism between noesis and noema would be
violated. Once this is granted, however, and Husserl himself grants it when he investigates "how the infinite, continually cohesive stream of lived-experience ... 'constitutes itself'" (Natorp 1973, 55), then it follows that "[t]his cohesion can never be
given as a whole through a singular pure look (§83)." Natorp then concludes, that
the necessity of this cohesion's being "intentionally graspable in the mode of the
'*endless*' *progress* of immanent intuitions" and thus "not as a singular lived-
experience" means the following: "the same necessity is not accorded to every statement, which intends and pretends *immediately to bring to cognition* the streaming
stream of consciousness, *as it is in itself*, in the middle of its streaming, in its 'absolute' concretion and continuity."

Natorp's critique can be summarized as follows. One, knowledge of lived-
experience, as well as knowledge of its essence, has as its indispensable condition
acts of reflection. Two, reflective acts are themselves lived-experiences, which are
directed to unreflected lived-experiences in a manner that grasps them as their
object. Three, the essence of lived-experience is not abstract but concrete, which
means that both the coherent whole of lived-experience (*Erlebnizusammenhang*)
and its parts must be *thought* of as a streaming stream. Four, reflection, and more
specifically, its cognitive intention, necessarily *changes* its reflected object by stop-
ping the streaming of its stream in order to hold it fast in knowledge. And, five, one
consequence of this is that Husserl is wrong to understand the givenness of lived-
experience to be absolute in any sense, but especially in the sense of it being given
in advance of its apprehension by reflection, such that to this apprehension an element of passive *reception* would belong.

10 Heidegger's Fateful Misappropriation of Natorp's Critique

In light of the already mentioned influence of Heidegger's appropriation of Natorp's critique, it's significant to note that Natorp's critique nowhere argues that the epistemological limit of reflection to which he is calling attention is that it is "objectifying." Natorp, of course, does follow Husserl in calling the reflected lived-experience the "object" of the higher order act that reflects it; however, "objectivation" is terminologically reserved by Natorp for his own method of "reconstruction," which he explicitly relates to Husserl's notion of "constitution."[10] The *change* that Natorp maintains reflection introduces into the coherent whole of lived-experiences concerns the arresting of the infinitude composing the whole's streaming stream, which renders it as something contrary to its nature, namely, as something finite. Therefore, rather than the "stilled stream of lived-experience" (*ZBP*, 101) becoming "a series of singly intended objects [*einer Reihe einzelner gemeinter Objekte*]," as Heidegger puts it, the change according to Natorp is that the infinitude of the streaming stream is *dissolved* into the finitude of "a sum [*eine Summe*] of *abstractions*" (Natorp 1973, 53). Because a sum is precisely not a series but something singular that unifies a multitude, the contrast here between Natorp's critique and Heidegger's appropriation of it could not be greater. Natorp frames his critique in terms of reflection's limited capacity to cognize the unity of the infinitude of unreflected lived-experience. Heidegger recasts Natorp's criticism in terms of reflection making "reflectionless lived lived-experience [*reflexionlos erlebts Erlebnis*] into something 'looked at'" (*ZBP*, 100), such that "in reflection it stands before us as an object of reflection … standing over and against us." The conclusions that Heidegger draws from this, "thus, in reflection we are theoretically oriented," and that this orientation is "objectifying" in a manner that is intrinsically alienated from the "lived" moment of lived-experience, are therefore not found in Natorp's critique of Husserl's *Ideas I*. However, this opposition, between reflection as intrinsically theoretical and objectifying and therefore in principle alienated from non-objective and non-theoretical phenomena like life, existence, the lived-body, the other, etc., is—to the detriment of transcendental phenomenology and thus to phenomenological philosophy—tragically something that is found everywhere in contemporary philosophy.

Putting aside for the moment Heidegger's fateful misappropriation of Natorp's critique of the scope and limits of reflection as it functions in Husserl's presentation

---

[10] Natorp therefore does not extend his critique (in *Allgemeine Psychologie nach kritishcher Methode* [Tübingen: Mohr/Siebeck, 1912) of the "objectivation" of the subjective that drives traditional psychology and Husserl's presentation of phenomenology as "descriptive psychology" in *Logical Investigations* to Husserl's presentation of phenomenology in *Ideas for a Pure Phenomenology*. (Regarding the earlier critique, see Sebastian Luft, in "Reconstruction and Reduction: Natorp and Husserl on Method and the Question of Subjectivity," *Neo-Kantianism in Contemporary Philosophy* [Bloomington: Indiana University Press, 2010], 64–66. Hereafter cited as "Luft.")

of transcendental phenomenology in *Ideas I*, the question before us now is the extent to which, if at all, Natorp's critique, considered on its own terms, is justified. In 1919 Heidegger said, "until now Natorp is the only person to have brought scientifically noteworthy objections against phenomenology. Husserl himself has not yet commented on these" (*ZBP*, 101). And I am unaware of Husserl having ever commented anywhere on the specific objection that is my concern here. Husserl's comments about Natorp's understanding of his thought in a September 9, 1918 letter to Heidegger, may provide a clue about Husserl's lack of a response to Natorp's review. He writes:

> How odd it is: Natorp, an eminently honorable man (truly an *anima candida* [sterling soul]), a great intellect who has seriously studied my writings and honestly takes pains to use them, nonetheless thinks my phenomenology is an *unclarified* prelude to his own psychology, which is clear and firmly grounded on the deepest foundations! For my part, I consider his psychology not even a prelude, but as an extremely vague *premonition*—embellished with philosophical constructs—of one problem-level in my phenomenology.[11]

Not to put too fine a point on it but given his assessment of Natorp's lack of understanding of his thought and his own critical assessment of Natorp's thought, Husserl may well have lacked the motivation to engage Natorp's critique. Be that as it may, on my view Heidegger is correct about the scientific noteworthiness of Natorp's critique.

11 A Husserlian Response to Natorp's Critique

11.1 Part One: What Natorp Gets Right

A proper Husserlian response to Natorp's critique must acknowledge that its presentation of the methodological function of reflection in Husserl's phenomenology is essentially accurate. By 'reflection' Husserl means both various modifications that lived-experiences undergo independent of methodical intervention (in methodological spontaneity, as it were), as well as the scientifically interested carrying out of phenomenological reflection, which transforms the provisional (i.e., before entering the phenomenological "terrain" [*Ideas*, 144]) results of Husserl's investigations "into exemplary cases of essential universalities that we have to make our own in the framework of pure intuition and to study systematically" (146).

Husserl's account of reflection in the first sense includes the "reflecting look [*reflektierenden Blick*]" (145) in which lived-experience "gives itself [*gibt sich*]." For him, lived-experience gives itself to reflection in this first sense, as being temporally modalized. Thus, it is given as something "actually lived through, as

---

[11] "September 10, 1918: Edmund Husserl to Martin Heidegger," in *Becoming Heidegger*, ed. Theodore Kisiel and Thomas Sheehan, (Evanston: Northwestern University Press, 2007), 361.

'now' being," as well as "itself as just *having been*," and finally, as something "anticipated" as "coming in the future." Significant in this regard, Husserl characterizes a further aspect of the way in which lived-experience gives itself as "just having been"; he notes, "insofar as it was not looked at [*es unerblicktes war*], it gives itself precisely as such, as having been unreflected [*als unreflektiert gewesenes*]." Husserl, moreover, distinguishes these reflections in which lived-experience gives itself from the immanent reflections in retention and protention. Thus, there is "the immanent reflection within *retention* (the 'primary' remembering)," in which the lived-experience gives itself "as 'just' having been." Likewise, there is in protention "the reflecting regard [*Blick*]" (146), which "is turned toward the 'future' lived-experience of perception." Natorp gets all of this (see Natorp 1973, 53).

In reflection in the second sense, the attitude of *phenomenological* reflection, Husserl maintains, "[w]e carry out all reductions and see what lies in the pure essence of the phenomenological matters." To these matters belong reflection in the first sense, in the guise of the "many sorts of distinctively built-up [*gebauten*] reflective acts that themselves belong in turn to the stream of lived-experience and that can and also must be made into objects of phenomenological analyses, in corresponding reflections of a higher level" (147). Because "every mode of immanent apprehension of essence falls under the concept of reflection, as does every mode of immanent experience [*Erfahrung*]" (148), Husserl maintains "the study of the essences of reflections" assumes "[t]he fundamental methodological meaning" "for phenomenology." This study not only confirms that "in the phenomenological attitude" (94) "we carry out acts of *reflection*," and "[w]e live now completely in such acts of the second level, where what is given is the infinite field of absolute lived-experiences—*the basic field of phenomenology*" (95). But also, it confirms that "[e]very lived-experience is in itself a flow of becoming; it is what it is in an *original production* of an essential type that cannot change, namely, a constant flow of retentions and protentions mediated by a phase of an originary sort, that is itself flowing, in which consciousness of the living now of lived experience comes about, over against its 'before' and 'afterward'" (149). Natorp likewise gets all of this (see Natorp 1973, 49, 54).

Natorp thus gets reflection's "*universal* methodological function: the phenomenological method moves entirely in acts of reflection" (*Ideas*, 144) for Husserl. Natorp gets as well that this function is what, for Husserl, permits "[t]he entire stream of lived-experience, with its—in the *mode of unreflected consciousness*—lived lived-experience" (147), to "be subjected to a scientific, essential study" (147). But as we've seen, he rejects—because of its flowing nature—Husserl's claim that lived-experience can come to be *given* to *phenomenological* reflection in a manner that does not arrest its flowing nature and therefore *change* that nature into its opposite. As we've also seen, Natorp is aware that Husserl has a ready response to his objection, namely, that it presupposes that which it denies, specifically, reflective knowledge of unreflected lived-experience.

11.2 Part Two: The Cryptic Relation Between Induction and Reflection in the Critique

Natorp's response to Husserl's anticipated response, that it's not sufficiently radical, invites closer scrutiny. Specifically, it hinges on the distinction Natorp introduces between an epistemic 'hypothesis' and its inductive proof. His claim is that Husserl's argument is incomplete, because what it establishes is an hypothesis that is in need of proof, rather than the requisite proof necessary to support the hypothesis. In order to assess Natorp's distinction, let's parse closely Husserl's argument. Its first part makes the general claim that the genuine expression of doubt about something presupposes the existence of what is being doubted. As Husserl puts it, "every genuine skepticism, of whatever kind and orientation, shows itself by way of the intrinsic absurdity of implicitly presupposing, in its argumentation, as conditions of the possibility of its validity, just what, in its theses, it denies" (*Ideas*, 155). Its second part then considers the argument against the possibility of reflective knowledge of unreflected lived-experiences as a variation of the more general claim. Thus, Husserl's specific argument comes about, that doubt about the possibility of reflective knowledge of unreflected lived-experience cannot but avoid presupposing, in its very expression of what is doubted, viz., the possibility of knowledge of unreflected lived-experience, precisely sufficient reflective knowledge of unreflected lived-experience to justify the claim that it cannot be known. In Husserl's words,

> in the arguments, the talk is invariably about reflection as a fact, and about what it is or could be indebted to. With this, naturally, there is talk of 'unconscious', unreflected lived-experiences, again as facts, namely, as those from which the reflected lived-experiences emerge. Thus, *knowledge* of unreflected lived-experiences, including unreflected reflections, is constantly presupposed, while the possibility of such knowledge is at the same time put in question. (Ibid.)

On Natorp's view, what Husserl establishes here, however, is not that reflection is capable of accomplishing what its doubters argue it cannot, namely, knowledge of ureflective lived-experiences, but only that *both* reflection and reflective knowledge of unreflected lived-experiences are hypothetically presupposed in the objection expressed by their doubt. What Natorp calls the "'thesis' of reflection" formulated in Husserl's argument needs to be proved and Husserl not only has not done that, but as we've seen, Natorp thinks it's incapable of proof. Hence, Natorp's claim, that Husserl's response to the critics of self-observation is not radical enough is itself based in the claim that the scope and limits of reflection *cannot* be determined without an appeal to "genuine [*echt*] induction." What Natorp means by "genuine induction" in this context, however, is rather cryptic. Clearly, he is seeking to distinguish the type of induction he is appealing to from the empirical psychological variety that Husserl criticizes (in *Ideas Pertaining to a Pure Phenomenology* and indeed in §79 in his response to the difficulties of self-observation). Thus, Natorp makes it clear that "genuine induction" does not produce general propositions from "single facts [*einzelnen*

Fakten]" (Natorp 1973, 53), suggesting that such induction is somehow based rather in a multitude of some kind. But beyond that, however, Natorp gives no indication of how genuine induction is supposed to able to prove or disprove what he characterizes as Husserl's "thesis." In fact, as we've seen, Natorp grants that induction can only yield truth on the presumption of "reliable reflection" (Natorp 1973, 53).

Granting not only Natorp's presumption but also that he himself was in the possession of it, his critique of the methodological role Husserl assigns to reflection in transcendental phenomenology seems to come down to the following. Reflection is the means by which lived-experience is *explicitly* experienced and thus made available for cognition. As such, reflection is a higher order act than the lived-experience that it makes available to cognition. The exercise of reflection is limited by its nature as an act to single looks at that which it reflects. Because that which is reflected in reflective looking, however, *is* a stream of lived-experience whose coherent whole is itself streaming, this streaming of the stream cannot, in principle, either give itself to reflection's single looks or be given by those same looks as something that is there, antecedent to the act of reflection's singularity. Husserl's claim, therefore, that lived-experience, or the pure consciousness that is the phenomenological residuum of lived-experience subsequent to the phenomenological *epoché*, give themselves to reflection "absolutely," cannot withstand critical scrutiny.

On my view, it is legitimate to ask at this point about the critical basis of Natorp's claims about the scope and limits of reflection. If genuine induction presupposes reliable reflection, then it would seem that his own critique is vulnerable to Husserl's thesis that *reflective* claims about the limits of reflection vis-á-vis unreflected lived-experience presuppose sufficient *critical* access to what is unreflected to be able to make the claim that it is of such a nature as to be beyond the scope of reflective "looking."[12] Natorp's review, however, remains silent on the issue of how he has achieved sufficient philosophical access to the streaming stream that composes the coherent whole of lived-experience to be able to refute Husserl's claims about it.

---

[12] To argue that Natorp's claims about the limits of reflection vis-à-vis knowledge of the streaming of the stream presuppose eidetic knowledge of unreflective lived-experience, that is, the knowledge that "'consciousness is essentially a stream'," (Staiti, 84) does not really get at the heart of his critique of Husserl. Natorp's claim, as we've seen, is *not* that consciousness is essentially a stream, but that a dimension of it is, and it is precisely that dimension, in its streaming, that reflection on it stops and therefore changes from its non-reflective flowing nature. I show below that Husserl's account of reflection addresses what Natorp's critique of it does not, namely, how the access to the streaming dimension of lived-experience presupposed by his method comes about. Moreover, I show that according to Husserl's account, the change in the nature of unreflectively lived-experience induced by its reflective objectivation is itself presented by Husserl as a *phenomenon*, the recognition of which takes place in "higher" acts of reflection.

12   Husserl's Account of Reflection as the Method of Knowing Consciousness at all

Husserl, however, does not remain silent on the issue of how reflection is able to achieve knowledge of unreflected lived-experience, including its flowing. Reflection for him is, as he puts it, "the name for consciousness' method of knowing consciousness at all" (*Ideas*, 147). As such, its illuminating intention, its "ray of regard [*Blickstrahl*]," is inseparable from any and all cognizance of consciousness. Reflection, moreover, "becomes itself an object of possible studies precisely in this method." Reflection, as a "*modification of consciousness*" (148), is "of the sort that *each consciousness* can in principle undergo." Husserl speaks "here of modification insofar as each reflection essentially emerges from changes in focus [*Einstellungsänderungen*]," about which he could not be clearer or more explicit: in these changes,

> a pre-given lived-experience or datum of lived-experience (which is unreflected) undergoes a certain transformation, precisely in the mode of reflected consciousness (or of that which reflective consciousness is conscious). The pre-given lived-experience can itself already have the character of a reflected consciousness of something, so that the modification is of a higher level. But ultimately we come back to absolutely unreflected lived-experiences and to what can be given in them [...] (142)

Thus, for Husserl, "we know something of the stream of lived-experience and of its necessary relatedness to the pure ego, only through acts that *experience [erfahren]* reflectively." Husserl explicitly ties such acts, that is, the reflective modifications of unreflected lived-experiences, to our being "convinced that" (150) what is experienced in these acts "retain their sense and *authority [Recht]*, and, in the form of a general, essential universality, we apprehend the *authority* of experience of this sort in general just as, in a way parallel to this, we apprehend the authority of *discerning essences*, related to experiences in general." On Husserl's view, then, acts of reflection, which is to say, lived-experiences intentionally directed to *a* "pre-given" lived-experience or to *a* datum of lived-experience, are what convince us—that is, we who reflect—that both the *experience [Erfahrung]* of *what* is reflected and the *experience* of the consciousness *in* which it is reflected, have authority. This reflectively experienced authority characterizes for Husserl both the givenness of lived-experience to reflecting acts and the givenness of the essences of these given lived-experiences (also to reflective acts).

Husserl provides an instructive account of both methodologically spontaneous acts of reflection and phenomenological reflection at work. The account's point of departure is the phenomenologist's transportation into a lively intuition of any kind of act's implementation. The intuition may be imagined. Husserl's example is the enjoyment of a sequence of theoretical thoughts that are "freely and fruitfully elapsing" (146). The phenomenologist then carries out "all reductions" in order to "see what lies in the pure essence of the phenomenological matters." What is "first" according to Husserl is "a being turned toward the elapsing thoughts." Developing "the exemplary phenomenon further: while the thoughts joyously elapse, a reflecting look [*Blick*] turns toward the joy." The reflected joy "becomes a lived-experience that is looked at and immanently perceived, fluctuating in such and such and manner in the look of reflection and fading away." With this, "[t]he freedom and the flow of thoughts suffers in the process, we become conscious of it now in a modified manner, the joyousness inherent in its progression is also essentially affected." Husserl reports that the corroboration of all of this requires the implementation of "new changes in reflective looks." He also reports that rather than continue in this vein the following can be noted. The "first reflection on the joy finds it as currently [*aktuelle*] present, *but not as just beginning.*" Thus "[i]t stands there as enduring and before that as already lived, only not held in view [*in Auge gefaßte*]." What is given in this first reflection is assessed by Husserl in terms of the evident possibility "to pursue the past duration and manner of givenness of what is enjoyed, to attend to the earlier stretches of the succession of theoretical thoughts as well as to the [reflective] look that was turned toward it." Moreover, Husserl relates, "it is also possible to attend to the [subsequent] turn toward joy, and in the contrast [between the joy looked at and not looked at], to apprehend in the elapsing phenomenon the lack of a look turned toward it." On top of this, Husserl maintains it's possible to carry "out a reflection on the reflection objectifying [*objektivierende*]" the joy, that is, "the joy that has subsequently become an object" of reflection. This reflection on another reflection clarifies "the difference between joy that is *lived* but not looked at [*erblickter*] and joy that is *looked* at [*erblickter*]."

13   The Husserlian Phenomenon's Determination in the Double-Sided Foundational "Logic" Proper to the Relationship Between Unreflected and Reflective Lived-Experiences

In light of Natorp's critique, Heidegger's appropriation of it, and the general acceptance of the French introduction of the unit of meaning "pre-reflective" into the phenomenological lexicon, three things stand out in what Husserl's says here about self-objectivation.

One, the flowing aspect of a lived-experience can *only* be given in an act of reflection that looks at it. This is the case because a lived-experience becomes conscious, and, according to the essences of the matter, can *only* become conscious, by giving itself to an act of reflection. The temporally modalized character of givenness, which again can only become conscious in an act of reflection, gives itself in terms of the three-dimensional flowing proper to the present-past-future. Moreover, consciousness of both the flowing past and flowing future is reflectively given in, respectively, immanently reflective retentions and protentions. Thus, contra Natorp, the essentially reflective condition of givenness includes rather than precludes the givenness of the streaming stream proper to lived-experience.

Two, when a flowing phenomenon becomes an *object* of reflection by being looked at, an essential aspect of it as a phenomenon that is looked at is the *difference* between how it is now, as looked at, and how it was when it was *lived* but not looked at. This difference, and the contrast behind it that makes it possible, is something given to consciousness only in reflections, plural, that is, in a reflection on the reflection objectifying the flowing phenomenon. Thus, contra Heidegger, the very phenomenon of reflective objectivation and the changes it introduces in the reflected phenomenon, can only be reflectively given. That is, cognizance of the phenomenon of reflective objectivation is essentially a *reflective* affair, in the sense that the very recognition of 'reflective objectivation' as such presupposes both the reflective givenness of reflected and unreflected lived-experiences *and* the higher-level reflection that attends to their phenomenal contrast.

Three, Husserl nowhere refers to a "pre-given" lived-experience as "pre-reflective." In fact, as already noted, he does not use the term "pre-reflective" at all. He does so for good reason, namely, because phenomenologically—that is, in terms of phenomenology in *his* sense—the unit of meaning 'pre-reflective' is unintelligible. A lived-experience that is pre-given is so in the mode of *unreflectively* lived lived-experience. *This is how it's given to consciousness, indeed, to "reflectively modified"* consciousness; it is given precisely *as not reflectively modified.* Of course, this does not mean that unreflectively lived lived-experience is somehow being characterized by Husserl here as "reflective." Rather, what it means is that for Husserl the givenness of any phenomenon, in this case, the unreflectively modified lived-experience *as a phenomenon*, has, as the necessary *phenomenological* condition for *its* givenness, that it "gives itself" to an act of reflection. There can be nothing *phenomenologically* "pre" or "prior" about it *vis-à-vis the reflection* to which it gives itself. Should it undergo reflective modification, the lived-experience in question would become, of course, reflective. But again, to give itself as such, that is, to give itself *as* a reflectively modified consciousness, another, "higher" level act of reflection is required—and essentially so—for it to give itself to. Because as a *phenomenon* the unreflective lived-experience *presupposes* the reflective lived-experience to which it *necessarily* must give itself in order to be presented as a phenomenon at all, the predication of the adjective "pre" to its status in relation to the act of reflection that reflects its givenness is completely unwarranted.

Talk of the priority of a mode of consciousness to reflection is therefore unintelligible in Husserlian phenomenology because it defies the "*logic*" of phenomenological givenness in Husserl's sense. In this logic, the relationship between pre-given, unreflectively modified *lived* lived-experience and the reflectively modified *lived* lived-experience, is foundationally double-sided. That is, each side of the relationship reciprocally founds the other, such that the "logic" of the phenomenon requires both sides together, with neither having a foundational priority over the other. Put differently, if, per the impossible, something nevertheless managed to exercise a logically foundational priority over one or both terms of the double-sided foundational relationship between unreflectively and reflectively modified consciousness, that something, in accord with eidetic necessity, would have to be something other than a phenomenon.

14   The Gap in Husserl's Account of the Modification of Reflection in its Change Over to Phenomenological Reflection

That said, important philosophical questions remain about Husserl's account of reflection in *Ideas I*. Husserl's account of reflection treats it as a "concept" (148) under which various "sorts of lived-experience [*Erlebnisarten*] "fall" (147). This of course invites the suggestion that the different sorts of 'reflection' share a general structural commonality. This suggestion, however, is borne out neither by the distinctions Husserl makes between "the diverse 'reflections'" nor by his analysis of them "in systematic order" (148). Broadly speaking, Husserl distinguishes two kinds of reflection. On the one hand, he characterizes reflection—with the significant qualification "we may say" (147)—as consciousness' method of knowing itself. On the other hand, there is "phenomenological reflection," which is the phenomenologist's method of knowing the pure phenomena of consciousness. As Husserl's qualification about consciousness' method makes clear, the first "method" belongs to consciousness while the second method, more properly speaking, belongs to the phenomenologist. They are clearly related in his eyes, of course, since both kinds of reflection are evidently manifest as modifications of consciousness characterized by a change in focus [*Einstellungsänderung* (see 147)]. However, consciousness' "method" of knowing itself, e.g., immanent reflection in retention and protention, or the givenness of the modalities of time to reflection in the natural attitude, is essentially different from the phenomenologist's method of knowing pure consciousness.

Of course, it could be argued that Husserl not only was aware of this in the *Ideas I* but that he identified the difference in question: natural reflection is characterized by an attitude that naively accepts the thesis of the world, whereas phenomenological reflection involves a change in attitude that puts that thesis out of play. But this will not do, since it invites the interpretation, which Husserl himself at times succumbed to, that the change of focus that allows phenomenological reflection to look at pure essences is analogous with the change of focus that generates natural reflection. On such an interpretation, the change in focus responsible for phenomenological reflection would be structurally equivalent, for instance, to the change that occurs with the shift in focus from a series of theoretical thoughts establishing Heidegger's distortion of Natorp's critique of phenomenological reflection to the living joy elicited by those thoughts. The emergence of reflection *in* the natural attitude, as we've seen, involves a change in *Einstellung*—best translated in this context as "focus"—in which the reflective *Blick* catches a glimpse of something that gives itself as having been, before its change in *Einstellung* (in the sense of focus), from an engagement in the flowing thoughts to reflecting on the joy they are eliciting. (NB: this change in *Einstellung* should not to be confused with the change in *Einstellung*—here best translated as "attitude"—determinative of the natural attitude *per se* that Husserl identifies with the emergence of the phenomenological attitude.) What is reflected upon, as we have seen, therefore gives itself according to

Husserl as having been an unreflectively ongoing affair before being taken up in reflection. Can the same be said of the change in *Einstellung* in the sense of attitude involved in the move from natural to phenomenological reflection? Do the pure *essences* give themselves to phenomenological reflection as having been and thus as being unreflectively there, before the change in focus that looks at and therefore sees them? Husserl in *Ideas I* certainly talks that way at times, as Natorp so astutely noted.

I agree with Natorp's critique, however, that to do so was an error on Husserl's part. The source of the error, I submit, is a gap in Husserl's account of the transformation of acts of reflection given in the natural attitude into phenomenological acts of reflection. As we've seen, Husserl understood the essence of the acts of natural reflection to be a "modification" rooted in a change of *Einstellung* in the sense of focus. We've also seen, this change involves a shift in consciousness' "ray of regard," from its straightforward objective directedness to the explicitly subjective consciousness of its objective directedness. In line with his understanding of phenomenological reflection as falling under the same concept of reflection as natural reflection, Husserl also understood its essence to involve a focal modification, and, indeed, a modification that is structurally analogous with the modification that generates natural reflection. Specifically, a modification that allows the given to be seen and investigated *by reflection* in its givenness *as it was before giving itself to reflection*. But in the case of the givenness of the pure essence of consciousness to phenomenological reflection, precisely this is ruled out. It is ruled out, as Husserl will make clear after his *Ideas I*, because inseparable from seeing essences (*Wesenserschauung*) is both a manifold and a model (*Vorblid*) that functions as a guiding clue (*Leitfaden*) to raise into prominence the essence (*eidos*) "running through" the manifold. The manifold, as is well known, is generated by eidetic variation, whose source is manifestly *not* pre-given lived-experience but its imaginative extension. And its guiding clue is *not* something generated by lived-experience and its extension but rather is something singled out and therefore chosen by *thought*.[13] That thought, and the thinking behind it, is, I submit, what links Husserl's

---

[13] The attempt to fashion a Husserlian response to Natorp's critique of the status of the givenness of the essence in Husserl by invoking the distinction between *Wesensschau* and *Wesenserkenntnis* begs the question, on my view, that Natorp justifiably raises concerning Husserl's talk in *Ideas for a Pure Phenomenology* about the essence's absolute mode of givenness. As we've seen, Natorp is questioning how it's possible for the essence to be said to be absolute, in the sense of being given "ready-made" *in advance* of the seeing that sees it. To say that it's first seen, in a seeing that provides the basis for its cognition but is sufficiently different from it to be non-conceptual, does not address the question of the mode of the putative non-conceptual givenness. To characterize the givenness of the essence in terms of "a move from unthematic to the thematic" (Staiti, 82), a move that functions "to increase the clarity of the given essence," presupposes rather than addresses the question of the givenness proper to the essence's unthematic status. It presupposes that the essence is somehow there and "ready-made," waiting to be thematized and conceptually clarified. But this seems to be precisely what Husserl's post *Ideas* account of *Wesensschau* rules out, namely, that, in advance of methodological intervention, the *eidos* is somehow already pre-constituted. Indeed, Husserl's most developed account of *Wesensschau* (in *Experience and Judgment*) makes no mention at all of degrees of thematic clarity being a factor in the seeing of an *eidos*.

Ideas I to philosophy, and indeed to *traditional* philosophy. Natorp again, on my view, was right to call attention to the Aristotelian nature of the clue that guided Husserl's eidetics in that book and to point out its limits for bringing to knowledge the infinitude of the pure phenomenological field that that book nevertheless opened up. The significance of Husserl's turn to the Platonic understanding of the *eidos* as his guiding clue in his detailed accounts of the method of seeing essences, and the answer to the question of whether his understanding of that understanding was sufficient to provide the groundwork for cognition by phenomenological reflection of the infinite manifolds demanded by *his* phenomenology, however, is a topic for another discussion.

References

Heidegger, Martin (1987). *Zur Bestimmug der Philosophie.* Frankfurt am Main: Vittorio Klostermann.
Husserl, Edmund (1952). *Ideen zu einer reinen Phänomenologie und phänomenologischen Philosophie II: Phänomenologische Untersuchungen zur Konstitution.* Nijhoff, Den Haag, 1952.
Husserl, Edmund (2014). *Grenzprobleme der Phänomenologie: Analysen des Unbewusstseins und der Instinkte. Metaphysik. Späte Ethik (Texte aus dem Nachlass 1908–1937).* Dordrecht, Springer.
Husserl, Edmund (1976) *Ideen zu einer reinen Phänomenologie und phänomenologischen Philosophie: Ergänzende Texte (1912–1929).* The Hague, M. Nijhoff.
Kisiel, Theodore and Thomas Sheehan (2007). *Becoming Heidegger.* Evanston: Northwestern University Press.
Luft, Sebastian (2010). "Reconstruction and Reduction: Natorp and Husserl on Method and the Question of Subjectivity. In *Neo-Kantianism in Contemporary Philosophy* Bloomington: Indiana University Press: 59–91.
Natorp, Paul (2004a). *Platos Ideen Lehre. Eine Einführun in den Idealismus.* Hamburg: Felix Meiner.

Interestingly in this connection, Husserl writes the following in the margin of his copy of Natorp's *Allgemeine Psychologie*:

> The opposition of object-subject that is at play here finds its comprehensive resolution only through the phenomenological reduction, viz., in contrasting the natural attitude—which has givennesses, entities, objects as pregiven—the transcendental attitude, which goes back to the *ego cogito*, i.e., which passes over to absolute reflection, which posits primal facts and primal cognition, i.e., absolute cognition of possible cognition that has nothing pregiven but that is purely self-having cognition (*sich selbst habendes Erkennen).* (Luft 2010, 74.)

Husserl most likely wrote this note in 1918, when, as he relates in his letter to Heidegger referred to above, he "took up" (361) Natorp's book and studied it. Thus, some five years after the publication of his *Ideas for a Pure Phenomenology,* Husserl—at least in the thinking behind the writing of this note—seems to have given up on the idea of the "pregiven" in connection with "absolute cognition." Since this would presumably include the absolute cognition of essences, it appears that Husserl had moved significantly beyond the position presented in his *Ideas for a Pure Phenomenology* that was the target of Natorp's critique.

Natorp, Paul (2004b). *Plato's Theory of Ideas. An Introduction to Idealism*, trans. Vasilis Politis and John Connolly. Sankt Augustin, Academia Verlag.

Natorp, Paul (1912). *Allgemeine Psychologie nach kritishcher Methode*. Tübingen: Mohr/Siebeck.

Natorp, Paul (1914) Husserls *Ideen zu einer reinen Phänomenologie*. In *Die Geisteswissenschften* I: 426–448.

Natorp, Paul (1917–18). Husserls *Ideen zu einer reinen Phänomenologie*. In *Logos: International Zeitschrift für Philosophie der Kultur* 7: 224–246.

Natorp, Paul (1973). Husserls *Ideen zu einer reinen Phänomenologie*. In *Husserl*, ed. H. Noack. Darmstadt, WBG: 36–60.

Sartre, Jean-Paul (1956). *Being and Nothingness*, trans. H. E. Barnes. New York: Philosophical Library.

Staiti, Andrea (2013). The *Ideen* and Neo-Kantianism. In *Husserl's Ideen*, eds. L. Embree and T. Nenon. Dordrecht, Springer: 21–90.

Zahavi, Dan (1999) *Self-Awareness and Alterity*. Evanston: Northwestern University Press.

Critical Ontology and Critical Realism. The Responses of Nicolai Hartmann and Vasily Sesemann to Husserl's Idealism

Dalius Jonkus

Abstract Sesemann's philosophy is similar to Hartmann's in many respects. They were both influenced by the Marburg Neo-Kantians and they both discovered phenomenology as an alternative to Neo-Kantian idealism. However, the reception of phenomenology in their works is critical. Observing from a realist standpoint, they understood phenomenology as a method for describing objects of experience and their a priori structures. Hartmann described his philosophical position as a "critical ontology," whereas Sesemann called himself a "critical realist." Hartmannn and Sesemann understand Husserl's phenomenology as the practice of intuitive knowledge, which can be contrasted to conceptual construction. Both authors seek to join intuition and conceptual knowledge using the concept of dialectics or the genesis of knowing. However, their positions differ concerning the relationship between intuition and construction. Hartmann emphasizes the perspective of the natural sciences as a necessary element of knowledge, and Sesemann criticizes naturalistic scientific knowledge as objectifying and therefore insufficient to understand consciousness and values. I first discuss how Hartmann understands the dialectical tension between givenness and conceptual construction. Then, I analyze how Sesemann criticizes phenomenological idealism. Finally, I discuss the genesis of knowledge and the realist interpretation of phenomenological intuition in Sesemann's Philosophy.

Keywords Knowledge · Phenomenology · Neo-Kantianism · Realism · Idealism · Intuition · Construction

I wish to give special thanks to Frederic Tremblay and the anonymous reviewers for their suggestions for improving this paper.

D. Jonkus (✉)
Vytautas Magnus University, Kaunas, Lithuania

© Springer Nature Switzerland AG 2021
R. K. B. Parker (ed.), *The Idealism-Realism Debate Among Edmund Husserl's Early Followers and Critics*, Contributions to Phenomenology 112,
https://doi.org/10.1007/978-3-030-62159-9_5

99

1 Introduction

Herbert Spiegelberg's book *The Phenomenological Movement* rather thoroughly presents the relationship between Nicolai Hartmann's (1882–1950) philosophy and phenomenology. On the one hand, Spiegelberg acknowledges that Hartmann positively evaluated the phenomenological method and himself used the phenomenological method in his descriptive analysis of phenomena as well as eidetic intuition. Spiegelberg also recognizes, on the other hand, that Hartmann rejected the transcendental reduction and criticized the idealist factions of phenomenology. However, in his evaluation of Hartmann's critique of phenomenology, Spiegelberg correctly states that, in Hartmann's writings, there is more phenomenology than he himself admits (Spiegelberg 1960, 386). A similar conclusion is made by other authors who have studied Hartmann's relationship with phenomenology. Michael Landmann, for instance, argues that Hartmann was polemical about historical phenomenology, but that he did so from a phenomenological standpoint, thus the overcoming of phenomenology in Hartmann's work should rather be treated as a continuation of it (Landmann 1951, 69). Christian Möckel, in an article dealing with the question of whether Hartmann was a phenomenologist, also reaches the conclusion that Hartmann had creatively used the phenomenological method without ever being an orthodox phenomenologist (Möckel 2012, 125). Agreeing with these conclusions, I argue in this paper that, with his critique of phenomenology, Hartmann raises anew the question of intuition [*Anschauung*] and of its significance for phenomenology. Hartmann recognizes the significance of phenomenological intuition and, at the same time, indicates its limits. The discussion about intuition leads to the question of phenomenological givenness [*Gegbenheit*]. Is givenness a sufficient basis for knowledge? Must the question of givenness be related to the knowing of the *un*given, the existence of which is entailed by the given and which must be conceptually reconstructed? I maintain that, Spiegelberg mistakenly states that Hartmann fully recognizes phenomenological intuition. I argue that the significance of such intuition in Hartmann's aesthetics is irrefutable, but that, in his critical ontology, Hartmann seeks to combine the description of phenomenological givenness with a dialectics that intends to reconstruct the contexts of givenness and conceptually explain the layers of being.

  In order to better understand the relationship of Hartmann's philosophy to phenomenology, I cross-examine the latter using another philosopher who is little known and undeservedly forgotten, namely Vasily Sesemann (1884–1963), who from his teenage years until his death sustained friendly relations with Hartmann. Sesemann was born in 1884 in Vyborg, Finland. He studied philosophy at St. Petersburg Imperial University with Nikolai Lossky and in Marburg with the Neo-Kantians Hermann Cohen and Paul Natorp. Upon his return to St. Petersburg, Sesemann taught philosophy and classical languages at a high school until the outbreak of World War I, after which he was a volunteer in the Russian army (from 1914 to 1915). From 1915 to 1917, he taught philosophy as a *Privatdozent* at the University of St. Petersburg, and from 1918 to 1919 at the Viatka Pedagogical Institute. From 1922 to 1923, Sesemann had a teaching position at the Russian Institute in Berlin. In 1923 he was invited, on Hartmann's recommendation, to teach at the University of Lithuania in Kaunas and eventually became a professor there. In 1950, he was arrested and spent 6 years in the Gulag. After being released, he was allowed to work as a professor until his death on March 23, 1963, in Vilnius.[1]

Hartmann knew Sesemann from the time of his studies at the St. Petersburg German Gymnasium. Studying at Marburg (1909–1911), Sesemann also interacted with Hartmann, who at the time had just begun teaching at that university. Sesemann also belonged to the Hartmann-led group of philosophers who critically evaluated Neo-Kantian philosophy. Ortega y Gasset, who also studied at the University of Marburg in 1911, argued that the young philosophers who gathered around Hartmann were critical of Neo-Kantianism and had found an alternative in phenomenology (Ortega y Gasset 1965, 41). Sesemann's philosophy is in many respects similar to that of Hartmann. Both were influenced by the ideas of Nikolai Lossky, especially his ideas concerning intuition in knowing,[2] both took shape under the influence of the Marburg Neo-Kantians, and both discovered phenomenology as an alternative to Neo-Kantian idealism. It should be noted, however, that the reception of phenomenology in their works is critical. Recognizing the significance of phenomenological intuition and description, they both criticized the idealism of Husserl's phenomenology. They were well acquainted not only with the phenomenology of Husserl, but also with that of Max Scheler, Alexander Pfänder, Moritz Geiger, and other "realist" phenomenologists. As a result, they understood phenomenology as a method that helps solve philosophical problems. A comparison between Hartmann's and Sesemann's positions through the lens of phenomenology allows us to take a wider perspective and to see a more general tendency of the reception of Husserl's phenomenology. Herein I will not be concerned merely with similarities, but also with the differences between Husserlian phenomenology and the philosophies of Hartmann and Sesemann. Sesemann was often in dialogue with Hartmann's philosophy, directly and indirectly; he further developed some of his ideas and rejected others. Hartmann described his own philosophical position as a "critical ontology," whereas Sesemann called himself a "critical realist." Since the reception of Husserlian phenomenology in the philosophy of Hartmann has been discussed more than once,[3] I pay more attention here to the analysis of Sesemann's position.

---

[1] For further biographical details, see Botz-Bornstein 2006, 7–22.

[2] For the connection of Lossky's philosophy with Husserl's phenomenology, see: Tremblay 2016.

[3] See, for instance Jordan 1997.

2   The Dialectical Tension Between Givenness and the Theoretically Constructed Problem in Hartmann's Philosophy

Hartmann, unlike the Marburg Neo-Kantians who associated knowledge with the mathematized, theoretical construction of the natural sciences, argues that the problem of knowledge could be solved only by revealing its metaphysical preconditions. He emphasized the primacy of ontological issues. In this, he tried to separate himself both from the logical idealism represented by Neo-Kantianism and from the transcendental idealism represented by Husserlian phenomenology. Hartmann described his position as a "critical ontology." The point of departure of his thought is the problem of givenness, that is, direct access to the object of knowledge. Neo-Kantianism claimed that knowledge does not start from givenness, but rather from the comprehension of problems. Phenomenology made the opposite claim, i.e., that all knowledge is based on givenness. (Husserl Hua III/1, 51, 326). Hartmann sought to show that both were wrong. In *Grundzüge einer Metaphysik der Erkenntnis*, Hartmann argues that givenness is possible as partial givenness. On this account, it is incorrect to argue that nothing is given, but it is also wrong to presume that everything is given in experience. These are theses that show the aporetic nature of the concept of givenness (Hartmann 1949a, 42). He argues that the givenness of the object cannot be associated only with the subject's perspective, because the former is dependent on the understanding of the problem as a whole (Hartmann 1949a, 43). Phenomenology tries to overcome the theoretical formulation of the problem and return to the description of direct givenness, but such a reliance on givenness, according to Hartmann, denies objective reality and considers only the significance of phenomena. Therefore, Hartmann, contrary to the phenomenologists, claims that, in order to understand phenomena, the latter must be interpreted on the basis of theories that cover more than direct givenness. One of the possibilities for overcoming the antinomy of givenness and the theoretically constructed problem is to link the object of cognition to the progress of knowledge.

Hartmann often criticized Husserl's phenomenological idealism. In most cases, he wrongly criticized Husserl for only analyzing acts of consciousness and not focusing on transcendent objects. In a letter written to the French translator of *Grundzüge einer Metaphysik der Erkenntnis*, Raymond Vancourt, he described his relationship with phenomenology as follows:

> I nevertheless understood phenomenology differently than many of my contemporaries. Its representatives, first and foremost being Husserl, developed a theory that was semi-psychological, semi-transcendental. I had to reject this theory together with Husserl's conception of consciousness, because the new method was limited by the analysis of acts and the phenomena of acts. It seemed to me that it was necessary to better describe the phenomena of objects, and through that to rebuild the significance of the outer world that Husserl had lost due to the bracketing of reality. (Vancourt 1945, 8)

Hartmann expressed such criticism not only in *Grundzüge einer Metaphysik der Erkenntnis*, but in other books as well. For example, in his posthumously published

Ästhetik, he also criticized the orientation of phenomenology to the phenomena of consciousness. He argues that phenomenologists developed an analysis of subjective *acts* of aesthetic enjoyment but did not analyze the structure of aesthetic *objects*. With this criticism, Hartmann points out, however, that the phenomenological method allows analyzing not only the subjective acts, but also aesthetic objects (Hartmann 1966, 30). He notes that phenomenological description developed the analysis of subjective acts but lagged behind in the analysis of the aesthetic objects themselves. Hartmann set out to overcome this issue with his own aesthetics. In his opinion, this focus on the analysis of subjective acts is explained by the fact that phenomenologists rely on the prejudice of immanent philosophy, i.e., the prejudice that in immediate experience only the act can be given, and never the object in itself. Therefore, Husserl's desire to return to the things themselves remained unfulfilled.

Hartmann argues that the intentional object is different from the transcendent object in itself. He considers intentional objects to belong to the immanence of consciousness. Hartmann links phenomenology only with the descriptions of phenomena that do not allow the perception of their transcendent manifestations. In other words, the phenomenological method cannot help where reconstructive interpretation is needed. The Neo-Kantians formulated the theory of knowledge as a theory of problem-solving, and the phenomenologists as a description of givenness. In contrast, critical ontology, according to Hartmann, must start from what is given in the phenomena of direct experience and move toward a theoretical reconstruction. The reconciliation of the problems of direct givenness and reconstruction could be seen as Hartmann's contribution to the reflections on the phenomenological method. It should be noted that Eugen Fink followed a similar strategy in explaining the phenomenological method. In the *Sixth Cartesian Meditation*, Fink provids the outline of a constructive phenomenology, in which he follows a position similar to Hartmann. Fink also stats that it is not enough to rely on intuition as direct givenness, but to achieve understanding construction is also necessary (Fink 1988, 70).[4] Hartmann combines his critical ontology with a representational model of knowledge. By giving self-sufficiency and independence to the objects of cognition, he could not explain knowledge otherwise than by acknowledging the existence of images in consciousness; he understood consciousness as a storehouse for images representing reality.

Hartmann emphasized the difference between logical idealism and phenomenology. Neo-Kantian idealism is primarily a rationalism that understands being as a function of thought, reduces givenness to a problem and perception to the formulation of problems. In the Neo-Kantian conception, according to Hartmann, there is no room for irrationality. On the contrary, phenomenology extends the scope of logic beyond what is merely rational. Logical contents are not a characteristic of thinking, but of what can be intuitively experienced, or perceived. Instead of intellectualism, phenomenology presents us with intuitivism (Hartmann 1949a, 169).

---

[4] It is noteworthy that Sebastian Luft also analyzed the analogy between the Neo-Kantian idea of reconstruction and Husserl's genetic methodology. See Luft 2010.

Hartmann criticizes phenomenology from two sides. First, he criticizes the phenomenological concept of intuition, and second, he speaks against the phenomenological interpretation of phenomena, arguing that phenomenology associates phenomena solely with the immanence of consciousness. According to Hartmann, by preaching the primacy of intuition, phenomenology becomes an antiscientific doctrine and gives priority to the natural perception of the world. The phenomenological criticism of science turns into hostility to science in general (Hartmann 1949b, 590). The phenomenologists stated that the natural worldview was more primordial than the scientific. The method of intuition, according to Hartmann, is insufficient, because it can only confirm phenomena or indicate them. In his view, the phenomenological concept of intuition emphasizes not the structure of the object, but the function of consciousness, which implies that intentionality does not go beyond the immanence of consciousness. Unlike the phenomenologists, Hartmann made a radical distinction between the intentional and the transcendent object. In every phenomenon, there is a reference to something non-phenomenal beyond it. Therefore, by being satisfied only with the description of phenomena, phenomenology could not solve the problem of knowledge (Hartmann 1949a, 172). Hartmann's critique shows that he did not properly understand intentionality, since he was treating it as the immanence of consciousness. In Sect. 4, we will discuss how Sesemann criticizes Hartmann's position, because the former rejected the notion of closed consciousness, basing himself on the phenomenological concept of intuition.

Thus, on the one hand, Hartmann acknowledges the significance of phenomenology and, using the phenomenological method, criticized the Neo-Kantian theory of knowledge for not recognizing the importance of ontological assumptions. On the other hand, according to Hartmann, phenomenology has isolated individual intuitions and turned the description of phenomena into knowledge. Hartmann found a way out of these extremes through Platonic dialectics. Thought must be maximally based on phenomenal givenness but cannot be limited to this alone.

3   The Problem of Givenness and Philosophical Anthropology

Hartmann's second proposal, which has the potential of improving the solution to the problem of givenness, is associated with philosophical anthropology.[5] Hartmann proposes such a solution in his *Zum Problem der Realitätsgegebenheit*. Hartmann held the problem of givenness to be crucial in order to answer the question of reality. The problem of givenness is considered in the context of the

---

[5] For the relation of Hartmann's philosophy with philosophical anthropolgy, see Wunsch 2015 and Fischer 2011.

philosophy of knowledge, and here the most important issue is the dilemma of direct intuition and theoretical construction. Hartmann suggests solving the problem of givenness as it relates to epistemology using dialectics, through which the givenness of reality and its reconstruction are joined. This joining of intuition and reconstruction is the middle path between phenomenological intuitivism and Neo-Kantian constructivism. However, by criticizing the Neo-Kantians as much as the phenomenologists, Hartmann offers another solution to the problem of reality. One of Hartmann's main complaints about both theories is their idealistic attitude and their focus on issues pertaining to knowledge. Hartmann states that *things* are not only the objects of perception and knowledge, but also objects of human desire, suffering, and other emotional acts. Knowledge is an important relationship between subjects and the objects of reality, but a person is first emotionally bound to and affected by those objects. Therefore, the problem of givenness can be solved not only in the context of a theory of knowledge, but also through an analysis of the human being and its relationship with the reality of the world. The objects of the world, according to Hartmann, are primarily given not in knowledge, but through our practical use of them. Knowledge, he thinks, is the objectified and derived form of our practical relationship with the objects of the world (Hartmann 1931, 15). The givenness of reality is firstly experienced in life and only then does it become a problem of knowledge. Hartmann thus emphasizes the special importance of participation in situations and events. Being in a situation, here and now, a person transcends the bounds of givenness and the present. By acting, a person orients himself or herself towards the future (Hartmann 1931, 21–22). The analysis of the temporal dimension brings Hartmann's view close to Heidegger's ontology. Hartmann is also close to Scheler in arguing that reality is experienced through *resistance*. Like Scheler, Hartmann analyzes the phenomenon of labor, in which a twofold experience is revealed, namely the experience of the object of labor and the experience of the action of labor itself (Hartmann 1931, 22). Hartmann is much closer to those philosophers who treated phenomenological intuition as a relationship to reality itself. Those phenomenologists who are of a realist leaning, such as Scheler, Geiger, and Pfänder, did not acknowledge the transcendental turn and understood the intuition of essences from a realist standpoint (Smith 1997). Especially close to Hartmann are Scheler and Heidegger, who argue that intuition is not only the theoretical insight into essence, but also emotional and practical action in the world. Husserl's phenomenological influence is also noticeable in all of Hartmann's works, although it is particularly important in areas where Hartmann is concerned with values. The concept of ethical and aesthetic values would not be viable without Husserl's critique of psychologism, which revealed the autonomy of ideal objects and its irreducibility to the subject's psyche or to the object's material attributes.

4   The Critique of Neo-Kantianism and Hartmann's "Closed Consciousness" in Sesemann's Philosophy

As mentioned earlier, Sesemann studied at Marburg University, which, at the beginning of the twentieth century, was one of the most important centers of Neo-Kantian philosophy in Germany. Although Sesemann experienced the influence of Neo-Kantian philosophy, he can in no way be identified as a representative of this school. In *Gnoseologija*, Sesemann provides a comprehensive critique of the Marburg School (Sesemann 1987, 271–276). There he repeats the grievances that were poured out in his earlier articles, namely that Neo-Kantianism denies the real subject of cognition and reorients itself towards scientific knowledge, which is based upon pure theoretical thinking. The former, basing itself on *a priori* principles, constructs its own object. Thought is not given an object itself, but only a task and problem that it must solve. The Neo-Kantians state that thinking affects being and that being depends on thinking, and not *vice versa*. By reducing the problem of knowledge into the theory of the structure of scientific knowledge, Neo-Kantianism considerably narrows the problem. In this critique, Sesemann even more clearly points out that Neo-Kantian idealism ignores the basis of direct givenness or intuition in knowledge. As he says in *Gnoseologija*:

> Methodological idealism unilaterally interprets the very structure of knowledge. It does not pay attention to the basis of intuitive knowledge and is only concerned with the higher-order knowledge — the logical formation of primordial intuition. This means that it makes the same mistake as rationalism — it ignores the difference between real and ideal being, between the empirical and *a priori* moments of knowledge. (Sesemann 1987, 274)[6]

In his critique of Neo-Kantianism, Sesemann relied on Hartmann's philosophical insights about the presupposed ontological foundations of the theory of knowledge. But Sesemann noticed flaws in his friend's philosophy as well. According to him, Hartmann correctly criticized the idealist conceptions of knowledge, claiming that it is not the subject's act of cognition that constitutes the object, but that the object exists independently of cognition. However, as Sesemann noticed, in admitting that thought is immanent to the subject and that the object is transcendent, Hartmann returns to the representationalist theory of knowledge. Hartmann's orientation towards scientific knowledge also received criticism. Sesemann formulates the idea that aesthetics and ethics should be different from theoretical knowledge because each region of being requires a different mode of intuition. That which is irrational from the point of view of scientific knowledge can nevertheless be rational from an ethical or aesthetic perspective (Sesemann 1925, 234). Sesemann criticizes Hartmann's representational concept of knowledge on the basis of a phenomenological approach:

> Hartmann is undoubtedly right when he says that the object of knowledge and the thought that grasps it or the symbol that marks it are two different things. But a conclusion that the object as such is absolutely transcendent to the whole of the act of knowledge cannot be

---

[6] All translations of Sesemann from Lithunian and Russian into English are those of the author.

made. The law of consciousness, upon which Hartmann bases his reasoning, cannot be considered as certain as it seems at first glance. In this case, the conception of open consciousness that is common to intuitivism would be impossible and meaningless. It is precisely in the context of a phenomenological approach that it would be incorrect to assert that in the act of external perception or the insights of ideal meaning what is given is not the object itself but rather the symbol or the image that represents it. (Sesemann 1925, 234)

In his 1923 "Review of New German Philosophical Literature [*Обозрение новейшей германской философской литературы*]," Sesemann also criticizes the aforementioned shortcomings of Hartmann's philosophy. According to Sesemann, Hartmann uses phenomenology to uncover the ontological assumptions of the theory of knowledge and to show how knowledge goes beyond natural scientific knowledge, but Hartmann fails to critically evaluate the representationalist theory of knowledge (as Husserl did in the *Logical Investigations*), and therefore does not understand how consciousness goes beyond its own limits:

> If we agree with Hartmann that consciousness is completely enclosed within itself, then his proposed theory of representation (partially reviving Leibniz's conception) is the only way to explain the real meaning of knowledge. However, this very concept of "closed" consciousness is controversial. Phenomenological analysis seems to support the idea of an "open" consciousness, i.e., a consciousness directly reaching a thing that is different and independent from it; the theory of open consciousness, of course, meets great obstacles that so far have not been successfully defeated, but this does not yet mean that a more detailed phenomenological and gnoseological analysis will not succeed in one way or another. (Sesemann 1997a, 222)

It can be said that Sesemann criticizes both the Marburg Neo-Kantians and Hartmann's philosophy on the basis of the phenomenological idea of "open consciousness." Open consciousness is a kind of consciousness whereby things that exist independent of consciousness can be known without being immanent to consciousness and can only be known on the basis of a direct givenness, i.e., intuition.

5 Phenomenological Idealism and the Phenomenological Method

Sesemann repeatedly reacts positively to phenomenology and often calls the method he uses phenomenological. But his own approach to phenomenology was nevertheless critical. In discussing this critique, we should begin by distinguishing the phenomenological *method* from phenomenological philosophy. Sesemann criticized phenomenology on several grounds. His 1940 article "Fenomenologija," originally published as an entry in a Lithuanian encyclopedia, discusses what are, in his opinion, the most important features of phenomenology along with some critical remarks (Sesemann 1997b, 266–268). Sesemann points out that Husserl's phenomenology is a science that explains the essence of phenomena, thus justifying not only philosophy but also the other sciences. Phenomenology explores phenomena as direct data of consciousness. Therefore, in order to reveal its essence, phenomenology must examine the necessary and general structures of consciousness. Sesemann describes this connection between the givenness to consciousness and the structure of consciousness as the intentionality of consciousness.

> The basic feature of consciousness is its intentionality: its essence is directed toward something, has something in mind. Therefore, consciousness must be divided into two parts: the act of consciousness, or the intention, and the object to which the intention is directed. The act determines how the object appears to us; what we see depends on the object. Phenomenology deals equally with the structure of conscious acts and the structure of its objective content; because each act is also matched by a special content and the act determines the state of the content. (Sesemann 1997b, 266)

On this interpretation of the theory of intentionality, the role of consciousness and its acts becomes more important, because it is the acts that determine the state of the content. Therefore, the phenomenological method is understood as an immanent exploration of the data of direct consciousness in accurately describing the essence of phenomena and the types of phenomena connected to it. Phenomenological reduction here plays only an auxiliary role in emphasizing the pure structure of consciousness (Sesemann 1997b, 267). By limiting phenomenology to the eidetic method of insight into essences and revealing the structure of pure consciousness, Sesemann ignores the relationship between the act of consciousness and the transcendent object. In other words, this connection, according to him, remains immanent to consciousness and does not go beyond its bounds.

Sesemann therefore criticizes phenomenology first for not taking into account the transcendental moments manifested in phenomena.

> By being confined to the field of phenomena, phenomenology posits being only as what simply appears in consciousness. Such a strictly immanent approach is unilateral and cannot be justified by the nature of phenomena, because in the phenomena itself there is also a certain transcendental moment, referring to what is beyond the bounds consciousness. (Sesemann 1997b, 268)

Such a criticism can only be accepted in part. Husserl's phenomenology limits itself to the field of phenomena and to what is given in consciousness, but the phenomena themselves are not immanent to consciousness (Husserl Hua III/1, 87). Such a claim concerning the immanentness of phenomena and the denial of transcendence contradict the way in which Sesemann himself describes the phenomenological intuition in "Fenomenologija." He states that Husserl's intuition refers to every act of consciousness, the purpose of which is fully realized, i.e., "In which the intended object itself appears, and not this or that sign that represents it" (Sesemann 1997b, 267). In his entry on "Fenomenas" in the same encyclopedia, Sesemann also examined the contradiction between the direct givenness of the transcendental object inherent in intuition and the objects immanent in consciousness inherent to phenomena. In this article, Sesemann critically reviews various forms of phenomenalism and, in conclusion, presents the position that may be considered the closest to his own and which he calls "intuitive" or "realistic phenomenalism." As he says:

> According to intuitive phenomenalism, there is no strict boundary between the phenomenon and being itself. Being manifests itself through phenomena, even if in an incomplete form. The phenomenon gives us certain aspects of being that arise from human nature.

Their analysis allows us to somewhat determine what in their content and composition is objective and what is subjective. Since the person itself is a creature of the world and organically connected with its environment, it must be assumed that the principles of knowledge are somewhat consistent with the principles of being. The forms of intuitive or realistic phenomenalism are very diverse and differ primarily in that they define intuition and what role it attaches to the process of cognition [...]. (Sesemann 1997c, 265–266)

In criticizing Husserl's phenomenology, Sesemann distances himself from idealism, but acknowledged the significance of the phenomenological method and intuition. Sesemann describes himself as a critical realist, that is, he believes knowledge claims must be related to human beings in the world and reflect their ontological presuppositions. In describing his position as a critical realism, Sesemann often mentions Hartmann, Scheler, and Heidegger (the latter's importance for Sesemann's thought grew significantly after the appearance of *Being and Time*). Sesemann contrasts two variants of phenomenology: phenomenological idealism and ontological phenomenology. (Sesemann 1997d, 268). It could be argued that the realist branch of phenomenology is closer to Sesemann's philosophy. Sesemann gradually transformed epistemological and logical issues into ontological ones and associated phenomenology with philosophical anthropology.

Exactly what kind of complaints did Sesemann lodge against phenomenology? We can answer this question with the help of his *Gnoseologija*. First, it should be noted that Sesemann recognizes the importance of phenomenology for the descriptive study of knowledge. Second, he immediately refers to the shortcomings of the phenomenological approach. His main criticism of phenomenology is that it isolates knowledge and explores it separately from the processes of reality. This is required by the phenomenological method, which must reveal the structure and essence of pure knowledge. Therefore, according to Sesemann, phenomenology is not interested in the origin of knowledge, it does not analyze how specific circumstances affect knowledge and what its purpose is (Sesemann 1987, 212). However, such a critique of phenomenology does not take into account the difference between static and genetic phenomenology. In genetic phenomenology, which Husserl developed at a late stage in his career, and which remained unknown to Sesemann, questions were raised about the horizons of perception *wherefrom*, *wherein*, and *whereto* (cf. Geniušas 2012). Genetic phenomenology investigates the origin of knowledge and various implications connecting the separate acts of knowledge with the whole of life.

The second criticism pertains to the fact that the phenomenological analysis of knowledge isolates it and abstracts it from the specific environment of concrete life. According to Sesemann, these specific conditions of knowledge must be revealed by philosophical anthropology because they indicate that knowledge is based on the relation between a human organism and its environment. Despite his critical comments, Sesemann formulates a positive phenomenological research program. Phenomenology must reveal both the structure of pure knowledge and explain knowledge's "place and task in human life and culture. And this second aspect requires that the analysis be based on the data of perception so that, in other words, it will listen to what perception itself has to say and try to understand its language correctly, but will not add anything to it and would not involve itself at all" (Sesemann 1987, 213). Based on such statements from Sesemann about phenomenology, it becomes clear that, although he criticized phenomenological philosophy, he also appreciated the significance of the phenomenological method. Sesemann's position is close to phenomenology when he bases his philosophy on intuition and the description of the direct experience of things. However, in his epistemological research Sesemann not only admitted the significance of intuition, but also pointed out its insufficiency. In the 1935 study "New Directions in Contemporary Epistemology [*Mūsų laikų gnoseologijai naujai orientuojantis*]," in which he summarizes his long-term research into the theory of knowledge, Sesemann argues that phenomenological intuition isolates phenomena and orients itself towards an objective knowledge of ideal essences. According to Sesemann, in seeking specificity phenomenology should not only rely on ideal intuition, but also take into account the significance of the phenomena under investigation within the life of the experiencing subject. To quote Sesemann:

> On the one hand, ideal intuition is able to grasp the essence of phenomena only by lifting them out of their empirical surroundings and rejecting all those moments that are influenced by external factors. Thus, phenomenology cannot do without a certain *abstraction*, a certain *isolation* of the phenomena it investigates. On the other hand, ideal intuition could not reach its goal if it did not merge directly with the phenomena, if it did not embrace all their concreteness, i.e., all that in which the real essence and structure of phenomena assert themselves. Consequently, phenomenology must be especially careful that the abstraction and isolation of phenomena it uses does not destroy their concreteness. But, for the execution of this task, ideal intuition often does not suffice. There are many phenomena whose nature can be thoroughly understood only by their relations to other phenomena. Taken separately, a phenomenon is indistinct, opaque, and, as it were, silent; it does not tell the investigator what is important and essential to it. This feature is above all characteristic of those phenomena that are *significant*, i.e., whose essence also depends on what part they play in his life. (Sesemann 2010, 57)

In developing the theory of knowledge in this direction, phenomenologists must admit that what is most important is not the structure of pure consciousness, but the temporally and bodily situational being of a human in the world, which Sesemann, following in the footsteps of Heidegger, calls an ontological interpretation of facticity (Sesemann 2010, 59). The appearance of an anthropological dimension such as this one in phenomenology is associated with the transformation of phenomenology and the return to the meaningful reality of the surrounding world:

> Consequently, the vital, specific essence of knowledge can be grasped only upon taking into consideration the very nature of man. But the constancy and time-independence of man's nature is a myth that the science of our time does not allow us to believe in. Neither from the biological nor the sociological nor even the ethical point of view can we find in human nature an unchanging nucleus, i.e., a totality of constant features, that would unambiguously define its concrete essence. This is a decisively important consideration that forced philosophers to undertake a fundamental review of the current situation of philosophy in its entirety. Phenomenology, too, had to take account of it, with interesting consequences for the direction of its research. The older generation of phenomenologists (Edmund Husserl, Alexander Pfänder, and others) were interested mainly in analyzing the formal *a priori* elements of knowledge. The younger generation led by Max Scheler began to delve into the material side of the *a priori* sphere. That means that the focus of phenomenological thought

moved away from more abstract problems to those more concrete and closer to reality itself. And this reality, taken concretely, is the human environment, the *Umwelt*, the world the human being not only knows, but also judges and affects; in a word, it is that in which his whole life is rooted and unfolds. (Sesemann 2010, 59)

Sesemann understood the knowledge of reality not as the analysis of objects that are static and completely independent of human beings, but as the dynamic and temporal reconstruction of the becoming of reality. In admitting the limited nature of intuition, he returned to the logical formation of knowledge. Most important is the fact that Sesemann, in the interpretations of knowledge, emphasizes an organic relationship between all conceptual constructions and primordial intuition: "These constructions do not depend on a subjective attitude, but grow out of the intuition's inner flowering and bear fruit only insofar as they bring to light those moments that potentially lie in the content of intuition" (Sesemann 2010, 74). The relationship between intuition and reconstruction is complemented by the ontological dialectics of real and ideal being. Since being is understood as becoming, there is no longer a radical difference between real and ideal being. Ideal being is included in real being as the revelation of its possibilities. The creation of ideal schemes is an extension of the spheres of knowledge, because ideal schemes are implemented in actuality by replacing and transforming it. This is how Sesemann seeks to overcome the contraposition of pure contemplation and pure reconstructiveness. Treating knowledge as the becoming of reality, Sesemann thereby overcomes not only the contraposition of ideality and reality, passivity and activity, but also connects knowledge with cultural-creative dynamics. Knowledge of ideas means that they must be disclosed to others, which in turn means that ideas must be formulated and expressed in a specific way (Sesemann 2010, 79).

Sesemann also speaks of dialectics as the knowledge of the becoming of real being. The problem of dialectics, for him, arises when, while discussing questions of cognition, the weaknesses of a static kind of knowledge are revealed. In the article "Zum Problem der Dialektik," Sesemann examines the relationship between real dialectics and the dialectics of concepts..[7] Intuition and immediate participation in being, he argues, must be supplemented by conceptual and logical knowledge (Sesemann 1935).

6   Phenomenology – Idealism or Realism?

Sesemann further criticizes Husserl's phenomenology for its idealism. His criticism takes aim at the facts that (i) Husserl called his phenomenology "transcendental idealism"[8] and (ii) Husserl introduces the transcendental reduction in *Ideas I*.[9]

---

[7] Hartmann does the same in "Hegel und das Problem der Realdialektik." (Hartmann 1957)
[8] Husserl Hua I, 118.
[9] Husserl Hua III/1, 228–229.

The method of transcendental reduction would necessitate that the phenomenologist neutralize statements about a reality independent from consciousness and focus soley on the correlation of the acts of consciousness with intentional objects. It is no coincidence that Sesemann identified Husserl's position with the Cartesian project and Descartes' method of radical doubt. Sesemann associated Husserl's phenomenology with the search for an absolute foundation for knowledge, where consciousness itself is discovered as a prerequisite assumption for any knowledge. In his encyclopedia article "Husserl, Edmundas," Sesemann argues that Husserl, following Descartes, treats knowledge as a manifestation of consciousness and places all possible experience within the bounds of consciousness (Sesemann 1997d: 343). This position of Husserl was often equated with solipsism. In the same text, Sesemann warns against this danger, but believes that phenomenology is capable of solving the problem of solipsism:

> Rationally motivated obviousness is the ideal sought by scientific knowledge. However, in keeping a strictly immanent position, Husserl thinks that the logical necessity of knowledge initially applies only to my self, i.e., to the subject who perfectly fulfills the intention of knowledge and is certain of its evidentiality. Therefore, the universal or intersubjective power of knowledge needs more measurement. This problem can be solved and the specter of solipsism is removed by taking note that: 1) the "I" on which phenomenological analysis is based does not coincide with my empirical personality, but is the basis for it, and 2) that in revealing the logical structure and inner meaning of my "ego's" perception what appears is the "ego's" necessary connection with the alter ego, belonging to the same world, which forms the horizons of my "I." (Sesemann 1997d: 347)

In fact, the second point here seems especially important. Sesemann suggests a way to improve Husserl's position using the arguments concerning the intersubjective existence in the world. The problem of intersubjectivity can only be solved if the subject is in the world and shares it with others. Only dependence on the same world allows us to understand each other and to find the necessary connection between ego and alter ego.

Rather than following Husserl, Sesemann aligns himself with Scheler and Heidegger in their analysis of existence in the world and its horizons. In "Husserl, Edmundas," he states:

> In the first works, in which Husserl attempts to sketch an outline of the phenomenological method, his basic philosophical position is not yet fully apparent. But, in his last writings, he insistently spoke in favor of phenomenological idealism: that which shapes and gives meaning to the world in which we live and act is the mind itself. Husserl's disciples expressed their opinions on this question: some are in favor of his idealism, while others explain phenomenology ontologically (realistically), for example, Scheler, Heidegger [...]. (Sesemann 1997d: 347)

Although Sesemann is critical of Husserl's phenomenology, he does not reject phenomenology altogether. He acknowledged the significance of the phenomenological method and argues that by focusing on the concrete plane of givenness and our being in the world that we share with others, it is possible to overcome the problematic aspects of Husserl's phenomenology.

Thus, phenomenology, according to Sesemann, should attempt to overcome idealism by using intuition as a mode of unrepresentative consciousness and as a relationship between human beings and their environment. In Scheler's philosophy, Sesemann discovered such an understanding of knowledge, which is based on assumptions completely different from scientific knowledge. In his article "Max Scheler [*Макс Шелер*]," Sesemann writes that: "Philosophical knowledge, precisely because it is pure knowledge, is not closed within itself, but lies in a certain real, emotionally-willing relationship with the world, which is thus opened to the subject" (Sesemann 1928, 7). Similarly, in Heidegger's philosophy Sesemann discovered such an adaptation of the phenomenological method that was not focused on the objectified consciousness, but on the intentional opening of the concrete world.

> The starting point for the interpretation of being, according to Heidegger, has to be used by being that is simply accessible to us, and whose ability to know, to perceive, is inherent; that is us ourselves — humans, being-as-consciousness or conscious being. Philosophy, therefore, in its essence, is philosophical anthropology. Heidegger acknowledges a care as the main factor that determines the general structure of the consciousness of being and all its concrete manifestations. From his phenomenological analysis it becomes clear that being-as-consciousness is linked to the external world with an essential link that enables it to know. At first, this knowledge does not separate from the everyday practical activity of a human: in dealing with things, the person first understands them as what is "useful" to him, only to later see the significance of things that is released from practical meaning, the form of being that becomes the object of the natural sciences. (Sesemann 1997e: 322–323)

Sesemann here understands realism as the theory according to which there is a direct presence in the world of things, where these are not represented, but directly given in practical activities. This practical relationship with a meaningful world makes it possible to critically evaluate the objectivistic methodology of the natural sciences and the Neo-Kantianism that uses it. Scientific knowledge is here tantamount to derivative knowledge based on participation in the living world. We can thus say that, with Sesemann, we are faced with a realist interpretation of phenomenological intuition.

7   Conclusion

Hartmann and Sesemann both develop a rather traditional interpretation of Husserl's phenomenology. In their view, the early Husserl relied on intuition as the evident and direct givenness of things and gave priority to the consciousness of the experiencing subject. Thus, phenomenology returned to idealism, analyzed only immanent objects, and the transcendent objects of the world remained beyond the scope of phenomenological inquiry. But, although Hartmann and Sesemann both criticize Husserl's phenomenological idealism, they formulate their criticisms differently. Hartmann argues for the priority of transcendent objects and focuses on ontology, which — for him — precedes epistemology. He denies the primacy of intuition and returns to the representational theory of knowledge. In contrast, Sesemann further develops the concept of direct intuition. He argues that any formed conceptual knowledge is based on direct pre-reflective intuition as primarily oriented in the world. He considers intuition as a kind of understanding that includes perceived circumstances as well as the attitudes of the subject itself. Sesemann describes intuition not only as the direct givenness of things in themselves, but also as a correlation between the structures of the perceived objects and the modes of perception. He furthermore describes intuition not as a theoretical approach, but as a practical activity in the world. Hartmann's position differs from this because, in recognizing the priority of transcendent objects and the primordiality of material physical reality, he acknowledges the priority of the natural sciences with respect to all other sciences. Sesemann, in contrast, consistently criticizes scientific naturalism and shows that the alleged objective position of the natural sciences does not qualify as a pure form of knowledge, because it is based on attitudes that are common to all knowledge. So, whereas Sesemann criticizes the idealism of Husserl's phenomenology, his proposed version of critical realism resembles genetic phenomenology, which shows how any form of knowledge is not only correlated with an appropriate attitude but must also be understood by reconstructing the genesis of knowledge.

To summarize the reception of Husserl's phenomenology in the philosophy of Hartmann and Sesemann, several important aspects must be distinguished:

1. Both philosophers value phenomenology as a method for describing directly experienced phenomena.
2. Both rely on Husserl's critique of psychologism and the subsequent theory of ideal objects that Husserl endorses in defending the autonomy of ethical and aesthetic values.
3. Both criticize Husserl's phenomenology for analyzing knowledge too statically and without concern for the context in which the object is embedded.
4. Both understand Husserl's phenomenology as the practice of intuitive knowledge, which can be contrasted to conceptual construction. Both authors seek to combine intuition and conceptual knowledge using dialectics or the genesis of knowledge.
5. Their positions differ with regards to valuing either intuition or construction. Hartmann leans toward the perspective of the natural sciences as a necessary element of knowledge, and Sesemann criticizes scientific knowledge as objectifying and, therefore, as insufficient for understanding consciousness and values. Also, Sesemann develops a non-objectifying conception of self-knowledge and pre-reflective self-consciousness that also supplements the conception of phenomenological reflection.[10]

---

[10] For Sesemann's conception of self-knowledge and pre-reflective self-consciousness, see Jonkus 2015.

References

Botz-Bornstein, T. 2006, *Vasily Sesemann: Experience, Formalism, and the Question of Being*. Amsterdam/New York: Rodopi.

Fink, E. (1988). *VI Cartesianische Meditation. Teil 1. Die Idee einer transcendentalen Methodenlehre*. Dordrecht, Boston, London: Kluwer Academic Publishers.

Fischer J., 2011, "Nicolai Hartmann: A Crucial Figure in German Philosophical Anthropology," in *The Philosophy of Nicolai Hartmann*, edited by R. Poli, C. Scognamiglio, F. Tremblay, Berlin: Walter de Gruyter.

Geniusas, S., 2012, *The Origins of the Horizon in Husserl's Phenomenology*. Dordrecht: Springer.

Hartmann, N., 1931, *Zum Problem der Realitätsgegebenheit*. Berlin: Pan-Verlagsgesellschaft M. B. H.

Hartmann, N., 1949a, *Grundzüge einer Metaphysik der Erkenntnis*. Berlin: Walter de Gruyter.

Hartmann, N., 1949b, *Der Aufbau der realen Welt*. Meisenheim am Glan: Westkulturverlag.

Hartmann, N., 1957, *"Hegel und das Problem der Realdialektik."* In: *N. Hartmann, Kleinere Schriften*, Bd. 2, Berlin: Walter de Gruyter, 323–346

Hartmann N., 1966, *Ästhetik*, Berlin: Walter de Gruyter.

Husserl, E., Hua I; 1973, *Cartesianische Meditationen und Pariser Vorträge*. Den Haag: Nijhoff.

Husserl, E., Hua III/1; 1976, *Ideen zu einer reinen Phänomenologie und phänomenologischen Philosophie I: Allgemeine Einführung in die reine Phänomenologie*. Den Haag: Nijhoff.

Jonkus, D., 2015, "Phenomenological Approaches to Self-consciousness and the Unconscious (Moritz Geiger and Vasily Sesemann)." *Studia phenomenologica*. 2015, vol. 15: Early Phenomenology, 225–237.

Jordan, R., W., 1997, "Nicolai Hartmann." *Encyclopedia of Phenomenology*, eds Lester Embree, Elizabeth A. Behnke, Thomas Seebohm, Jitendra Nath Mohanty, Joseph J. Kockelmans, et al. Contributions to Phenomenology, vol. 18, Dordrecht; Boston: Kluwer Academic Publishers; 288–292.

Landmann M. 1951. Das phänomenologische Moment bei Nicolai Hartmann. In: Erkenntnis und Erlebnis: Phänomenologische Studien. Berlin : De Gruyter, 39–84.

Luft, S., 2010, "Reconstruction and Reduction: Natorp and Husserl on Method and the Question of Subjectivity," in: Rudolf A. Makkreel and Sebastian Luft (eds.), *Neo-Kantianism in Contemporary Philosophy*, Bloomington and Indianapolis: Indiana University Press, 59–91.

Möckel, Ch., 2012, "Nicolai Hartmann — ein Phänomenologe? Zu den termini Phänomen und Phänomenologie in der *Metaphysik der Erkenntnis*." G. Hartung, M. Wunsch, C. Strube (Hg.), *Von der Systemphilosophie zur systematischen Philosophie — Nicolai Hartmann*. Berlin/New York: Walter de Gruyter, 105–127.

Ortega y Gasset J., 1965, "Prologo para Alemanes," *Obras completas*, T.8. Madrid: Revista de Occidente, 15–58.

Sesemann, V. [Сеземан, В.] 1923, "Обозрение новейшей германской философской литературы," *София: Проблемы духовной культуры и религиозной философии*. Вып. I, с. 173–183.

Sesemann, V., [Сеземан, В.] 1925, "Nicolai Hartmann. Grundzüge Einer Metaphysik der Erkenntnis (Berlin, 1921)." In: *Логос* 1, 229–235.

Sesemann, V., [Сеземан, В.] 1928, "Макс Шелер." *Евразия* 2, 7–8.

Sesemann, V., 1935, "Zum Problem der Dialektik," *Blätter für Deutsche Philosophie*, Berlin, Bd. 9, Heft 1, 28–61.

Sesemann, V., [Sezemanas, V.] 1987: *Gnoseologija*. In: *Raštai. Gnoseologija*, Vilnius: Mintis, 209–334.

Sesemann, V., [Sezemanas, V.] 1997a: "Naujausios vokiečių filosofinės literatūros apžvalga." In: *Raštai: Filosofijos istorija. Kultūra*, Vilnius: Mintis, 191–214.

Sesemann, V., [Sezemanas, V.] 1997b: "Fenomenas." In: *Raštai: Filosofijos istorija. Kultūra*, Vilnius: Mintis, 262–266.

Sesemann, V., [Sezemanas, V.] 1997c: "Fenomenologija." In: *Raštai: Filosofijos istorija. Kultūra*, Vilnius: Mintis, 266–268.

Sesemann, V., [Sezemanas, V.] 1997d: "Husserl Edmundas." In: *Raštai: Filosofijos istorija. Kultūra*, Vilnius: Mintis, 343–348.

Sesemann, V., [Sezemanas, V.] 1997e: "Heidegger, Martinas." In: *Raštai: Filosofijos istorija. Kultūra*, Vilnius: Mintis, 322–324.

Sesemann, V. 2010: "New Directions in Contemporary Epistemology." In: *Selected papers*, M. Drunga, Amsterdam/New York: Rodopi. 55–80.

Smith, B., 1997, "Realistic Phenomenology." In: Lester Embree (ed.), *Encyclopedia of Phenomenology*. Springer Science & Business Media, 586–590.

Spiegelberg, H., 1960, *The Phenomenological Movement: A Historical Introduction*, Dordrecht: Springer.

Tremblay, F., 2016, "Nikolai Lossky's Reception and Criticism of Husserl," *Husserl Studies*, vol. 32, n. 2, 149–163.

Vancourt, R., 1945, "Préface du traducteur." In: Hartmann N. *Les principes d'une métaphysique de la connaissance*, traduction et préface de Raymond Vancourt, Tome I, Paris: Aubier Montaigne.

Wunsch, M., 2015, "Anthropologie des geistigen Seins und Ontologie des Menschen bei Helmuth Plessner und Nicolai Hartmann." In: K. Köchy und F. Michelini (Hg.), *Zwischen den Kulturen. Plessners „Stufen des Organischen" im zeithistorischen Kontext*. Freiburg/München: Karl Alber, 243–272.

Part III
The Munich Circle Reception of Husserl's Idealism. Back to the Things Themselves

The Problem of Reality. Scheler's Critique of Husserl in *Idealismus – Realismus*

Susan Gottlöber

Abstract Scheler had always emphasized that he had developed his phenomenological method independently from Husserl. Even though references to Husserl in works such as *Der Formalismus in der Ethik und die materiale Wertethik* are surprisingly sparse, the critical remarks are balanced with ones that remain largely appreciative of Husserl's philosophical project. This, however, seems to have changed significantly in Scheler's later works. The following paper investigates Scheler's position with respect to Husserl in the posthumously published work *Idealismus - Realismus* from the year 1928. In critiquing the binary opposing positions of *"Bewusstseinsidealismus"* on the one hand and *"kritischer Realismus"* on the other, Scheler explicitly includes Husserl among those who are not able to solve the so-called problem of reality. He argues that Husserl, rather than investigating what we mean by this moment of reality and the acts through which reality is given to us, is content with the vague and erroneous statement that being real means "to have a place in time." Husserl, according to Scheler, loses reality completely. Reconstructing Scheler's position on reality not only gives insight into Scheler's interpretation of Husserl but also sheds light on Scheler's central philosophical concerns in his later work.

Keywords Idealism · Realism · Phenomenology · Resistance · Consciousness · Intentionality · Drive · Perception · Essence · Existence

In Husserl's absolute consciousness reality would disappear in the same way as it would in an absolute land of plenty.[1]

---

[1] "In dem absoluten Bewußtsein Husserls wäre die Realität ebensowohl verschwunden als im absoluten Schlaraffenland." Scheler 1995, 279.

S. Gottlöber (✉)
Maynooth University, Maynooth, Ireland
e-mail: susan.gottlober@mu.ie

© Springer Nature Switzerland AG 2021
R. K. B. Parker (ed.), *The Idealism-Realism Debate Among Edmund Husserl's Early Followers and Critics*, Contributions to Phenomenology 112,
https://doi.org/10.1007/978-3-030-62159-9_6

119

1 Introduction

It is well documented and often commented upon how the relationship between Max Scheler and Edmund Husserl was one characterized first by respect and support but, as time went by, increasingly also by reciprocal feelings of rivalry and criticism.[2] Even though he readily acknowledged the great influence and debt owed to Husserl, Scheler always maintained that he was never a "student" of Husserl and reportedly took it personally if he was ever called one.[3]

As Scheler recalls in *Die deutsche Philosophie der Gegenwart* (1922), he met Husserl in 1901 in Halle at the house of the philosopher and Kant scholar Hans Vaihinger (1852–1933). They engaged, according to Scheler, in a debate on intuition (*Anschauung*) and apperception (*Wahrnehmung*) and it was from this moment onwards that there existed a spiritual and intellectual connection between the two thinkers that turned out to be – despite all the discordances – incredibly fruitful for Scheler.[4] In the same text, Scheler credits Husserl for having sought out (again) the essence of philosophy[5] and instituted with his *Logische Untersuchungen* the starting point for one of the most important and effective philosophical movements of the 20th century. And of course, it was indeed Husserl who, despite their later differences, recommended Scheler to Theodor Lipps for the position in Munich, which Scheler held from 1906–1910.[6]

The references to Husserl in Scheler's main work, *Der Formalismus in der Ethik und die materiale Wertethik* (1916/17), are surprisingly sparse, and the critical remarks are balanced with observations that are mainly appreciative of Husserl's philosophical

---

[2] Cf., e.g., Spiegelberg 1994, 269ff. However, that initial respect may have been one-sided. According to Spiegelberg "Husserl's opinion of Scheler, never too high from the start, dropped in proportion to Scheler's rising fame." Ibid.

[3] Mader 1995, 30.

[4] Cf., Scheler 1973, 308. As Spiegelberg points out, Husserl's point of view on this account is not known. Scheler describes in this passage the connection with Husserl as ongoingly highly beneficial (*ungemein fruchtbar*). It is also in this passage that Scheler stated that he already at this stage had been so dissatisfied by the Kantian philosophy to which he had been close, that he had withdrawn his half printed (sic!) work on logic. According to Mader, Scheler had withdrawn the planned publication with Metzger and Wittig in Leipzig although the publisher had already provided the proofs. Cf., Mader 1995, 30.

[5] "[das] fast verloren gegangene Wesen der Philosophie in der Gegenwart erst wieder aufgesucht werden mußte." Scheler 1973, 267.

[6] That Husserl recommended Scheler for his post in Munich is mentioned by a number of scholars. Cf., for example, Henckmann 1998, 20 or Hand 2017, 247. Hand points to an additional recommendation by Husserl from 1910 for an international post. Cf., ibid. Hand refers to the signature Ana 315 E II, 1 in the Scheler *Nachlass*. The precise nature of the relationship and its development between Scheler and Husserl, including philosophical, scholarly, and personal tensions, growing especially after Scheler moved from Munich to Göttingen is not the topic of this paper. However, both are well documented. See, for example, Mader 1995, 30; Staude 1967, 19–21; 26–28; Spiegelberg 1994, 269ff. For a precise analysis of the philosophical relationship of the early Scheler to Husserl see Willer 1981.

project. In his Introduction to the first edition of the *Formalismus* Scheler affirms how much he is indebted to Husserl. As Scheler makes clear, it is Husserl who ought to be given credit for articulating the methodological consciousness of unity and the meaning of the phenomenological attitude, a sentiment that seems to unite (and Scheler seems to imply here despite their differences) the authors and editors of the *Jahrbuch für Philosophie und phänomenologische Forschung* in a shared project. He also praises Hussserl for his critique of Kant's notion of the *a priori*, for being the first to distinguish between category as term (*Begriff*) and content/thingness (*Gehalt/Dingheit*) in his *Logische Untersuchungen*, his critique of Berkeley and in general the nominalist tradition Scheler saw developed by Berkeley, Locke, and Hume, and his critique of critical realism.[7]

Of course, Scheler's view on the nature and aims of phenomenology differed substantially from Husserl: rather than being a well-defined science or a school, phenomenology for Scheler was a movement that was characterized by a new technē or attitude (*Einstellung*) of the observing consciousness instead a particular method of thinking.[8] Without naming him, Scheler is, of course, critical here of Husserl's long held definition of phenomenology as "a new kind of descriptive method [...] and an a priori science derived from it."[9] Although Scheler had always been outspoken, his critical remarks become even more prominent in his later work, especially when addressing concerns related to the so-called transcendental turn of Husserl; a reaction that Scheler had in common with many of Husserl's former pupils, among them Edith Stein and Roman Ingarden.[10]

One of the places where we can find Scheler's critique expressed in both an explicit and implicit manner is Scheler's late essay *Idealismus - Realismus* from the years 1927/1928. As Scheler reflects in *Die deutsche Philosophie der Gegenwart*, the question concerning realism played an essential and significant role in the

---

[7] Cf., Scheler 1980b, 69, 513 f. and Scheler 1973, 307ff. Scheler references *Logische Untersuchungen* II, 6. Cf., Husserl 1913b. See on this topic also Zhang 2011.

[8] "Die Phänomenologie ist weniger eine abgegrenzte Wissenschaft als eine neue philosophische *Einstellung*, mehr eine neue Techne des schauenden Bewußtseins als eine bestimmte Methode des Denkens." Scheler 1973, 309. It is interesting that Scheler in the same passage, just like Spiegelberg 30 years later, characterized phenomenology as a *movement*, an interpretation that Spiegelberg defended throughout his career. Cf., Spiegelberg 1994; Spiegelberg 1983. I am not aware if Scheler references to the phenomenological movement earlier than in *Die deutsche Philosophie der Gegenwart* which was first published in 1922 in *Deutsches Leben der Gegenwart*, ed. by Ph. Witkop. Rodney Parker makes the interesting observation that Husserl already uses this phrase in 1905 when referring to the so-called "Munich Invasion" in a letter to William E. Hocking (Cf., Hua Dok III.3 (Husserl 1994), 157) and that, to his knowledge, it first appeared in print 1918 in Johannes Volkelt's essay 'Die phänomenologische Gewissheit'. Cf., Volkelt 1918, 174. Scheler knew Volkelt's work and referenced him repeatedly.

[9] Husserl 1997, 159. The definition quoted here is from Draft D of Husserl's *Encyclopedia Britannica* article, written in 1927.

[10] On the latter cf., De Palma 2017. De Palma argues that Husserl's phenomenology, despite many opposite claims, is actually not idealistic. However, these questions are not the main focus of this paper and will therefore be left unaddressed.

contemporary philosophical currents in Germany.[11] As a means to clarify his notion of reality in his essay, *Idealismus - Realismus*, Scheler provides a critique of the opposing approaches to reality, idealism of consciousness (*Bewusstseinsidealismus*) and critical realism (*kritischer Realismus*), not only in respect to their opposition but also in respect to their stance regarding reality as such. Both, according to Scheler, rely on the same mistakes (which will be explicated in greater detail further below).[12] Scheler explicitly includes Husserl among those who are not able to solve the "problem" of reality,[13] which for Scheler, as we will see, is centered on the experience of resistance (*Widerständigkeit*) and its relationship to consciousness.

The goal of the following paper is to reconstruct Scheler's Husserl-critique as it pertains in particular to Scheler's position regarding reality as developed mainly in *Idealismus - Realismus*. Therefore, this critique will need to be situated in the context of *Idealismus - Realismus* as a whole, namely (i) the aforementioned debate on the realism of his time and Scheler's analysis of it and (ii) Scheler's critical analysis of Wilhelm Dilthey which he uses in order to establish his own understanding of resistance as the key experience of reality. Placing the following investigation in these two contexts will then enable us to develop a more detailed understanding of Scheler's position regarding Husserl. It can be shown that Scheler's critique is substantial and unfolds on a number of different levels: methodological, epistemological, anthropological, psychological, and ontological.

2   The Realism Debate in Early 20th Century German Philosophy and Scheler's Critique of Husserl

As Manfred Frings indicates in the epilogue of volume 9 of the *Collected Works*, only parts II and III of the treatise *Idealismus - Realismus* were published together in the *Philosophische Anzeiger* in 1927/28. Scheler himself had announced in the opening pages of the *Philosophische Anzeiger* version that parts I, IV and V were to follow soon, with the latter focusing on Heidegger's *Sein und Zeit*.[14] A number of works give evidence that the problem of reality was a growing preoccupation of Scheler's in his later period, a period wherein Scheler developed a wide range of

---

[11] Scheler 1973, 280–302.

[12] Scheler 1995,185.

[13] Ibid., 191 f. When Scheler speaks of the "problem of reality" he seems to mean both, different theories relating to questions regarding reality (*Realitätslehren*) as well as what he calls the "the actual problem of reality," namely the givenness of reality and the relationship of this givenness to consciousness. It is here that resistance and how it is experienced emerges as the central tenet for Scheler's own answer to the actual problem of reality. Cf., ibid., 208ff. In addressing the idealism-realism debate, the problems (plural) of reality are a subset of issues that Scheler further splits into a number of subcategories, such as, e.g., the questions of the givenness of reality, in which acts it is given, what kind of being (*Sein*) we consider reality to be etc. Cf. for the full set, ibid., 204 f.

[14] Scheler 1927/28, 257.

topics such as epistemology and philosophical anthropology, but also the question of aging and death. Thus, *Idealismus - Realismus* picks up on a number of positions on reality that Scheler had already developed in *Erkenntnis und Arbeit. Eine Studie über Wert und Grenzen des pragmatischen Motivs in der Erkenntnis der Welt*, published in 1926.

The context of *Idealismus - Realismus* is stated by Scheler himself at the beginning of the text: the decline of idealism accompanied by a revival of realism which he had witnessed over the last years and which in the German philosophy of his time had expressed itself in two distinct subspecies: the idealism of consciousness (*Bewusstseinsidealismus*) on the one side and the critical realism (*kritischer Realismus*) on the other.[15] Scheler describes "idealism of consciousness" as the Berkeleyan (and perhaps Kantian) position that all possible being is being for consciousness, thus there is no existence independent of consciousness – esse = percipi. Therefore, consciousness is essentially a correlate of all existence.[16] He identifies this as the position held by Heinrich Rickert, Wilhelm Schuppe, and Hans Cornelius. Concerning realism, Scheler points out that there was a rise in the number of new realistic trends, which can be distinguished along three lines: (1) the revitalization of the old *Scholastic realism* (Désiré-Joseph Mercier, Georg von Hertling, Joseph Geyser, Joseph Gredt), (2) *critical realism* (Oswald Külpe, Benno Erdmann, Carl Stumpf, Alexius Meinong), and (3) *intuitionist* (Henri Bergson, Nikolai Lossky, Johannes Volkelt) and *voluntative* realism (Wilhelm Dilthey, Max Frischeisen-Köhler, Erich Jaensch and Scheler himself).[17] As Sepp notes, a number of the phenomenologists were involved around 1930 in the revived idealism-realism debate, not only Husserl, Scheler, and Heidegger but also Ingarden, Stein, Celms, and Conrad-Martius, to name but a few.[18]

The goal of his own essay, as Scheler states in the beginning, is twofold. First, to show that it would be wrong to opt for either of the "elements of this opposition," i.e., idealism of consciousness or critical realism.[19] Why this is the case becomes clear in the second point: both positions are based, according to Scheler, on three mistakes:

1. The wrong questions;

---

[15] Scheler 1995, 185.

[16] "Also muß auch alles mögliche Dasein in mente sein, also gibt es kein bewußtseinstranszendentes, kein vom Bewußtsein unabhängiges Dasein (esse = percipi); Bewußtsein (überindividuelles Bewußtsein oder Bewußtsein überhaupt) ist also wesensnotwendig Korrelat auch *alles* Daseins." (Scheler 1995, 186) Husserl similarly identifies *Bewusstseinsidealismus* as the position associated with Berkeley and Kant. See, Hua Mat 3 (Husserl 2001), 238–239. However, Husserl denies that his philosophy is equivalent to this. See, Hua XXXIV (Husserl 2002), 114.

[17] Scheler 1973, 297–301.

[18] Sepp 2014, 206–207.

[19] Cf., Scheler 1995, 185.

2. Insufficient divisions (*Sonderwege*) in the partial problems (*sachliche Teilprobleme*);[20]

3. The erroneous presupposition that essence (*Sosein*)[21] and existence (*Dasein*) are inseparable in relation to the intellect (perception, thinking, memorizing).[22]

The last point is the most important for Scheler. He states that a precise grasping (*die scharfe Erfassung*) of this problem would give the whole problem of reality a fundamentally new meaning and lead to the final overcoming of the dichotomy. It is on this point that Scheler most severely criticizes Husserl, who he maintains comes to a position close to the epistemological idealism of Berkeley and Kant in *Ideen I*.[23]

For Scheler, issues surrounding reality are crucial to Husserl's phenomenology (specifically, according to Scheler, with respect to the phenomenological reduction)[24] for "in order to suspend the moment of reality so that the essence (*Wesen*) can appear, we have to find out *what* this moment of reality is and *in which acts* (*worin*) it is given."[25] Scheler believes that, rather than investigating what we mean by this "moment" of reality and the acts through which reality is given to us in consciousness, Husserl is content with the vague and erroneous statement that to be "real" means "to have a place in time."[26] Thus, Husserl has formulated this fundamental problem of theoretical philosophy in an original and profound way but has not solved it and actually has not answered it whatsoever.[27]

Scheler is convinced that we need a fundamental change in attitude (namely, his own phenomenological approach) in order to address the problem. It is here that we

---

[20] Which are divided as follows: 1. Order of evidence (*Evidenzordnung*); 2. Knowledge and consciousness (*Wissen und Bewusstsein*); 3. The problem of transcendental objects and transcendental consciousness (*Problem der transzdentalen Gegenstände und des Transzendenzbewusstseins*); 4. The problem of the spheres (*das Sphärenproblem*), 5. Relativity of being (*Seinsrelativität*); 6. Cognition and its standards (*Erkenntnis und ihre Maßstäbe*); 7. The problem of the a priori (*das Apriorismusproblem*) and 8. The problems of reality (*Realitätsprobleme*), the main issue of the text. Cf., Scheler 1995, 187–208.

[21] Which Scheler distinguishes in *zufälliges Sosein* and *echte Essentia*. The translation as essence is thus somewhat unfortunate as this distinction is not kept. Cf., ibid., 185, fn 1.

[22] Ibid., 185.

[23] "Er ist dadurch besonders gesteigert worden, daß E. Husserl in seinem letzten Werk über «Ideen» usw. sich dem erkenntnistheoretischen Idealismus Berkeleys und Kants, sowie der Ichlehre Natorps wieder bedeutend genähert hat und die Phänomenologie nur als Wesenslehre von den Bewußtseinsstrukturen (die durch zufällige Erfahrungen unwandelbar sind) auffaßt, gleichzeitig aber, ähnlich wie Kant, diese *Bewußtseinsstrukturen* zu Voraussetzungen auch der Gegenstände der Erfahrung selber macht. Auch ihm werden so die Gesetze der Erfahrung der Gegenstände zugleich Gesetze der Gegenstände aller möglichen Erfahrung («kopernikanische Wendung» Kants). Diese eigenartige Wendung Husserls, nach der auch bei Aufhebung aller Dinge ein «*absolutes Bewußtsein*» erhalten bliebe, ist fast von allen von ihm angeregten Forschern abgelehnt worden und sie ist zugleich ein Haupthindernis für den Aufbau einer Metaphysik auf wesenstheoretischer Basis." (Scheler 1973, 311).

[24] Ibid., 309.

[25] Scheler 1995, 206.

[26] Ibid., 207.

[27] Ibid.

turn with Scheler to the resistance theory of the givenness of reality. And while for Scheler a number of thinkers addressed the problem even better than Dilthey (such as Maine de Biran)[28] it is to Dilthey that Scheler turns as his point of reference. Therefore, we will now follow Scheler's analysis of Dilthey's conception of reality as resistance. Developing Scheler's "distancing" from Dilthey will clarify the grounds for Scheler's own understanding of reality and his critique of Husserl.

3   Reality as Resistance. Scheler's Analysis of Dilthey

As indicated above, Scheler identifies a number of problems that precede the problem of reality and it is, he argues, thanks to the lack of "separation and false logical order of the sub-questions" that the problem of idealism-realism could not be properly solved.[29] In the following we will focus only a few selected issues that are of relevance to Scheler's critique of Dilthey and (subsequently) of Husserl.

For Dilthey, the question of the origin of our belief in the existence of reality is one that should generate the highest interest even though to the layman the reality of the external world is self-evident and raising the question regarding our belief in this reality of the external world is rather pointless.[30] Responding to developments in transcendental philosophy that state that the existence of things only becomes meaningful within the categories of relation, thus turning reality into notional formulas of the functions of reason, Dilthey develops a concept of reality which establishes that reality, although given through the senses, is experienced as resistance: "The scheme of my experiences in which I as an individual comes to be distinguished from the object lies in the relationship between the consciousness of the discretionary movement and resistance that it encounters."[31]Scheler observes that, at least at the outset, Dilthey fails to recognize that the experience of resistance is not given to the senses but a fundamental experience of our drives and striving (*Drängen* and *Streben*), even though Dilthey made the important distinction between the experience of resistance and the accompanying sensations. Scheler follows Dilthey's example of a stick being pushed against a wall: I experience the resistance at the end of the stick and not in the palm of my hand.[32]

In *Idealismus - Realismus*, Scheler remarks that he has developed this theory in greater detail elsewhere (namely, his work *Erkenntnis und Arbeit* from 1926 where

---

[28] It is not actually clear from Scheler's brief mention of Maine de Biran (1766–1824) if he read the "French Kant" directly, as the only references are to two dissertations on Maine de Biran which were being prepared in Cologne. Cf., ibid., 209.

[29] Ibid., 187.

[30] Dilthey 1964, 90.

[31] "Das Schema meiner Erfahrungen, in welchen mein Selbst von sich das Objekt unterscheidet, liegt in der Beziehung zwischen dem Bewußtsein der willkürlichen Bewegung und dem des Widerstandes, auf welchen diese trifft." Ibid., 98.

[32] Scheler 1995, 210–211.

his main focus regarding the problem of reality is also Dilthey) and thus only briefly summarizes his insights. In Scheler's eyes, Dilthey makes four major mistakes.[33] First, he posits the experience of resistance is a mediated experience. But, Scheler argues, since the experience of reality is not bound to or by any specific sensation, it has to be regarded as immediate; the experience of resistance is *sui generis* for the spontaneous and involuntary life of our drives (*Triebimpulse*). The inhibition (*Hemmung*) of our intentionality gives evidence that there is something independent that is not given in my own immediate experience of the will.

Second, Dilthey mixes his theory of reality, according to Scheler, with the erroneous principle that all that is given is immanent to consciousness. However, experiencing reality is first and foremost an *ecstatic experience*, a "having" rather than a "knowing". This insight is also fundamental for Scheler's argument against Husserl: since the experience of resistance is given to the drives (*triebhaftes Verhalten*) it is not the case that a consciousness of drives (*Triebbewusstsein*) corresponds with the experience of resistance but rather that all consciousness originally arises out of experienced resistance and ecstatic knowledge.[34] This experience of resistance in turn motivates conscious reflection. Or to phrase it slightly differently: *all consciousness emerges from an antecedent experience (vorgängiges Erleiden) of resisting objects*. Thus, the experience of resistance necessarily precedes consciousness.[35]

Third, Dilthey understands resistance as an experience of the will, *viz.* an experience of the conscious central Will or deliberative willing (*bewusster zentraler Wille* or *bewusstes Wollen*). For Scheler this is impossible since, as he has already shown, we experience the resistance against our spontaneous involuntary (*unwillkürlich*) drives.[36]

Finally, Dilthey too narrowly relates the experience of reality to the experience of the external world (*Außenwelt*). However, reality can be experienced in all of the following different spheres:

1. *Ens a se* – relative being: This means that even when it comes to our assessment of existence (*Dasein*) we can have true and false judgments regarding their relativity, e.g., the sun going down, Apollo being dependent on Greek mythology etc.
2. External – internal world: We can presume the pre-givenness of the external world before the internal world. But while the external world can only be developed from specific essences (*Soseins*) it is not the case the we can deduce the external sphere from the internal one.

---

[33] Sepp provides an excellent overview and analysis of Scheler's position on reality and his critique of Dilthey. Cf., Sepp 2014, 199–236; on Scheler's critique of Dilthey cf., especially, 199–208.

[34] Ecstatic knowledge is that knowledge, according to Scheler, which does not include consciousness (*Bewusst-Sein*); such as to be found in animals, primitives, children and particular mental states such as awakening out of a general anesthetic. Cf., Scheler 1995, 189.

[35] Cf., ibid., 211–14.

[36] Scheler emphasizes here the difference between the will that has an element of consciousness and the life of the drives as involuntary (*unwillkürliches Triebleben*) or pre-conscious. Cf., ibid., 214–15.

3. Living beings – environment.
4. I-you – community (*Gemeinschaftssphäre*).[37]

The most important point to note is that the different spheres are irreducible to one another. Reflecting in this way on the different spheres allows Scheler to draw a number of conclusions. First, he can now make an argument for both expanding the concept of reality beyond the external world (including, e.g., experiencing the reality of aging, past memories, etc.) and, secondly, draw attention to the fact that the problem of the different spheres has to be treated separately from the problem of reality. The distinction between real and unreal/irreal can be made in all the different spheres and is not one exclusively concerning the external world.[38]

Having developed his critical assessment of Dilthey, Scheler can now establish his own position regarding reality in such a manner that experiencing reality becomes *the* fundamental experience. It is here that we can now draw out in detail Scheler's assessment of Husserl.

4   Scheler's Critique of Husserl in the Context of the Idealism-Realism Debate

Despite judging Husserl to belong to (or at least having come very close to) the idealists,[39] Scheler credits Husserl for having made valuable contributions to the idealism-realism-debate. In his positive evaluation of Husserl, Scheler focuses on two main points, one epistemological (I) and the other ontological (II) in nature.

(I) The first point embraces the idealist critique (as Scheler sees it) against the critical realists. This leads us back to the sub-question of cognition and its standards (as mentioned above). Scheler states here that for him cognition (*Erkenntnis*), understood as knowledge *of* something "as" something, always relies on two types of knowledge: knowledge through perception and knowledge through thought. It is thus the *mutual* correspondence of some correlate of perception, i.e., an image, and thought (*gegenseitige Deckungseinheit von Bild und Gedanke*).[40] He sees himself here very much in agreement with Nicolai

---

[37] Ibid., 194ff.

[38] The being of each empirical object is pre-given; real and unreal exist in a "peculiar mixture" in each. They exist each in each and have their own causality; e.g., a past memory can be experienced to put pressure on a present experience and once that is experienced it cannot be changed just by an act of will while a fata morgana or a shadow or a rainbow can be experienced as appearances but are not real in the defined sense above.

[39] With this judgment Scheler is not alone. A number of philosophers and phenomenologists share this perception, among them Conrad-Martius, Stein, Landgrebe, and Fink. However, as already mentioned earlier, this assessment of Husserl is debatable, as a number of scholars such as De Palma have pointed out.

[40] Cf., Scheler 1995, 200.

Hartmann and his position as developed in the *Grundzüge einer Metaphysik der Erkenntnis* from 1921. Scheler declares that the position of those critical realists who claim that cognition functions as the one-sided correspondence of representations immanent to conscious with objects (*Seinsbeständen*) that are independent from all possible knowledge is insufficient. A number of the idealists such as Kant and Husserl have already pointed out that this image theory in itself depends on a likeness and presupposes the cognition of both the image and the object such as, e.g., the picture of an object.[41]

(II) The second point concerns the question of (experiencing) reality as such. Here Scheler recognizes that Husserl criticized the idea that being real cannot be explained through reality but rather through suffering the effects (*Wirkungen erleiden*) of something real. What is not able to be effective is not real and thus reality and causality belong essentially together.[42]

However, Scheler also raises a number of critical points which are more comprehensive and substantial in nature, combining psychological and epistemological (I), ontological (II), methodological (III), and anthropological (and as its consequence again epistemological) elements (IV).

(I) The first issue concerns the question of transcendental consciousness. Scheler assumes the transcendence of objects, no matter if they are real, ideal, or fictional. Moreover, because the transcendence of objects is independent of their existential (*Dasein*) modification, transcendental consciousness is not useful at all to solve the problem of reality. Indeed, in other words, the problem of reality is entirely different from the transcendence of the objects, a problem that has escaped Husserl, according to Scheler. All that is left to transcendental consciousness is to bring that which is given as real into an objective form.[43]

(II) The second point Scheler raises relies on the assumption that reality as resistance functions as the ultimate foundational experience. Since resistance, as shown earlier, underlies consciousness, it is only in a world of possible resistance that being real and being conscious is possible at all. If we would assume the absolute consciousness of Husserl, reality would disappear in the same way as it would in an absolute land of plenty (*Schlaraffenland*), in the paradise of Quran or the state of enlightenment of the Buddha, as in all of them there is no possible resistance. Scheler sympathizes with Heidegger in his rejection of an autonomous sphere of "ideal meanings", "ideal Being" or logical idealspheres which have been "exaggerated to the point of the absurd."[44] Scheler states that he has always fought in the strongest terms against those approaches

---

[41] Cf., Scheler 1995, 200–202.

[42] Ibid., 236 f.

[43] "[…] das so als 'real' Gegebene auch zu einem realen 'Gegenstand' erheben zu können. Damit ist aber auch die Leistung des Transzendenzbewußtseins für das Realitätsproblem zu Ende." Scheler 1995, 192.

[44] Ibid., 286.

that claim there is a sphere of ideas, values, truths, etc., independent from all acts. Thus, both Scheler and Heidegger break completely with all those approaches which follow Husserl, and here he lists Adolf Reinach and "partially" Alexander Pfänder, Moritz Geiger and Nicolai Hartmann.[45]

(III) This question leads Scheler back to the methodological question of what phenomenology is. Scheler severely critiques what he sees as the "one-sided 'idealistic orientation' of all being towards an 'absolute consciousness'" in Husserl.[46] Indeed, while being quite critical of Heidegger (e.g., he rejects Heidegger's idea to assume care (*Sorge*) as the source of the experience of the real) – a number of passages from the unpublished parts of *Idealismus - Realismus* deal with Heidegger in great depth – Scheler states that he himself is much closer to Heidegger than Husserl on the question of *what* phenomenology actually is, while Heidegger's distance from Husserl is "incredible".[47]

(IV) The fourth point of criticism brings us to the relationship between drives and consciousness in relation to the givenness of reality. In many ways this is the core argument upon which Scheler's entire approach hinges. The question that Dilthey raised and which was taken up by Husserl concerning drives is the following: are the drives themselves and everything that is given to them immanent within consciousness? This is how Scheler interprets Husserl's position, tracing it back to Descartes' proposition that all that is given is first and primordially immanent within consciousness.[48] Or, is it the resisting to the drives that is experienced in the ecstatic knowledge which leads to the emergence of true consciousness as reflective knowledge, i.e., consciousness presupposes (ecstatic) knowledge?[49]

Scheler, as we have already indicated, chooses the latter position, developed not only in *Idealismus - Realismus* but also *Erkenntnis und Arbeit* and *Die Stellung des Menschen im Kosmos*[50]. Looking at all three works we can trace the following points which he establishes against Husserl:[51]

1. Since resistance is accessible neither to consciousness nor to knowledge, but rather to the drives only, the relationship of the drives to resistance is not a relation to an essence (*Sosein*) or meaning (*Sinn*) but rather is characterized by being pre-conscious and pre-known; *we experience that which is real as pure*

---

[45] Ibid., see also fn 2.

[46] Ibid., 282.

[47] Ibid.

[48] Ibid., 208.

[49] Cf., ibid., 189; Sepp 2014, 204–205; Henckmann 1998, 76. Scheler makes the distinction between knowledge and consciousness very clear in the beginning of *Idealismus - Realismus* where he distinguishes between *Wissen* (scientia) and *reflexives Wissen* (Be-wußt-sein as con-scientia). Cf., Scheler 1995, 186.

[50] Especially in *Erkenntnis und Arbeit* (Scheler 1980a).

[51] The following points have been excellently summarized by Hans Rainer Sepp. Cf., Sepp 2014, 204–209.

meaningless resisting, we grasp what is real "before we perceive it with our senses or think its essence."[52]

2. Thus, Scheler takes issue with Husserl's claim in *Ideen I* that all real unities are unities of meaning.[53] On the contrary: the experience of reality is not meaningful in itself at all as we experience the object itself rather than the meaning of that object. Now we can also see why for Scheler we ask the wrong question if we ask how something real can be conveyed to perception and thinking in a meaningful way. In this context Sepp rightly points out the following: because this encounter with reality is not an encounter with meaning, we do not have to ask the misleading question of how the real can be mediated to perception and thinking. It is rather the experience of resistance (that is free of meaning) that founds any possible relationship to meaning.[54]

3. This means that Scheler has established a relationship between knowledge and consciousness on one side and the experience of resistance on the other without the latter being relativized in relation to the former. Thus, the experience of resistance is not an experience immanent to consciousness or one that assumes a hermeneutical relation.[55] Rather, resistance remains transcendental to consciousness at all times.

4. This then leads finally to the core epistemological argument of Scheler against Husserl. As knowledge is a relationship to reality that has been established by the experience of resistance, Husserl's "principle of all principles" that every originary intuition (*Anschauung*) is a justified source for cognition, is wrong.[56]

5 Conclusion

Much more could be done to analyze critically Scheler's assessment of Husserl, but that is beyond my present scope. Being mainly concerned with developing his own approach, Scheler's account of Husserl is incomplete and guilty, at least in parts, of creating a strawman of Husserl's position. Likewise, Scheler's own proposed solution to the problem of realism raises as many questions as it answers.[57] However,

---

[52] "Wir erfassen das *Real*sein eines unbestimmten Etwas [...] *bevor* wir sein *So*sein sinnlich wahrnehmen oder denken." Scheler 1980b, 372. Cf. also ibid., 373.

[53] "In gewisser Art und mit einiger Vorsicht im Wortgebrauche kann man sagen: 'Alle realen Einheiten sind Einheiten des Sinnes'." Husserl 1913a, § 55.

[54] Cf., Sepp 2014, 205–206.

[55] Cf., Sepp 2014, 205.

[56] "[...] daß jede originäre gebende Anschauung eine Rechtsquelle der Erkenntnis sei, daß alles, was sich uns in der 'Intuition' originär (sozusagen in seiner leibhaften Wirklichkeit) darbietet, einfach hinzunehmen sei, als was es sich gibt, aber auch nur in den Schranken, in denen es sich gibt, kann uns keine erdenkliche Theorie irre machen." Husserl 1913a, § 24.

[57] See, for example, Henckmann on the relationship between the genetic understanding of knowledge types and the functionalisation of the spirit (*Geist*). Henckmann 1998, 76.

there is something compelling in the way Scheler, inspired by Dilthey, establishes the idea of the pre-givenness of reality through resistance as the foundation of consciousness and, in turn, makes this assumption the core of his critique of Husserl.

It seems that with the concepts presented in *Ideen I*, Scheler became more critical of Husserl, stating that with using the phenomenological reduction to uncover transcendental absolute consciousness Husserl does not only move into a transcendental idealism but also loses reality completely since, for Scheler, reality, rather than being constituted by consciousness, itself constitutes consciousness. This leads us back to the third (and for our present purposes, most important) shared mistake made by both the idealists and the critical realists, namely the erroneous presupposition that essence *and existence* are inseparable from consciousness.[58]

Instead, taking the experience of resistance as the foundational principle, Scheler can now conclude that when it comes to the essence (*Sosein*) of a thing, it can be *in mente* and *extra mentem* but existence (*Dasein*) can only be *extra mentem*. If that is the case and the *ens reale* is consequentially always *extra mentem* it cannot be recovered through knowledge or meaning bestowing (*Sinnstiftung*), but is only experienced through resistance.[59] This, of course, does not mean that reality equates with independence *per se* or that being real follows the independence of being, but rather, that the real *is* independent but does not exhaust itself in it.[60] This stance may lead to the question of how we can know anything about reality at all (as it is always trans-intelligible),[61] since essence (*Sosein*) can be both *in mente* and *extra mentem* without the real existence following it. However, this does not exclude the possibility that there *can* be a connection between the essence (*Sosein*) and the existence (*Dasein*) but only that the *realitas* of the object, its *existence*, can never be *in mente*.[62] Reality, Scheler states, is always *trans*intelligible: only the *what* of existence is intelligible for us, never the existence of the what.[63]

In terms of assessing Husserl, these are potentially devastating criticisms given that they seek to undermine Husserl's position as a whole. Thinking these ideas through to the end, Scheler also attributes intentionality not to transcendental consciousness but to the experience of resistance with consequences for "ideal being." Since ideas for Scheler are neither *ante res* nor *in rebus* but only *cum rebus*[64] and the existence of beings is transcendental and not mind-immanent, only in the encounter with reality as resistance can we actually have ideas and meaning.

---

[58] Cf., Sepp 2014, 207.

[59] Thus, Scheler distinguishes between the *ens reale* and the *ens intentionale*. Cf., Scheler 1995, 188.

[60] Cf., ibid., 203; Sepp 2014, 206.

[61] Cf., Scheler 1995, 205.

[62] "Es kann *sehr wohl* das Sosein des Seienden 'in mente' und zugleich 'exra mentem' sein; es kann sehr wohl in mente 'einspringen' und 'ausspringen' ohne daß das *reale* Dasein diesen Sprüngen folgt, und zwar im strengsten Sinne das Sosein *selbst* [i.e., the true essentia]." Ibid., 202.

[63] "nur das *Was* des Daseins, nicht das *Dasein* des Was ist intelligibel." Ibid., 204. The emphasis is Scheler's.

[64] Ibid., 252.

Furthermore – and maybe this is the most important point at all – in losing reality Husserl cannot get back to the things themselves either, thus abolishing *the* key motivation and defining principle of phenomenology. For Scheler, it is not clear what will become different by regarding the flowering apple tree (an example Husserl uses); there is no new world of objects which is being revealed but only the accidental essence (*Sosein*) comes out more clearly as it keeps its place in space and time.

Scheler's solution is a methodological one but as Sepp rightly points out, one which is rooted in his anthropological conceptions.[65] Husserl's reduction, according to Scheler, is a "logical process" that needs to be replaced with a *techné* of reduction that is able to change our attitude to the world. As we have seen earlier, for Scheler phenomenology is essentially an attitude (*Einstellung*) and not a method. In order to practice it we cannot go through Husserl's absolute consciousness but through the spiritual ability to say "no" to the world – the human being as the ascetic of life – which means that to discover the essence of beings we need annihilate the moment of existence of that object altogether, which has been given to us originally through our drives. We are thus not just taking back the judgment of existence (*Existenzurteil*) as Husserl would have it, but "block out" reality itself. Although he does not make this explicit in *Idealismus - Realismus*, Scheler does commit himself to the view that only the person who unifies the distinct movements of the life-drives and spirit is able to perform this task, thus leading us back ever more deeply into Scheler's philosophical anthropology.[66]

References

Dilthey, Wilhelm. 1964. *Beiträge zur Lösung der Frage vom Ursprung unseres Glaubens an die Realität der Außenwelt und seinem Recht* (1890). In *Gesammelte Schriften*, vol. V: *Die geistige Welt. Einleitung in die Philosophie des Lebens. Erste Hälfte*, ed. Georg Misch, 90–138. Stuttgart: B. G. Teubner Verlagsgesellschaft.

Hand, Annika. 2017. Max Scheler. Begegnung mit Husserl. *Husserl-Handbuch. Leben—Werk—Wirkung*, ed. by Sebastian Luft and Maren Wehrle, 246–251. Stuttgart: J. B. Metzler.

Henckmann, Wolfhart. 1998. *Max Scheler*. Munich: C. H. Beck.

Husserl, Edmund. 1913a. *Ideen zu einer reinen Phänomenologie und phänomenologischen Philosophie. Erstes Buch*. Jahrbuch für Philosophie und phänomenologische Forschung 1,1: 1–323.

Husserl, Edmund. 1913b. *Logische Untersuchungen, zweiter Band: Untersuchungen zur Phänomenologie und Theorie der Erkenntnis, I. Teil*. Zweite, umgearbeitete Auflage. Halle: Max Niemeyer.

Husserl, Edmund. Hua Dok III.3; 1994. *Briefwechsel Teil 3, Die Göttingen Schule*, ed. K. Schuhmann. Dordrecht: Kluwer.

---

[65] Cf., Sepp 2014, 208.

[66] I would like to express my gratitude to Rodney Parker and Zachary Davis for their very helpful comments and suggestions.

Husserl, Edmund. 1997. *Psychological and Transcendental Phenomenology and the Confrontation with Heidegger (1927–1931)*, trans. T. Sheehan & R. Palmer. Dordrecht: Kluwer.

Husserl, Edmund. Hua Mat III. 2001. *Allgemeine Erkenntnistheorie Vorlesung 1902/03*, ed. E. Schuhmann. Dordrecht: Kluwer.

Husserl, Edmund. Hua XXXIV. 2002. *Zur phänomenologischen Reduktion: Texte aus dem Nachlass (1926–1935)*, ed. S. Luft. Dordrecht: Kluwer.

Mader, Wilhelm. 1995 *Max Scheler*. Reinbeck: Rowohlt.

De Palma, Vittorio. 2017. Phänomenologie und Realismus. Die Frage nach der Wirklichkeit im Streit zwischen Husserl und Ingarden. *Husserl Studies* 33/1: 1–18.

Scheler, Max. 1927/28. Idealismus-Realismus. *Philosophischer Anzeiger* 2 (3), pp. 255–324.

Scheler, Max. 1995. Idealismus–Realismus. In *Gesammelte Werke*, vol. IX, ed. by Manfred Frings, 183–340. Bonn: Bouvier.

Scheler, Max. 1973. Die deutsche Philosophie der Gegenwart. In *Gesammelte Werke*, vol. VII, ed. by Manfred Frings, 259–330. Bern/München: Francke Verlag.

Scheler, Max. 1980a. Erkenntnis und Arbeit. In *Gesammelte Werke*, vol. VIII, ed. by Maria Scheler, 191–382. Bern/München: Francke Verlag.

Scheler, Max. 1980b. *Der Formalismus in der Ethik und die materiale Werethik. Neuer Versuch der Grundlegung eines ethischen Personalismus* (*Gesammelte Werke*, vol. II), ed. by Maria Scheler. Bern/München: Francke Verlag.

Sepp, Hans Rainer. 2014. *Über die Grenze*. Nordhausen: Traugott Bautz.

Spiegelberg, Herbert. 1994. *The Phenomenological Movement. A Historical Introduction*, 3rd ed. Dordrecht: Kluwer Academic Publishers.

Spiegelberg, Herbert. 1983. Movements in Philosophy: Phenomenology and its Parallels. *Philosophy and Phenomenological Research* 43/3: 281–297.

Staude, John Raphael. 1967. *Max Scheler, An Intellectual Portrait*. New York: the Free Press.

Volkelt, Johannes. 1918. Die phänomenologische Gewissheit. *Zeitschrift für Philosophie und philosophische Kritik* 165: 174–189

Willer, Jörg. 1981. Der Bezug auf Husserl im Frühwerk Schelers. *Kant-Studien* 72: 175–185

Zhang, Wi. 2011. Schelers Kritik an der phänomenologischen Auffassung des gegenständlichen Apriori bei Husserl. *Prolegomena* 10/2: 265–280.

The Question of Reality. A Postscript to Schuhmann and Smith on Daubert's Response to Husserl's *Ideas I*

Daniel R. Sobota

Abstract This paper deals with the Munich phenomenologist Johannes Daubert's attitude towards Husserl's turn to idealism as well as the problem of reality, taking Karl Schuhmann and Barry Smith's article *Against Idealism: Johannes Daubert vs. Husserl's Ideas I* (1985) as its point of departure. Indeed, the present work constitutes a supplement or addendum to Schuhmann and Smith's text, relating the theses presented therein to Daubert's investigations into the issue of questioning. Here we bring together two overarching motifs found in Daubert's vast unpublished writings, namely "the consciousness of reality [*Wirklichkeitsbewusstsein*]" and the problem of the question. According to Daubert, it is not the case that being is constituted on the level of transcendental consciousness, the latter he regarded as purely fictitious. Instead, being is found in openness, which is in turn established by the direct, felt encounter of incarnate human beings with reality.

Keywords Johannes Daubert · Karl Schuhmann · Barry Smith · Edmund Husserl · Critique of transcendental idealism · Question · Consciousness of reality · Openness

1 Introduction

The research was funded by the National Centre of Science on the basis of the decision DEC-2015/16//S/HS1/00257.

The purpose of this paper is not to present a detailed account of Johannes Daubert's critical standpoint with respect to Husserl's idealism. That topic has been clearly and exhaustively covered by Karl Schuhmann and Barry Smith in their article

D. R. Sobota (✉)
Polish Academy of Sciences, Warsaw, Poland
e-mail: dsobota@ifispan.edu.pl

© Springer Nature Switzerland AG 2021
R. K. B. Parker (ed.), *The Idealism-Realism Debate Among Edmund Husserl's Early Followers and Critics*, Contributions to Phenomenology 112,
https://doi.org/10.1007/978-3-030-62159-9_7

Against Idealism: Johannes Daubert vs. Husserl's Ideas I.[1] Instead, the present work constitutes a supplement or addendum to Schuhmann and Smith's text, placing their considerations into the larger context of Daubert's thought. In particular, the aim here is to offer a coherent reading of Daubert's vast unpublished philosophical writings that brings together his work on the "consciousness of reality [*Wirklichkeitsbewusstsein*]" and his investigations on the problem of the question. Combining these two overarching themes enables us to portray Daubert's philosophy not as a loose collection of undeveloped ideas but rather as a coherent philosophical standpoint that contains – among other things – a critique of Husserl's idealism. According to Daubert, it is not the case that being is constituted on the level of transcendental consciousness, the latter of which he regarded as purely fictitious. Instead, being is found in openness, which is in turn established by the direct, felt encounter of incarnate human beings with reality.[2]

This paper begins with an overview of Schuhmann and Smith's paper on Daubert's reading of *Ideas I*. The goal here is not to defend or critically engage Daubert's interpretation of Husserl, but, rather, to highlight some key features of Daubert's own phenomenological position that he develops in response to Husserl's idealism. Following this, I discuss Daubert's *Nachlass* (otherwise known as the Daubertiana) and attempt to give a glimpse into the larger philosophical whole of which his criticisms of Husserl are only a part. Whereas Schuhmann and Smith suggest that Daubert's engagement with the realism-idealism controversy via his work on the consciousness of reality can act as the unifying theme in his writings, I argue that this is only partially correct. Daubert's interest in the relationship between consciousness and reality is only one aspect of his larger interest in the act of *questioning* and the nature of *questions*. The merging of Daubert's concerns with our consciousness of reality and questions lead him, like Heidegger, to the question concerning the meaning of being. For Daubert, one's bodily encounter with the world is the primary question.

2   Against Idealism

Schuhmann and Smith's work on Daubert brilliantly illuminates in step-by-step fashion why Daubert could not come to terms with Husserl's apparent idealist turn and how he "stands Husserl on his head."[3] Their discussion focuses on 29 pages from Daubertiana A I 3 (ca. 1930–31), which make explicit reference to Husserl's *Ideas I*. The majority of Daubert's comments deal with the concepts of the natural attitude and epoché, the relationship between consciousness and the world, positing

---

[1] Schuhmann and Smith (1985). This paper was reprinted as Schuhmann and Smith (2004).

[2] These themes will not be fully developed in this paper due to limitations of space, but a more thorough exposition can be found in Sobota (2017). A German translation of this work is scheduled to appear in 2022.

[3] Schuhmann and Smith (1985, p. 38).

(*setzende*) acts, and the phenomenology of reason. As Schuhmann and Smith note, the overall aim of the papers contained in A I 3 is the development of a phenomenology of evidence, which Daubert had planned to contribute to the *Festschrift* celebrating Alexander Pfänder's 60th birthday under the title "Zur Phänomenologie der Evidenz."[4]

In his discussion of perception and the relationship between consciousness and the world, Husserl introduces a fundamental distinction between the *perceived as perceived* or the perceptual *sense*, which is in consciousness, undergoes change, and constitutes a distinct noematic layer of experience, and the real object in the natural world, which remains what it is in all its adumbrations. Husserl elucidates this by employing the well-known example of the apple tree in his chapter on "Noesis and Noema" in *Ideas I*.[5] While phenomenology presupposes perception as the original mode of our acquaintance with the world, "this perceptual acquaintance with reality cannot legitimate its own contents."[6] According to Daubert, there is no point in introducing this sort of epistemological dualism since everything we know about this tree is given in the experience of the particular existent tree over there. It is only for the sake of our cognitive interest in this tree that we draw the above-mentioned distinction, but the distinction corresponds to nothing in reality. As Daubert writes, "Precisely that which I perceive and which is given to me by way of perception is real and has its place in reality; it has its chemical structure, it burns, etc. There is nothing behind it."[7] This is not to say that there is no real world, rather, that there is no distinction between the real object and perceptual sense. The two are fundamentally entangled.

Daubert's rejection of the distinction between the real object and perceptual sense allows him to call into question the existence – whether real or transcendental – of what "perceived reality [*wahrgenommene Wirkliche*]" (A I 3/10v; D I 3/57)[8] manifests itself in, namely, consciousness. While Daubert and Husserl might agree on the primacy of perception, what is primary in perception for Daubert is not consciousness, but reality. Consciousness, according to Daubert, is "a function directed towards reality" (A I 3/62v; D I 3/225).[9] The absolute existence in-itself of consciousness is that which is constituted by consciousness alone and is that which ought to be bracketed as a belief originating from the natural attitude.

Daubert further criticizes Husserl's account of hyletic (perceptual) data. Because consciousness is nothing real, hyletic data cannot be real component parts of it. Nor does Daubert think that hyletic data can be grasped through reflective acts of

---

[4] Schuhmann and Smith (2004, p. 37). The *Festschrift* (Heller and Löw 1933) was published without a contribution from Daubert.

[5] Husserl (1983, pp. 214–217). For a thorough discussion of Daubert's critique of Husserl's concept of noema, see Schuhmann (1989).

[6] Schuhmann and Smith (2004, p. 38).

[7] Schuhmann and Smith (2004, p. 38).

[8] References of this form throughout are to Daubert's *Nachlass* also known as the Daubertiana. Items in convolute D are the transcriptions of the handwritten manuscripts in A.

[9] Cf. Schuhmann and Smith (2004, p. 40).

consciousness, since consciousness can only grasp objects that are already formed out of the hyletic data. The hyletic data themselves lack any intentional unity. On Daubert's view, hyletic data are, for Husserl, merely a construct that emerges due to both a reflective turn of consciousness towards itself and the thematization of its own cognitive processes. Daubert does not, however, reject the concept of hyletic data. He contends that, once coupled with a form, they are indeed elements of reality itself.[10]

For Daubert, the encounter of corporeal beings in an always already existing physical realm is the precondition for the fact that the world appears to us in this way or that.[11] This encounter is perceived by a subject in its direct acquaintance with the world and is prior to cognitive acts and to the subject-object relation. Direct acquaintance is "the point where a participation in reality takes place" (A I 3/16v; D I 3/90). As Schumann and Smith argue, "the priority of direct awareness will yield for Daubert a decisive argument against Husserl's idealism."[12] Daubert calls this direct acquaintance with or awareness of reality *Innesein* or *Spürung* (emotional self-givenness). It constitutes the ineliminable background of our actions, including cognitive acts. By no means can it be suspended or neutralized. For Daubert, the discovery and description of this direct awareness is the task of phenomenology proper, which aims not to explore the field of transcendental subjectivity but rather explores "real reality [*wirkliche Wirklichkeit*]."[13] The "real reality," the real things-themselves (*die Sachen selbst*), is the fundamental subject matter of philosophy. Husserl's phenomenology after *Ideas I* seems to have forgotten this in making the inward, idealist turn. Given these criticisms of Husserl's transcendental phenomenology, one might wonder to what extent Daubert realized the sort of object-oriented phenomenology just described.

3   The Problem of Daubert's Manuscripts

Schuhmann and Smith's article was published nearly 20 years after Daubert's *Nachlass* arrived at the Bayerische Staatsbibliothek in Munich, and only a few years after Schuhmann had established an interpretative key that enabled him to transcribe Daubert's cryptic shorthand. With the assistance of Elisabeth Schuhmann and Reinhold Nikolaus Smid, all 20 files contained in Daubertiana A I, his research manuscripts, have been transcribed. According to Eberhard Avé-Lallemant, these papers constitute a highly original philosophical corpus. In addition to the as yet untranscribed notebooks from Daubert's years studying in Munich (A II), the *Nachlass* contains his correspondence with Husserl and members of the Munich

---

[10] Schuhmann and Smith (2004, p. 45).
[11] Schuhmann and Smith (2004, p. 51).
[12] Schuhmann and Smith (2004, p. 52).
[13] Schuhmann and Smith (2004, p. 58).

Circle of phenomenologists, a short diary written by Daubert during World War I, and two diaries from his student years.[14] The content of the latter can be surmised from a long abstract written by Daubert.[15] The Word War I diary was written by Daubert while fighting on the western front and studying Husserl's *Ideas I*. This diary remains to be transcribed, however, judging from the headings and drawings that relate to battle scenes, ballistics, troop movements, etc., one can reasonably assume that it does not contain significant remarks of a philosophical nature. As Daubert himself admits to Husserl in a letter sent from the battlefield, the war deprived him of the quiet and the peace of mind needed for philosophical concentration and caused him to focus on his own life rather than philosophical matters.[16]

Since the publication of Schuhmann and Smith's original article on Daubert's reaction to *Ideas I*, more than 30 years have passed. Undoubtedly, the later half of the 1980s was the most fruitful time in terms of establishing the legacy of Daubert as one of the most influential members and "true architect of the phenomenological movement."[17] Thanks to renewed interest in early phenomenology since the turn of the twenty-first century, Daubert's philosophy has ceased to be *terra incognita*.[18] Yet, like the works of other important Munich phenomenologists, such as Alexander Pfänder and Adolf Reinach, Daubert's work has not received widespread attention among Husserl scholars.

Despite the steps taken to restore the name of Daubert to its proper place in the history of the phenomenological movement, almost none of the papers from his *Nachlass* have been published or translated. This state of affairs is similar to that of the writings of the other early phenomenologists whose writings are held in Bayerische Staatsbibliothek, but with one major difference. Unlike, for instance, Theodor Conrad or Moritz Geiger, Daubert never published a single sentence during his lifetime. All we have is his unpublished literary estate. Thanks to Schuhmann's efforts, a chronology of Daubert's life and work[19] along with some notes from Daubert's *Nachlass* have appeared in print, such as his "Phenomenological and Transcendental Method in Theory of Cognition"[20] and "Notes from Husserl's

---

[14] Cf. Avé-Lallemant (1975, pp. 131–138).

[15] The diaries themselves, which contain personal reflections from the years 1896–1898, 1900–1901 and early 1906, are were not given over Bayerische Staatsbibliothek when Daubert's *Nachlass* arrived in 1967. They remained in the possession of Daubert's widow, Stephanie Daubert, as well as Daubert's personal copy of Husserl's *Logical Investigations* containing his with marginal notes. (Avé-Lallemant 1975, p. 128).

[16] Husserl (1994, p. 75). I would like to thank Kimberly Baltzer-Jaray for drawing my attention to this letter.

[17] Schuhmann and Smith (2004, p. 35).

[18] In addition to the publication of another paper by Schuhmann, this time on Daubert and Husserl's *Logical Investigations* (Schuhmann 2003), see the articles by Fréchette (2001) and Bower (2019).

[19] Schuhmann (2004b).

[20] Schuhmann (1985, pp. 7–8).

Mathematical-Philosophical Exercises SS 1905."[21] However, the majority of Daubert's writings (several thousand pages, much of which are only rough notes) remain virtually inaccessible to researchers. This is in part due to issues of copyright, but also due to the state of the manuscripts themselves. Here we face a number of problems.

The first problem concerns the complex and idiosyncratic nature of Daubert's notes. Schuhmann and Smid's work needs collating, and the cipher that Schuhmann discovered for transcribing Daubert's handwriting should be subjected to thorough scrutiny. Of course, this is a technical rather than a philosophical matter. Nevertheless, a tedious and time-consuming verification process is required before we can be confident about the accuracy of the transcriptions that currently exist. A second and equally important problem is deciding what material should be published and how it should be organized. At first glance, the diversity in Daubert's writings is striking. In addition to the few essays and outlines of essays, we are confronted with a loose collection of philosophical notes and observations not presented in any systematic way. Among them there are notes written in a personal tone, not intended for an audience. Then there are the excerpts (*Exzerpte*) on books that Daubert intensively studied, project outlines, drafts of letters, and countless polemics against both well-known and forgotten figures in the history of philosophy. Despite the fact that these texts were arranged into separate folders, most of which bear handwritten titles given to them by Daubert himself, one cannot help noticing that these titles neither establish an internal ordering for nor accurately reflect the substantive contents of the folders. In most cases, there seems to be no order at all to the pages contained therein. Sometimes it happens that pages related thematically within a folder are separated by comments on a completely different subject. Other times, pages dealing with the same theme are scattered across a number of folders.

One thing for which Daubert was reportedly known and that garnered the respect of his peers and teachers is his (sometimes excessively) detailed analysis and criticism. Detailed analyses are certainly not lacking in his papers. When reading them, one often has the impression that the descriptions will run-on without end, and often without purpose. These same ideas are often repeated with the author apparently oblivious to the fact that they have already been described. Daubert's thought gets lost in the maze of details, which in turn – in the absence of a thesis or guiding idea – begin to represent and serve only themselves. Such is the nature of his phenomenological analyses, which can be compared perhaps only to Husserl's unpublished notes. These problems do not allow the reader of Daubert's texts to agree or disagree with his philosophical positions. Rather, his writings lack any clear conclusions and avoiding taking a firm position on any issue. The *Daubertiana* is marked by temporariness and impermanence. The reader is left wondering whether Daubert is a proponent of the ideas he is discussing and is preparing them for publication, or if they are ruminations on ideas he rejected.

---

[21] Daubert (2004). Sobota (2017) includes transcripts of numerous additional fragments from Daubert's *Nachlass*.

The fact that Daubert never published any of his investigations might lead us to conjecture that he was never satisfied with the writings that make up his *Nachlass*. Only careful research could even suggest to us if he ever seriously intended to publish any of these writings.[22] It follows that if one were to ever take on the task of preparing any of the fragments from Daubert's *Nachlass* for publication, it would be difficult to definitively determine whether it is indeed Daubert's thought. Although we know that all the preserved texts came from Daubert's hand, it is difficult to identify a single philosophical mind that would have taken full responsibility for it. These difficulties pose serious problems for potential editors and publishers of Daubert's *Nachlass*.

4 Towards a Philosophical Whole

The problems outlined above are, strictly speaking, of an archival and editorial nature. But they point to an important philosophical-hermeneutic issue as well. Despite the huge body of knowledge about the individual issues that make up Daubert's philosophical corpus, until only recently, there has been no attempt to approach his thought as a unified whole.[23] His unpublished works represent a variety of topics and issues that, at first glance, do not form any sort of coherent whole. What is more, one can venture to make the following assertion – its individual parts could have been written by various authors. Both stylistically and thematically, there appears to be no single thread that ties them together. Reviewing the existing literature on Daubert, one should note that no comprehensive elaboration of Daubert's thought exists that takes into account the entirety of his *Nachlass*. Only when we have such an overarching perspective on Daubert's thought can we properly assess the relationship between his philosophy (if he is indeed a genuine philosopher and not merely a secondary thinker – a scholastic or a critic) and the work of other members of the phenomenological movement, especially Husserl, and his place in the history of not only the movement but philosophy as such.

Constructing a philosophical system requires – according to well-known directives of hermeneutics – the establishment of a guiding narrative or problem. We know that a number of the manuscripts in Daubert's *Nachlass* were to serve as the foundation for his uncompleted dissertation on the consciousness of reality (*Wirklichkeitsbewusstsein*).[24] In light of this, it would make sense to have the consciousness of reality, and hence the realism-idealism debate, serve as the guiding

---

[22] We only know of three items that were promised for publication: Daubert's draft dissertation on the consciousness of reality (A I 7), a draft of an article on the phenomenology of the "question" intended for the first volume of Husserl's *Jahrbuch* (A I 2), and (as mentioned above) the drafts of an article on the phenomenology of evidence (A I 3).

[23] Cf. Sobota (2017).

[24] Daubert worked on this topic under the supervision of Theodor Lipps from 1899–1908. (Schuhmann 2003, p. 109)

theme of Daubert's philosophy. After all, this is not only an important issue in philosophy in general, but one of particular importance within early phenomenology. The relationship between consciousness and reality corresponds to the fundamental problems that defined the development and reception of Husserl's phenomenology. If we proceed down this path, then efforts to interpret Daubert's philosophical corpus as a systematic whole might well amount to completing his dissertation for him. This guiding narrative has the benefit of allowing us to assess how Daubert's ideas diverge from and converge with discussions our consciousness of reality in twentieth century philosophy, and promises to demonstrate the impact that Daubert had on other phenomenologists and the development of the phenomenological movement (presuming he shared these thoughts either in conversation or in writing). This way of reading Daubert is present in Schuhmann and Smith's article,[25] where Daubert is decidedly against Husserl's idealism and is perhaps one of the catalysts for the realism-idealism debate between Husserl and the members of the Munich and Göttingen Circles.

We should not give up on the general methodological goal of looking for a guiding idea in Daubert's writings, nor should we reject the suggestion of Schuhmann and Smith that the realism-idealism debate might serve as such a unifying thread. It is without question that this issue was at the center of the development, and dismemberment, of early phenomenology. The question of *Wirklichkeitsbewusstsein*, which Daubert intended to be a main pillar of his dissertation, may well serve as a way of presenting the whole of his thought. That said, I argue that the suggestion of Schuhmann and Smith as only partially correct. In addition to this, I would like to draw attention to a related line of thought present in Daubert's writings, and which is one of the most important *topoi* of continental philosophy in the twentieth century[26] – the act of *questioning* and the phenomena of the *question* itself.[27] This aspect of Daubert's thought is presented in another, perhaps equally well-known, article by Schuhmann and Smith.[28] Commenting on this latter article, John Bruin writes that Daubert's work is "the most ambitious work on the subject of the Q [question] in the phenomenological literature."[29]

---

[25] We find a similar reading of Daubert in Schuhmann (1989).

[26] The problem of the question as such became an important topic in twentieth century philosophy and contributed to the sharp division between the so-called Anglo-American "analytic" and "continental" traditions. See Sobota (2014).

[27] The connection between the consciousness of reality and the question is hinted at in Schuhmann (1996, pp. 78–80).

[28] Schuhmann and Smith (1987).

[29] Bruin (2001, p. 16).

5   The Problem of the Question

Given that Daubert did not start work on a "phenomenology of the question" until March 1911, and thus relatively late in his philosophical career, this alone might constitute an argument in favor of rejecting it as the key to his thought.[30] However, a more thorough examination of the development of Daubert's philosophy shows that the problem of the question was from much earlier on an important part of his thought. As early as 1904, the phenomenological analysis of questions was an issue for Daubert in reading Husserl's *Logical Investigations*. Paying attention to the topic of questions, one can see the reason for Daubert's having distanced himself from Husserl as well as the point of departure for Daubert's own philosophical project.[31]

The significance of the question in relations to Daubert's criticism of the Husserl is reconstructed by Smid, Schuhmann and Smith.[32] In the *Logical Investigations*, Husserl distinguishes between those intentional acts that refer directly to an object – what he calls 'objectifying acts' or 'representations' – and all other acts that refer to an object only *via* the former. Taking into consideration the possibilities of producing utterances, it is only objectifying acts that are meaning-bestowing acts and therefore, each utterance must be accompanied by such an act. It follows that only propositions directly express the acts of judgements underlying them since the latter belong to the class of objectifying acts. All other utterances – because their significance is derived from the acts of judgement – only indirectly refer to the acts underlying them. Hence, for example, any interrogative sentence does not directly express the act of questioning that founds said sentence. Instead, it does so only indirectly, that is, by dint of an objectifying act of questioning within an act of judgement. From the perspective of logic, an interrogative sentence is not a question but a proposition about the internal perception of the act of questioning.[33]

According to Daubert, Husserl's theory does not do justice to the phenomena. Requests, commands, questioning, wishing, and so on – Daubert claims – have their own meanings and do not have to be founded upon acts of judgement. From the logical perspective, these utterances are as legitimate as propositions. The consciousness of their occurrence is not a reflective consciousness; in other words, it not an internal perception of an act of requesting, commanding, questioning or wishing but rather it is of pre-reflective nature. We know that we request, command, or ask because each experience is accompanied with a certain pre-reflective self-consciousness – quite similar to the one that accompanies our emotions. Daubert argues that this pre-reflective consciousness is not of an intellectual but an

---

[30] Schuhmann and Smith (1987, p. 358).

[31] Smid (1985, pp. 282–284). In distancing himself from Husserl, Daubert finds himself more in line with the phenomenology of his teacher, Lipps (Smid 1985, p. 268–271), as well as the members of the Brentano school (Schuhmann 1996, p.75).

[32] Schuhmann and Smith (1987, pp. 354–358); Smith (1988, pp. 126–133).

[33] Smid (1985); Schuhmann and Smith (1987, pp. 355–357).

emotional nature (*Zumutesein, Spürung*), and it is this nature that bestows meaning on requests, commands, wishes and questions. As a result, this implies that we would be ill-advised to look for the source of our knowledge of internal psychic states or for the origins of our utterances only in objectifying acts. Instead, we would be well-advised to look for their origins in extra-theoretical and extra-intellectual emotional life. Therefore, we must open up a broad field for researching the genesis of higher forms of logical reasoning, cognitive acts and language in preconscious layers of our life as well as in its natural and cultural history.

Yet another thing is critical for accepting the notion of question as the key to interpreting the entirety of Daubert's thought, namely the incontrovertible philosophical significance of the problem of the question for both the phenomenological movement and the whole of the twentieth century philosophy. This way of construing Daubert's work is not entirely new. Smith, for example, emphasizes the merits of Daubert's contributions to the theory of speech acts.[34] In this sense, like his contemporary Adolf Reinach, Daubert could be included among the forgotten forefathers of the so-called "linguistic turn" – though, for obvious reasons, we know that Ludwig Wittgenstein, J. L. Austin, and others never read his work. Daubert was first among the early phenomenologists to take up a phenomenological investigation of the question in a detailed and comprehensive manner.[35] For Daubert, the problem of the question is not a specific problem within logic or epistemology, related to concerns over the nature of question as such, what is its logical structure, what is its function in cognition and in psychological life, what are its types and sources, etc., but is, rather, an issue that intersects with the most fundamental philosophical problems. The problematic of the question ranges from the problematic of acts and emotions, which are dealt with in psychology, through the problem of a method (reduction), the issue of the distinction between logic and grammar, communicative acts, which are subject to the laws governing social life, up to complex metaphysical issues (such as the relation between consciousness and reality). It not only plays a central, if not definitive, role within Daubert's extant writings, but it is an important theme in the later half of twentieth century philosophy.[36] Through his phenomenology of questions, Daubert anticipated many developments in philosophy in the second half of the twentieth century concerning the essence of questionness (*Fraglichkeit*). As Wilhelm Wieschedel puts it: "The fundamental experience of contemporary thought is [...] the experience of radical questionness [*Die*

---

[34] Smith (1988, pp. 130–134).

[35] Schuhmann and Smith (1987, p. 354). By "early phenomenologists" here we mean the early students of Husserl and the members of the Munich and Göttingen Circles. If we broaden this to include the School of Brentano, then we find Daubert's discussions taking place within a larger tradition including figures such as Alexius Meinong. See Schuhmann 1996.

[36] On the history of the philosophy of the question, see: Struyker-Boudier (1988), Kusch (1997), and Sobota (2012–13). Within the phenomenological movement, those who contributed to this issue of note were Heidegger, Ingarden, Patočka, Sartre, Merleau-Ponty, Levinas, Gadamer, Rombach, Ricoeur, Derrida, or Waldenfels. Outside phenomenology, the question constituted an important thread in the thought of P. Tillich, K. Rahner, W. Weischedel, E. Coreth.

Grunderfahrung des gegenwärtigen Denkens ist so die Erfahrung der radikalen Fraglichkeit."[37] Taking the question as the guiding theme in Daubert's work thus helps us to situate him both within the phenomenological movement, and within the broader history of philosophy.

6   The Question of Being (*Seinsfrage*)

Focusing on the problem of the question does not divert us from the topic of Daubert's draft dissertation, that is, our consciousness of reality. In fact, the two topics are closely linked. The link between questions and reality is a crucial moment in Heidegger's thought and in the phenomenological movement, insofar as it marks the turn to existential phenomenology.[38] It is the famous question of Being (*Seinsfrage*).[39]

Daubert read Heidegger's *Being and Time* during the short interlude between the sale of his old and the purchase of a new farm around 1930.[40] At the time, he was also researching the concept of evidence (*Evidenz*) and what it means to be evident. The last page of A I 3, with the heading *Kritisches zu Husserl*, indicates Daubert's solution to the problem of the consciousness of reality.[41] Because evidence is closely related to the issue of truth, and the latter has, for Daubert – as for Husserl and Heidegger –, at first glance an object-related dimension, the problem of evidence turns out to be closely related to the problem of reality. The condition of truth is to be found in the truth. Daubert quotes Heidegger: "»*Consciousness of Reality [Realitätsbewußtsein]*« *is itself a way of being-in-the-world*."[42] The latter is characterized by disclosedness or openness (*Erschlossenheit*; *Offensein*; *Offenheit*),[43]

---

[37] Weischedel (1976, p. 38).

[38] Waldenfels (1983, p. 47).

[39] The question of being is not only taken up by Heidegger in *Being and Time* (1927), but by Hedwig Conrad-Martius well. Among the pages of Daubertiana A I 3 we find notes on her radio lecture *Seinsphilosophie* (24 July 1931) (Conrad-Martius 1963, pp. 15–31) as well as the references to her *Realontologie* (Conrad-Martius 1923).

[40] Schuhmann and Smith (2004, p.36).

[41] "Heidegger, Scheler und Dilthey: Realität wird primär nicht im Denken und Erfassen gegeben. Nur aus der Fundamentalanalyse des Lebens (Dilthey). Das ist richtig: Das Organ für die Realität ist ein anderes als Wahrnehmen und Denken. Aber durch Widerstandserfahrung (Dilthey) oder durch voluntatives Verhalten (Scheler) ist nur höchstens ein besonderes Verhalten bezeichnet, in dem Realität zugänglich wird. Heidegger hat hiergegen recht mit seiner tieferen Analyse Realität = Dasein. Widerstandserfahrung ist nur möglich auf dem Grund der Erschlossenheit der Welt. Erkennen ist nicht Urteilen (Scheler) ist radikal richtig gegenüber Husserl. Wissen ist ein Seinsverhältnis (Scheler) ist problematisch, geht aber zentral gegen Husserl. »Realitätsbewußtsein ist selbst eine Weise des In-der-Welt-seins« (Heidegger, S. 211)." (Daubertiana A I 3/172r; D I 3/530)

[42] Daubertiana D I 3/530. Heidegger (1927, 211).

[43] Daubertiana D I 3/129. Cf. Heidegger (1927, p. 133; 220).

which in turn is the essence of the question.[44] This means that, for Daubert, the consciousness of reality is not the way of objectifying-cognitive reference of consciousness to the object, but the original, emotional openness of *Dasein*, which is a kind of original questioning.[45] It provides for the possibility of relating to reality or being real, thus including the actual asking and ultimately phenomenological-ontological question about the same openness (i.e., Being). In other words, the consciousness of reality – defined now by Daubert as the primary, bodily, emotional encounter (*Begegnung*) with myself, other people and the world of things – is the original openness, the primary question. It is no longer a theoretical question, but the bodily, mindful being-in-the-world, being within the reality that turns out to be for *Dasein* both closest and most alien.

By combining the two main themes of his philosophy – consciousness of reality and questioning – Daubert detheorizes and eroterizes (from *erotesis* – question) Husserl's theory of intentionality.[46] The detheorization consists in repudiating the primacy of logic and of apophantic ontology, and simultaneously in assigning a higher function to the sphere of emotion, which constitutes a condition of possibility for self-consciousness and reflection and is also a source of meanings of our language. The eroterization of intentionality protects it from the doomed simplifying, schematizing and objectifying search for theoretical certainty. The direct encounter with reality, to which Daubert often refers, does not have the character of certainty. However, as *openness*, it is an attitude of readiness for what is surprising and unexpected. Around this same time, while indulging himself in critically reading Husserl's and Heidegger's works, Daubert bade farewell to philosophy in favor of a quieter, "mute existence."[47] Being in question calls for the answer that comes from reality itself. However, it does not mean that Daubert simply took over the solution that Heidegger had put forward. Daubert's attitude towards Heidegger is a critical one. For instance, Daubert believed Heidegger never exhaustively captured the philosophy of the subject or the philosophy of reflection. Therefore, Daubert criticizes these motifs, which Heidegger himself, after the-so called turn (*Kehre*) recognized as the ones in need of being overcome.[48]

---

[44] Gadamer (2006, p. 356).

[45] Daubert refers to this as "being-in-a-mood [*Zumutesein*]" (Daubertiana A I 5 83v). Cf. Smid (1985, p. 238)

[46] Sobota (2017, pp. 672–702).

[47] Hofmannsthal (2005, p. 127), Sobota (2017, pp. 173–179).

[48] Schuhmann (2004a, p. 199). Sobota (2017, pp. 659–672).

7   Conclusion

Based on the above, we can clearly see Daubert's affinity to the transformations that occurred in philosophy in the wake of Husserl's phenomenology. Criticizing Husserl's emphasis on the primacy of consciousness, objectifying acts and expressions in the form of propositions, Daubert points to the felt, pre-reflexive anchoring of our consciousness of reality. In doing so, Daubert follows the path that was first shaped by his early interest in aesthetics, particularly the concept of empathy (*Einfühlung*) developed by Robert Vischer and Lipps.[49] Over time, empathy proved to be useful not only for describing aesthetic experience, but became the key to solving the problems of intersubjectivity and the experience of an objective, shared reality in phenomenology. In post-war French phenomenology, this gave rise to a new phenomenological metaphysics, what is now referred to as the "new" phenomenology of Emmanuel Levinas, Michel Henry, Jacques Derrida, Jean-Luc Marion, and Jean-Louis Chrétien.[50] The roots of this movement can be found in Daubert and others like him, and their reaction to Husserlian idealism.

Daubert's phenomenology, which bears witness to both his fascination with and critical stance toward Husserl's philosophy, and which he described as "phenomenology of phenomena," "phenomenology proper" or "phenomenology of understanding," opens onto the era of the struggle for a new metaphysical paradigm. Despite Husserl's purported metaphysical neutrality, the greater part of the phenomenological movement became a movement devoted to metaphysics, and its basic phenomenon appears to be a phenomenon of openness. For Daubert, the concept of *Seinsfrage* merges the basic theme of philosophy, which is being as such, with the issue of the question. *Seinsfrage* is not just some isolated idea, but a paradigm of ontological phenomenology and phenomenological metaphysics.

Seinsfrage expresses the peculiar relationship between thought and being, logic and ontology. According to Husserl, the only possible logical correlate of ontology is apophantic logic, i.e., the logic of constative utterances or propositions. Ontology and logic are two sides of the same coin.[51] But what would happen if we undermine the primacy of constative utterances? What if the understanding of being as permanent presence (*Anwesenheit*) – as implied by the proposition – forcefully imposes itself on our perception of reality, and stops us from being open to other areas of what exists? What happens if this primacy of the proposition is contested, and we replace it with a spectrum of different, previously discriminated logical forms, such as questions, requests, commands, wishes, and so on? These are the types of questions posed by Daubert in response to Husserl's phenomenology.

---

[49] Sobota (2017, Chapter 3).
[50] Simmons and Benson (2013); Migasiński and Pokropski (2017).
[51] Husserl (1969, §§37–64).

References

Avé-Lallemant, E. (1975) *Die Nachlässe der Münchener Phänomenologen in der Bayerischen Staatsbibliothek*. Weisbaden: Harrassowitz.
Bower, M. (2019) Daubert's Naïve Realist Challenge to Husserl. *Grazer Philosophische Studien, 96/2*, 211-243.
Bruin, J. (2001). *Homo Interrogans: Questioning and the intentional Structure of Cognition.* Ottawa: University of Ottawa Press.
Conrad-Martius, H. (1923) Realontologie. *Jahrbuch für Philosophie und phänomenologische Forschung 6*, pp. 159-333.
Conrad-Martius, H. (1963). Schriften zur Philosophie. Erster Band. Munich: Kösel.
Daubert, J. (2004). Notizen zu Husserls Mathematisch-philosophischen Übungen vom SS 1905/ Notes from Husserl's Mathematical-Philosophical Exercises, Summer Semester 1905. *The New Yearbook for Phenomenology and Phenomenological Philosophy, 4*, 288-317.
Frechette, G. (2001). Daubert et les limites de la phénoménology: Etiude sur le donné et L'évidence. *Philosophiques, 28/2*, 303-326.
Gadamer, H.-G (2006). *Truth and Method.* Translated by J. Weinsheimer, G. Marshall. New York: Continuum.
Heidegger, M. (1927). *Sein und Zeit*. Halle: Niemeyer.
Heller, E., and Löw, F. (eds) (1933). *Neue Münchener Philosophische Abhandlungen: Alexander Pfänder zu seinem sechzigsten Geburtstag gewindet von Freunden und Schülern.* Leipzig: Barth.
Hofmannsthal, H. (2005) *The Lord Chandos Letter and Other Writings*. New York: New York Review of Books.
Husserl, E. (1983) *Ideas pertaining to a pure phenomenology and to a phenomenological philosophy, First Book: General introduction to a pure phenomenology*. Translated by F. Kersten. The Hague: Martinus Nijhoff.
Husserl, E. (1969), *Formal and Transcendental Logic*. Translated by D. Cairns, The Hague: Martinus Nijhoff.
Husserl, E. (1994) *Briefwechsel II. Die Münchener Phänomenelogen*. Dordrecht: Kluwer (Husserliana Dokumente, III/2).
Kusch, M. (1997). Theories of Questions in German-Speaking Philosophy Around the Turn of the Century. *Poznań Studies in the Philosophy of the Sciences and the Humanities, 51*, 41-60.
Migasiński, J. and Pokropski M. (Ed.). (2017). *Główne problemy współczesnej fenomenologii.* Warszawa: Warsaw University Press.
Schuhmann, K. (1985). Structuring the Phenomenological Field: Reflections on a Daubert Manuscript. In W. S. Hamrick (Ed.), *Phaenomenologica: Vol. 92. Phenomenology in Practice and Theory* (pp. 3–17). Dordrecht: Kluwer.
Schuhmann, K. (1989). Husserl's Concept of the Noema: A Daubertian Critique. *Topoi, 8*, 53–61.
Schuhmann, K. (1996). Daubert and Meinong. *Axiomathes, 7*(1–2), 75–88.
Schuhmann, K. (2003) Johannes Daubert und die *Logischen Untersuchungen*. In D. Fisette (ed.), *Husserl's Logical Investigations Reconsidered* (pp. 109-131). Dordrecht: Kluwer.
Schuhmann, K. (2004a). Daubert und Heidegger. In C. Leijenhorst and P. Steenbakkers (Eds.), *Karl Schuhmann. Selected Papers on Phenomenology* (pp. 185–199). Dordrecht: Kluwer.
Schuhmann, K. (2004b). Daubert-Chronik. In C. Leijenhorst and P. Steenbakkers (Eds.), *Karl Schuhmann. Selected Papers on Phenomenology* (pp. 279–354). Dordrecht: Kluwer.
Schuhmann, K., and Smith, B. (1985). Against Idealism: Johannes Daubert vs. Husserl's Ideas I. *Review of Metaphysics, 38*(4), 763–793.
Schuhmann, K., and Smith, B. (1987). Questions: An Essay in Daubertian Phenomenology. *Philosophy and Phenomenological Research, 47*(3), 353–384.
Schuhmann, K., and Smith, B. (2004). Against Idealism: Johannes Daubert vs. Husserl's Ideas I. In C. Leijenhorst and P. Steenbakkers (Eds.), *Karl Schuhmann. Selected Papers on Phenomenology* (pp. 35–59). Dordrecht: Kluwer.

Simmons, J. A. and Benson, B. E. (2013) *The New Phenomenology: A Philosophical Introduction*. New York: Bloomsbury.

Smid, R. N. (1985). An Early Interpretation of Husserl's Phenomenology. Johannes Daubert and the "Logical Investigations". *Husserl Studies*, 2, 267–290.

Smith, B. (1988), Materials towards a history of speech act theory. In A. Eschbach (Eds.), *Karl Bühler's Theory of Language* (pp. 125-152). Amsterdam/Philadelphia: John Benjamins Publishing Company.

Sobota, D. R. (2012–13). *Źródła i inspiracje Heideggerowskiego pytania o bycie*. Vol. 1–2. Bydgoszcz: Fundacja Kultury Yakiza.

Sobota, D. R. (2014). Heidegger i neopozytywizm. U źródeł rozłamu filozofii XX wieku. *Przegląd Filozoficzny - Nowa Seria*, R. 23, Nr 2 (90),189–205.

Sobota, D. R. (2017). *Narodziny fenomenologii z ducha pytania. Johannes Daubert i fenomenologiczny rozruch*. Warsaw: Polish Academy of Sciences.

Struyker-Boudier, C.E.M. (1988). Toward a History of the Question. In M. Meyer (Eds.), *Question and Questioning* (pp. 9–35). Berlin: De Gruyter.

Waldenfels, B. (1983). *Phänomenologie in Frankreich*. Frankfurt am Main: Suhrkamp.

Weischedel, W. (1976). *Skeptische Ethik*, Frankfurt am Main: Suhrkamp.

Bogged Down in Ontologism and Realism. Reinach's Phenomenological Realist Response to Husserl

Kimberly Baltzer-Jaray

> *Consider the case, where we become cognizant [erkennen] of being filled with a feeling of delight, or that we see [something] red, or that sound and colour are distinct, or something like that. The individual cases of cognition [Erkennens] and their existence do not matter here, however it is in them that we intuitively discern [erschauen], in every instance, the What, the essence of the cognition, which consists in taking in [Aufnehmen], in a receiving [Empfangen] and making one's own, what offers itself. It is towards this essence that we must move, it is what we must investigate; but we must not substitute for it anything foreign to it.*
>
> *~ Adolf Reinach, Über Phänomenologie (1914)*

Abstract Adolf Reinach began his education in phenomenology with the teachings of Theodor Lipps before encountering Edmund Husserl's *Logical Investigations* in 1902. What attracted Reinach to the *Logical Investigations* was the philosophical realism he saw accompanying Husserl's criticism of psychologism and discussions of the formal structures of meaning therein. However, shortly after Reinach and a number of the Munich Circle members began studying with him in Göttingen, it became clear that the position Husserl espoused was shifting into transcendental idealism. Reinach maintained a theoretical independence from Husserl while embarking on the richest kind of dialogue with his revolutionary texts and teachings. By bringing out the strengths of some of Husserl's ideas and finding ways to repair the weaknesses of others, Reinach discovered new applications for the realism he found so attractive and significant in the *Logical Investigations*. I argue that this was how Reinach's response to Husserl took shape and grew, and set the foundation for

---

Reinach 1989, 549. All translations of Reinach are those of the author unless otherwise noted.

K. Baltzer-Jaray (✉)
King's University College, Western University, London, ON, Canada
e-mail: kbaltzer@uwo.ca

© Springer Nature Switzerland AG 2021
R. K. B. Parker (ed.), *The Idealism-Realism Debate Among Edmund Husserl's Early Followers and Critics*, Contributions to Phenomenology 112,
https://doi.org/10.1007/978-3-030-62159-9_8

151

the version of phenomenology that Reinach would continue to build upon with his own students until he left for the battlefield of World War I. This article sets forth and explores Reinach's realist response to Husserl by focusing on his expansion of the *a priori*, and his ontological work on essence and states of affairs – including his original contributions to jurisprudence.

Keywords Adolf Reinach · Ontology · Realism · Munich circle · Phenomenology · Edmund Husserl · Essence · Necessity

1   Introduction

Adolf Reinach, like some of his fellow Munich Circle members – Johannes Daubert, Moritz Geiger, and Theodor Conrad – began his education in phenomenology with the teachings of Theodor Lipps before encountering Edmund Husserl. Prior to the turn of the twentieth century, Lipps had developed his own phenomenology, whereby he understood 'purely phenomenological' as "the unprejudiced description of the contents of consciousness."[1] This point is substantiated in a letter that Reinach wrote to Conrad in 1907 where he states that "it could be questioned whether the phenomenology proper, as practiced in Munich, originated with Husserl."[2] Lipps also established and regularly attended a group known as the *Akademischer Verein für Psychologie* (*Academic Association for Psychology*), which met weekly outside of classes to host guest lectures and discuss each member's current projects. The atmosphere of this group was one of interdisciplinary collaboration, openness to new ideas, and constructive dialogue meant to strengthen research. The style and orientation of these group meetings would benefit the students greatly, allowing them to be creative while engaging a critical eye.

   Thanks to Daubert, the group of Lipps' students was already familiar with and discussing the philosophy of Franz Brentano and the ontological work of his students – specifically, that of Anton Marty, Carl Stumpf, and Alexius Meinong – before they discovered Husserl.[3] Daubert discovered the *Logical Investigations*

---

[1] Smid 1985, 268.

[2] "[…] man eigentlich bezweifeln könne, ob die eigentliche Phänomenologie, wie man sie in München betreibe, bei Husserl ihre Wurzel habe." Correspondence from Reinach to Conrad can be found at the Bavarian State Library under the signature Ana 379 C I 1. The lines preceding this statement reference a conversation Reinach had with Daubert about matters that he and Conrad had already discussed, mainly issues they both had with Husserl's work.

[3] In his chapter "Contents of Consciousness and States of Affairs: Marty and Daubert," Schuhmann writes: "The early Munich phenomenologists, in contrast, adopted a much more favourable stand toward Brentano and his followers. This attitude (which is of course in line with their general opposition to all that is of a transcendental bent) was no doubt inspired by Johannes Daubert." (Mulligan 1990, 198) In this chapter, Schuhmann also states that Daubert's criticisms of Husserl's *Logical Investigations* have roots in his positive attitude towards the Brentanists: "And as early as

(1900/1901) in 1902 and travelled to Göttingen to visit Husserl in order to discuss the work with him. Upon returning to Munich, Daubert proceeded to familiarize his fellow students with it.[4] Husserl's work was well received by the group, some even declaring the text to be a much-needed "tonic bath" [*Stahlbad*].[5] What attracted them so much was the philosophical realism[6] they understood as accompanying Husserl's criticism of psychologism and analyses of the formal structures of meaning, which was a refreshing change from the varieties of idealism that dominated the German philosophical landscape – such as that of some Neo-Kantians. However, these students did not embrace Husserl uncritically. Both Daubert and Reinach took issue with the way Husserl discussed the relation between object and signification;[7]

1904 he was criticizing Husserl for his 'partially misguided interpretations of Brentano' in the *Logical Investigations*. And concerning his own projects Daubert noted that his investigations 'are in large measure to follow Brentano.'" (Mulligan 1990, 199) Later, in his introduction to the translation of "Johannes Daubert's Lecture 'On The Psychology of Apperception and Judgment' From July 1902", when speaking about the familiarity of the Munich Circle students with the adjectival and adverbial forms of 'phenomenological,' Karl Schuhmann writes: "At the same time, however, it also indicates that Daubert must have already familiarized Lipps' students to some degree with Husserl's *Logical Investigations* and phenomenology before July 1902. This is also suggested by the fact that the title of Husserl's work is not mentioned a single time in the lecture [...] One of the preconditions for that is to be sought, of course, in the fact that the constant background of Husserl's thought, the ideas of the Brentano school, were also very much present in the Munich Circle. In Daubert's lecture this is manifest above all in his insistence on the distinction between intentional content and intentional object, as well as in his reference to a book by Alexius Meinong that had just appeared (probably in March 1902), *On Assumptions*." (Schuhmann 2002, 340–341) To bring the point back to Reinach, the intellectual biography of Reinach that Schuhmann and Smith assembled indicates that, "It was Daubert who was to be of most significance for Reinach's later philosophical development. Already in this period [1901–1903] Daubert was working on just those topics – positive and negative judgments, impersonalia, dispositions, *Sachverhalt* and *Gegenstand* – which were later to play a central role in Reinach's work." (Schuhmann and Smith 1987, 5)

[4] Spiegelberg 1994, 169. Husserl is here quoted as saying that Daubert was "the first person who had really read and understood the book." Similar points are also made in Schuhmann 2002.

[5] Smid 1985, 270.

[6] The specific character of Husserl's realist position in *Logical Investigations* has been adequately treated elsewhere. For instance, see Willard 2012 and Cobb-Stevens 2002. See also, Ingarden 1975. However, I will not be discussing the realist reading of the *Logical Investigations* here. Rather, I will simply echo the statements of James DuBois: "But whatever the stance one takes towards the *Logical Investigations*, we must insist that, whether Husserl intended to develop a phenomenological *realism* within these investigations is to some extent irrelevant to our understanding of Reinach. In any case, the *Logical Investigations* inspired a philosophical realism." (DuBois 1995, 146)

[7] During the summer term of 1905, a conversation took place between Daubert and Reinach where the two shared an objection to how Husserl had in several instances described the object by reflecting on the signification. Daubert used as an example the relation of similarity, and how the relation changes when the objects involved do. Another example the two men used to illustrate their point involves Kaiser Wilhelm: If I think of Kaiser Wilhelm, the son of Kaiser Fredrich III and the grandson of Queen Victoria, the object "Kaiser Wilhelm" does not imply the significations "son of Kaiser Fredrich III" and "grandson of Queen Victoria." (For further details, see Smid 1985, 278.) Daubert also criticized Husserl along Meinongian lines: he argued that Husserl showed a bias in

a number of Munich Circle members questioned the distinctions Husserl drew between statements expressing judgment, wishing, questioning, and commanding – specifically, by examining the issue of how these different types of grammatical constructions come to have meaning. These critiques reveal that the Circle members were not blindly swept up in their excitement; rather, they were careful, thoughtful and reflective individuals who saw a variety of avenues for expanding and improving Husserl's thought.

It was this phenomenological training under Lipps and the environment of the *Verein* that enabled Reinach and the others to maintain a theoretical independence from Husserl while embarking on the richest kind of dialogue with his revolutionary texts and teachings. Spiegelberg notes that phenomenology for early members like Reinach was primarily about a universal philosophy of essences, not merely the essence of consciousness: "It thus included ontology in Husserl's sense; and in fact it did so increasingly. To the first announcement of Husserl's phenomenological transcendentalism and idealism the group responded with growing consternation."[8] The Munich phenomenologists found ways to sustain their independence and realism even after a few key members moved to Göttingen, where they started to teach phenomenology, and after Husserl had committed to a more idealist, transcendental phenomenology. To this point, Dietrich von Hildebrand writes:

> One meaning of phenomenology is that which Husserl gave to this term after 1913, in his *Ideen*, and all subsequent works. [...] But a completely different meaning of phenomenology is in strict, radical opposition to any idealism. It signifies in fact the most outspoken objectivism and realism. It is this meaning of phenomenology which we find in the writings of Adolf Reinach, Alexander Pfänder, myself, and several others, and which we, at least, identified with the meaning of phenomenology in the first edition of Husserl's *Logische Untersuchungen*.[9]

It would appear in light of this context that Reinach was representative of the response to Husserl. His most direct way of doing this was simply to stay the course he perceived as mapped out in the *Logical Investigations*. In this work, Husserl stated that phenomenology

> has, as its exclusive concern, experiences that can be intuitively grasped and analyzed in pure generality pertaining to essence, not experiences empirically apperceived as real facts [...]. [T]his phenomenology brings *descriptively* to pure expression – through concepts and lawfully governed statements pertaining to essence – the essences directly grasped in intuition, and the interconnections grounded purely in such essences. Each such statement is *a priori* in the most preeminent sense of the word.[10]

At this stage of Husserl's thinking, phenomenology reveals the sources of the basic concepts and laws of pure logic so that they can be traced and made clear, thus allowing for epistemological critique. "*Ideating* or *generalizing abstraction*

---

favour of real existing objects when distinguishing between signification and object, failing to take into consideration possible objects or significations.

[8] Spiegelberg 1994, 168.

[9] Hildebrand 1991, 222–223.

[10] Husserl 2001, Vol. I, 166 (translation modified).

[ideation]" is an "act whose intention is directed solely to the 'idea' or the 'universal,'" and in which "we apprehend directly, 'itself,' the specific [*spezifische*] unity of *redness* on the basis of the singular intuition of something red. We look at the moment of red, but we perform a peculiar act [...]. Abstraction in the sense of this act is altogether different from the mere attention to, or emphasis on, the moment of red."[11] Later, in the Sixth Investigation §52, Husserl further clarifies: "Naturally I do not here mean 'abstraction' merely in the sense of a setting-in-relief of some non-independent moment in a sensible object, but ideating abstraction, where instead of the non-independent moment, its idea, its universal, is brought to consciousness, and achieves *actual givenness*."[12] In order to apprehend essences, such as the essence *red*, we must return to the intuitive experiences in which they are instantiated, and in doing so apprehend the underlying formal structures of our cognition and grasp what the corresponding words we use really *mean*. Reinach employed ideation as the preferred method for his realist ontology.

With the publication of *Ideas I,* and the subsequent turn towards a more subjectivist philosophy,[13] this response grew more forceful via an increasingly entrenched realism. In January 1914, when Reinach delivers his Marburg lecture *Concerning Phenomenology* [*Über Phänomenologie*], he speaks of a new realm opening up in philosophy, that of an *a priori* theory of objects, and that same year Husserl too describes a new realm open to philosophical investigation, that of pure consciousness. Schuhmann writes that "this seems to justify Husserl's final view that Reinach fell back into an ontologism" and, moreover, "If you compare Reinach's path from the theory of judgement to the treatise on justice with Husserl's journey from the *Logical Investigations* to *Ideas*, it is apparent that both developed not so much parallel to each other but rather in opposite directions."[14]

---

[11] Husserl 2001, Vol. I, 312, translation modified.

[12] Husserl 2001, Vol. II, 292, translation modified.

[13] To illustrate, in *Ideas I* Husserl writes: "On the other hand, the whole *spatiotemporal world*, which includes human being and human Ego as subordinate single realities, is, *according to its sense*, *merely intentional being*, thus one that has the merely secondary, relative sense of a being *for* a consciousness. It is a being posited by consciousness in its experiences [*Erfahrungen*] which is in principle intuited and determined only as something identical, motivated by manifolds of appearances: *beyond that* it is a nothing" (Husserl 1983, 112, translation modified).

With the appearance of *Ideas I*, Husserl was subjected to a concerted pushback by many of his Göttingen students against what they perceived as a serious drift toward a radical form of idealism. These charges against Husserl may well be made compelling – but they must be fair. Husserl was not impervious to these objections, as evidenced by changes he made to the text in his personal copies of the book in order to mitigate these reproaches. To mention two such changes in the passage I have cited, which apply to single words, among other more extensive ones, Husserl encloses the word 'for' in quotation marks and replaces the word 'nothing' [*Nichts*] with 'absurdity' [*Widersinn*] – changes that arguably dampen the thrust of the arguments against him. Curiously, I have yet to see these acknowledged in the critical literature, even though F. Kersten cites them in footnotes (Husserl 1983, 112, notes 29–31) of his translation (they cannot have gone unnoticed, despite his translation having fallen into disfavor).

[14] "Das scheint Husserls schließliche Auffassung zu rechtfertigen, daß Reinach in einen Ontologismus zurückgefallen sei. [...]. Vergleicht man Reinach's Gang von der Urteilstheorie zum

However, it should be noted that Reinach was always respectful of Husserl; he never wrote a harsh word in any publication about Husserl's choice to pursue transcendental phenomenology (in fact, I have not come across a direct mention of Husserl's *Ideas I* in any of his work).[15] Reinach reserved critical discussion of Husserl's work for face-to-face conversations with Husserl himself and his fellow Munich Circle members, or sometimes even with upper-level students in seminars. Above all, he valued their friendship, and respected Husserl's role as The Master even when he did not agree with him philosophically.

By bringing out the strengths of some of Husserl's ideas and finding ways to repair the weaknesses of others, Reinach discovered new applications for the realism he found so attractive and significant in *Logical Investigations*. I would argue that this was how Reinach's response to Husserl took shape and grew, and set the foundation that he would continue to build upon with his own students until he left for the battlefield of World War I. This article will set forth and explore Reinach's phenomenological realism response to Husserl in more detail, and it will do so by focusing on his expansion of the *a priori*, his ontological work on essence and states of affairs, and his original contributions to jurisprudence.

2 Phenomenological Realism

The commitment to phenomenological realism is the core of Reinach's response to Husserl, but what exactly is this standpoint? To be a phenomenological realist involves a commitment to at least the following two commonly accepted fundamental positions. First, the real world exists independently of human consciousness and its interactions therein and with others. Second, within that world we find different types of being: some things (such as tables and giraffes) exist and other entities (such as relations and states of affairs) subsist or absist (i.e., *Außersein*, as translated by Roderick Chisholm, such as impossible objects like valley-less mountains and square circles).[16] What becomes immediately clear is that phenomenological realism has both metaphysical and epistemological components. Understanding these is

---

Rechtsbuch mit Husserls Weg von den Logischen Untersuchungen zu den Ideen, so fällt auf, daß beide sich nicht so sehr parallel zueinander als vielmehr in entgegengesetzter Richtung entwickelten." He adds, " Reinachs philosophisches Hauptproblem war offenbar der Versuch, mit jener 'Bewußtseinsseite' ins Reine zu kommen. Auch wenn ihm der Weg zu einer endgültigen Lösung dieser Frage durch seinen Kriegstod abgeschnitten war, so war er sich doch von Anfang an darüber im Klaren, daß eine kantianisierende Antwort auf das Bewußtseinsproblem ausgeschlossen blieb, da sie mehr Schwierigkeiten schüfe als löste." (Mulligan 1987, 252)

[15] In *Concerning Phenomenology* – Reinach's last work before leaving for war – only Husserl's *Logical Investigations* is mentioned.

[16] These two fundamental positions of a phenomenological realist are the first two in a list of seven characteristics that summarize the "Austrian Aristotelianism" of the Brentano School. Reinach's phenomenology exhibits all of them, and this sometimes renders his work more in the spirit of

of the utmost importance for discussing the method of any phenomenological realist.

Most commonly we see philosophers speak dichotomously with regard to being: there is real being (e.g., tables and pineapples exist) and ideal being (e.g., numbers and logical axioms subsist). However, that does not exhaust what can be said of being. When I speak of the impossibility of square circles, my statement refers to an abstract "object" that cannot ever come to exist, and yet I understand the characteristics of the "object" and the logic of its nonexistence: when I judge "square circles do not exist" my judgment grasps the content of this impossible object, indicating it has a kind of being or subsistence.[17] Similarly, phenomenological realists – taking ontological cues from Meinong (alluding specifically to absistence) and, more importantly, Aristotle – describe a third kind of being, that which states of affairs, essences, and 'forms' have. These entities do not require consciousness to constitute them, implying that their being cannot be reduced solely to the operations of consciousness and, more importantly, that consciousness is not required for their presence in the world. When I look at a red rose in my garden, I perceive the physical rose, and I apprehend (employing insight [*Einsicht*]) that the state of affairs [*Sachverhalt*] *being-red* obtains.[18] The physical rose exists, and the state of affairs obtains or subsists, regardless of my experience with them: they are 'there', and not because I think them into being. With this brief mention of the activities of consciousness, we arrive at the epistemological side of phenomenological realism.

Fritz Wenisch, in his article, "Insight and Objective Necessity," describes the epistemological position of phenomenological realism as upholding the following:

1. There are propositions that, by their very nature, can be recognized as true but more importantly, as necessarily true. (e.g., 'Responsibility presupposes freedom');
2. Insight is the most fundamental method of philosophy;
3. A relationship holds between method and formal object such that a given object determines the method to be used for gaining knowledge of it.[19]

Austrian phenomenology than Husserl's. For further elaboration on these characteristics, see Smith 1996.

[17] Meinong 1960, 76–117. When we delve into the ontological jungle of Meinong we get another kind of being, one that is beyond existence and subsistence: absistence [*Außersein*]. According to Meinong, there is more than the simple disjunction between real and ideal being. There is also 'being-thus' [*Sosein*], which is properly distinct from 'being' [*Sein*] and 'non-being' [*Nichtsein*]. The being-thus of an object refers to the characteristics it has, such as the blackness of the cat or the largeness of the tree, and these characteristics are not affected by the object's being or non-being. For example, in the judgment "round squares do not exist" the object whose being is denied has characteristics – roundness and squareness – but these characteristics are not affected by its non-being.

[18] Reinach 1989, 114–115.

[19] Wenisch 1988, 108–109.

If insight[20] is the method of choice for the phenomenological realist, the formal object corresponding to it must be considered as comprising the center of objects being investigated by philosophy, and this formal object is characterized by necessity. If we take the example 'responsibility presupposes freedom', we see that it is a proposition that, by way of insight, reveals the necessity of the constituting states of affairs: the truth of this proposition is self-evident, and cannot possibly be otherwise. The necessity found here is as much an aspect of the objective world as it is of the states of affairs.[21] Hence, necessary states of affairs can be said to be the conditions for the possibility of insight. This enables Wenisch to conclude that phenomenological realism is an investigation of necessary states of affairs, and we come to apprehend these by way of insight.[22]

This fundamental method that utilizes insight is crucial to understanding the difference in the phenomenological approaches practiced by Reinach and Husserl, and is thus also the key to understanding Reinach's response. In *Logical Investigations*, Husserl writes that epistemology must not be taken as a discipline coinciding or following on the heels of metaphysics, but one that precedes it, as well as psychology and all other disciplines.[23] Reinach, on the other hand, exercises an approach that does epistemology at the same time as metaphysics. The reason for following such practice stems from the understanding that different types of objects are given to us in different ways – sounds heard, sweetness tasted, ideal laws intuited, states of affairs apprehended, etc. – and the only way we can uncover the different modes of gaining knowledge is by engaging with the variety of beings that are to be known. Hence, Reinach does metaphysics and epistemology simultaneously, or more pre-

---

[20] Intuition and insight are related but not the same. To possess or acquire insight [*Einsicht*] we must invoke discerning intuition [*Erschauung*]. Reinach speaks of the discerning intuition of essence [*Wesenserschauung*]: we grasp or lift the 'whatness' from the material object and bring it to ultimate givenness. That which we grasp through such intuition is amenable to the strongest sense of *Evidenz*. When we do this, we can also apprehend the subsisting states of affairs and the *a priori* connections that obtain. Apprehension is a special kind of intuition for Reinach, and this is performed with respect to states of affairs: it is as if I read them off the material objects.

[21] Reinach distinguishes between two types of insight: formal and essential. The difference boils down to that of form (purely logical) and material content. If we take a simple syllogism ($P \rightarrow Q$, $P \vdash Q$), looking only to the form of the argument, we can see it is valid. This insight that we gain concerns the formal connections only and has nothing to do with content – they are insightful all by themselves, and the evidence is directly there. There is also necessity and universal validity, and this means they are also *a priori*. If we flesh out the syllogism with content (e.g., If a woman floats in water then she must be made of wood. Abigail floats in water. Therefore she is made of wood.), then the truth or falsity we arrive at is not formal, but material – we know something about the 'things' or the natures of what P and Q stand for, which is how we know Abigail floats for reasons other than being made of wood. There are also instances of universality and necessity within the material realm but, when they pertain to the content, Reinach would call them material *a priori* truths. Essential insight, unlike formal insight, requires knowledge of the essences that ground the obtaining state of affairs. Confusion and/or conflation of these two types of insight have caused many misinterpretations of Reinach. For a brief discussion of this, see DuBois 1995, 108–110.

[22] Wenisch 1988, 109.

[23] Husserl 2001, Vol. I, 16–17.

cisely, he specifies that we must regard all epistemological and logical terms as primarily ontological.[24]

According to Reinach, pure intuition into essences is the means for attaining insight into the necessary laws that govern them and their instantiations, and these laws are *a priori* in character. In *Concerning Phenomenology*, Reinach writes:

> Experience, as sense perception, refers in the first instance to something individual, to the this-here [*Diesda*], and seeks to grasp it as this one. The subject endeavors to draw toward itself what is to be experienced, as it were: by its very essence, sense perception is only possible from some vantage point; and where we humans perceive, this starting point of the perception must be in the close vicinity of the perceived. [...] In order to grasp the essence, however, no sense perception is required; here we are dealing with intuitive acts of a completely different kind, which can be carried out at any time, wherever the subject effecting the presentation may happen to be.[25]

To illustrate this point, Reinach describes the act of mentally representing the colour orange as falling qualitatively between yellow and red. This does not require me to reflect on any particular instances of red, yellow, and orange that I may have gained through experience, even though a single case can suffice for apprehending *a priori* laws. David Hume's example of the missing shade of blue works here as well since, when shown a palate of blue shades with one missing, my mind fills in what shade ought to be there without having ever experienced it.

When Reinach identified pure intuition as the sole requisite for grasping essences and states of affairs, he also implied that reductions or bracketing were unnecessary. In *Concerning Phenomenology*, he makes comments about reducing and reductions that are not directed at Husserl by name, but one can easily gather given the eidetic reduction and talk of bracketing in *Ideas I* that Husserl is one of the intended targets (amongst the mathematicians and physicists).[26] In the very least, Reinach gives the impression with his unfavourable talk of reductions that he is against such approaches, especially in the context of essences: "People wanted to learn from the natural sciences, and wanted to 'reduce' [*zurückführen*] experience to the furthest possible extent. And yet this formulation of the task is senseless. [...] Let us leave undecided the deeper meaning of reduction [*Zurückführens*] – it certainly has no

---

[24] Vandervort Brettler, Lucinda Ann 1973, 116.

[25] Reinach 1989, 543.

[26] In the notes compiled by Schuhmann and Smith under the title "Die Vieldeutigkeit des Wesensbegriffs" [*The Ambiguity of the Concept of Essence*], taken from Reinach's seminar notes from winter 1912/1913, we see a brief comment about eidetic reduction, a rare example of Reinach referring to *Ideas I*, but, once again, without naming it: "{Thus becomes clear the} ambiguity of the expression "essence". {Is the concept of essence in phenomenology perhaps an} idea that plays a role but to which nothing {really} belongs? Phenomenology and eidetics {are following} Husserl to be distinguished. Eidetics is supposed to investigate relations of essences. {But the} sciences of essences of jurisprudence or national economy {would} never {become} accessible without phenomenological methodology. {Nevertheless it would not} be right to call all propositions achieved in this manner phenomenological. Mathematics {for example, possesses equally well} eidetic propositions as synthetic propositions *a priori*" (Reinach 1989, 362; Baltzer-Jaray 2016b, 137).

application to essentialities [*Wesenheiten*]."[27] In order to highlight the methodological difference between the phenomenologist and the physicist, between intuitive
discerning of essence and reducing [*zurückführen*], he later adds: "What is grounded
in the essence of objects can be brought to ultimate givenness in the intuitive discerning of essence [*Wesenserschauung*]."[28] Given that what follows in this lecture
are statements about *a priori* truths that involve material content, and this content
goes far beyond formal/logical connections – in fact, for Reinach *a priori* judgments concern material content more so than valid forms – reducing in Husserl's
sense becomes unnecessary. 'Orange is similar to yellow', for example, is not a
proposition that holds because of a compulsive feeling that belongs strictly to my
thinking; it is not a law of thought. Rather, it is a requirement of *being-orange*: the
similarity of orange to yellow is grounded in the being of the colour orange and the
being of the colour yellow, and it obtains regardless of whether anyone thinks it so.
A priori knowledge is amenable to irrefutable *Evidenz*, according to Reinach, in that
its content can be intuitively given in the strongest possible sense.[29] This not only
makes reductions a moot point, but, when *a priori* judgments and truths are linked
to material content, reductions become dangerous.[30]

Although Reinach never formulated his own phenomenological method outright,
we can gather from his published articles and unpublished notes that he was not
supportive of most of the additions and changes Husserl made to the phenomenological method in *Ideas I*. Specifically, he disapproved of bracketing and other
reductions.[31] The essential intuition to which Reinach refers is very much like (if not

---

[27] Reinach 1989, 534.

[28] Reinach 1989, 546.

[29] Reinach 1989, 545–546.

[30] It is interesting to note, as Spiegelberg does, that the famous song from 1907, *Phänomenologenlied*, written by Alfred von Sybel, was a piece of satire aimed at Husserl and his new innovations. That summer Husserl first presented his lectures on "The Idea of Phenomenology," and the song reflects the skeptical attitudes of the early members (Spiegelberg 1994, 258). The lyrics are as follows: *Wie blüht doch die Philosophie, / Seit sie Phänomenologie, / Man reduziert sich diese Welt / Und Existenz in Frag' man stellt. / Man hält sich an Essenzen, Essenzen, [Essenzen] – bis / Essenz von Punsch und von Likör / Gehören freilich nicht hierher. / Die Essenz, die man brauchen kann, / Die trifft man ganz wo anders an, / Da geht man zu den Müttern, den Müttern, [den Müttern] – bis / Die Mütter sitzen still and stumm, / Wohl um ein Klärbassin herum; / Drin muss man rühren früh und spat, / Bis man Essenz gefunden hat, / Und ziemlich ausfiltrieret, filtrieret, [filtrieret] – bis / Sie bilden dann die DingStruktur, (scil. Die Essenzen) / Grad wie bei einer Perlenschnur; / Die Schichten stecken an 'nem Speer, / Der geht wohl mitten durch sie quer, / Und das ist die Intentio, Intentio, [Intentio] – bis / Schon wächst empor das neue Haus, / Da plötzlich stürzt es ein, o Graus, / Denn auch, die Schichten in der Tief' / Sie lagen alle gänzlich schief, / Weil vag die Evidenzen, Videnzen, [Videnzen] – bis / Von neuem sich die Arbeit regt, / Die Schichten werden umgelegt, / Die Reihenfolg hat keened Sinn, / Und alles muss wo anders hin, / Und so geht's immer weiter, Ja weiter, [Ja weiter] – bis.* (Bavarian State Library, Conrad, Ana 378 C I 3)

[31] Although Reinach was rather vigilant not to show directly that he is at odds with Husserl, the following citation from Dorion Cairns attests to the growing divide between them: "Husserl [...] soon saw that the group did not progress with him. Already when he first read on the phenomeno-

the same as) the 'ideation' Husserl described in the *Logical Investigations*.[32] This early conception in the development of the phenomenological method was the preferred method for most of the Munich and some of the Göttingen phenomenologists, demonstrating a commitment to realist phenomenology as they saw being outlined in *Logical Investigations* and a refusal to follow Husserl into transcendental idealism.

When we look to Husserl and his transcendental idealism, the possibility of achieving philosophical insight depends primarily upon certain acts of the knowing subject's consciousness: performing an act of reflection, the phenomenological or transcendental reduction, bracketing everything pertaining to the existence of the object of knowledge, and so on. Reinach, conversely, seeks out features of the object of knowledge that give rise to instances of philosophical insight and make it possible. This kind of direct insight is not possible with every object of knowledge; however, Reinach is able to isolate instances where we stand the greatest chance of it: essences that serve to ground necessary and immutable laws, those which ground necessary states of affairs and give rise to informative synthetic *a priori* knowledge. For instance, in his Marburg lecture, he says: "Laws hold of essentialities, laws of a unique character and dignity that distinguish them radically [*durchaus*] from all empirical interconnections and empirical lawfulness. The pure intuitive discerning of essence is the means to achieve the intuitive and adequate comprehension [*Erfassung*] of these laws."[33]

In this vein, Reinach calls our attention to *material* necessity, the kind of necessity that occurs and belongs to material content found in the world around us – in contrast to the *modal* necessity that belongs to the realm of mathematics and logic. We experience this type of necessity daily, as noted by Hume, with cause and effect relationships (e.g., fire produces smoke, diphosphorus pentoxide reacts with water), where we can arrive at knowledge not by finding the predicate in the subject (e.g., looking for smoke in the essence of fire, looking for the reaction to water in the diphosphorus pentoxide) but by insight into the necessary connections holding between them. Reinach will extend this notion and find a practical application for direct insight in the sphere of law – to describe the essences that ground the necessary states of affairs and *a priori* structures pertaining to promises, obligations, and other juridical acts as a segment of the broader social world. More on this later.

So, with this understanding of what it means to be a phenomenological realist, I now want to turn to some specifics of Reinach's ontology in order to further demonstrate his realist commitment and flesh out in greater detail his response to Husserl.

---

logical reduction, many did not come along. After the publication of the *Ideen*, Reinach and, following him, others broke away from the new developments" (Cairns 1976, 10).

[32] Although Husserl's characterization has been provided above, from the Second Investigation, another take on this act concludes the book at the end of the Sixth Investigation, §66: "the peculiarity of pure 'ideation' [is] the adequate intuitive discerning of essences and of valid generalities lawfully grounded in essences" (Husserl 2001, Vol. II, 319, translation modified).

[33] Reinach 1989, 535.

3   Ontology of the *A Priori*, States of Affairs, and Essences

Reinach's phenomenological realism is largely expressed in an ontology comprised
of expanded notions of *a priori*, states of affairs, and essences. These entities inter-
lace with one another, and thus it is rather difficult to talk about them without reference to each other. Although the title of this section singles out ontology, the
discussion will not be purely ontological, but will rather mirror and further illustrate
Reinach's approach of doing metaphysics and epistemology simultaneously.

The *a priori* is traditionally understood from an epistemological standpoint: Kant
described it as a kind of knowledge that is *independent* of experience (i.e., it does not
require experience).[34] Sometimes it is also understood as obtaining *prior* to experience, and hence derivable from reason alone. Kant claimed that instances of *a priori*
cognitions are to be found almost exclusively in mathematics[35] and synthetic *a priori*
judgments are found in both mathematics and physics (natural science).[36] Reinach's
critique of Kant's conception of the *a priori* is twofold. First, the *a priori* is ontological rather than strictly epistemological, thus rendering it as not simply having to do
with thought, but with being and the laws that govern essential connections. *A-priority*
is a property of states of affairs and is such by virtue of the essential connections that
occur among states of affairs. In other words, the essential connections among states
of affairs act as carriers [*Träger*] of the *a priori* property. Second, the scope of the *a
priori* far exceeds the domains of mathematics and natural science, extending to
include the sphere of jurisprudence and several other disciplines. Reinach addresses
this point in *The A Priori Foundations of Civil Law*:

> As ontology or *a priori* theory of objects, philosophy has to be concerned with the analysis
> of all possible kinds of objects as such [...]. Also the laws that apply to these objects [juridi-
> cal structures] are of the highest philosophical interest. They are *a priori* laws, indeed – as
> we may add – *a priori* laws that are of a synthetic nature. Even if until now no one cast
> doubt on where Kant had restricted far too narrowly the sphere of these propositions, this
> doubt is now fully vindicated by the discovery of the *a priori* theory of justice [*Rechtslehre*].
> Alongside pure mathematics and pure natural science, there is also a pure jurisprudence, as
> assembled like the others – out of strictly *a priori* and synthetic propositions, and serving
> as foundation for disciplines that are not *a priori*, indeed situated even beyond the antithesis
> of the *a priori* and the empirical.[37]

Configuring the *a priori* as ontological rather than merely epistemological allows
Reinach to correct what he deems to be the gross errors committed in the name of
the *a priori*, thereby allowing it to extend the domain proper to it: the foundations
of the laws in our society are synthetic *a priori* propositions, and the natural consequence of this extension is that many other disciplines, not thought to have anything
a priori about them, must now be recognized as having an *a priori* foundation.

---

[34] Kant 1996, 45 [B2–B3].

[35] Kant 1996, 49–50 [A4/B8–A5/B9].

[36] Kant 1996, 55–55 [B14–B18].

[37] Reinach 1989, 145–146.

As detailed in the previous section, Reinach's position is that one can come to intuit *a priori* connections, and from this one can come to study the essential relations occurring among phenomena. These connections obtain whether or not persons or other subjects acknowledge them, and this of course is something we can say of all objective truths, not just *a priori* ones. He writes, "With the *a priori*, on the other hand, it is a matter of the sighting [*wesensschau*] and cognition of essence."[38] Furthermore, "The *a priori* in and for itself has nothing in the least to do with thinking and cognizing [...] in truth, it has nothing at all to do with laws of thought. At issue is that for something to be or to comport itself in such and such a way is grounded in its essence [...]."[39] *A priori* connections are ontological, universal in scope (i.e., strictly necessary), and this necessity derives from being and not thought. Here, Reinach establishes again his stance that the *a priori* is ontological and not just epistemological. The laws that govern essences are unfettered by any factual connections of which sense perception informs us; they hold true – and by necessity. Moreover, "That there are these laws is of the utmost importance to philosophy, and – if we think this through to its conclusion – of the utmost importance in the world at large. To present them in their purity is therefore a momentous task of philosophy [...]."[40] The *a priori* concerns necessity in the world, not only necessity in thought, and construing it as such conforms to one of the phenomenological realist's key commitments.

As previously mentioned, *a-priority* is a property of states of affairs. Reinach conceives of states of affairs as substantiating the relationship between judgments and the objects judged. They also act to correlate propositions and subsist in a way that is neither real nor ideal: they are intentional. States of affairs are essential connections subsisting between the thing judged and the properties judged – such as in the example the '*being-red* of the rose' – and thus are different from both the material rose and the proposition 'that rose is red'.

Reinach describes six essential characteristics of states of affairs. This short list is by no means exhaustive, nor does it constitute a definition. These six are essential marks meant to distinguish states of affairs from propositions and objects, and they are sufficient in the sense that every entity to which any one of them applies would be a state of affairs. These characteristics are described by Reinach in his 1911 essay "Toward the Theory of Negative Judgment." A state of affairs is:

1. that which is believed or asserted in judgments (Reinach 1981, 34);
2. that which can stand in the relationship of ground and consequent (Reinach 1981, 34–35);
3. that which can take on modalities, such as possibility and necessity (Reinach 1981, 35);
4. that which stands in the relation of the logically contradictory positive and negative (Reinach 1981, 35–36);

---

[38] Reinach 1989, 543.

[39] Reinach 1989, 545

[40] Reinach 1989, 543.

5. that which obtains or does not obtain (as opposed to existing)[41] – and given (4) above, either a positive or a negative state of affairs obtains (Reinach 1981, 36);
6. that which is apprehended or intuitively discerned, not seen or perceived through the senses (Reinach 1981, 37).[42]

Being *a priori* in nature entails that states of affairs are independent of any judgment or cognition on our part, and that they follow strict laws – ones that also obtain independently of our acknowledgment. States of affairs have a special mode of being that enables them to relate to both ideal and real objects but are not themselves real or ideal. As *intentional* entities, states of affairs can participate with[43] a wide array of ontologically different 'objects'. By employing words like 'obtain', the list of characteristics reiterates that we must not mistakenly regard states of affairs as existing; it is rather the objects to which they stand in relation that exist.[44] Reinach adds to this point: "As we immerse ourselves into the essence of these entities [*Gebilde*], we intuitively discern [*erschauen*] what holds for them as a matter of strict law; we grasp interconnections analogously to the way we do through the immersion into the essence of numbers and geometric entities: the being-thus [*So-Sein*] is here grounded in the essence of that which is thus [*So-Seienden*]."[45] Once again we see Reinach emphasizing the type of immaterial subsistence states of affairs have, and that states of affairs and the laws to which they are subject are immutable and strictly necessary. States of affairs, like the *a priori* laws they

---

[41] An important way in which Reinach differentiates objects from states of affairs is to refer differently to their modes of being: physical objects *exist*; states of affairs *obtain* or *subsist* (Reinach 1989, 118).

[42] I have modified Don Ferrari's translation of characteristic 6. The original German from which Ferrari gleans characteristic 6 reads: "*Indem ich die rote Rose sehe, 'erschaue' ich ihr Rotsein, wird es von mir 'erkannt'. Gegenstände werden gesehen oder geschaut, Sachverhalte dagegen werden erschaut oder erkannt*" (Reinach 1989, 118). Ferrari translates *erschaue* as "observe," and I don't agree with this choice. It does not capture the meaning accurately. His choice of translating *erkannt* as "apprehended" is acceptable but it should be noted that Reinach's notion of apprehending as applied to states of affairs is not the same as applied to concepts. For example, to apprehend the concept 'man' is not the same as to apprehend the state of affairs 'being-man'. The way intuition apprehends states of affairs differs from the way concepts are apprehended because in the former what is grasped or discerned are essential connections but in the latter it is abstract ideas. Intuition must operate differently when apprehending states of affairs because these are not necessarily static, but rather occur in connection and participation with other entities.

[43] The choice of preposition here – 'participate *with*' – is a deliberate one and is intended to reflect the idea that an individual thing or being is not static, but rather is engaged in essential activity: "the activity in and through which its matter was being informed" (Mitscherling 2010, 83). This should more clearly capture the sense of Aristotle's Formal Causality and Plato's notion of Participation. My hope is to avoid the confusion or conflation of participation with imitation, which happens when phrasing like 'participate *in*' is used – as if the essence preexisted the thing or entity. To subsist or obtain at all, essence must do so *through* participation. See Baltzer-Jaray (2016b).

[44] In a set of rough notes, Reinach writes that the form of states of affairs can be either temporal or atemporal, and it is their content or 'matter' that determines this. See Reinach 1989, 351.

[45] Reinach 1989, 144.

participate with, come to be known through insight: they are brought to ultimate givenness when we perform essence intuition and come to apprehend states of affairs as distinct from the objects with which they participate. Moreover, because the apprehending of states of affairs is grounded in my perception of objects (e.g., of the red rose I see in the garden), the presentation of states of affairs is grounded in the presentation of objects. I do not need to have the rose be present before me in order to have a representation of *being*-red. I can recall it in memory, and from this recollection I can at any time repeat an intuition of the essence.

While *a priori* knowledge gained through the use of insight is amenable to the highest form of evidence, such insight is by no means always easy: "The fact that a direct grasp of essence [*Wesen*] is so unusual and difficult that for some it seems impossible can be at once explained by the deep-rooted orientation [*Einstellung*] of practical life, which is more into availing itself of objects and manipulating them than into intuiting them contemplatively and penetrating into the being that is appropriate [*Eigensein*] to them."[46] Simply put, the reason intuiting essences can be difficult has to do with the fact that we are not used to 'looking' for them, or rather have not trained ourselves to be receptive to their presence. This is why their subsistence in the world may be open to skepticism. Reinach adds that this difficulty of grasping essences is "further explained by the fact that some scientific disciplines – in contrast to those discussed thus far – avoid *as a matter of principle* [*prinzipiell*] all direct intuitive discerning of essences, and thus produce in all who devote themselves to these disciplines a deep aversion to any direct grasping of them."[47] Here he is alluding to both mathematics and the natural sciences, fields that rely for their truths and certainties on axioms and empirical relationships rather than on essences. It is therefore by design that natural science does not seek out essences, but rather looks for material facts – and thus has a bias for the real (over the intentional). Mathematics, as Reinach notes, uses the term 'thing' not in the philosophical sense of a "determinate categorial form", but as a contentless concept in general, and to this 'thing' many types of things are ascribed – and a system is formed.[48] Thus, we see the reason why Reinach italicizes 'as a matter of principle': science and mathematics, in virtue of the axioms and laws that found and regulate their disciplines, have in principle, that is *fundamentally*, nothing to do with intuiting essences.

For Reinach essences do not inhabit some separate realm as timeless, immutable, disembodied entities; rather, they subsist in the relations that obtains between the form and matter of objects: "Wherever we happen to be in the world, everywhere and always the doorway to the world of essentialities [*Wesenheiten*] and their laws stands open to us."[49] If we return to our earlier example of the red rose, there is the material red rose (i.e., the one growing in my garden), a state of affairs that obtains (i.e., the *being-red* of the rose), and a judgment about the rose (i.e., 'this rose is red')

---

[46] Reinach 1989, 535

[47] Reinach 1989, 535.

[48] Reinach 1989, 535–536.

[49] Reinach 1989, 543.

that refers to this state of affairs. I intuit the essence of the rose to be the very item that we attribute to its *whatness* (e.g., smell, type of petal, thorns, genus, etc.) as necessary. Once again: I perceive the existing rose before me as red in colour; I apprehend the obtaining state of affairs *being-red*; I intuit the subsisting essences. There is also a sense of material necessity to the redness of the rose that I apprehend: the rose before me *is* red; it is necessarily so (i.e., it is not white, it is not yellow), and is not otherwise – although it could have been. When I apprehend the obtaining state of affairs, this necessity is conveyed via the *a priori* (i.e., the essential interconnections amongst the states of affairs pertaining to the red rose). Once again, both of the core phenomenological realist commitments are upheld here: the world around me exists independently, and *a-priority*, essences, and states of affairs are among the entities to be encountered in this world by means of insight. Hence, the ontology expressed in Reinach's phenomenological realism is incompatible with the phenomenological idealism Husserl espouses in *Ideas I*.

4   Jurisprudence

As discussed, Reinach wanted to demonstrate that the *a priori* was much broader in scope than originally conceived and that it had a firm footing in ontology. One domain in which he found the clearest exemplification of this was jurisprudence. Reinach's *a priori* theory of justice [*Recht*], which culminated in *The Apriori Foundations of Civil Law* (1913), was a phenomenological realist investigation into an intentional entity that subsisted in the world, one that could be apprehended with insight and described using the phenomenological device of ideation. In this essay, Reinach takes aim at the view that laws derive their meaning and power through codification: laws are created and enforced by persons, and the only way we can have contracts or proxy arrangements with any binding power is by having written laws about them.[50] This positive law movement produced the infamous German Civil Law code of 1900 – the *Bürgerliches Gesetzbuch*.

This positivist position denies not only the traditional sense of natural law, but also justice [*Recht*] understood as a transcendent unity or harmony that subsists in the world, one we rationally participate with as an activity of thinking where we employ insight to apprehend this unity. The main tool at Reinach's disposal for this investigation was his 'new and improved' sense of the *a priori*:

> That a claim is settled by a waiver is grounded in the essence of the claim as such and thus holds necessarily and universally. *A priori propositions hold for juridical structures [rechtlichen Gebilden]*. This a-priority should convey nothing dark or mystical, it is guided by the plain facts we have mentioned: every state of affairs that is universal and obtains [*besteht*] necessarily in the sense adduced is designated by us as *a priori*. We will see that there is a rich abundance of such *a priori* propositions, capable of strict formulation and amenable to self-evident insight [*evident einsichtig*], independent of all apprehending

---

[50] See Baltzer-Jaray 2016a.

consciousness, and above all independent of any positive law – just as are the juridical structures of which they hold.[51]

This sense of justice should, according to Reinach, always be the foundation for our codified laws [*Gesetzt*], and thereby the written law would reflect the greater sense of justice at work in the universe. Reinach, as a phenomenological realist, supported the notion of justice [*Recht*] as subsisting in the universe, and sought to describe how we come to know justice and explain how our insight works to apprehend the transcendent harmony.[52] Once again we see that with the *a priori* Reinach is doing epistemology and ontology simultaneously, since he also talks about how we come to know the subsistence and truth of legal entities.

Say, we make a claim such as 'I promise to buy you a cigar'; once I fulfill the obligation created here (i.e., I keep my promise – buy the cigar and give it to you) the claim dissolves completely. Had I failed to meet the obligation I created – say I made the promise in bad faith and never even intended to go to the tobacconist – then the claim does not dissolve, but rather persists unfulfilled, and the person I am obligated to senses the injustice. Failing to keep a promise creates a situation of disharmony: a wrong has been done. In the case of promises, we know what it means to make them, keep them, or fail to keep them – we do not need a law book to tell us how promises work or how they should be resolved. Reinach adds to this point:

> There are indeed vast realms of social life that are untouched by any positive-juridical normativity [*Normierung*]. In them, too, we encounter those structures usually designated as specifically juridical, whose independence from positive law we assert, and needless to say those *a priori* laws hold here too. Just as their form is of interest for the theory of objects and for epistemology, so their content becomes significant for the sociologist. Along with some other laws, they represent the *a priori* of social comportment, even for spheres that lie beyond any positive juridical regulation.[53]

We can know justice and injustice with certainty by invoking insight. Codified law can enact rules about promises, it can incorporate or not incorporate elements of justice, but regardless, it cannot touch the being and objective truth these entities have. When the written law deviates too far from the transcendent unity of justice we end up with cases where something is lawful but unjust: with insight we know

---

[51] Reinach 1989, 144. Reinach's denotation for the word 'claim' [*Anspruch*] is not the conventional one. It takes on a legal significance for him when it is linked to promise: it is a demand or request for something considered one's due, a right to something as part of an oral or written contract. It is a bond formed between two parties where, "the one can demand something and the other is obliged to fulfill it or grant it. This bond shows up as *consequence* or *product* (as it were) of the promising." (Reinach 1989, 147) Claim and obligation are causally linked when a promise is made. Once the promise is fulfilled, the claim is waived and the obligation is cancelled by being satisfied.

[52] Berkowitz (2010) describes Leibniz's lifelong involvement with attempting to write a science of justice (*ius*): "What does it mean that *ius* is knowable and measurable by a science of justice? What does it mean that *ius* comes to be an object of scientific knowing?" are questions that preoccupied Leibniz (Berkowitz 2010, 28). The first is an epistemological question, and the second is an inquiry into the essence of *ius* itself. The latter is what preoccupied Leibniz, and later also Reinach.

[53] Reinach 1989, 146.

when laws miss their mark, we experience it rationally as well as emotionally. We feel that agitating sense of discord.

Regarding ontology, we see once more the entities we discussed earlier: essences, states of affairs, and the *a priori*. With this, Reinach is attempting to restore authority to the old sense of justice [*Recht*] by way of phenomenological realism – through demonstrating the objective, intentional status it has. In doing so, he makes clear that the status of these entities is entirely independent and makes clear at the same time how they participate with us. He writes:

> We will show that the structures which are commonly designated as specifically juridical possess a being no less than numbers, trees or houses do; that this being is independent of whether or not it is grasped by humans, that it is independent, in particular, of all positive laws. It is not only false but, for all intents and purposes, meaningless to designate juridical structures as inventions of positive law – just as meaningless as it would be to call the establishment of the German Reich, or some other historical event, a fabrication of historical science. We really do have before us what is so fervently denied: positive law finds the juridical concepts that enter into it; it *in no way produces* them. [...] We assert only one thing – and we place the greatest importance on it: the so-called specifically juridical basic concepts have a being extrinsic to that of positive-juridical [concepts], just as numbers possess a being independently of mathematical science. [...] And further: There are eternal[54] laws that hold for these juridical structures, which [laws] are independent of our grasping them – exactly like the laws of mathematics. [...] We shall see that here [with juridical structures] philosophy encounters a whole new kind of objects – objects that do not belong to nature in the authentic sense, that are neither physical nor psychical, and that at the same time – owing to their temporality – also differ from all ideal objects.[55]

Justice, in the greater sense of transcendent harmony, is comprised of structures that have a being that is neither physical, psychical, or ideal; they are intentional entities subsisting in the universe. Therefore, justice too has a unique ontological status that defies the dichotomy of real and ideal. It subsists in the world independently of the mind; we become aware of it when we engage with its intentional structure, and then we can exercise insight to apprehend it and the necessary laws that hold for it. Due to its independent subsistence in the universe and its intentional being, justice makes altogether possible the concretization of laws and legal principles, and through the course of experience it also guides and informs our behavior. When I employ insight to grasp justice, my potential behavior and actions take on form.

In pursuing this line of argument and particular ontology, Reinach not only responds to the positive law movement and its rather gross underestimation and misappropriation of justice, but also to Husserl – simply by continuing to pursue an approach of phenomenological realism, rather than embarking on one of phenomenological idealism. In fact, Reinach's strong commitment to such a realist ontology did not go unmentioned when Husserl spoke to his later students: referring

---

[54] *Ewige*: Reinach's use of the term – which I translate literally – is unfortunate because it may imply some sort of Platonist bent to his thinking. Reinach was not a Platonist!

[55] Reinach 1989, 143–145.

Spiegelberg to Reinach's work on law, he described it as an ontology in need of a phenomenology of legal consciousness.[56]

5 Conclusion

In his obituary for Reinach, published in 1919, Husserl wrote that, "Yet even the first essays gave evidence of the independence and power of his mind as well as of the seriousness of his scientific striving, to which only the most fundamental research could give satisfaction."[57] He continues:

> He was one of the first who was able to comprehend fully the peculiar sense of the new phenomenological method and to see its philosophic import. The phenomenological manner of thought and research were soon second nature to him and never henceforth did the conviction – so very pleasing to him – that he had reached the true continent of philosophy and now knew himself, as researcher, to be surrounded by an infinite horizon of possible and, for a rigorous scientific philosophy, decisive discoveries, fall into doubt. Thus, his Göttingen writings breathe a completely new spirit and at the same time manifest his efforts to dedicate himself to clearly bounded problems and, through taking the work in hand, to make the ultimate foundation fruitful.[58]

In these sorrow-filled lines, it is evident that Husserl was well aware of the theoretical divide that had grown between himself and Reinach, but that never diminished any of the respect he felt for him as a scholar and colleague. After all, it was *Logical Investigations* that inspired and captivated Reinach, so much so that he could not move past it. The phenomenological realism he saw alive in those pages was open to many possibilities and domains, ones Husserl did not explore at the time. I attribute Husserl's neglect of these issues largely to context: Reinach's background in legal studies revealed to him a kind of ontology and epistemology in which Husserl did not show much interest prior to 1917. However, after he pursued this avenue and brought to light the power and potential of phenomenological realism, Husserl was increasingly in awe of Reinach's accomplishments. This is already reflected in the above tribute.

Much as Reinach's response to Husserl (via his continued phenomenological realist position) was conveyed in a duly respectful manner, Husserl also seemed to be disappointed by it: he is quoted as referring to Alexander Pfänder and the Munich phenomenologists as bogged down [*stecken geblieben*] in ontologism and realism, having ignored the revolutionizing transformations in his new phenomenology.[59]

---

[56] "Als Rechtsstudenten wies er mich auf Adolf Reinach hin. Doch fügte er bei, daß noch etwas ganz anderes benötigt sei als Reinachs Ontologie, eine Phänomenologie des Rechtsbewußtseins, von der er improvisierend ein mich damals faszinierendes Bild entwarf" (Spiegelberg 1959, 59).

[57] Husserl 1975, 571.

[58] Husserl 1975, 572.

[59] Spiegelberg 1994, 171–172. Spiegelberg adds that in the 1920s Husserl was also disappointed in Pfänder's apparent disinterest in the problems of the transcendental reductions and constitution

Husserl very much wanted the brilliant mind of Reinach, and the other Munich Circle members, to see the awesome potential that his new idealist path foretold, to be as enthusiastic about that path as they were about his *Logical Investigations* a decade earlier. Of course, they were not; and especially Reinach seemed unwilling to shift approaches because he envisioned how much more was left to be done by following Husserl's original approach. This task then fell to Reinach and to the other realist phenomenologists to complete.

Acknowledgements I dedicate this article to the memory of Professor Dr. Fritz Wenisch (1944–2020), who sadly passed away during its preparation for print. Fritz received his doctorate in philosophy from the University of Salzburg in 1968, with a dissertation on *Die Objektivität der Werte,* and was awarded his habilitation in 1975 for *Die Philosophie und ihre Methode.* He was a professor in the department of philosophy at the University of Rhode Island from 1971 until 2019. He was also highly instrumental in the inauguration of NASEP. He considered himself a phenomenological realist in the tradition of the Munich Circle, and a follower of Dietrich von Hildebrand. I dedicate this paper to him in honour of the wonderful and enlightening discussions we had about Adolf Reinach, Edith Stein, Gerda Walther, and all the other early phenomenologists we both so greatly admired. Fritz was a brilliant and generous colleague, a talented poet, and a dear friend. He will be sorely missed – but never forgotten.

References

Avé-Lallemant, Eberhard. 1975. *Die Nachlässe der Münchener Phänomenologen in der Bayerischen Staatsbibliothek.* Wiesbaden: Harrassowitz.
Baltzer-Jaray, Kimberly. 2016a. Phenomenological Jurisprudence: A Reinterpretation of Reinach's *Jahrbuch* Essay. In *Phenomenology For The Twenty-First Century.* Eds. J. Edward Hackett and J. Aaron Simmons. London: Palgrave Macmillan. 117–137.
Baltzer-Jaray, Kimberly. 2016b. The Intentional Being of Justice and the Foreseen. In *Essays on Aesthetic Genesis.* Eds. Charlene Elsby and Aaron Massecar. Lanham: University Press of America. 65–76.
Baltzer-Jaray, Kimberly. 2016c. Reinach and Hering on Essence. *Discipline Filosofiche XXVI, 1, 2016: Phenomenological Ontologies: Individuality, Essence, Idea.* Volume Editors: Simona Bertolini and Faustino Fabbianelli. 123–143.
Berkowitz, Roger. 2010. *The Gift of Science: Leibniz and the Modern Legal Tradition,* New York: Fordham University Press.
Cairns, Dorion. 1976. *Conversations with Husserl and Fink.* The Hague: Martinus Nijhoff.
Cobb-Stevens, Richard. 2002. "Aristotelian" Themes in Husserl's Logical Investigations. In *One Hundred Years of Phenomenology,* ed. D. Zahavi and F. Stjemfelt. Dordrecht: Kluwer. 79–92.
Daubert, Johannes. 2002. 'Remarks on the Psychology of Apperception and Judgment.' Ed. Karl Schuhmann and Trans. Marcus Brainard. *The New Yearbook for Phenomenology and Phenomenological Philosophy II.* 338–364.
DuBois, James M. 1995. *Judgment and Sachverhalt: An Introduction to Adolf Reinach's Phenomenological Realism.* Dordrecht: Kluwer Academic Publishers.

that were absorbing Husserl at the time. The distance between these two grew, and by 1931 Husserl and Pfänder stopped communicating altogether.

Hildebrand, Dietrich von. 1991. *What is Philosophy?* Chicago: Franciscan Herald Press.

Husserl, Edmund. 1975. Adolph Reinach. Trans. Lucinda Vandervort Brettler. *Philosophy and Phenomenological Research*, Vol. 35, No. 4. 571–574.

Husserl, Edmund. 1983. *Ideas Pertaining to a Pure Phenomenology and to a Phenomenological Philosophy: First Book: General Introduction to a Pure Phenomenology.* Trans. F. Kersten. Dordrecht: Kluwer Academic Publishers Group.

Husserl, Edmund. 2001. *Logical Investigations.* Trans. J. N. Findlay. Ed. Dermot Moran. London: Routledge.

Ingarden, Roman. 1975. *On the Motives Which Led Husserl to Transcendental Idealism.* Trans. A. Hannibalsson. The Hague: Nijhoff.

Kant, Immanuel. 1996. *The Critique of Pure Reason.* Trans. Werner S. Pluhar. Indianapolis: Hackett Publishing Company Inc.

Meinong, Alexius. 1960. The Theory of Objects. Ed. Roderick Chisholm. In *Realism and the Background of Phenomenology.* Illinois: The Free Press of Glencoe. 76–117.

Mitscherling, Jeff. 2010. *Aesthetic Genesis: The Origin of Consciousness in the Intentional Being of Nature.* New York: University Press of America Inc.

Mulligan, Kevin, ed. 1990. *Mind, Meaning, and Metaphysics: The Philosophy and Theory of Language of Anton Marty.* Dordrecht: Kluwer Academic Publishers.

Mulligan, Kevin, ed. 1987. *Speech Act and Sachverhalt: Reinach and The Foundations of Realist Phenomenology.* Dordrecht: Martinus Nijhoff Publishers.

Reinach, Adolf. 1981. On the Theory of Negative Judgment. Trans. Don Ferrari. Epistemology. *Aletheia: An International Journal of Philosophy*, Volume II: 9–64.

Reinach, Adolf. 1989. *Sämtliche Werke: Textkritische Ausgabe in 2 Bänden.* Eds. Karl Schuhmann and Barry Smith. Munich: Philosophia Verlag.

Schuhmann, Karl. 1996 Daubert and Meinong. *Axiomathes*, No. 1–2, 75–88.

Schuhmann, Karl. 2002. Introduction: Johannes Daubert's Lecture 'On the Psychology of Apperception and Judgment' from July 1902. *The New Yearbook for Phenomenology and Phenomenological Philosophy II.* 338–343.

Smid, Reinhold, N. 1985. An Early Interpretation of Husserl's Phenomenology: Johannes Daubert and The Logical Investigations. *Husserl Studies* 2 (3): 267–290.

Smith, Barry. 1996. *Austrian Philosophy: The Legacy of Franz Brentano.* Chicago: Open Court.

Spiegelberg, Herbert. 1994. *The Phenomenological Movement: A Historical Introduction*, 3rd ed. Dordrecht: Kluwer Academic Publishers.

Spiegelberg, Herbert. 1959. Perspektivenwandel: Konstitution eines Husserlsbildes. *Edmund Husserl 1859 – 1959.* The Hague: Martinus Nijhoff. 56–63.

Vandervort Brettler, Lucinda Ann. 1973. *The Phenomenology of Adolf Reinach: Chapters in the Theory of Knowledge and Legal Philosophy.* Ph.D. Dissertation, McGill University.

Wenisch, Fritz. 1988. Insight and Objective Necessity: A Demonstration of the Existence of Propositions Which Are Simultaneously Informative and Necessarily True. Epistemology and Logic. *Aletheia: An International Journal of Philosophy*, Volume IV: 107–197.

Willard, Dallas. 2012. Realism Sustained? Interpreting Husserl's Progression Into Idealism. *Quaestiones Disputatae* 3:1. 20–32.

Evidence-Based Phenomenology and Certainty-Based Phenomenology. Moritz Geiger's Reaction to Idealism in *Ideas I*

Michele Averchi

Abstract At first glance, Moritz Geiger's reaction to Husserl's *Ideas I* appears to be neither systematically articulated nor particularly original. Geiger talks about Husserl's idealism in *Ideas I* in just a few passages from his book *Die Wirklickheit der Wissenschaften und die Metaphysik* (1930), and in a short essay in praise of Alexander Pfänder, *Alexander Pfänders Methodische Stellung* (1933). There, Geiger seems to follow a general line of criticism shared by several so-called early phenomenologists, and most fully articulated by Jean Hering, Roman Ingarden, Theodor Celms and Max Scheler. In this paper I argue that Geiger's reaction to *Ideas I* contains some well-developed and original contributions to phenomenological thought. In particular, I defend three theses. First, Geiger's criticism of Husserl's idealism is much more original and sophisticated than it at first appears, because it rests on a complex phenomenology of "attitudes" [*Einstellungen*]. Second, Geiger offers a unique account of phenomenology as a variation of "stance" [*Haltung*], rather than a variation of attitude. Third, Geiger points to an alternative kind of phenomenology, which I call certainty-based phenomenology as opposed to an evidence-based phenomenology. Elements of this certainty-based phenomenology can be found in thinkers such as Merleau-Ponty and Ricoeur, but many of their views are significantly anticipated by Geiger.

Keywords Husserl · Geiger · Idealism · Worldview · Certainty · Evidence · Stance · Givenness

M. Averchi (✉)
The Catholic University of America, Washington, DC, USA
e-mail: averchi@cua.edu

© Springer Nature Switzerland AG 2021
R. K. B. Parker (ed.), *The Idealism-Realism Debate Among Edmund Husserl's Early Followers and Critics*, Contributions to Phenomenology 112,
https://doi.org/10.1007/978-3-030-62159-9_9

1   Why Moritz Geiger?

At first glance, Moritz Geiger's reaction to Husserl's *Ideas I* appears to be neither systematically articulated nor particularly original. His comments on *Ideas I* can be found mainly in two of his later works: a book, titled *Die Wirklicheit der Wissenschaften und die Metaphysik* (1930), and a short essay in praise of Alexander Pfänder, *Alexander Pfänders Methodische Stellung* (1933).

A first set of problems in understanding his view is connected to the scarcity and fragmentariness of the sources. Neither text mentioned above seems to have much to offer by way of a systematic critique of Husserl. In his book there are a few scattered passages, in which Geiger talks about Husserl's idealism. These can be confidently taken as references to *Ideas I*. There Geiger describes Husserl's idealism as a form of self-misinterpretation of the phenomenological stance. For Geiger, phenomenology is a certain way of looking at things. When it misinterprets itself in too radical terms—when it takes itself too seriously, so to speak— it becomes "givenness idealism," a peculiar version of idealism to be distinguished from transcendental idealism. In the short essay, there is an explicit discussion of the infamous §24 of *Ideas I*, the so-called "principle of all principles": "whatever presents itself to us in "Intuition" in an originary way (so to speak, in its actuality in person) is to be taken simply as what it affords itself as, but only within the limitations in which it affords itself there" (Husserl 2014, 43). With this principle, Husserl claims a validity for intuition as a source of knowledge, but also limits such validity to those objects given to it in evidence. Geiger criticizes Husserl's obsession with evidence and argues that phenomenology should find a place for non-evidential components of experience. The whole discussion, however, takes less than a page of the article. Thus, the overall material dedicated to a discussion of Husserl's *Ideas I* seems too limited to amount to a fully articulated response. This also connects to the more general problem of the fragmentary nature of Geiger's philosophy. Edward Casey, borrowing a term from Herbert Spiegelberg, has aptly compared it to a "torso".[1] Geiger's philosophical production is characterized by several almost self-contained contributions to disparate domains, from aesthetic experience, to relativity theory, to existential philosophy, without any explicit presentation of his main philosophical tenets. One could even question whether there is any overarching unity in Geiger's philosophy. This situation compounds the difficulty of reconstructing his thoughts on *Ideas I*.

A second set of problems is connected with the apparently unoriginal character of Geiger's remarks. In his short discussions of *Ideas I*, Geiger seems to follow a general line of criticism shared by several so-called early phenomenologists: criticisms shared by Husserl's followers in Munich and Göttingen, and most fully articulated by Hering, Ingarden, Celms and Scheler. According to this line of criticism, Husserl had abandoned the groundbreaking realism offered in the *Logical*

---

[1] See Casey's Translator's Introduction to Dufrenne 1973, xix. Compare this with Spiegelberg's description of Pfänder, Reinach, and Geiger's works (Spiegelberg 1994, 185, 192, 201).

Investigations in favor of a disappointing idealism in *Ideas I*. Since Husserl had claimed that an endorsement of idealism was a necessary conclusion for everybody endorsing a fully-fledged phenomenological philosophy, the shared effort by his opponents consisted in showing that the turn to idealism was by no means necessary, and that a realist phenomenology was more consistent with Husserl's original insight. This seems to be precisely what Geiger is also doing; he shows that idealism is not a necessary final destination of phenomenology, but rather the outcome of a self-misunderstanding. Thus, Geiger seems to be perfectly in line with the anti-idealist strategy of many early phenomenologists. Moreover, in his aforementioned article about Pfänder, Geiger offers an enthusiastic endorsement of Theodor Celms' book *Der Phänomenologische Idealismus Husserls* (Celms 1928), which he describes as "extraordinary" [*ausgezeichnet*] (Geiger 1933, 15). Pfänder himself had written a review of the book (Pfänder 1929), basically challenging Husserl to provide a convincing answer to it instead of dismissing it as a misunderstanding of his philosophy. In his book, Celms articulated a detailed presentation of Husserl's philosophy (including the latest developments), along with a criticism of its idealism. In his short article, Geiger simply encouraged any readers, who were curious to know more, to read Celms' book. Thus, the impression arises that Geiger had read Celms' book and modeled his own criticism of *Ideas I* after it. If this is the case, however, it would seem more reasonable simply to turn to Celms' book instead of trying to extract the same criticisms from Geiger's comments.[2]

To sum up: the scarcity and fragmentariness of Geiger's remarks on *Ideas I*, along with the apparently unoriginal character of his criticisms, seems to discourage the pursuit of the investigation any further. At the very least, any attempt must face these two difficulties. We must ask ourselves: is Geiger's reaction to *Ideas I* only worth exploring for the sake of historical completeness? Or does it contain some developed and original contribution to phenomenological thought?

In this paper, I argue that, notwithstanding these difficulties, the answer to the last question is affirmative. My overall claim is that Geiger's reaction to *Ideas I* contains a philosophically important contribution to phenomenology. In particular, I defend three theses. First, Geiger's criticism of Husserl's idealism is much more original and sophisticated than it looks, because it rests on a complex phenomenology of "attitudes" [*Einstellungen*]. Second, Geiger offers a unique account of phenomenology: it takes place as a variation of "stance" [*Haltung*], rather than a variation of attitude. Third and finally, Geiger's criticism of Husserl points to an alternative kind of phenomenology, which I would like to call a certainty-based phenomenology as opposed to an evidence-based phenomenology. Elements of this certainty-based phenomenology can be found in thinkers such as Merleau-Ponty and Ricoeur, but many of their views are significantly anticipated by Geiger, whose writings have the advantage of clarity and brevity. Thus, a fresh look at Geiger's reaction to *Ideas I* will have the consequence of re-opening questions about the goals and method of phenomenology, especially in these years in which phenomenology is on the rise.

---

[2] For a discussion of Celms' critique of Husserl, see Parker 2020.

2   Idealism and Realism

Geiger's reaction to *Ideas I* must be located in the context of the so-called "idealism-realism" debate in phenomenology. In fact, the relevance of Geiger's reaction to *Ideas I* can be seen in terms of its original contribution to the "idealism-realism" debate. More detailed reconstructions of this debate have been provided elsewhere, but it is necessary to mention some facts about it in order to situate Geiger's comments.

As I have mentioned above, several early phenomenologists expressed puzzlement and disappointment at Husserl's alleged idealist turn in *Ideas I*, and they distanced themselves from this development of his phenomenology.[3] Their criticisms started to take printed form more than a decade after the original publication of *Ideas I* in 1913. One of the first critical appraisals of Husserl's *Ideas I* from a realist-phenomenological standpoint can be found in Jean Hering's *Phénoménologie et Philosophie Religieuse*, which devotes an appendix to the primacy of consciousness in the infamous §49 of *Ideas I* (Hering 1925, 83–86). Hering's move is threefold. First, he enucleates an argument for idealism from §49 of *Ideas I*. Second, he argues that the rest of Husserl's phenomenology (especially the *Logical Investigations*) does not depend on that argument, so that one can reject it and still appropriate Husserl's phenomenology as a whole. Third, he directly argues against the argument for idealism enucleated from §49 of *Ideas I*. The whole strategy of the realist-phenomenological reaction to Husserl's idealism is already present here. To mention some of the most important developments of the debate: Theodor Celms would produce a book-length presentation and criticism of Husserl's idealism (the aforementioned *Der Phänomenologische Idealismus Husserls*) along very similar lines to Hering's criticism, and so would Roman Ingarden, in his later *On the Motives which led Husserl to Transcendental Idealism* (Ingarden 1975).[4] Other prominent phenomenologists would provide their contributions to the debate as well: for instance, Max Scheler in his "Idealismus-Realismus" (Scheler 1927).

A historical reconstruction of the different phases of the "idealism-realism" debate lies beyond the scope of this paper. In order to understand Geiger's contribution to it, let us instead take a step back and briefly consider Husserl's alleged argument for idealism in §49, the so-called "annihilation of the world." Why did it seem

---

[3] Moritz Geiger (1880–1937) studied philosophy and psychology in Munich under Theodor Lipps in 1899–1904 and experimental psychology in Leipzig under Wilhelm Wundt in 1901–02. Back in Munich, he joined the group of Lipps' students who became interested in Husserl's *Logical Investigations* and became known as the "Munich Circle" of phenomenology. In 1906 he took one class with Husserl during the summer semester. He also became one of the co-editors of the *Jahrbuch für Philosophie und phänomenologische Forschung*. He taught in Munich (1915) and Göttingen (1923). After the National Socialist party came to power in Germany he emigrated to the United States and taught at Vassar College until his death. A bibliography of his works can be found at Spiegelberg 1994, 212.

[4] Originally published in Polish as *O motywach, które doprowadziły Husserla do transcendentalnego idealizmu* (1963).

so controversial to some of Husserl's own followers? Confronting this question will make it possible to better appreciate Geiger's sophisticated answer to the problem.

In order to understand Husserl's apparently idealist conclusions in §49, we need to consider Husserl's argument as a whole, as he builds it in the course of the second section of *Ideas I*. Husserl's own presentation is much more nuanced and sophisticated. For reasons of space, I will condense it into three passages, the ones on which the later idealism-realism debate revolves.

Husserl's argument for idealism begins with §42, after the phenomenological reduction has already been performed. In §42, Husserl claims that an eidetic analysis of phenomena reveals an essential difference between two kinds of entities: being as experience and being as thing. In other words, entities belonging to the kind "experience" and entities belonging to the kind "thing" present an essentially different eidetic structure. In short, experiences and things manifest themselves in two essentially different ways. As Husserl puts it: "A fundamentally essential difference thus surfaces between being as experience and being as thing. The regional essence of experience (specifically, the particular region of the *cogitatio*) has the intrinsic property of being perceivable in immanent perception, whereas the essence of a spatial thing does not have this property" (Husserl 2014, 74). "Experiences" [*Erlebnisse*] are the intentional acts that manifest themselves in our stream of consciousness, and through which we have access to worldly things: perceptions, recollections, volitions, imaginings, categorial acts etc. "Things" [*Dinge*] are the real entities which populate the world around us: a house, a tree, a dog, other people…in short, everything that is there in objective space. Husserl remarks that an essential feature of experiences is that they are perceivable in immanent perception, while this is not the case with things. When I reflect upon my experience, I can have an experience as the object of my higher-order intentional act. For instance, suppose I am perceiving a house. I can reflect upon my experience and have the perception (i.e. the perceiving) of the house as a higher-order intentional object (so that I can say "I am perceiving a house"). The same is possible with all the other sorts of experiences. Husserl's point is that experiences can be adequately perceived through immanent perception. When I reflect upon my perception of the house, I grasp my perception (the experience) just as it is, as it is given. To see the point here, let's contrast this with the case of things. Things are not perceivable in immanent perception, because things are never adequately manifested through it. In other words, things always present themselves through profiles, with hidden parts. For instance, I can never perceive a house from all its sides at once. For Husserl, this fact is not just an empirical limitation of our subjectivity, but rather belongs essentially to the way of givenness of things: being a thing and manifesting itself through profiles are one and the same. If this is the case, it follows that experiences can be adequately given through inner perception, while things are always only imperfectly given. In Husserl's words: "To be imperfect in this manner *in infinitum* is inherent to the ineradicable essence of the correlation between a thing and perception of it" (Husserl 2014, 78).

In the second step of his argument for idealism, Husserl claims that experiences have intrinsically absolute existence, while things do not. In other words, their manifestation is a sufficient condition for their existence. Once an experience is manifested in our stream of consciousness, it can never be the case that a future course of events will show that such experience did not exist. In Husserl's words: "If the reflecting apprehension is directed at my experience, then I have apprehended an absolute self, the existence of which is intrinsically undeniable. In other words, discerning its nonexistence is intrinsically impossible. It would be absurd to consider it possible that an experience, thus given, would truly not be" (Husserl 2014, 82). The existence of experiences, once it is grasped, is thus absolute because it is intrinsically undeniable. In the example of a perception of a house, imagine that I find out that it was just a hallucination. There is no house out there. Still, Husserl claims, this will not revoke the perception-like existence of that experience: I have had the experience of perceiving a house, even if there is no house. For experiences, manifestation and being are one and the same. Things, on the other hand, have an intrinsically contingent existence. This is related to their essentially being manifested through profiles. The house I perceive is never fully adequately given in perception. It could be that I walk around it and realize it was only a façade. Or I could find out that I have always misperceived its color due to poor illumination. Or I could find out that it is an incredibly persistent hallucination. With real things their manifestation is never enough to vouchsafe for their existence. As Husserl puts it: "It holds, as a matter of an essential law, that thingly existence is never an existence necessarily demanded by the givenness but is instead in a certain way always contingent. That means that it is always possible that the further course of experience [*Erfahrung*] necessitates giving up what has been posited already as experientially correct" (Husserl 2014, 83).

In the third and final step of his argument for idealism, Husserl claims that a necessary conclusion follows from the two previous steps: the existence of consciousness is independent of the existence of the external world, while the existence of the external world is relative to the existence of consciousness. According to Husserl, in our everyday life we take things to have absolute existence. We believe that things are out there as things in themselves, and that the world would exist as such even if there were no consciousness to which it could be an intentional correlate. However, the two previous steps have shown that things essentially manifest themselves only through profiles, and thus that their existence is only contingent, never absolute. Husserl concludes that, since things are not complete in themselves, a reference to the existence of a consciousness capable of perceiving them is intrinsic to their essence.

In simpler terms, things are intentional correlates of consciousness, and nothing more. Thus, their existence requires the existence of consciousness. As Husserl puts it: "the entire spatiotemporal world [...] is, in terms of its sense, a merely intentional being, that is to say, the sort of being that has the merely secondary, relative sense of a being for a consciousness. It is a being that consciousness posits in its experiences, a being that is in principle only capable of being intuited and determined as something identical on the basis of motivated manifolds of appearance, but beyond this is a nothing" (Husserl 2014, 90). On the other hand, experiences have absolute existence, as seen in the previous steps. This means that their existence is independent of the existence of things, so that consciousness would survive an annihilation of the world. In the infamous §49, Husserl's conclusion could not be more explicit: "The immanent being is, therefore, without doubt absolute being in the sense that, in principle, *nulla "re" indiget ad existendum* [it needs no "thing" to exist]. On the other hand, the world of the transcendent "res" is utterly dependent upon consciousness, and, indeed, not some logically thought up consciousness, but a currently actual consciousness" (Husserl 2014, 89). To sum up Husserl's argument for idealism: (1) an eidetic analysis of phenomena reveals an essential difference between two kinds of entities: being as experience, and being as thing; (2) experiences have intrinsically absolute existence, while things do not; (3) the existence of consciousness is independent of the existence of the external world, while the existence of the external world is relative to the existence of consciousness.

This was, roughly speaking, Husserl's argument for idealism as it was understood by the "early phenomenologists." As seen earlier, their sense of disagreement eventually turned into an open debate, after the publication of Hering's book. Husserl himself felt the need to qualify and clarify his position, for instance in the so-called *Nachwort* from 1930, in which he acknowledged shortcomings in the presentation of *Ideas I*, although he still maintained the necessity of endorsing a very special form of idealism for phenomenology. The discussion seemed to have taken the form of a traditional metaphysical debate, albeit carried out with phenomenological tools. In fact, it was about a disagreement about what there is, and, more in particular, about the kind of being proper to things: phenomenological realists claimed that things are absolute beings, while phenomenological idealists claimed that things are relative beings.

On this background, we can appreciate the originality of Geiger's contribution. Unlike several other participants, Geiger did not engage in a straightforward phenomenological-metaphysical debate. For instance, he did not try to argue in a straightforward way that we must attribute absolute being to things, rather than relative being. In fact, Geiger thought that such a straightforward metaphysical debate was doomed to fail, because no involved party would be able to convince the opponent by the sheer force of philosophical argument. In this regard, Geiger seems to be thinking of Kant's dialectic of pure reason, in which all-encompassing metaphysical models unceasingly overturn one another, with no possibility to settle the argument. In his aforementioned book, *Die Wirklichkeit der Wissenschaften und die Metaphysik*, Geiger remarks: "the all-encompassing philosophical systems are predelineated in their fundamental direction of resolution by the attitudes. In other words, the immanent ontological structure given through an attitude determines the transcendent ontological structure, and makes up for their character as a self-sufficient, independent foundation, free from every preconception" (Geiger 1966, 144).

Thus, the all-encompassing philosophical systems present themselves as purely rational constructions, free of all presupposition. If this were the case, it should be possible to settle the dispute among them by means of philosophical arguments. However, in fact philosophical systems are "predelineated" as Geiger puts it, by pre-theoretical implicit assumptions. Such preliminary assumptions guide the development of philosophical systems, without their developers necessarily being fully aware of them. As a result, proponents of opposite philosophical systems necessarily fail to convince one another, because they move within different sets of presuppositions. Instead of a straightforward philosophical debate, what is therefore needed is an analysis of the implicit preliminary assumptions of the opposing philosophical systems. This is precisely Geiger's strategy in the phenomenological idealism-realism debate. Geiger shares the early phenomenologists' disappointment with Husserl's argument for idealism in *Ideas I*, but instead of developing a counter argument Geiger works to provide a genealogy of both idealism and realism. He wants to show how both philosophical positions are outcomes of preliminary assumptions played out at an implicit pre-theoretical level. Only after an analysis of this implicit pre-theoretical level is in place does a convincing criticism of Husserl's idealism becomes possible. However, since such assumptions are implicit, it is not possible to address them in a straightforward way, as if they were axioms of a theory. Geiger's tool for such genealogy is, rather, a notion familiar to phenomenologists and crucial for Husserl himself, that is, the notion of an attitude. Geiger's stance towards the idealism-realism debate makes sense in light of his account of attitudes.

3   Attitudes

The notion of attitude [*Einstellung*] is a crucial one both for Husserl and Geiger, but neither provides a fully-fledged definition of it. "Attitude" was a common word in different domains in the German-speaking milieu at the beginning of the twentieth century. Most notably, it was commonly used in photography and in psychology.[5] In psychology, in particular, "attitude" was and is used to designate a preliminary disposition that influences mental and bodily processes. The first uses can be traced back to Darwin and to Ludwig Lange, an experimental psychologist affiliated with Wilhem Wundt's so-called Würzburg School. Lange found out that subjects prepared to press a telegraph key at a signal reacted more quickly than subjects whose attention was focused on the signal rather than on the key (Lange, 1888). At the time Husserl and Geiger were writing, the study of attitudes had expanded significantly, mainly through the further work of Wilhelm Wundt's followers. In general terms, an attitude is a readiness or inclination to respond to the world in a certain way.

Husserl made the concept of attitude relevant in phenomenology presumably due to the influence of the empiriocriticist philosopher Richard Avenarius. In fact, one of Husserl's first important discussions of attitudes occurs in a comment on Avenarius' idea of a "natural concept of world" in the important 1910/11 course "Basic Problems of Phenomenology." There, Husserl begins by talking about the

---

[5] See "Einige Grundbegriffe der Transzendentalen Phaenomenologie: Intentionalität, Einstellung und Reduktion" in Broekman 1963.

"different attitudes in which experience and cognition can take place" (Hua XIII, 112) and contrasts in particular the natural attitude "in which we all live" (Hua XIII, 112) with the phenomenological attitude, which we access when we "perform the philosophical change of gaze [*Blickänderung*]" (Hua XIII, 112). According to the attitude we are in, the natural attitude or the phenomenological attitude, we respond to the world in a different way. As Husserl points out, the natural attitude is the "default" attitude in which we find ourselves firstly and for the most part, while the phenomenological attitude can be accessed only through a peculiar change of gaze.

A complete discussion of Husserl's account of attitudes is beyond the scope of this paper.[6] What is important here is to see the connection between the idealism-realism debate and the phenomenological account of attitudes. As the doctrine of attitudes shows, realism, before being a philosophical doctrine, is a main feature of our natural attitude: we are, by default, realists. In other words, we tend to take things in the world around us as real entities, as "things in themselves." This holds true even if this tendency is disappointed on occasion by dreams, hallucinations, illusions, etc. As already noted in the course of Husserl's argument for idealism, we have a constant tendency to take things around us as "absolute beings." Thus, this implicit ontological commitment[7] is an important feature of the natural attitude. By the very fact that we are in the natural attitude, we are committed to the view that things in the world around us are things in themselves. Or, in other words, the reason why we take things around us to be real and existing is not first and foremost because we have particular reasons or evidence for their reality, but rather because we find ourselves in the natural attitude. Husserl calls this implicit ontological commitment the "general thesis" of the natural attitude, which he articulates as follows: "I find constantly on hand opposite me the one spatiotemporal actuality to which I myself belong, as do all other human beings who find themselves in it and related to it in a similar way. I find the 'actuality' (the word already says as much) to be there in advance and I also take [it] as it affords itself to me, as being there. No doubt or rejection of anything given in the natural world changes anything in the natural attitude's general thesis" (Husserl 2014, 53). As long as we are in the natural attitude, such ontological commitment is unshakeable, no matter how much evidence there might be against it.

According to Husserl, phenomenology is carried out from within a different attitude than the natural one. When we do phenomenology, we leave the attitude of our everyday existence, and we assume a new attitude. In this new attitude, we respond to the surrounding world in a different way. In particular—and this is crucial—in the phenomenological attitude we leave behind the realism of the natural attitude. We are no longer straightforward realists. The transition from the natural attitude to

---

[6] For an excellent and recent discussion of this topic, see Staiti 2014, Chapter 3.

[7] I consider the expression "ontological commitment" clearer than the expression "metaphysical presupposition." Here the discussion is about the existence in themselves of certain entities. Metaphysics traditionally includes discussions of further dimensions of being, such as essence, which are not at stake here. Thus, I think that the expression "ontological commitment" is more precise, as it univocally refers to existence.

the phenomenological attitude implies a suspension of the ontological commitment proper to the natural attitude. In Husserl's terms, we must "bracket" or suspend the general thesis of the natural attitude, so that the realism of the natural attitude is of no use for us anymore.

Before moving to Geiger's account of attitudes, four points are worth stressing here. First, an account of attitudes provides a genealogy of realism. Realism is the outcome of the implicit ontological commitment, called the "general thesis," which underlies our everyday life. Second, according to Husserl such realism can be suspended. For philosophical purposes, we can temporarily "bracket" the general thesis and put it out of play. Third, according to Husserl phenomenology takes place within its own proper attitude, different from the natural attitude. Indeed, an essential feature of phenomenology is precisely the suspension of the ontological commitment proper to the natural attitude. In other words, phenomenology does not take place within a straightforward realism (which Husserl significantly calls "naive realism"). Fourth, Husserl's argument for idealism takes place from within the phenomenological attitude, when the ontological commitment of the natural attitude has already been suspended. If it were not the case, the argument for idealism would lose all its strength, because nothing can confute realism from within the natural attitude. This will be a crucial point in Geiger's answer to Husserl; his strategy is to show that, in fact, we do not leave the natural attitude when we do phenomenology, so that the argument for idealism does not need to be taken too seriously.

Geiger's most articulated account of attitudes can be found in his aforementioned 1930 book *Die Wirklichkeit der Wissenschaften und die Metaphysik*. I will focus primarily on the elements useful for a reconstruction of Geiger's stance in the idealism-realism debate. In fact, in his book Geiger provides a genealogy of both realism and idealism, together with a rebuttal of Husserl's idealism as a self-misunderstanding of phenomenology. As already stated, the connection between an account of attitudes and a rebuttal of Husserl's idealism is an important element of originality in Geiger's reaction to *Ideas I*.

The framework of Geiger's account of attitudes is, again, the realization of a widespread clash between opposing worldviews. For Geiger the contrast between idealism and realism is a local episode within a greater tension, characteristic of modern culture, between the natural sciences and the human sciences. In particular, the natural sciences present themselves more and more as the ultimate criterion for answering metaphysical questions, namely questions of "what there is." In other words, the natural sciences are increasingly expected to provide an answer to the question on what reality really is. This high expectation is fostered on one hand by the impressive success of the natural sciences and, on the other hand, by a self-understanding of the natural sciences as a purely rational, evidence-based and pre-suppositionless form of knowledge. Natural sciences are understood to be unbiased and rigorous, so that no other worldview can compete with their pronouncements about reality: "there is no knowledge of reality except the one carried out by sciences" (Geiger 1966, 6). Geiger strongly disagrees with this view, which he labels "scientism" (with the -ism proper of ideology) and which he considers a dangerous dogmatism. His rebuttal of scientism goes through an account of attitudes. Geiger wants to show that, far from being presuppositionless as they claim, the natural sciences too take place within an attitude, a tendency to respond to the world in a certain way. Thus, the natural sciences rely on implicit preliminary assumptions to which they are committed without any evidence: the evidence provided by experiments relies on such preliminary assumptions, far from founding or justifying them. As the reader might have noticed, Geiger is perhaps drawing upon the discussion about the role of paradigms in the sciences, a concept popularized by Alexandre Koyré and Thomas Kuhn.[8] Instead of "paradigm" Geiger uses the familiar notion of "attitude."

In his book, Geiger contrasts two basic attitudes, the so-called "naturalistic attitude" and the so-called "immediate attitude." The two attitudes look at the world from two different sets of preliminary assumptions. Most importantly, the two attitudes differ in their implicit ontological commitments. As noted before, for Husserl too ontological commitments are crucial components of attitudes. It is important to stress once again that those are preliminary commitments: *by the very fact* that I am in a certain attitude, I have an implicit answer to the question "what is there?" It is not that I give such an answer because I have reasons or evidence for it. I might have those, but this is not the reason why I answer in such a way. The reason is, rather, the fact that I find myself in a certain attitude, and therefore that I endorse the corresponding set of ontological commitments. What are, according to Geiger, the ontological commitments proper to the "naturalistic attitude" and to the "immediate attitude"?

The *naturalistic attitude* is, needless to say, the attitude from within which the natural sciences are developed. It entails two ontological commitments: a) there is an external world, existing in-itself and founded in-itself; b) there is a second ontological domain, the mental, which is not necessary for the existence of the external world. Once again, these are *not* outcomes of scientific investigation, but rather implicit assumptions in the naturalistic attitude. From within this attitude, only external things necessarily exist, while everything else might or might not. The *immediate attitude* is, first and foremost, the attitude of our everyday life. It closely resembles Husserl's "natural attitude," and the human sciences are developed from within this attitude. Its ontological commitments are: a) there is both a subjective and an objective world; b) there are multiple non-physical objective realms. So, the answer to the question "what is there?" proper to the immediate attitude is fivefold: psychic entities (e.g. the mental image of a house), physical objects (e.g. a house), real spiritual objects (e.g. a house renovation agreement), ideal objects (e.g. the concept of a house as such) and mental objects (e.g. the mental act of perceiving of a house). In the immediate attitude, we take all these different sorts of entities to be "existing" in a genuine sense, even if their modes of existence are vastly different from one another. As with Husserl's natural attitude, the immediate attitude entails

---

[8] In his review of Geiger's book, Patočka describes it as a "polemic against scientism" (Patočka 1999, 421).

a "general thesis," that is, a commitment to the existence of these different sorts of entities.

With this, Geiger has provided the first half of the genealogy for the idealism-realism debate. In agreement with Husserl, Geiger argues that realism is not first of all a philosophical doctrine, but rather an essential feature of our everyday life. We are realists not because of compelling reasons or evidence, but rather because such an ontological commitment belongs by default to the immediate attitude, in which we usually find ourselves. The multifaceted realism proper to the human sciences builds on the ground of the implicit preliminary assumptions proper to this pre-philosophical realism. In Geiger's words, such assumptions are not full-blown concepts (*Begriffe*) but rather anticipatory grasps (*Vor-Griffe*). In order to understand the second half of Geiger's genealogy, namely the origin of idealism, another question needs to be answered: what is the place of phenomenology in Geiger's account of attitudes? Here, Geiger's answer is intentionally and strikingly different from Husserl's.

Geiger complicates his account of the immediate attitude, claiming that there are different versions of it. We can be in the immediate attitude in three different ways, by focusing on different aspects of our experience of the world. Geiger calls these three different ways of being in the immediate attitude "stances" [*Haltungen*]. The first stance is the *objective stance*. In it, our primary focus is on the objects of our intentional acts. This is the most straightforward stance. For instance, I look at a house and my thematic focus is on the house itself. The second stance is the *subjective stance*. In it, our primary focus is on ourselves, the subjects. For instance, I look at a house, and I focus on my own experience of the house: what can I see of it and what I cannot, how I like it, what relevance it has to me, etc. I am still looking at the world around me, but I am here focusing on my perspective on it. The third and last stance is the *givenness stance* [*Gegebenheitshaltung*]. In it, I focus neither on the object nor on the subject, but rather on the intuitive content of my experience. For instance, I look at a house, and I focus on its color, its shape, its varying profiles as I move around it etc. Geiger goes to great lengths carefully to distinguish the subjective stance and the givenness stance. He offers the following example. In the subjective stance, I look at a table in front of me, and I know that there is a smaller one behind me, but I realize that I cannot see it. I take for granted the existence of the objective world, and I focus on my perspective on it. In the givenness stance, instead, I focus merely on the content of my perception and "I don't know anything of the objective world" (Geiger 1966, 61). In the subjective stance, I am focusing on my perspective on the objective world while minding that the objective world is out there, but in the givenness stance I am focusing on the intuitive fulness of the given and *ignoring* the objective world. Geiger's account of stances fits his more general purpose of accounting for the root of different disciplines and worldviews in attitudes. Thus, for instance, as the natural sciences are rooted in the naturalistic attitude, human sciences such as psychology and history are rooted in the subjective stance of the immediate attitude. Psychology, for instance, presupposes the objective world, but focuses on how a subject is experiencing it. The givenness stance is instead the kind of response proper to the visual artist: when a painter is painting a house, for instance, he or she just focuses on "what is intuitively given as such, not insofar as it is in a strong sense objective or subjective.

In his account of the givenness stance, Geiger draws on his previous research on aesthetic contemplation, presented in his study *Beiträge zur Phänomenologie des äestetisches Genusses* (1913). There, confusingly enough, he had defined aesthetic contemplation as an "attitude," and characterized it in the following terms: "while before we immediately looked at the object through the intuitive data, now the ray of consciousness stops at the sensuous data and takes interest in the intuitive fulfill-ment, rather than in the something appearing in this intuitive fulfillment" (Geiger 1913, 645). In his example, I can switch from looking at the man in front of me, to the intuitive fulfillment through which the man is now given to me." This switch of gaze is proper to the visual artist and to the enjoyer of art: it is what we perform every time we enjoy a painting. So, if subjective stance is at the origin of human sciences as psychology and history, what is givenness stance at the origin of? What discipline is born of the givenness stance? Geiger's answer is unequivocal: it is phenomenology. Phenomenology has as its condition of possibility the transition from the objective stance to the givenness stance. As Geiger puts it, "there is only one science that investigates the given as such: phenomenology in its original for-mation, elements of which can already be found in Aristotle" (Geiger 1966, 64). Phenomenologists train themselves to abide in the givenness stance, in order to develop a scientific, systematic account of the domain of the given as such, which is a task not yet fulfilled by any other discipline.

The importance of this account of the origin of phenomenology can hardly be exaggerated, for it is here that we find one of the most relevant aspects of Geiger's reaction to *Ideas I*, as well as the basis for his original contribution to the idealism-realism debate. Two points are particularly worth stressing.

First, a characteristic feature of the givenness stance is that it focuses on the given as such, beyond the subjective/objective divide. In Geiger's words, "I don't know anything of the objective world" (Geiger 1966, 61): I look at a house, or at a painting, or at the content of my imagination with the same focus on the intuitive fulfillment. As said earlier, the givenness stance is the one within which phenome-nology takes place. From this, it follows that phenomenology partakes in the prima facie metaphysical neutrality of the givenness stance. Insofar as it takes place within the givenness stance, phenomenology as such "does not know anything of the objec-tive world," but simply accounts for the essential features of the given qua given. In making this claim, Geiger distances himself from a straightforward realistic under-standing of phenomenology, as the one proper to other early phenomenologists such as Reinach or Conrad-Martius. For those straightforward realists, phenomenology revolves around a peculiar kind of intuition, the intuition of essences [*Wesensanschauung*], that gives access to ideal entities as a kind of real entity. Geiger's understanding of phenomenology is different, in that it is halfway between such straightforward realism and Husserl's doctrine of the phenomenological reduc-tion. For Geiger, even before the intuition of essence, there is the transition from the objective stance to the givenness stance, in which the focus shifts from the objective world to the given as such. For this reason, Geiger could neither endorse the idea

that a strong realism essentially belongs to phenomenology nor that Husserl's idealism was a sheer betrayal of phenomenology. Rather, Geiger acknowledges that
something here inclines us toward idealism, because the givenness stance implies a
variation within our everyday look at things. Thus, Geiger's position in the debate
appears more moderate than others.

Second, however, Geiger carefully crafts his account of the origin of phenomenology as an alternative to Husserl's account in *Ideas I*. In opposition to Husserl,
Geiger argues that phenomenology is a stance, rather than an attitude, which means
that phenomenology takes place from within the immediate attitude of everyday
life. As discussed earlier, Husserl thinks that the natural attitude of everyday life is
characterized by a "general thesis," an implicit realistic ontological commitment.
The transition to the phenomenological attitude implies a suspension of such ontological commitment, and this paves the way to a phenomenological idealism: once
the general thesis is suspended, a phenomenological consideration of the essential
features of givenness leads to Husserl's argument for idealism. Geiger's account,
however, is different. Geiger agrees with Husserl that the immediate attitude of
everyday life entails an implicit realistic ontological commitment—more precisely,
a fivefold one. In Geiger's view, however, phenomenology takes place within a variation of stance, rather than a variation of attitude. The givenness stance, from which
phenomenology originates, is an inner variation of the immediate attitude. The distance from *Ideas I* could not be more explicit: for Geiger, there is no such thing as a
phenomenological attitude different from the natural attitude. Rather, phenomenology operates within the immediate attitude. This means that phenomenology, as
seen earlier, "ignores" the ontological commitment of the immediate attitude but
does not at all suspend or bracket it. Phenomenology in itself is metaphysically
neutral, but it is always embedded in the broader context of the realism proper to the
immediate attitude. As seen earlier, the realism of everyday life is not the outcome
of reasons or evidence, even if they might be there, too. Rather, it intrinsically
belongs, as a presupposition, to the immediate attitude. Geiger is arguing that, as
phenomenologists, we never leave the ground of that presupposition. According to
Geiger, this conclusion results from the very description of the shift of gaze from the
straightforward immediate attitude to the givenness stance. In fact, such a shift
never includes any suspension of our belief in the existence of the world, but rather
just an ignoring of such belief: suspending a belief and ignoring a belief are two
different processes, because in the second case I am still implicitly committed to its
validity. Phenomenology never frees itself from that implicit realism, nor does it
have to. It is a variation of the immediate attitude and not an alternative to it.

The consequences for the idealism-realism debate are crucial, since Geiger uses
the genealogy of the phenomenological stance to settle that debate. The usual strategy, from Hering to Celms to Ingarden, was to show that idealism does not necessarily follow from the phenomenological method, and that there are arguments
against idealism and in favor of realism. Geiger's strategy, instead, is to show that
we are by default committed to realism, and that we never abandon this commitment while doing phenomenology. Thus, there is no need for positive arguments in
favor of realism and against idealism. For Geiger, Husserl's argument for idealism

is simply a non-starter, an intellectual enterprise that should not be taken too seriously, precisely because realism is more than a metaphysical system: it is the air we live and breathe. If this is the case, there is no room for any idealism-realism debate. While other phenomenologists reply to Husserl's argument with counter-arguments, Geiger's reply is an analysis of attitudes, which shows: a) that realism is an implicit commitment of our everyday life; b) that we never leave it in doing phenomenology. If this holds true, the whole problem of idealism loses much of its grip and its urgency.

A final component of Geiger's reaction to *Ideas I* needs to be explored, namely his account of the origin of idealism. So far, we saw how his account of attitudes traces the origin of realism. Geiger claims that there are two basic attitudes, the naturalistic attitude and the immediate attitude. The immediate attitude harbors the kind of everyday realism we have been dealing with, while the naturalistic attitude harbors a reduced form of realism, limited to physical entities. What about idealism? If we abide in realism, how is idealism even conceivable? As anticipated, Geiger also thinks that something in the givenness attitude lends itself to a misunderstanding in the direction of idealism. Thus, for Geiger, idealism is ultimately a self-misunderstanding of phenomenology, but an understandable one. Ultimately, a difference stands out in the very understanding of phenomenology. I propose to call Geiger's understanding a "certainty-based" phenomenology, as opposed to the "evidence-based" phenomenology exhibited by Husserl in *Ideas I*. A discussion of Geiger's account of idealism shall present this alternative in more detail.

4   Idealism

As seen earlier, the givenness stance is metaphysically neutral. As Geiger puts it, "only the being-given to a subject is relevant to it; the oppositions between realism and idealism lay outside its sphere of vision" (Geiger 1966, 65). While in the givenness stance, we ignore the realist ontological commitment proper to the immediate attitude, which we nonetheless still inhabit. The ontological commitment is still there, but is, as it were, out of focus. Phenomenology is the science that develops a systematic account of the world from within the givenness stance. For this reason, Geiger warns, there is an inherent risk to phenomenology, namely that it loses track of the ontological commitment of the immediate attitude. In other words, the givenness stance lends itself to a self-misunderstanding that leads to idealism. Since in the givenness stance the world is taken into account only insofar as it is given to a subject, it is tempting to think that this is all that the world is, and that "being" means "being given to a subject" (or, in Berkeley's famous expression, "*esse est percipi*.") For this reason, phenomenology always runs the risk of slipping into, or being deformed (*Umformung*) into, idealism. For Geiger, the reality of the world is not in itself part of the given. Rather, the reality of the world is part of the ontological commitment proper to the immediate attitude, within which the givenness stance takes place. Thus, the idealism arising from the givenness stance is a misunderstanding that takes the part for the whole. In fact, such idealism just focuses on the given, and, since it cannot find the reality of the world as part of the given, hastily moves to dismiss it—being forgetful that its own operations are embedded within the framework of the immediate attitude and within its inherent realism. On several occasions, including his *Nachwort*, Husserl carefully distinguishes his phenomenological idealism from Berkeley's idealism and from neo-Kantian idealism. Geiger agrees with such differentiations and considers the genealogy of these three different kinds of idealism. According to him, neo-Kantian idealism has its roots in the aforementioned subjective stance, which focuses on the subjective perspective on the world. This is different from Berkeley's and Husserl's idealism, which moves from the givenness stance and focuses on givenness. According to Geiger, this explains the different role of the subject in these two versions of idealism. In subjective idealism, the reality of the world is never suspended or denied, but rather interpreted as the outcome of a subjective position: the world is real, and it is so because the subject posits it as so. In givenness idealism, the key role is played by consciousness rather than by the subject. Here there is not necessarily an activity on the part of a strong egological principle, but rather the succession of experiences. The reality of the world is suspended and unmasked as "naïve," while objects are interpreted as givenness for a subject. This holds true both for Berkeley's and Husserl's idealism. In stressing this difference, Geiger makes room for Husserl's distance from neo-Kantian idealism and especially for his accusation that that kind of idealism is naïve, because it takes the existence of the world for granted. At the same time, Geiger argues that Husserl's version of idealism is not a real overcoming of that naivety, because it misunderstands the givenness stance in absolute terms.

Two important consequences follow from Geiger's genealogy of idealism. First, his position towards Husserl's idealism is more moderate than that of other early phenomenologists. He does not take idealism to be a betrayal of the original intuition of phenomenology or as some big theoretical mistake. Rather, Geiger acknowledges that in phenomenology something lends itself to an idealist tendency. According to him, Husserl has fallen prey to the temptation of following that tendency. Thus, an adequate answer to Husserl is a genealogy of idealism, rather than a straightforward attack or refutation: it is a matter of showing Husserl what he himself was unable to see. Secondly, as already stressed, this moderation is shown by the fact that the givenness stance is metaphysically neutral. The problem of the reality of the world simply does not play a role in it, because the reality of the world is not a "given," but rather an implicit assumption. This seems to suggest that phenomenology does not have the resources within itself to cope with the problem of the reality of the world. In Geiger's view, a phenomenological dispute about that seems to be hopeless. If phenomenology takes place within the givenness stance, and the givenness stance necessarily ignores the reality of the world, it follows that phenomenology ultimately has no ultimate grip on this metaphysical question. Geiger's implicit conclusion seems to be, thus, that phenomenology cannot aspire to be "first philosophy."

An alternative to phenomenological idealism can be found, according to Geiger, in Pfänder and in the Munich Circle of early phenomenologists. I would like to call this alternative "certainty-based phenomenology." The basic difference from Husserl, according to Geiger, is that this approach starts with a pure description of givenness, rather than with logical and epistemological problems. Husserl's initial concern with a theory of science leads him to use phenomenology to have undoubtable evidence as a foundation for science, and this in turn leads him to idealism. The alternative approach, instead, starts with the givenness stance and develops a systematic account of the world from within it. This different starting point has, for Geiger, far-reaching consequences. As Geiger had argued in his book, in our everyday life we find ourselves in the so-called immediate attitude. A core component of it is a fivefold realistic ontological commitment: we take different kinds of entities to be real, including things in the external world. For Geiger we do not leave the immediate attitude when we do phenomenology, because the givenness stance is an inner variation of the immediate attitude. Thus, our belief in the reality of the external world is both unfounded on evidence and undoubtable. We believe in the reality of the external world because we are in the immediate attitude, and, since we don't leave it while doing phenomenology, there is no point in doubting it: we are certain of the reality of the external world.

A crucial difference between an "evidence-based phenomenology" and a "certainty-based phenomenology" becomes clear here. An evidence-based phenomenology takes skepticism and a Cartesian-type universal doubt very seriously, so that it tries to provide evidence-based justification for our beliefs. A certainty-based phenomenology, instead, proceeds by showing that skepticism and universal doubt do not need to be taken too seriously, because they are never able fully to undermine our ontological commitment to realism. If this is the case, we do not need to provide any justification or positive evidence for our belief in the reality of the external world. Rather, we keep it undisturbed. Note that this alternative form of phenomenology is not "naive" or "commonsensical": it is not the case that it ignores the problem of the universal doubt. Rather, the strategy is different. Both evidence-based phenomenology and certainty-based phenomenology answer to the challenge of universal doubt with trying to provide reasons, but they do so in two different ways: evidence-based phenomenology looks for evidence for our beliefs, while certainty-based evidence provides reasons why we can dismiss the doubt. As Geiger puts it: "Pfänder takes a different way: a seen house is given as real, so it must therefore be taken as real. If we hold on rigorously to this standpoint, we come upon a realistic interpretation of the world, like the one Pfänder and the Munich school—including, in those years, Scheler—have endorsed" (Geiger 1933, 15). I look at a house and I take it to be real. Then a Cartesian-type doubt arises, that maybe my whole perception is unreliable and the external world is in fact not real. However, as long as I stay in the immediate attitude, as happens while I am doing phenomenology, I do not need to take that doubt seriously, so that I can keep taking the house as real. Husserl's evidence-based approach led him to dismiss the "reality moment" as extra-phenomenological—because it was not grounded in evidence—and thus to idealism. The Munich phenomenologists' certainty-based approach instead led them to keep the reality moment even if not grounded in evidence, because it is part of our immediate attitude, thus ending in a "realistic understanding of the world" (Geiger 1933, 15).

5   Conclusion

It is time now to draw some conclusions. Geiger's reaction to *Ideas I* takes place in the context of the intra-phenomenological idealism-realism debate prompted by Husserl's argument for idealism in the book. Geiger shares with many other early phenomenologists an endorsement of realism and a critical stance towards Husserl's proposal of a phenomenological idealism. However, there are two important elements of philosophical originality in Geiger's reaction. The first one is an account of the idealism-realism debate through an analysis of attitudes. Geiger argues that this debate cannot be solved with straightforward argumentation, because realism and idealism are rooted in a pre-theoretical dimension of subjectivity. In particular, he shows that realism takes place as a fivefold ontological commitment within our everyday immediate attitude, and that phenomenology takes place through an internal variation of it, called the givenness stance. Phenomenological idealism, far from being a legitimate alternative to such realism, is the outcome of a misunderstanding of that stance. Since in the givenness stance the reality of the world is ignored, the tendency is there to end up thinking that the reality of the world has been suspended. Husserl fell prey to this very mistake. Thus, for Geiger, phenomenological idealism is both not a real threat to realism, and somehow a constant temptation for phenomenologists. His position is also, as we have seen, more moderate than that of other early phenomenologists. The second element of philosophical originality in Geiger's reaction to *Ideas I* is his contrast between two approaches to phenomenology, which I call "evidence-based phenomenology" and "certainty-based phenomenology." Evidence-based phenomenology leads to idealism, while certainty-based phenomenology remains consistent with realism as an implicit presupposition. The main difference between the two approaches is their stance towards skepticism and Cartesian-type universal doubt. Husserl's evidence-based approach takes these seriously and tries to answer them by providing undoubtable evidence as a foundation to science. For this reason, it ends up dismissing our everyday belief in the reality of the external world as non-evidence-based, and therefore leads to idealism. Early phenomenologists' certainty-based approach, instead, provides reasons to dismiss skepticism and the Cartesian-type universal doubt, so that it preserves our everyday belief in the reality of the external world even if it is not evidence-based.

Let me finish by pointing to a far-reaching consequence of Geiger's approach: in it, phenomenology cannot aspire to be "first philosophy." Phenomenology takes place within the immediate attitude, so that it has nothing to say about the reality of the world. Other philosophical resources are needed for that. Geiger's reaction to *Ideas I* is therefore also a demarcation of the boundaries of phenomenology that seems to part ways with Husserl's understanding of phenomenology as the ultimate philosophy. It is, thus, not a coincidence that Geiger's later work tends towards metaphysics and existential philosophy. Geiger hands over the question of the boundaries of phenomenology to the phenomenology of today.

References

Broekman, Jan M. (1963). *Phänomenologie und Egologie. Faktisches und Transzendentales Ego bei Edmund Husserl.* Springer.

Celms, Theodor (1928). *Der Phänomenologische Idealismus Husserls.* Walter und Rapa, Riga.

Dufrenne, Mikel (1973). *The Phenomenology of Aesthetic Experience.* Northwestern University Press, Evanston.

Geiger, Moritz (1933). "Alexander Pfänders Methodische Stellung." In: Heller, E., Löw F., *Neue Münchener Philosophishce Abhandlungen, Alexander Pfänder zu seinem sechzigsten Geburtstag gewindet von Freunden und Schülern.* Johann Ambrosius Barth, Leipzig. Pp. 1–16.

Geiger, Moritz (1913). "Beiträge zur Phänomenologie des äestetisches Genusses." In: *Jahrbuch für Phänomenologie und Phänomenologische Forschung* 1. Pp. 567–684.

Geiger, Moritz (1966). *Die Wirklichkeit der Wissenschaften und die Metaphysik.* Georg Olms Verlagsbuchhandlung, Hildesheim.

Hering, Jean (1925). *Phénoménologie et Philosophie Religieuse.* Imprimerie alsacienne, Strasbourg.

Husserl, Edmund (2014). *Ideas for a Pure Phenomenology and Phenomenological Philosophy. First Book: General Introduction to Pure Phenomenology.* Translated by D. Dahlstrom. Hackett, Indianapolis.

Husserl, Edmund (1930). "Nachwort." In: Biemel, M., ed., (Hua V; 1971), *Ideen zu einer reinen Phänomenologie und phänomenologischen Philosophie, III, Die Phänomenologie und die Fundamente der Wissenschaften,* Nijhoff, Den Haag. Pp. 138–162

Husserl, Edmund (Hua XIII; 1973). *Zur Phänomenologie der Intersubjektivität. Texte aus dem Nachlass, Erster Teil: 1905–1920.* Nijhoff, Den Haag.

Ingarden, Roman (1975). *On the motives which led Husserl to Transcendental Idealism.* Springer, Dordrecht.

Ludwig Lange (1888) "Neue Experimente über den Vorgang der einfachen Reaktion auf Sinneseindrücke." *Philosophische Studien* 4, 479–510.

Parker, Rodney (2020). "Does Husserl's Phenomenological Idealism Lead to Pluralistic Solipsism? Assessing the Criticism by Theodor Celms." In: *The Subject(s) of Phenomenology.* Springer, Dordrecht. Pp. 155–184.

Patočka, Jan (1999). *Texte-Dokumente-Bibliographie.* Karl Alber, Freiburg

Pfänder, Alexander. (1929). "Theodor Celms. Der Phänomenologische Idealismus Husserls." In: *Deutsche Literaturzeitung* Jg 50, Heft 43, Berlin. Pp. 2048–2050.

Scheler, Max (1927). Idealismus-Realismus. *Philosophischer Anzeiger* 2 (3), pp. 255–324.

Spiegelberg, Herbert (1994). *The Phenomenological Movement. A Historical Introduction, 3rd ed.* Kluwer, Dordrecht.

Staiti, Andrea. (2014). *Husserl's Transcendental Phenomenology. Nature, Spirit and Life.* Cambridge University Press, Cambridge.

The Metaphysical Absolutizing of the Ideal. Hedwig Conrad-Martius' Criticism of Husserl's Idealism

Ronny Miron

Abstract This article discusses the main arguments of Hedwig Conrad-Martius against the worldview (*Weltanschauung*) of idealism in connection to her phenomenological idea of reality. The discussion focuses on her most far-reaching critical argument concerning the damage caused by idealism to the possibility for metaphysics by turning the real (*das Wirkliche*) into the ideal (*Ideelles*), thereby reducing reality to an idea. This article analyses Conrad-Martius' understanding of the evolution of idealism and of her criticism regarding the metaphysical absolutizing of the ideal in idealism. Her subsequent response to idealism attempts to rehabilitate the *facticity* (*Faktizität*) of real reality (*wirkliche Wirklichkeit*) within metaphysics.

Keywords Idealism · Hedwig Conrad-Martius · Pure consciousness · *Proton pseudos* · Edmund Husserl · Facticity · Real reality · Abyss

1 Introduction

In her radio lectures on "Seinsphilosophie," Hedwig Conrad-Martius[1] states that "we can no longer leave this land [*Boden*] that has been won by means of wholly idealist and epistemological [*erkenntniskritische*] research [...]. In terms of methodology, we cannot simply go back to the land of medieval ontologies"

---

[1] From WS 1909/10 until SS 1910, Conrad-Martius studied at the Ludwig Maximilian University of Munich. During this time, she participated in the Munich Circle of phenomenologists. She then transferred to the University of Göttingen, where she studied with Edmund Husserl and Adolf Reinach from WS 1910/11 until SS 1912 before submitting her dissertation under Alexander Pfänder back in Munich. During her time in Göttingen Conrad-Martius was a central figure in the Göttingen Circle of phenomenologists, becoming the leader (*Leiterin*) of the group in WS 1911/12. Cf. Avé-Lallemant 1975, 193; Hart 2020, 1–4.

R. Miron (✉)
Bar Ilan University, Ramat Gan, Israel
e-mail: ronny.miron@biu.ac.il

© Springer Nature Switzerland AG 2021
R. K. B. Parker (ed.), *The Idealism-Realism Debate Among Edmund Husserl's Early Followers and Critics*, Contributions to Phenomenology 112,
https://doi.org/10.1007/978-3-030-62159-9_10

193

(Conrad-Martius 1931, 21–22).[2] This sober insight regarding the irreversibility of philosophical progress results from Conrad-Martius' acknowledgment that phenomenology is "still carrying the eggshells of its idealist origins [*Geburtsursprungs*]" (Conrad-Martius 1951, 5) and that the contemporary philosophical trends of her time, namely existentialism and phenomenology, emanate from idealism and are even its zenith (Conrad-Martius 1934, 229). Moreover, she determines that like any genuine philosophy, idealism deals with Being in its absoluteness (Conrad-Martius 1931, 15–16) and has the "cognitional commitment [*erkenntnismäßige Hingabe*]" to establish an approach that seeks an essential *a priori* grounding (Conrad-Martius 1932A, 33). She adds that "it is in fact indisputable that subjective idealism again and again in all its forms since Plato (albeit the mostly false subjectivist interpretation of his epistemology) upholds that the human spirit [*Geist*] in its own depth meets with the most mysterious fullness of all intelligibility" (Conrad-Martius 1938, 271). In her opinion, the Platonic-idealist way of thinking "surely leads to a great abundance of objectively valuable insights" (Conrad-Martius 1931, 22). Hence, she argues that "Platonism and idealism have time and again trusted the most profound and essential arteries of the process of coming to know [*Erkenntnisvorgangs*]" (Conrad-Martius 1956A, 310). Also, she agrees with idealism that "the spiritual being genuinely depicts an 'elevated' form of substantiality" and regards the idealist position as preferable to material realism, which in her opinion "darkens the view" (Conrad-Martius 1957, 135) and disregards the spiritual element. Finally, she establishes the importance of completing and supporting objective realist epistemology with an idealist subjective epistemology that "emanates from the last essential truth" (Conrad-Martius 1938, 271).

Nonetheless, Conrad-Martius is unwilling to consider as genuine philosophy of Being (*Seinsphilosophie*) the post-Kantian approaches within which reason "*remains* the measure" of Being (Conrad-Martius 1931, 19). In this regard, she argues that "modern philosophy totally divests itself of the inconvenient 'in-itself'. Instead, this aspect has been 'transcendentally idealized' in idealism concomitantly with turning it to an 'eternally escaping target'" (Conrad-Martius 1932, 61), until finally the metaphysical thesis regarding the existence of the world has been rejected "in favor of a converted transcendental antithesis" (Conrad-Martius 1932, 78). She explains that the confinement of the study of Being to the boundaries of pure consciousness underlying the transcendental stance, which in many respects reinforces the philosophical vision of idealism, suggests a solution to the philosophical problem of Being "that in truth does not exist" (Conrad-Martius 1932, 75).

Against this background, Conrad-Martius presents her own approach as executing a "necessary methodical turn" that stands in opposition to "idealist philosophy" (Conrad-Martius 1931, 23); as overcoming the "idealist world-aspect [*Weltaspekt*] in general that became blind to the true (substantial) Being" (Conrad-Martius

---

[2] References to Conrad-Martius' works in the body of the text are dated according to the year of their authorship, not the year of publication. See the bibliography for details. References to unpublished manuscripts from Conrad-Martius' *Nachlass* are indicated with the letter 'N' following the year of authorship. All translations from German into English are my own.

1932B, 195) that brings about desubstantialization of the "I" and of Being in general (Conrad-Martius 1932B, 195–196) and finally as responding to the what she critically refers to as the "blinding darkness" generated by idealism's distinction between the ideal and the real that blocked any access to the question of reality (Conrad-Martius 1923, 160). However, while Conrad-Martius' discussion of idealism addresses it as a "way of thinking [*Geisteshaltung*]" often without engaging in a detailed account of the specific ideas that took shape within idealism (Conrad-Martius 1932A, 32), her references to Husserl seem to bear some ambivalence and reservations that are often accompanied by a positive evaluation. Thus, on the one hand she counts Husserl within the idealist tradition and regards his work as describing not only "its last and utmost blossom, but also the fulfillment of its most genuine and deep essential content."[3] Subsequently, she adds: "Here truly, in the most purest, most factual [*sachlichste*], and most accurate sense, to the extent that these are generally only possible, consciousness became the measure [*Maß*] of all Being" (Conrad-Martius 1931, 21).[4] On the other hand, unlike the sweeping determinations about idealism as a whole or representative figures such as Kant and Hegel, regarding Husserl, Conrad-Martius emphasizes not just the disagreements between her philosophy and his, but also their shared aspects. For example, she declares her affinity to Husserl's early idea of phenomenology that was anchored in the method of "essence intuition [*Wesenserfassung*]" and not in epistemology (Conrad-Martius 1916, 355n1).[5] Following Husserl's general thesis of the rationality of the world,[6] Conrad-Martius argues that the presence of essences in real beings is primary and

---

[3] The question of whether Husserl was an idealist or realist is widely and continuously being discussed in the scholarly literature. See, for example, Ingarden 1975, Drummond 1988, Moran 2005, Hopkins 2010, Zahavi 2017. However, for the present article on Conrad-Martius' stance towards idealism, it is unnecessary to take a position on this matter. Rather, it accepts methodically Conrad-Martius' view of Husserl as an idealist.

[4] See also Conrad-Martius' reference to Husserl in Conrad-Martius 1916N, 2. Conrad-Martius' criticism of Husserl's idealism refers to his transcendental phenomenology as presented in *Ideas I*. In the view of the members of the Munich Circle as a whole, *Ideas I* essentially withdraws the establishing principles of the *Logical Investigations*, to the point of a "turn" that brings about an insurmountable abyss within Husserl's phenomenology. Conrad-Martius suggests that Husserl's shift to idealism is already present in the second volume of the first edition of the *Logical Investigations* (Conrad-Martius 1958, 395). Avé-Lallemant also discusses the difference between the two volumes of *Logical Investigations* (Avé-Lallemant 1971, 14ff). See also Herbert Spiegelberg, who observed that the two volumes constitute two periods in Husserl's phenomenology – the pre-phenomenological and the phenomenological (Spiegelberg 1960, 74).

[5] Conrad-Martius was committed to the method of essence intuition that localizes and analyzes the "what" that establishes the real being by searching for the indispensable *a priori* and primordial foundations, thanks to which the real being can become a specific object. (For Husserl's relation to this method, see Husserl 1901, 165–179; Husserl 1983, §§ 1–17). Conrad-Martius regards this method as a "genuine philosophical mission" (Conrad-Martius 1916, 348). See also Conrad-Martius 1916, 346–348; 1923, 159; 1956B, 377; 1956, 347. For further reading on the issue, especially in reference to the realist school of phenomenology, see Hart 2020, 18–19; Reinach 1951, 71–73; Reinach 1913, 1–163; Pfänder 1913, 325–404; Pfeiffer 2005, 1–13; Schmücker 1956, 1–33; Ebel 1965, 1–25.

[6] See for example: Husserl 1983, §§ 136–137; §139; §142.

perceivable (Conrad-Martius 1931N1, 2–3) as well as foundational to the intelligibility of Being in general (Conrad-Martius 1934, 230). Also, she explains that "The same logos, in the thinkable and most universal sense, with which the *world* due to essence and Being is pervaded, lies concealed with the same universality also in human reason" (Conrad-Martius 1958, 400–401).[7] In this regard, she establishes that "the objective-intelligible logos is a primordial idea [*Uridee*] according to which the world was created," and that "endless diversity is inherent in it" to the extent that "every single thing and part of the world in accordance with its specific nature reflects this essence" (Conrad-Martius 1956A, 307). Moreover, she explicitly admits that within the study of the essence of consciousness it is completely legitimate to leave outside the real or any other meaning of the existing world (Conrad-Martius 1958, 401–402), namely: just as Husserl did. Therefore, she justifies and even practices herself the epoché, while explaining that despite being beyond all doubt, the reality of the world cannot be known evidently (Conrad-Martius 1958, 400–401).[8]

Nonetheless, the position that is granted to consciousness in Husserl's thinking over the world violates Conrad-Martius' most primordial insight regarding the essential precedence of reality over any other aspect that might concern philosophy. Also, for her, the phenomenological commitment to the given / Datum should be directed to reality as an absolute, autonomous, and independent being (Conrad-Martius 1916, 391–392), while Husserl's "principle of all principles" clearly adheres to the appearance before one's consciousness.[9] Consequently, she distinguishes between two types of phenomenologies: the "transcendental phenomenology" that she attributes to Husserl and idealism in general and the "ontological phenomenology" with which she herself identifies, declaring: "We deliberately and firmly accept the position of the ontologist" (Conrad-Martius 1934, 231). In any event, her unequivocal assertion that the two phenomenologies should separate themselves from each other (Conrad-Martius 1958, 399) does not indicate the removal of her primordial ambivalence towards Husserl and even towards transcendentalism as a whole. Rather, she devotes her thinking to the rehabilitation of philosophical issues that in her view were misconceived in idealism, Husserl's phenomenology included.

---

[7] The understanding that the same logos that pervades the world also characterizes the human spirit is also central to Conrad-Martius' philosophy of the "I". See Conrad-Martius 1956A; 1956, 335–350. For further reading, see Miron 2021, 137–181 (or Miron 2017; Miron 2019).

[8] Conrad-Martius distinguished between the épOche and the phenomenological reduction. While the former indicates the justified suspension of any existential judgment, the latter includes judgment regarding real beings (Conrad-Martius 1958, 397f). Similar to Conrad-Martius and independently of her, Theodor Celms distinguished between the two concepts (Celms 1928, 347–379). In his view, Husserl's ambiguity regarding the épOche and the phenomenological reduction led him to "metaphysical spiritualism" (Celms 1928, 427–435). Helmut Kuhn presents a more radical stance that demands "giving away" not only the reduction but also the thinking of the épOche, which he regards as "an artificial methodical concept" that is incapable of moving beyond the phenomena into the essential forms that appear in them. See Kuhn 1971, 6.

[9] Husserl 1983, §24.

In what follows, we will unveil what might be called, following Kant, Conrad-Martius' view of the architectonic of idealism, that is, the unifying goal that consolidates idealism into a philosophical system.[10] In particular, her view of idealism as evolving from an initial empirical starting point will be scrutinized. This view distinguishes between appearances and true Being, and finally evolves into a position where pure consciousness is provided with a be-all and end-all status. Subsequently, the main consequence of idealism, as conceived by Conrad-Martius, namely, the damage it does to the possibility of metaphysics, will be discussed. Finally, I will discuss the alternative to idealism outlined in her thinking, which seeks to overcome the deficiencies resulting from the centrality of pure consciousness. Specifically, she rejects the metaphysical absolutizing of the ideal in favor of rehabilitating the *facticity* (*Faktizität*) of real reality (*wirkliche Wirklichkeit*) within metaphysics. Instead of metaphysical idealism, Conrad-Martius argues for a phenomenological realism.

2   The Architectonic of Idealism and Its Damage to the Consolidation of Metaphysics

In her essay "*Die aktuelle Krisis des idealistischen Denkens*," Conrad-Martius asks: "How can we characterize the innermost ingredient of idealism?", "where is the basis [*Ausgangsebene*] from which idealism has always, in all its forms, been generated?", what is the thing that brings about from itself "the internal dialectic of idealism in an unstoppable way?" (Conrad-Martius 1932A, 34). Rather than a historical account of the establishing roots of idealism or suggesting an analysis of its foundational arguments, Conrad-Martius addresses idealism primarily as a worldview (*Weltanschauung*) that has exerted a foundational influence over modern thinking as a whole. The starting point of her critique of idealism concerns its evolution from an empirical stance in which only sense-data are acknowledged as the immediately given and true Being, as "an acosmic, ateleological, and aformal fundamental view" (Conrad-Martius 1931N2, 1), and as "mere sensory phenomenality, mere appearance [*Scheinhaftigkeit*] of the world of experience" (Conrad-Martius 1932A, 34). Conrad-Martius argues that this stance "necessarily 'misplaces [*verlegt*]' all the 'rest' (forms [*Formen*], purposes, values) in the perceiving subject and thus *subjectivism* emerges out of itself" from which any sensory moment seems to be eliminated in favor of an "indissoluble totality" (Conrad-Martius 1931N2, 1). This "totality" concerns exactly the essential necessity of judgments that can no longer

---

[10] Kant described the architectonic of reason as follows: "By an architectonic I understand the art of systems. Since systematic unity is that which first makes ordinary cognition into science, i.e., makes a system out of a mere aggregate of it, architectonic is the doctrine of that which is scientific in our cognition in general […]. I understand by a system, however, the unity of the manifold cognitions under one idea. This is the rational concept of the form of a whole, insofar as through this the domain of the manifold as well as the position of the parts with respect to each other is determined a priori". Kant 1998, 619 (A832/B860).

be anchored in reality itself. Rather, these judgments are established as "necessary *thinking contents*" that thereby ground "a new realm of the ideal" that becomes "the realm of *ideality*" (Conrad-Martius 1931N2, 2). In other words, aspects and contents of thinking are associated with the human subject, while their connection to the world external to the subject is disregarded. In fact, from the standpoint of idealism even the human being is reduced to nothing more than an idea, thereby removing it from the world and robbing it of its factual reality. Consequently, a comprehensive split between perceptibility and conceivability seems to take place to the point of bifurcation and hence a "dualism of the given world, a split into 'Being' [*Sein*] and 'appearance' [*Schein*] [...] in the sense that the sensory given [*sinnlich Gegebene*] is the genuine 'Being'; everything else (forms, purposes, values) are mere subjective appearance" (Conrad-Martius 1931N2, 1).

Up to this point, Conrad-Martius' characterization of the evolution of idealism seems to imply that initially her criticism is not addressed to an extreme version of idealism in which the concrete world can and should be deduced from thinking only.[11] However, it soon transpires that the initial duality does not persist. In this regard, she describes a subsequent "insight into the indissoluble totality of the eliminated sensory moment" that brings about the shift from subjectivism to idealism, which she calls "a modified [...] *aprioristic* form of subjectivism" (Conrad-Martius 1931N2, 1–2). This idiosyncratic phrasing concerns the decisive stage that establishes the worldview of idealism as a purified philosophical stance. More specifically, Conrad-Martius points here to the main consequence of the removal of any aspect of sense perception and thereby of worldliness and externality whatsoever, from the realm of the human subject, namely: the transposition to the realm of *a priori* thinking. At this point, idealism is declared to be a "new form of *phenomenalism*" in which the "the empirical sphere is regarded as an accidental facticity [*Faktizität*] of mere 'appearance'" (Conrad-Martius 1931N2, 2) to the extent that "the real [*das wirkliche*] now *thoroughly* becomes an ideal [*Ideelles*] (concept!)" (Conrad-Martius 1932A, 36). Subsequent to this conceptualization of the real, the ideal itself goes through a process of "metaphysical absolutization." Consequently, the ideal emerges as the only necessary absolute based on the *a priori* necessity of thinking contents that, in Conrad-Martius' judgement, "can be termed a *loss of the world* [*Entwirklichung der Welt*]" (Conrad-Martius 1931N2, 1–2). Eventually, also the elimination of the "sensory moment" from pure consciousness – that detaches it not only from any aspect of sense experience but also from the real world itself, the human subject is included – clarifies that its "purity" is but its being wiped of any aspect of reality.

The philosophical dynamic sketched above, as a result of which idealism is depicted by Conrad-Martius as trapped in subjectivism to the point of "*losing the world*," seems to deprive real or worldly things of their essential intelligibility. This is apparent from her indication of a "necessity of another reasoning (extra-cosmic, extra-subjective, extra-empirical) and securing thereof" (Conrad-Martius 1931N2,

---

[11] For a general survey of the different sorts of idealism, see: Kupperman 1957; Brown 1973.

1) that is raised by idealism. The accentuation of the "extra" seems to be responding exactly to the "indissoluble totality" (Conrad-Martius 1931N2, 1) that concerns the problematic of a lack of worldliness that typifies idealism as a closed worldview. Consequently, a new element comes into play and unavoidably dissipates the described initial duality, i.e., pure consciousness. This mental construct, which appears purports to extricate idealism from the self-imposed boundaries resulting from its binary starting point, is depicted by Conrad-Martius as "a new (over-empirical, over-real, over-sensory) realm, the realm of the Ideal, or the realm of *Ideality*" (Conrad-Martius 1931N2, 2). Also, "for pure consciousness all – the physical *and* the psychic, the interior *and* the external – are immediately given and attainable, as it is in-itself, just as it is given in-itself" (Conrad-Martius 1931, 20), hence "here precisely consciousness is taken for Being!" (Conrad-Martius 1931, 21). She explains that, under the influence of Descartes, the indubitable pure consciousness serves as the secure foundation not only for all claims of what we can *know*, but for all claims about what *is*. Conrad-Martius agrees that an absolute grounding in an indubitable epistemological realm is attainable within the realm of pure consciousness, regarding which she determines: "here and *only* here *exists* an absolute Being" (Conrad-Martius 1931, 21). She also admits that this move "certainly leads to a great abundance of factual valuable insights," hence the "Platonic-idealist way of thinking [*Geisteshaltung*]" is not entirely unjustified. Nevertheless, Conrad-Martius is confident that "it does not lead and cannot lead to the fundamental problem of Being and facticity" (Conrad-Martius 1931, 22) that in her view is indispensable in any metaphysical account. Thus, these unequivocally articulated arguments mark an unmistakable boundary between her view of idealism and her understanding of what metaphysics is all about.

The suggested interpretation of Conrad-Martius' view of the evolution of idealism from a empiricism, is further supported in her indication of the vanishing of the idealist dualism (Conrad-Martius 1932A, 36) by filling the "abyss [*Abgrund*]" between the "mere appearing" and the "in-itself" with knowing reason (Conrad-Martius 1931, 18). I argue that both the insertion of pure consciousness into idealist thinking and the difficulty in maintaining the bifurcated point of departure are connected in Conrad-Martius' view of idealism. That is to say that pure consciousness is posited to overcome this duality. Moreover, the objective of this positing is uncovered also in her characterization of the aim of idealism as viewing the realm of pure consciousness for epistemologically oriented studies (Conrad-Martius 1931, 19). Obviously, this epistemological task cannot be fulfilled in a torn domain. Rather, precisely a vision of cognition that is purified from any doubt can be realized under the jurisdiction of a purified consciousness. Ultimately, the sphere of thinking that is governed by the absolutized single element of pure consciousness, within which no room exists anymore for the factual world that is imbued with diversity and plurality, is all that remains. Conrad-Martius then refers to the subsequent expulsion of the world in-itself from idealist thinking as "absolutizing the 'meta'" (i.e., the "meta" in metaphysics), whereby everything that is beyond experience is marked as an ideal possibility inaccessible to consciousness (Conrad-Martius 1932, 53). Alternatively, since absoluteness cannot be achieved out of what is beyond experience – namely: from the "thing-in-itself" – it has been altogether expelled from the homogeneous and indubitable sphere of pure consciousness.

Concomitantly with the establishment of pure consciousness in idealism, its idea of world, which has been consolidated as "pure facticity" and "pure being-here [*Da-sein*]," soon becomes "a philosophical stumbling block" that rational, idealist, autonomic, and pure thinking has always tried to dissolve into the plane of reason (Conrad-Martius 1931A, 39). Alternatively, such a world boosts the attempts "to interpret-away [*fortzuinterpretieren*] reality idealistically" (Conrad-Martius 1931A, 41). In her view, once the sensory qualities fall completely on the subjective side, it follows that "the empirical qualification is no longer substantially genuinely rooted in the thing" itself and we arrive at "the complete desubstantializing [*Entsubstanzialisierung*] of Being" (Conrad-Martius 1932A, 35). The above discussed "*loss of the world*" transpires, then, as but the final result of eradicating facticity as such from the domain of the worldview of idealism. Moreover, this eradication is tantamount to what Conrad-Martius denotes as "the metaphysical absolutizing of the ideal" (Conrad-Martius 1931N2, 2), which can also be considered as the ultimate expression of freedom from any doubt. This seems to be enabled precisely due to the reconfiguration of reality as ideal, referred to as "true reality [*wahre Wirklichkeit*]," which "is at the same time a rational reality, since precisely in its thinkable necessity it is understandable [*einsehbare*] and deducible [*ableitbare*] [...] from the highest principles, that are through and through *reasonable* [*vernunftgemässe*]" (Conrad-Martius 1931N2, 3). For Conrad-Martius, it is obvious that reality, which "from the start and on its own grounds has been shaped in a non-substantial and non-real way [...] can never be recovered from the ideal [...] since ideality can never release reality from itself," rather it only "remains (a basically illusory) pseudo-shape [*pseudogestalt*]" (Conrad-Martius 1932A, 36). Finally, her analysis of the evolution of idealism arrives at the unavoidable ruling out of idealism as metaphysics.

Against this background, I argue that within the discussed process of elimination of "sensory moments" that eventually dissipated the related duality that Conrad-Martius observes in idealism, another process emerges that is even more radical and far-reaching in its overall consequences, namely, a transposition from the epistemological plain to the ontological one. To a certain extent, what is implied here is that even what is presented in idealism as a methodical stance, which as such has particularly epistemological bearings, is eventually consolidated as an ontological or metaphysical positioning in the sense that it determines the only beings whose existence reason is permitted to confirm. In this spirit, Conrad-Martius accepts the interpretation according to which "Kant did not present epistemology but a theory of Being" that blocks the "departure [*Aufbruch*] and breakthrough [*Durchbruch*] to a true comprehensive doctrine of Being" (Conrad-Martius 1936, 366).

In this way, also pure consciousness appears to be transformed from a mental construct to an legitimizing force that decides what is reality itself. Obviously, this is already implied in her statements regarding the loss of the world in idealism. However, at this point, this insight is lifted to an explicit ontological argument and thus the initial moderated version of idealism, which can also be regarded as epistemological, gives way to metaphysical idealism in which idea and Being are equated to the extent that reality is constituted as an idea. In Conrad-Martius' words, in idealism thinking becomes the only "determination of Being [*Seinsbestimmtheit*]" (Conrad-Martius 1932A, 36), or alternatively: "within the endeavor for a universal being-directed stance of cognition, idealism attempts to reclaim [*Zurückerobern*] the cosmic and metaphysical reality" (Conrad-Martius 1932A, 34). Eventually, the idealist world of things lacks what Conrad-Martius calls "that typical factor of reality [*Wirklichkeitsfactor*]" (Conrad-Martius 1931, 24).

The traces of the above discussed complex processes in idealism, in particular the transformation of the epistemological into the ontological or metaphysical, resonates also in Conrad-Martius' discussion of the foundation of Husserl's notions of the phenomenological reduction and the transcendental ego. In the first place, she establishes that Husserl's choice of "bracketing" reality was conducted to provide a firm and absolute ground for his philosophy, by locating reality outside and beyond consciousness and regarding it as that which essentially cannot be indubitably reached (Conrad-Martius 1931, 20–21). However, she is suspicious about Husserl's sacrifice of the so-called naive "belief in the world" in favor of a pure study of the world, arguing that "what's odd is then that here absolute and indubitable judgments about *factual* being, about the present at-hand [*Vorhandenheiten*], can be made pleasing" (Conrad-Martius 1931, 20).[12] Moreover, the idealist leap from the epistemological to the ontological plain is apparent also from Conrad-Martius' observation that Husserl did not only practice the legitimate methodological stage of the epoché, but rather made, conspicuously in the phenomenological reduction, a metaphysical decision whereby "the world with all its parts included is hypothetically posed as existing" but eventually "suspended [*enthoben*]" (Conrad-Martius 1958, 398). In her view, the result of Husserl's choice to supplement the epoché with phenomenological reduction is apparent in his employment of pure consciousness. As she puts it: "What is fundamental for the analytical study of pure consciousness, becomes an inducement [*Anlaß*] to radical factual reversal [*Verkehrung*] when this reduced field turns out to be an ontological and metaphysical *absolute*! This is indeed the overall intention of Edmund Husserl" (Conrad-Martius 1931A, 43–44n3).[13] The transposition into the ontological in Husserl's phenomenology is further reinforced in connection to his concept of the transcendental ego, whose cognitive limits determine the boundaries of reality. Accordingly, the real world is transformed into a noematic phenomenon whose being is dependent on conscious-

---

[12] Marvin Farber, too, regarded the reality of the external world as a basic fact (Farber 1967, 65). Yet, while Conrad-Martius turns the acknowledgment of the facticity of the external world into the firm ground upon which her metaphysical thinking stands, for Farber, "The philosophical problem of the existence of the external world resulted from an unsettling of a natural world belief, and has been complicated by underlying premises and theories" (Farber 1967, 63).

[13] Kuhn disagrees with Conrad-Martius on this point. He argues that Husserl does not present an idealist position but a methodical requirement that paved the way to transcendental phenomenology. Yet he argues that there is no justification for encapsulating all of reality within the realm of phenomena (Kuhn 1971, 4–5).

ness and the phenomenological investigation as a whole is restricted to the intentional framework.[14] In this regard, Conrad-Martius establishes that the expression "transcendental" denotes the "descending [*untersteigen*]" of the physical and psychical world as well as the empirical and ideal into the subjective (Conrad-Martius 1958, 400). This determination concerns the loss of the world taking place in Husserl's phenomenology after conducting the phenomenological reduction, regarding which Conrad-Martius (rhetorically) asks if the "noematic world that is also *really* real [*wirklich* wirklich], remains entirely undecided?" (Conrad-Martius 1958, 396), or alternatively "where does the world remain?" (Conrad-Martius 1956B, 371).[15] The fundamental similarity between Conrad-Martius' view of the idealist notion of pure consciousness and her understanding of Husserl's conception of transcendentalism is thus apparent, i.e., both are cleared of any aspect of real reality. Consequently, Husserl's phenomenology, regarded by her as merely the offspring of previous forms of idealism, is helplessly trapped within the realm of consciousness.

To be sure, of the various deficiencies that Conrad-Martius detects in idealism, the most bothersome is the destruction of the possibility of metaphysics. She argues that metaphysics includes the absolute in-itself, which we are somehow able to cognize, not as a regulative idea, but as an "inherent, freestanding, quantity [*seinshaften – stehenden – Größe*]" (Conrad-Martius 1932, 52). Idealism, whose ultimate product is an absolutized pure consciousness, eliminates any existing-in-itself dimension of reality and thereby thwarts the possibility of achieving metaphysics. In opposition to this, metaphysics can be established only within a realm that assumes the existence of Being, where Being has the "typical factor of reality [*Wirklichkeitsfactor*]" (Conrad-Martius 1931, 24) as an inherent part, namely, an aspect of substantiality. Conrad-Martius explains that idealism unavoidably and insolvably arrives at *proton pseudos*.[16] As a result, concrete reality is pushed outside, thereby the idealist realm of reality loses its substantial ground to the extent that reality cannot be found in it anymore (Conrad-Martius 1932A, 36). That is to

---

[14] See in particular: Husserl 1983, §§35–47. For further reading, see the interpretation that regarded Husserl's transcendental turn as a result of his reassessment of the issue of intentionality: Becker 1930.

[15] Husserl, for his part, was very critical of Conrad-Martius' metaphysical approach, see: Husserl 1994, 20. In his view, the phenomenologists from Munich "remain stuck in half-measures [*Halbheiten*]," namely, they were dogmatic for refusing to accept the phenomenological reduction (Husserl 1930, 285). Therefore, he could not consider them as genuine phenomenologists nor even as philosophers. See Avé-Lallemant 1975A, 28. Other phenomenological works were also evaluated by him as "pseudo-phenomenologies" and "essentially different" from his own, including those of his chosen co-editors of the *Jahrbuch für Philosophie* and *Phenomenologische Forschung*. Concerning Geiger and Pfänder, see: Miron 2021, xxxix–xliii and Schuhmann 1990, 23–24; as for Scheler being considered a "fake phenomenologist" (*Talmiphenomenologen*), see: Spiegelberg 1959, 59.

[16] The term *proton pseudos* is what Aristotle uses to refer to a set of false starting premises or an original error that necessarily leads to false conclusions despite the formal soundness of the intermediary steps in reasoning. For further reading see Sowa 2010.

say, the intelligible unity that is achieved by idealism, which is but a rationalization of reality (Conrad-Martius 1932A, 36–37), lacks any real foundation. In other words, the positioning of reality that takes place in idealism is subordinated to epistemological requirements and therefore cannot meet the ultimate requirement for something to be real, i.e., standing on its own foundations and not on anything else, rational or other. Finally, Conrad-Martius accuses idealism of ignoring in its account of reality the aspect of irrationality into which facticity is absorbed and therefore referred to as the *brutum*. Moreover, this aspect exists within itself and out of itself in an incommensurable individuality that is but a manifestation of the most essential characteristics of reality as independent, autonomous, absolute (Conrad-Martius 1916, 392), closed in-itself, and transcendent to human consciousness and spirit (Conrad-Martius 1916, 424). As opposed to that, the ideal and purely defining force of idealism is completely helpless and innocent about the related incommensurable aspect of reality (Conrad-Martius 1932A, 37). In this regard, she asks "how should a bridge be found between an internal de-substantialized and de-organized (in an exhausted pure space-scheme) matter and pure thinking, which for its part can be extracted from any substantial context of reality [*Wirklichketszusammenhang*]!?" (Conrad-Martius 1932A, 36). Evidently, such a "bridge" cannot be erected by idealist thinking that is portrayed by Conrad-Martius as assuming exactly the opposite, namely that "only higher reality," i.e., such that is consolidated by means of pure consciousness, is "capable of being substantiated and established commensurably" only (Conrad-Martius 1932A, 37). Conrad-Martius concludes, then, that as far as reality is concerned, the "Idealist worldview [...] in its consequences is practically only so 'ominous [*unheilvoller*],' since here again what is at stake is the *whole [das Ganze]*" (Conrad-Martius 1932A, 36), in which both the rational and the incommensurable irrational should be included.

3   Conrad-Martius' Alternative to Idealism: Securing the Possibility for Metaphysics

The most decisive point of departure of Conrad-Martius' philosophical project concerns what she calls the "thesis of existence [*Daseinthesis*]," according to which reality does not concern degrees of objectivity, but rather "something totally different" (Conrad-Martius 1923, 180) that stands in an absolute and unbridgeable primordial-opposition (*Urgegensatz*) to nothingness (Conrad-Martius 1923, 160).[17] This thesis is her response to what she identifies as the "Platonic-idealist metaphysics" (Conrad-Martius 1931, 22) that took root in modern philosophy concerning the opposition between the ideal and the real, which in her view blocked any access to the philosophical deciphering of reality.

---

[17] For a detailed discussion of Conrad-Martius' view of reality as "elevating" from nonexistence or merely ideal and formal existence (Conrad-Martius 1923, 173), see Miron 2014.

The immediate consequence of the "thesis of existence" concerns the requirement to reintegrate the world of facts into the philosophical discourse about reality
after its removal by idealism. Conrad-Martius derives from Husserl's constitutive
determination that *"nulla 're' indigent ad existendum,"* that immanent being is absolute, since it never brings any "thing" into being, that he left out facts, and that the
entire empirical field is left out.[18] Therefore, Conrad-Martius extracts from the same
insight an inverse argument that emphasizes the impossibility of establishing any
real aspect of consciousness, or alternatively, determining the inevitability of the
"collapse" of the real within a discourse that is based on an absolute consciousness
(Conrad-Martius 1916N, 2). Moreover, bringing facts back to the fore of the philosophical study of reality seems as an immediate response to what she observes as
the loss of fullness, depth, and content taking place within the approach of the for-
malistic idealist thinking about reality (Conrad-Martius 1923, 192). Thus, while
idealism appears in Conrad-Martius' discussion as immersed in mere abstract and
ideal objectivity regarding objects and reality, her realist stance emphasizes the
"material objectivity" that might be reached by what she describes as "the positive
outward departure" from pure nothingness of the real thing that posits itself in reality (Conrad-Martius 1923, 182).

Indeed, Conrad-Martius hesitates from the outset about the choice to eliminate
from the philosophical discourse the world of facts, which she calls the "immovable
rock *[unentwurzelbar erhebende Fels]* of factual existence in the face of which we
find ourselves" (Conrad-Martius 1931A, 39). She chooses to state what is for her
the obvious, by means of phrasing a series of rhetorical questions while omitting the
question marks, such as "how is this strange separation [...] upon which the phenomenological reduction relies at all possible! How is it possible that I can bracket
and set aside the positioning of facticity of the entire world and nevertheless have
the entire world left over; the very same world, only that it is on the uplifted plane
of pure consciousness!" (Conrad-Martius 1931, 24). As opposed to this, she determines: "it is no longer acceptable that we, in ascending to the essence and confining
ourselves to the descriptive analysis of pure essential relationships, set aside the
question of facticity or the question of Being *[Seinsfrage]* or leave it behind us"

---

[18] Conrad-Martius here cites Husserl 1983, §49, 110. Husserl expressed his negative attitude
towards facts in Husserl 1983, §3. See also Mohanty, 3–9. Conrad-Martius later clarified that
Husserl never rejected or doubted the reality of the world but regarded it as a hypothetical being
(Conrad-Martius 1958, 398). She clarifies in this regard that unlike Husserl, she does not see any
problem with empirical experience (Conrad-Martius 1956, 351) and even regards the then-new
natural sciences as elucidating the real foundations of such experience (Conrad-Martius 1958,
401). However, it is far from being unequivocal that Husserl sweepingly dismissed empirical sciences or observed a contradiction between phenomenology and the concrete scientific practice.
Rather, merely the reductionism and objectivism that characterize certain scientific worldviews
were dismissed. Husserl writes: "When it is really natural science that speaks, we listen willingly
and as disciples. But, the language of the natural scientists is not always that of natural science
itself and is assuredly not so when they speak of 'natural philosophy' and the 'theory of knowledge
of natural science'" (Husserl 1983, §20, 38–39). For further reading on the issue, see Harvey 1989,
Rinofner-Kreidl 2014; Choi 2007; Feist 2004 (mentioned in Urban 2016, 468).

(Conrad-Martius 1931, 22). Moreover, for her facticity is a philosophical "primordial situation" that stimulates two effects. On the one hand, it confronts the observer with "the primordial doubtfulness" or the "non-justifiability" of the immediate thing. On the other hand, precisely this state of affairs propels us towards continuous metaphysical questioning (Conrad-Martius 1931A, 39). Conrad-Martius was convinced that the being of factual existents can never be grasped in its full peculiarity if it is transcendentally evaluated by means of pure consciousness. She argues that pure consciousness is "always only carried out [*vollzogen*]" as an "intentional [*akthaft*] mode of existence"but never truly "*is*". Therefore, reality must be anchored in in facts, thinghood (*Dinglichkeit*) or substance (Conrad-Martius 1931, 25); in forces that are independent of consciousness and its merely intentional mode of being. This means that her philosophical journey begins precisely at the point from which idealism recoils. She criticizes what might be called Heidegger's "draining away of life [*Ent-lebung*]," which seems to her as the cessation of the required philosophical efforts for deciphering the Being that is inherent in finitude and facticity. In this regard, she asks why not "dig deeper" into the innermost finiteness of Being? How can one position oneself out of full awareness and resoluteness into the nothingness of Being? She wonders whether here there is not a spoiling of the metaphysical and divine procedures. Finally, unlike Heidegger's "deepening absolutizing of finitude, temporality, and historicity of the I," she argues that only with genuine penetration into the essence of facticity that is "*not* I-adhering [*nichtichhafter*]" can the desired "true entry" to Being be inaugurated (Conrad-Martius 1931, 30–31).

Against the background of above explanation of Conrad-Martius' philosophical stance towards facticity, which was consolidated vis-à-vis her criticism of idealism mainly in her writings from the 1930s, stands her earlier observation from *"Zur Ontologie und Erscheinungslehre der realen Außenwelt"* according to which "the *factual presence [tatsächliche Vorhandensein]* of entirely *peculiar* and *in-itself factually unanimous* phenomenon of the 'real external-worldliness' became undeniable" (Conrad-Martius 1916, 396).[19] The importance of the early reference to the issue of facticity concerns its anchoring in a detailed discussion of "the sensory given," which is grasped as a kind of "sense givenness" (Conrad-Martius 1916, 399). In other words, the focus is given to the thing sensed as an object and not to the subjective experience of it.[20] Conrad-Martius attaches the ability to achieve "real contact" with the external world (Conrad-Martius 1916, 423) to what she calls "the unique and original [*ureigenen*] nature of the sensory given" (Conrad-Martius 1916,

---

[19] *Zur Ontologie und Erscheinungslehre der realen Außenwelt* is an exploration of the first chapter of her earlier prize essay *Die erkenntnistheoretischen Grundlagen des Positivismus* (Conrad-Martius 1920, 10–14), which served as her doctoral dissertation in 1913.

[20] Krings illuminated that the focus on the real existing object is not tantamount to the inversion of the Kant's idea of the "I" as directed to its objects. Rather, the presumption here is that there is a real relation between the existent and the essence referring to it. Yet this assumption does not contain an argument about the possibility of knowing this existent, see: Krings 1960, 193ff.

398).[21] She explains that the capability of the "sensory given" to make obvious its real being in its "here and now" and be outwardly felt from itself enables it to approach the "I" as a content of givenness (Conrad-Martius 1916, 412–413). Moreover, the sensory given declares itself by itself as factually existing and appears in person before the "I" as self-presenting (Conrad-Martius 1916, 422).[22] Even more so, Conrad-Martius establishes that the sensory given is the only means that ensures for me the external world in its time-space facticity, since its essence is to "present" the external-world's Being. Thus, assuming the essential belonging of an essence to some specific phenomenal situations (Conrad-Martius 1916, 349), she argues that we must have confidence in the "existence" of something in order to argue for its givenness. She trusts that this requirement is not in vain, since the sensory given is already structured as a content of givenness or alternatively has a real connection to the real world (Conrad-Martius 1916, 423).[23] Finally, Conrad-Martius' understanding that the sensory given is the ultimate mediating link to external reality and Being itself will become crucial to mature thinking, which unlike idealism, regards the sensory given as an inseparable part of Being (Conrad-Martius 1932A, 35).

The return of facticity and sensation – clearly conducted vis-à-vis idealism – is finally complemented and generalized as the philosophical homecoming of the idea of the world. Conrad-Martius established unequivocally: "we cannot go behind this Ego […] that is such that constitutes anything and everything" (Conrad-Martius 1958, 400). Also, she affirms that within the framework of ontological phenomenology the world itself exists primarily and by its very being is independent of consciousness and of the "I" (Conrad-Martius 1956, 374).[24] In this regard, she distinguishes between two concepts of reality: "reality [*Wirklichkeit*] as a noematic existence" and "the noematic moments of reality that are transcendent to consciousness" that she call "the *real* reality [*wirkliche Wirklichkeit*]" (Conrad-Martius 1958, 397). This terminological duplication refers exclusively to the non-mental reality

---

[21] Based on a similar realist point of departure, Spiegelberg justifies relying on the sensory for achieving contact with the immediate phenomena of reality. See: Spiegelberg 1975, 153.

[22] Spiegelberg explains that phenomenon and reality do not exclude each other. What is real exists within itself and can be presented to us in its very existence out of itself. This means that real things in the world can remain exactly as they are, including in case of being presented and having relation to us. He terms the phenomena in which subjects are involved "subjectival" in the sense that they are objective parts of subjects and of their world (Spiegelberg 1975, 134–135). However, despite being evident (Spiegelberg 1975, 149), the subjectival phenomena encompass only small part of one's total reality and of Being in general (Spiegelberg 1975, 135).

[23] Like Conrad-Martius, Spiegelberg also emphasizes the "argument of reality" that is inherent in real being. A "phenomenon of reality" refers to the convergence of the capacity for the phenomenal object to present itself and its claim on being real. Hence, real phenomena are distinguished from "bare phenomena" that have no such claim to reality (Spiegelberg 1975, 133).

[24] Spiegelberg regards the related independence as a "fundamental and essential result of reality" (excluding real acts of the subject that depend on the subject itself) (Spiegelberg 1975, 132n2).

whose appearance and concretization outwards is possible.[25] Conrad-Martius emphasizes the independence and separateness of the two "realities" from each other. In her words, "the real reality [...] can never belong to the noematic-phenomenal totality [*Gesamtbestand*] of the world, because it concerns the factual 'standing-on-its-own' [»*Auf-sich-selber-Stehen*«] or ontological 'being grounded in-itself' [*seinsmäßige* »*in-sich-selber Gegründetsein*«]' of the world and all its parts [*Bestände*]. Herein *lies* the real reality of the world, whether it is factually given or not" (Conrad-Martius 1958, 397). Both ideas of reality are remote from the extreme version of idealism. However, while the former might be exhausted in the epistemological framework and thus at least partly have some affinities with the moderate shape of idealism, the latter inheres some stamp of Conrad-Martius' ontological-metaphysical stance, and hence can serve as a starting point in a realist philosophy of Being. In any event, the common title of "reality" might suggest that their separation from each other is not obvious.

However, unlike the real world that exists in-itself and for-itself, which Conrad-Martius refers to as the "'habit' of being independent ['*Habitus*' *der Seinsselbstständigkeit*]"[26] that refers to reality as such (Conrad-Martius 1916, 356), facticity is not there by-itself. At the very outset, she establishes that "'factual' [*Sachliche*] or as we also often say, 'objective' groundedness [*Habitus*] in genuine phenomenon does not mean [...] *real* groundedness" (Conrad-Martius 1916, 351). More specifically, factual existence indicates what she calls "sensory self-presenting [*ein sich selbst Präsentierendes*]." It is impossible for such existence to be confined to sense perception, which does not have the "job [*Beruf*]" of unearthing the "thing-in-itself" that underlie the perceptions, but rather of bringing "the 'world in-itself' into *exposure*" (Conrad-Martius 1916, 463). Moreover, she explains that the concretely given "does not always hold what it, as appearing [*Erscheinende*] thus and so, seems to promise" (Conrad-Martius 1916, 358). Sometimes the sensory given exposes merely what she calls the "*semblance of reality* [*Aussehen einer Realität*]" (Conrad-Martius 1916, 441n1) that does not entirely match "the *actually* present" (Conrad-Martius 1916, 356, 380). Indeed, the sensed is supposed to exist "only

---

[25] Kuhn explains that this expression of Conrad-Martius, which seems like a tautology, indicates the real that was not reduced to a phenomenon in which the "I" represents, but rather the real as standing on its own reality (Kuhn 1971, 2). However, he is suspicious of a potential "duplication of the quandry in attempting to solve the philosophical problem of reality (Kuhn 1971, 5). The expression "*wirkliche Wirklichkeit*" occurred previously in a lecture by Theodor Lipps from 1899 (Schuhmann and Smith 1985, 792) and the subsequent is in a manuscript of Johannes Daubert from 1904. It is mentioned also by Husserl in *Ideas-II* (see: Husserl 1952b, §18 55 / Husserl 2002a, §18, 16) in the sense of the objective material thing that transcends the initial subjectivity and indicates the intersubjective sphere (thus its translation as "actual reality"). However, while for Husserl this reality can exist solely as an intentional unity of sensory appearances, for Conrad-Martius, "real reality" refers to the independent and in-itself existence of real being that preconditions any possible fulfillment of spatial-temporal existence (Avé-Lallemant 1975A, 33n41).

[26] Spiegelberg regards the related independence as a "fundamental and essential result of reality" (excluding real acts of the subject that depend on the subject itself), see: Spiegelberg 1975, 132, n. 2.

through 'participation' in these eternal forms, values, and norms" (Conrad-Martius 1932A, 35) and in *a priori* essential relations (Conrad-Martius 1932A, 33) that as such are imperceptible. Similar to Husserl's "principle of all principles", according to which "presentive intuition is a legitimizing source of cognition, that *everything originarily [...] offered to us in 'intuition' is to be accepted simply as what it is presented as being, but also only within the limits in which it is presented there"* (Husserl 1983, 44), Conrad-Martius argues that the essence is initially given in the phenomenal appearance in a "covered and distant" manner. Husserl explains this inadequacy of appearance in terms of both the inadequacy of the object of experience (Husserl 1983, §§3, 44, 138) and subject of experience (Husserl 1983, §15).[27] For Conrad-Martius the same inadequacy results exclusively from the nature of the object itself, whose essence cannot be entirely unearthed at once, rather than from the limited capacities of the observing subject (Conrad-Martius 1916, 351–352).[28] However, despite the incompleteness of the appearance of the essence at the phenomenal layer, Conrad-Martius insists on the indispensability of the study of the phenomenal layer of appearance. She argues that the essence (*Wesensbeständen*) that underlie the appearances (Conrad-Martius 1916, 354) "bursts forth" already at the manifest "surface-appearance [*Erscheinungsoberfläche*]."[29] Moreover, any claim for matter-of-factness and objectivity must find some expression in the concrete reality (Conrad-Martius 1916, 351) in which finally the phenomenon "steps out in complete objectivity and totality" (Conrad-Martius 1916, 353).[30]

Obviously, in the absence of a full revealing of reality by means of its phenomenal appearances, the factual existence can be called into question. Hence, it is evident that the idealist stamp on Husserl's thinking, which prescribed the suspension and anything that admits of doubt, could not help but "bracket" any factual element of reality as an essential precondition for the constitution of pure consciousness (Conrad-Martius 1931, 24). In opposition to this, Conrad-Martius not only does not flee from the doubtfulness of facticity but seems to further emphasize and reinforce it. In addition to her employment of "incommensurability" that is rather familiar in philosophical discourses, she searches for proper words that might properly label

---

[27] Cf. Miron 2018b, 6–8.

[28] At this point, Conrad-Marius is clearly influenced by Reinach's view concerning the "gradual approximation to the object" (Reinach 1969, 220).

[29] In general, the manifest "surface-appearance" denotes the external side of the thing, behind which lies the interior realm that is imperceptible (Conrad-Martius 1916, 353–354). Conrad-Martius refers to this idea also within her discussion of materiality, where she establishes that the material being has internality and depth that lies in the dark, while its external surface is lightened and achieves appearance. However, she clarifies that there is a casual connection between the concealment in darkness and shining in the light to the extent that only because there is a depth there is also surface. See Conrad-Martius 1923, 205–209, 214, 235–136.

[30] Kuhn described the same state of affairs in the following words: "the things towards which the gaze is directed are always known in advance, we do not start at a null point. They show themselves to us, but they are concealed. They are standing up against us as known but also as mysterious and impose on us the distinction between what things are in their beginning and the essence that is uncovered by penetrating observation" (Kuhn 1969, 399).

the mysterious element that she observes in factual reality. In this connection, she refers to "something [*Etwas*]" that is there in facticity that turns it into *"the questionable* in the strict sense [*katexochen*]!" and raises questions such as: How does it arrive at Being? Why does it have Being? What does it substantiate in Being? What does it obtain in Being? Why is it the way it is, as it exists? She establishes that this problematic, referred to also as a primordial questioning (*Urfraglichkeit*), lies in the unjustifiability (*Unbegründbarkeit*) of the primordial situation (*Ursituation*) (Conrad-Martius 1931A, 39–40).[31] Likewise, she describes her philosophy as follows: "here we come across a pure, stubborn, unresolvable [*unaufschließbares*], readily acceptable 'that [*Daß*]'! And it is precisely in this pure, insoluble stubbornness of the 'that' that the 'offensiveness [*Anstößigkeit*]' of facticity lies" (Conrad-Martius 1931A, 42).[32] In any event, in her view, the related incommensurability, 'something', and 'such' that are inherent in facticity rob facticity of the possibility of achieving an internal uniformity and overall rationalization. Obviously, this offensiveness of reality cannot be detected from an idealist perspective, let alone deciphered by it. However, rather than suggesting an illumination of it, Conrad-Martius establishes the importance of acknowledging its presence in reality and consolidating this acknowledgment as a first datum in any philosophical approach to reality, that is to metaphysics. Consequently, she establishes that if the moment of rupture (*Bruch*) and ontological incommensurability is not inherent in the questioning and reasoning, then no metaphysics is possible at all (Conrad-Martius 1931A, 43).

As a genuine phenomenologist, Conrad-Martius gives herself over to what appears before her eyes rather than providing "solutions," and thus she harnesses philosophical argumentation for reinforcing the complexity that has been revealed to her. In this spirit, she declares "we must remain *with* Kant primarily vis-à-vis the hard fact of antinomy itself, that verifies *both* the thesis *just like the* anti-thesis to be proved" (Conrad-Martius 1932, 79). Also, she agrees with Kant that "the infinite dimension of the empirical has no direct metaphysical connection to the metaphysical absolutes" (Conrad-Martius 1932, 78), and that indeed there is no transfer from the real world and its patterns to the absolute and that it is impossible to extricate out of an anti-thesis a thesis of existence. However, while in her view these insights into the Kantian and idealist thinking carry out a "shifting back to reason [*in die ratio zurückverschob*]" (Conrad-Martius 1932, 79), she herself favors enduring in the dual realm, within which both appearance and Being are maintained. Therefore, the starting point of her metaphysics adheres to this original duality and aims at rehabilitating it in the form that she regards as an over-rationalizing influence that has been exerted by idealism. In this regard, she wonders what might be the genuine essence of a world that can no longer be accounted for by *a priori* forms of experience (Conrad-Martius 1932A, 35). She responds as follows:

---

[31] For additional references to the 'something', see Conrad-Martius 1931B, 89; 1927–1928, 158.

[32] For further reading about Conrad-Martius' search for a vocabulary that can appropriate her realist phenomenology, see Miron 2021, 95–114 (or: Miron 2015).

An irresolvable dualism of Being and appearing is constituted, whereby, depending on how much weight is given to the empirical [*sensualistischem*] or the ideal in the formation of the system, the character of mere appearance lies more on the side of the empirical [*Sensuellen*] or more on the side of the ideal. Therefore, conversely, "true Being [*wahre Sein*]" lies now on the side of immediate sense perception, now on the side of eternal ideas. (Conrad-Martius 1932A, 35)

The duality is, then, the tangible expression of her understanding of the real as essentially not revealing itself entirely in its sensory appearance, yet it still, as she puts it, "must possess 'somehow' its own position" (Conrad-Martius 1932A, 35). Indeed, the crucial infrastructure for the rehabilitation of the desired duality is implied already in the aforementioned contention that the sensory exists through its "'participation'" in eternal forms, values, and norms (Conrad-Martius 1932A, 35) and in *a priori* essential relations (Conrad-Martius 1932A, 33). However, while idealist thinking chooses to fill the abyss that separates the two constituents of the duality with cognizing reason, Conrad-Martius favors preserving and even reinforcing this abyss by maintaining the thesis and the anti-thesis "in their antonymic equilibrium," in which they were supposed to be from the outset as "proving and negating in the same sense" (Conrad-Martius 1932, 50). To be sure, what is at stake is not an epistemological balance, which can be altered to the point of the constitution of metaphysical idealism. On the contrary, especially as the elements involved here are existing in-themselves by their very nature, the essential abyss between them cannot be overcome. Consequently, the unearthing of the "fundamental duality in the possible configuration of real being" (Conrad-Martius 1957, 98), addresses the philosophical observation both outwards to the phenomenal shape of reality and inwards to its foundational essence.

Finally, the ultimate reinforcing of the duality between appearance and Being that Conrad-Martius argues for in response to the unifying force of pure consciousness in idealism is suggested when she writes:

Any 'groundlessness [*Grundlosigkeit*]' of Being, which is bounded by the nothing, must be located in the abyss or the non-ground [*Ungrund*] of the nothing, the groundlessness of Being that is incommensurable with nothing, however, is a foundation in the abyss of its own *Being*! (Conrad-Martius 1931B, 92)[33]

Being itself is portrayed as "resting on the grounds of the abyss" (Conrad-Martius 1923, 222). Thus, the ontological nature of the abyss, which enables it to serve as ground for real beings, is confirmed (Conrad-Martius 1923, 175, 222). Therefore, the rehabilitation of the duality is also the confirmation of the existence of an ontological abyss, the result of which being that neither a complete externalization nor an ideal unification of reality can take place.

One might wonder how facticity, which one tends to associate with ephemerality, became so important for a philosophy of Being that seeks the deciphering of reality in its absoluteness. Conrad-Martius' reply is straight to the point: Facticity is related

---

[33] Cf. my discussions of the term "abyss" in Conrad-Martius' thinking in Miron 2021, 107–108 (or: Miron 2015, 342–343); Miron 2018a.

to the very possibility of metaphysics. In her words: "We find the genuine field of metaphysics only *under the assumption of the factual reality of the world* in which we are and to which we ourselves belong" (Conrad-Martius 1931A, 38). Facticity motivates the metaphysical question to the extent that "it makes our not-questioning [*nichtfragen*] almost impossible" (Conrad-Martius 1931A, 42). Conrad-Martius explains that by its very nature, metaphysics refers to the real world within factual existence itself and for-itself. Once one deprives the world of this element, it becomes dependent being [*seinunselbständigen*] in an idealist sense, relative in its being [*daseinsrelativen*] to cognition, and thus we destroy the foundation for metaphysics. In contrast, in her view, what makes metaphysics possible is precisely the fact that the existence of the given world is problematic (Conrad-Martius 1931A, 40). Therefore, "the entire metaphysical problematic applies only in a world that exists in-itself and for-itself. Moreover, only in the view of that factual Being in its facticity can genuine metaphysical wonderment emanate" (Conrad-Martius 1931A, 39). This means that not only can no metaphysics be established without considering facticity, but also in the face of facticity we cannot help but establish metaphysics. As opposed to idealism, Conrad-Martius establishes, then, the importance of a conscious avoidance of the elimination of facticity as the first datum of metaphysics.

In this regard, she argues that "facticity is an *extensive partaking* [*mitbestimmender*] *factor in the qualitative basic set-up* [*Grundaufbau*] of the existing types of Being! *Hence* any new type of real Being precisely conditions a new kind of metaphysical reasoning" (Conrad-Martius 1931A, 44). Moreover, only coming to terms with the essential ontological constitution of the various types of facticity and confirming their factual existence might consolidate what Conrad-Martius calls the "entry point [*Eingangsstellen*] and breakthrough point [*Durchbruchsstellen*] into the realm of metaphysics" (Conrad-Martius 1931A, 44).

Nonetheless, metaphysics cannot find its safe-haven in facticity or in any empirical fulfillments of Being that unavoidably remain conditioned by contingent circumstances. Conrad-Martius clarifies that here the anchoring in facticity is dissimilar to any questioning in positive science, which is also based on facts (Conrad-Martius 1931A, 43) and in any event, we must take into account that fundamental datum that Being "could have not existed!" (Conrad-Martius 1931A, 41). Moreover, she explains that in metaphysics we do not deal with the question of the very existence of the external world or with providing evidence of its reality. Such evidence has never been achieved and in fact is impossible, since as much as facticity is here and now and acquires an essential immediate and phenomenal expression, it exists vis-à-vis an essential transcendent element. That is to say, Conrad-Martius demands confronting facticity itself with elements that are external to it, or aspects that have no factual expression. Thus, she contends that "the metaphysical problem [...] includes in itself *the permanent* positioning of transcendence [*beleibende Transzendenzstellung*] of the absolute" (Conrad-Martius 1932, 53). However, the above-construed duality, whose polarity is reinforced by the abyss that underlies it, leaves no possibility for a direct relation to the absolute but "a leap [*Absprung*]" that can be accomplished only by an "epistemological encroachment [*Übergriff*]" into another realm (Conrad-Martius 1932, 53).[34] As much as this transcendent element remains unspecified and rather obscure within Conrad-Martius' writings, it provide at least an initial protection from the related perils of the "*proton pseudos*" of idealism.

4 Epilogue

Conrad-Martius' striving to unveil the "offence [*Anstoß*]" of thinking (Conrad-Martius 1931, 17) or even its "primordial offence [*Uranstoß*]" (Conrad-Martius 1933/1934, 428), to pinpoint "where the philosophical stumbling block [*Stein des Anstoßes*] is located" (Conrad-Martius 1931A, 39) and illuminate it (Conrad-Martius 1931A, 41), or alternatively to come to terms with "the inner driving motive [*das treibende innere Motiv*]" (Conrad-Martius 1931A, 39) of philosophy, is typical of her writings. This attitude resonates in her overwhelming critique of idealism within which she attempts to demonstrate that idealism's sense of metaphysics, which dismisses any real aspect altogether, is "contradictory" (Conrad-Martius 1932, 51–52). Thus, subsequent to her critical description of the deficiencies of idealism she asks, "whether signs are increasing that our thinking about the world is becoming again truly substantial, cosmic, in short anti-idealist" (Conrad-Martius 1932A, 37). Yet, Conrad-Martius' argument that "the peril of the slipping of phenomenology into idealism […] is overwhelming" (Conrad-Martius 1932, 75n20) seems to threaten her own endeavors to achieve an "anti-idealist" philosophy insofar as she is a phenomenologist herself. Moreover, the friction indicated between phenomenology and idealism, which underlies the possibility for "slipping" from the one to the other, seems to imply that from a phenomenological point of view the conscious effort to establish an anti-idealist philosophy might also be unjustified. Indeed, also her own observation of phenomenology as "still carrying the eggshells of its idealist origins" (Conrad-Martius 1951, 5) clearly conflicts with this choice.

To a considerable extent, it is unclear on what exactly Conrad-Martius based her contention that only by regaining philosophical access to the empirical, the factual, and the genuinely transcendent, which in her view were eventually eroded in idealism, can we protect against "slipping" into idealism. What is it about facticity that can protect us from the "perils" of idealism? Conrad-Martius' response could have concerned their resistance to and escape from complete rationalization. However, the possible surprising or even mysterious aspects that are implicit in her view of facticity can deprive it of offering protection, unless it is acceptable that the desired metaphysics is deliberately fluid and bears no coherence whatsoever. Obviously, this is not the case as far as Conrad-Martius' idea of metaphysics is concerned. Despite characterizing the idealist striving for an "absolute and indubitable judgment about *factual* being" (Conrad-Martius 1931, 20) as odd, her essence-based

---

[34] Conrad-Martius uses the Greek expression μετάβασις εἰς ἄλλο γένος.

metaphysics and the assumed fluidity cannot go together. Therefore, it seems that Conrad-Martius' rehabilitation of the possibility of metaphysics out of the idealist worldview cannot rely solely on bringing facticity back to the fore of philosophizing.

In addition to the aspects that concern Conrad-Martius' declared philosophical predisposition, her view of the evolution of idealism, particularly the "elevation" of the empirical to the ideal, is also questionable. The main reservation in this regard is to what extent this "elevation" results from an informed decision, or from the human drive to decipher reality, which involves to one degree or another an abstraction articulated in ideal terms. Hence, the discussed turning of the real into an ideal, as a result of which reality turns out to be a mere concept for the idealist (Conrad-Martius 1932A, 36), not only applies to idealism but to the human experience, whose search for meaning is often not confined to facticity. Moreover, despite the apparent narrowing of the realm of reality by its rationalization and conceptualization in idealism, a restricted idea of reality does not necessarily deprive thinking from consolidating a metaphysical stance.

The final reservation concerns Conrad-Martius' accusation of idealism for "filling" again with reason (*Vernunft*) the "abyss" between the "mere appearing" and the "in-itself" (Conrad-Martius 1931, 18). Instead, as discussed above, her view of reality preserves and reinforces the ontological "abyss" and stresses the "incommensurability," the "something," and the "that" regarding reality. However, given that she herself assumes the possibility of the intelligibility of reality, due to the presence of essences in real beings (Conrad-Martius 1934, 230) that are considered as original and perceivable (Conrad-Martius 1931N1, 2–3), it seems that not much follows from this aspect of her criticism. In other words, acknowledging an aspect of incomprehensibility regarding facticity that prevails alongside the principle intelligibility of real beings seems more like a nuance that cannot support the sharp distinction between idealism and the anti-idealist thinking she strives to uphold.

Nonetheless, despite the indicated insufficiencies in Conrad-Martius' criticism of idealism, I argue that it should not be dismissed altogether. Rather, the issue requires a complementary study of other aspects in her thinking that might suggest broader grounds for understanding her view in connection to idealism. That is to say that Conrad-Martius' critique of idealism does not stand on its own but should be further explored and evaluated within the context of her work in its entirety. Also, it is worth mentioning the essential fact that important sections of her criticism of idealism still appear in unpublished documents (Conrad-Martius 1931N1, 1931N2), meaning that her critical view was never finalized. Nevertheless, both her published essays that deal with idealism and the archival and unfinalized documents open an important window to her realist phenomenology.

References

Avé-Lallemant, Eberhard. 1971. *Phänomenologie und Realität: Vergleichende Untersuchungen zur 'München-Göttinger' und 'Freiburger' Phänomenologie* (Habilitationsschrift), Munich.
———— 1975. *Die Nachlässe der Münchener Phänomenologen in der Bayerischen Staatsbibliothek.* Wiesbaden: Harrassowitz.
———— 1975A. Die Antithese Freiburg- München in der Geschichte der Phänomenologie. In *Die Münchener Phänomenologie*, ed. H. Kuhn, E. Avé-Lallemant, R. Gladiator. The Hague: Nijhoff, 19–38.
Avé-Lallemant, Ursula. 1965/66. Hedwig Conrad Martius. *Jahrbuch der Evangelischen Akademie Tutzing* XV: 203–212.
Becker, Oskar. 1930. Die Philosophie Edmund Husserls. *Kantstudien*, 35, 119-150.
Brown, Harold. 1973. Idealism, Empiricism and Materialism. *New Scholasticism* 47: 311–323.
Celms, Theodor. 1928. *Der phänomenologische idealismus Husserls*. Riga: Walters and Rapa.
Choi, Kyeong-Seop. 2007. *Unterwegs zum Dialog mit den Wissenschaften. Phänomenologische und neukantianische Wissenschaftsauffassung und Wissenschaftsauslegung am Beispiel von Husserls und Cassirers Philosophie*. Würzburg: Königshausen & Neumann.
Conrad-Martius, Hedwig. 1916. Zur Ontologie und Erscheinungslehre der realen Außenwelt. *Jahrbuch für Philosophie und phänomenologische Forschung* 3, 345–542.
———— 1916N. *Über Ontologie*. Conrad-Martiusiana A I 3, 1–14. Munich: Bavarian State Library.
———— 1920. *Die erkenntnisstheoretischen Grundlagen des Positivismus*. Bergzabern: Heinrich Müller (private print).
———— 1923. Realontologie. *Jahrbuch für Philosophie und phänomenologische Forschung* VI, 159–333.
———— 1927–1928. Die Zeit. In *Schriften zur Philosophie*, vol. 1 (1963). Munich: Kösel, 101–184.
———— 1930N. *Heideggers "Sein und Zeit", Metaphysische Quellpunkte*, Conrad-Martiusiana A III 6 (a), 1–42, Munich: Bavarian State Library.
———— 1931. Seinsphilosophie. In *Schriften zur Philosophie*, vol. 1 (1963). Munich: Kösel, 15–31.
———— 1931A. Was ist Metaphysik? In *Schriften zur Philosophie*, vol. 1 (1963). Munich: Kösel, 38–48.
———— 1931B. Seins und Nichts. In *Schriften zur Philosophie*, vol. 1 (1963). Munich: Kösel, 89–100.
———— 1931N1. Entwurf zu einer universalen Schematik realen Seins, Conrad-Martiusiana: A II 2, 1–10. Bavarian State Library: Munich.
———— 1931N2. Skizze über den Sensualizmus, Phänomenalismus, idealismus, Subjektivismus, Rationalizmus,Pantheismus einerseits und einer teleologischen, Kategorialen, realistischen, kosmischen Weltauffassung un dem Theismus enderseits, Conrad-Martiusiana A III 4, 1–14, Munich: Bavarian State Library.
———— 1932. Bemerkung über Metaphysik und ihre methodische Stelle. In *Schriften zur Philosophie*, vol. 1 (1963). Munich: Kösel, 49–88.
———— 1932A. Die aktuelle Krisis des idealistischen Denkens. In *Schriften zur Philosophie*, vol. 1 (1963). Munich: Kösel, 32–37.
———— 1932B. Dasein, Substantialität, Seele. In *Schriften zur Philosophie*, vol 1 (1963). Munich: Kösel, 194–227.
———— 1933/1934. Natur und Gnade. In *Schriften zur Philosophie*, vol 1 (1963). Munich: Kösel, 427–458.
———— 1934. Existentialle Tiefe und Untiefe von Dasein und Ich. In *Schriften zur Philosophie*, vol. 1 (1963). Munich: Kösel, 228–244.
———— 1936. Der Mensch in der heutige Naturwissenschft und Philosophie. In *Schriften zur Philosophie*, vol. 1 (1963). Munich: Kösel, 363–426.
———— 1938. Licht und Geist. In *Schriften zur Philosophie*, vol 3 (1965). Munich: Kösel, 261–274.
———— 1951. Vorwort. In Adolf Reinach, *Was ist Phänomenologie?* Munich: Kösel, 5–17.

————— 1956. Über das Wesen des Wesens. In *Schriften zur Philosophie*, vol 3 (1965). Munich: Kösel, 335–356.

————— 1956. Über das Wesen des Wesens. *Schriften zur Philosophie*, vol. 3 (1965). Munich: Kösel, 335–356.

————— 1956A. Wirkender und Empfangender Geist. In *Schriften zur Philosophie*, vol. 3 (1965). Munich: Kösel, 295–314.

————— 1956B. Phänomenologie und Spekulation. In *Schriften zur Philosophie*, vol. 3 (1965), Munich: Kösel, 370–384.

————— 1957. *Das Sein*. Munich: Kösel.

————— 1958. Die transzendentale und die ontologische Phänomenologie. *Schriften zur Philosophie*, vol. 3 (1965). Munich: Kösel, 393–402.

————— 1958N. *Von der Phänomenologie zur Metaphysik, Ansprache bei der Feier des 70. Geburtstages in der Universität München*. Conrad-Martiusiana D II 2, 1–5. Munich: Bavarian State Library.

Drummond, John. 1988. "Realism versus anti-realism: a Husserlian contribution." In R. Sokolowski (ed), *Edmund Husserl and the Phenomenological Tradition*. Washington DC: Catholic University of America Press, 87–106

Ebel, Gerhard. 1965. *Untersuchungen zu einer Realistischen Grundlegung der Phänomenologischen Wesensschau* (Dissertation). Munich.

Farber, Marvin. 1967. *Phenomenology and Existence, Toward a Philosophy within Nature*, New York: Harper & Row.

Feist, Richard (ed.). 2004. Husserl and the Sciences. Ottawa: University of Ottawa Press.

Hart, James G. 2020. *Hedwig Conrad-Martius' Ontological Phenomenology*. Cham: Springer.

Harvey, Charles W. 1989. Husserl's Phenomenology and the Foundation of Natural Sciences. Athens: Ohio University Press.

Holmes, Richard. 1975. Is transcendental phenomenology committed to idealism? *The Monist* 59 (1): 98–114.

Hopkins, Burt. 2010. *The Philosophy of Husserl*. Chesham: Acumen.

Husserl, Edmund. 1901. *Logical Investigations*, vol. 1 (1970). J. Findlay (trans.), London and New York: Routledge.

————— 1930. A letter to Dorion Cairns from 21.3.1930, in: *Husserl Edmund. 1859-1959. Recuiel Commémoratif Publié A L'occasion du Centenaire de la Naissance du Philosophie*, Martinus Nijhoff, La Haye (Phaenomenologica 4), 283–285.

————— 1994. *Briefwechsel Bd. 2: Die Münchener Phänomenologen*. Karl Schuhmann (ed.), The Hague: Kluwer.

————— [1989] 2002. *Ideas Pertaining to a Pure Phenomenology and to a phenomenological Philosophy, Second Book*. R. Rojcewicz and A. Schuwer (trans.). Dordrecht: Kluwer.

————— [1913] 1983. *Ideas Pertaining to a Pure Phenomenology and to a phenomenological Philosophy, First Book*. F. Kersten (trans.). The Hague: Nijhoff.

Ingarden, Roman. 1975. *On the Motives which led Husserl to Transcendental idealism*, Arnór Hannibalsson (trans.). The Hague: Nijhoff.

Kant, Immanuel. 1998. *Critique of pure reason*. P. Guyer and A. Wood (trans.). Cambridge: Cambridge University Press.

Krings, Hermann. 1960, "Studie über Vorstellung und Sein" in: *Sinn und Sein, Ein Philosophisches Symposion*, Richard Wisser [hrsg.], Tübingen, 193–208.

Kuhn, Helmut. 1969. Phänomenologie und Realität. *Zeitschrift für Philosophische Forschung* 23 (3): 397–402.

————— 1971. Phänomenologie und 'wirklich Wirklichkeit'. In *Die Münchener Phänomenologie*, ed. H. Kuhn, E. Avé-Lallemant, R. Gladiator. The Hague: Nijhoff, 1–7.

Kupperman, Joel. 1957. Realism vs. idealism. *American Philosophical Quarterly* 12 (3): 199–210.

Lovejoy, Arthur O. 1955 [1929]. *The Revolt against Dualism: An Inquiry Concerning the Existence of ideas*, The Open Court Publishing Company, La Salle, Illinois.

Miron Ronny. 2012. *Karl Jaspers: From Selfhood to Being*. Amsterdam: Rodopi.

Miron, Ronny. 2021. *Hedwig Conrad-Martius, The Phenomenological Gateway to Reality*. Cham: Springer.

———— 2014. The Gate of Reality – Hedwig Conrad-Martius' Idea of Reality in Realontologie. *Phänomenologische Forschungen*, 59–82.

———— 2015. The vocabulary of reality. *Human Studies*, 38/3: 335–336.

———— 2017. The Ontological Exclusivity of the I. *Phänomenologische Forschungen*, 97–116.

———— 2018a. Essence, Abyss and Self – Hedwig Conrad-Martius on the Non-Spatial Dimensions of Being. In *Woman Phenomenologists on Social Ontology*, Sebastian Luft and Ruth Hagengruber (eds.). Cham: Springer.

———— 2018b. *Husserl and Other Phenomenologists*, Ronny Miron (ed.) Routledge, Taylor and Francis, London and New York, 2018, "Introduction": 1–2; "Husserl and Other Phenomenologists": 3–16). (formerly appeared in The European Legacy: Towards New Paradigms, a special issue edited by Ronny Miron, 21, 5–6, 2016, "Introduction": 465–466; "Husserl and Other Phenomenologists": 467–480 (Miron 2016).

———— 2019. The Duality of the "I" in the Thinking of Hedwig Conrad-Martius. *Phänomenologische Forschungen*, 71–98.

Moran, Dermot. 2005. *Edmund Husserl: Founder of Phenomenology*. Cambridge: Polity.

Reinach, Adolf. 1913. *Die apriorischen Grundlagen des bürgerlichen Rechtes*. Halle: Niemeyer.

———— 1951. *Was ist Phänomenologie?* Munich: Kösel.

———— 1969. Concerning Phenomenology. *The Personalist*, 50/2, 194–211.

Pfänder, Alexander. 1913. Zur Psychologie der Gesinnung, *Jahrbuch für Philosophie und Phänomenologische Forschung*, I, 325–404.

Pfeiffer, Alexandra. 2005. *Hedwig Conrad-Martius, Eine Phänomenologische sicht auf Natur und Welt*. Würzburg: Königshausen & Neumann.

Schmücker, Franz Georg. 1956. *Die Phänomenologie als Methode der Wesenerkenntnis. unter besondere Berücksichtigung der Auffassung der München-Göttinger Phänomenologenchule* (Dissertation), Munich.

Schuhmann, Karl. 1990. Husserl's Yearbook. *Philosophy and Phenomenological Research* 50: 1–25.

Schuhmann, Karl, and Smith, Barry. 1985. Against Idealism: Johannes Daubert vs. Husserl's "Ideas" I, *Review of Metaphysics, A Philosophical Quarterly* 38 (4), 763-793.

Smith, David Woodruff and McIntyre, Ronald. 1971. Intentionality via Intentions. *Journal of Philosophy*, 68/18, 541-561.

Spiegelberg, Herbert. 1975. *Doing phenomenology: Essays on and in Phenomenology*, The Hague: Nijhoff.

Sowa, Rochus. 2010. The universal as 'what is in common': Comments on the proton-pseudos in Husserl's doctrine of the intuition of essence. In *Philosophy, Phenomenology, Sciences. Essays in Commemoration of Edmund Husserl*, ed. Carlo Ierna, Hanne Jacobs, and Filip Mattens. Dordrecht: Springer, 525–557.

———— 1959. Perspektivenwandel: Konstitution eines Husserlbildes. In *Husserl Edmund. 1859-1959. Recuiel Commémoratif Publié a L'occasion du Centenaire de la Naissance du Philosophe*. The Hague: Nijhoff, 56–63.

———— 1960. The Phenomenological Movement, A Historical Introduction, volume 1. The Hague: Nijhoff.

Plessner Helmuth. 1959. *Husserl in Göttingen*. Göttingen: Vandenhoeck & Ruprecht.

Rinofner-Kreidl, Sonja. 2014. What's Wrong with Naturalizing Epistemology? A Phenomenologist's Reply. In: R. Feist (ed.) *Husserl and the Sciences*, Ottawa: University of Ottawa Press, 41–68.

Urban, Peter. 2016. Phenomenology and interdisciplinarity. In Nielsen, C. C; Novotný, K.; Nenon, T. (ed.). *Kontexte des Leiblichen*. Nordhausen: Traugoot Bautz, 459–480.

Zahavi, Dan. 2017. *Husserl's Legacy: Phenomenology, Metaphysics, and Transcendental Philosophy*. Oxford: Oxford University Press.

Part IV
The Göttingen and Freiburg Followers. Appropriations and Amendments of Idealism

Gustav Shpet's Implicit Phenomenological Idealism: A Response to Husserl's *Ideas I*

Thomas Nemeth

Abstract The issue of whether the phenomenology presented in *Ideas I* was a metaphysical realism or an idealism came to the fore almost immediately upon its publication. The present essay is an examination of the relation of Gustav Shpet, one of Husserl's students from the Göttingen years to this issue via his understanding of phenomenology and, particularly, of the phenomenological reduction, as shown principally in his early published writings. For Shpet, phenomenology employs essential intuition without regard to experiential intuition. *If* we look on transcendental idealism as the label for this methodology, which disregards but does not deny either the empirical or its correlative species of intuition, then Shpet was such an idealist, all the while adhering to a metaphysical realism. In this way, Shpet could proclaim phenomenology to be the fundamental philosophical discipline without precluding the possibility of other philosophical disciplines insofar as they were conducted in relation to consciousness taken not as the "possession" of a human individual, but eidetically and thus not a "possession."

Keywords Phenomenological idealism · First philosophy · Ideal being · Intentionality · Eidetic description · Essential intuition · Transcendental reduction · Sense bestowal

1 Transcendental Phenomenology: A Realism or an Idealism?

As is widely known, many of Husserl's own followers in Munich and Göttingen were both perplexed and troubled by a number of the pronouncements they found in *Ideas I* upon its publication in 1913. Committed to a metaphysical realism, they looked askance on Husserl's seemingly idealistic turn in that work. In disbelief, at

Reprinted by permission (with slight modifications) from *Husserl Studies*, Thomas Nemeth, Gustav Shpet's Implicit Phenomenological Idealism, (2018) 34: 267–285.

T. Nemeth (✉)
Independent Scholar, Manchester, NJ, USA

© Springer Nature Switzerland AG 2021
R. K. B. Parker (ed.), *The Idealism-Realism Debate Among Edmund Husserl's Early Followers and Critics*, Contributions to Phenomenology 112,
https://doi.org/10.1007/978-3-030-62159-9_11

least some searched through it for statements that would buttress their own commitment to realism – hoping thereby to quell their anxiety and concomitantly affirm
their cherished wish that their acknowledged "master" had not completely abandoned what they conceived to be the basic ontological stance behind the *Logische
Untersuchungen*.[1] Among the most famous expressions of this endeavor was Gerda
Walther's 1922 index to *Ideas I*, in which she provided two subentries on "phenomenological idealism," one for passages allegedly supporting idealism and one "contra" idealism.[2] We need not say more than that Husserl himself, who became
increasingly enamored over the years with characterizing his phenomenology as an
idealism, was displeased with Walther's efforts, and in the 1928 edition it was
replaced by Landgrebe's compilation.

There were, indeed, reasonable grounds for the trepidations of Husserl's early
enthusiasts and disciples. Undoubtedly, already in his 1913 work Husserl labeled
his overall conception as "*transcendental* phenomenology" and wrote that "something transcendent necessarily must be experienceable [...] by any *actual* Ego as a
demonstrable unity relative to its concatenations of experience" (Hua III/I, pp. 6,
102/xx, 108). We could undoubtedly find many additional passages that lend support to an idealist – even solipsistic – reading of *Ideas I*, including the very title of
the next section, §49: "Absolute Consciousness as the Residuum After the
Annihilation of the World." In light of them, some of Husserl's early followers, such
as Roman Ingarden, refused to countenance and follow the path that they felt led
Husserl to idealism, viz., that of the phenomenological reduction.

Nevertheless, as Walther's index shows, a case could also be made for a realist
interpretation or understanding of *Ideas I*. For example, Husserl, earlier in §42,
wrote that "the physical thing is transcendent to the perception of it and consequently to any consciousness whatever related to it" (Hua III/I, pp. 86–87/89). And
in the next section, Husserl amplified this statement, saying that in intuitive acts we
grasp an "in itself," which, along with other expressions in that section, has prompted
Dermot Moran to write that "this appears to be a commitment to direct, empirical
realism" (Moran 2000, p. 122). Although an explicitly *metaphysical*-realist defense
and reading of *Ideas I* did not become part of the secondary literature, such an interpretation formed the background, as it were, for other young devotees of Husserl.
Simply identifying the phenomenological reduction with the eidetic reduction, they
conceived phenomenology, following Husserl's own words in his "Introduction," as
"a science of essences" that did not so much reject "matters of fact" as simply
expressed no particular interest in them (Hua III/I, p. 6/xx). Transcendental phenomenology, then, was the adoption of a purely eidetic attitude that merely *excluded*
but did *not* deny "every sort of transcendence" (cf. Hua III/I, p. 198/209).[3] One quite

---

[1] For a clear expression of this bewilderment on the part of one of Husserl's closest disciples, see
Stein (1986, p. 250).

[2] "The problem whether Husserl was an epistemological realist or idealist (as many thought) was
of particular importance to me, and I amassed all the assertions for each of the two conceptions"
(Walther 1960, p. 214). For a wealth of additional information on Walther, see Parker 2018.

[3] Recently, Luft wrote, "To this day, many presentations of the reduction repeat this faulty identification of both [the phenomenological and the eidetic] methods and equate 'eidetic intuition' with

recent convert to the phenomenological program, albeit possibly with qualification, was the relatively young Russian scholar Gustav Shpet, who had come to Göttingen initially for research on his eventual thesis dealing with what we, from the standpoint of early phenomenology, would conceivably regard as the incongruous topic of historical methodology. As we shall see in what follows, Shpet went on to display a rather idiosyncratic, but convoluted, attitude toward his German master's teachings.

In this essay, we shall examine Shpet's relation to Husserlian transcendental or phenomenological idealism via his understanding of phenomenology and the phenomenological reduction as shown principally in his early published writings.[4] Our focus here is not Shpet's disagreements with Husserl, but with what Shpet took to be the place and the role of phenomenology, as enunciated up to and with *Ideas I*, in philosophy as a whole.[5] We shall also look at remarks made in lecture notes, which have only recently come to light and which help to illuminate Shpet's position as expressed in his published writings.

2   Enter Shpet

Shpet arrived in Göttingen in late April 1912 to work, as mentioned, on his planned thesis, *Istorija kak problema logiki* [*History as a Problem of Logic*].[6] He stayed there together with his family apparently until August, returning to Moscow for approximately 1 or 2 months. There is no firm evidence that he even so much as met Husserl during this first stay in Göttingen, but, however it occurred, the two did become acquainted quite shortly after Shpet's return to Germany in late September. If he was familiar with Husserl's publications prior to this time, they could not have made a significant impression on him, since he did not seek out Husserl earlier.[7]

---

the reduction's establishment of the correlational *a priori*" (Luft 2012, p. 251). Of course, Luft is correct, but, as he admits, many have made this mistake. One question is whether Shpet was among this group making such a mistake – or did he, in effect, follow Husserl to a full phenomenological idealism.

[4] Savin writes, "the fact that Shpet studied with Husserl in Göttingen allows us to consider him a Russian representative of this [the Munich-Göttingen] school" (Savin 1997, p. 27). If we were to accept a period of study under Husserl in Göttingen as the necessary and sufficient condition for being a representative of the Munich-Göttingen school, we would have a great number of such representatives.

[5] For Shpet's specific disagreements with Husserl, see Nemeth (2009), the present essay being, in intent, complementary to it. Whereas the earlier essay criticized Shpet from a Husserlian perspective, here this author assumes Shpet's viewpoint.

[6] Shpet's extended stay in Western Europe was to pursue original source material for his dissertation. His stops included Berlin, Paris, Edinburgh in addition to Göttingen.

[7] There is little material on the basis of which one could speak with confidence of Shpet's philosophical views prior to his encounter with Husserl. In an essay from 1912 – and thus just prior to his encounter with Husserl – Shpet unhelpfully remarked that nowhere is philosophy so closely connected with life as in the Russian tradition, mentioning several names but not that of his teacher Georgij Chelpanov, to whom he was personally close. See Shpet 1912: 264. Indeed, there is no

Whatever the case, Shpet matriculated at the University for the academic year and began attending – whatever the motivation – Husserl's lecture-course *"Logik und Einleitung in der Wissenschaftslehre"* that winter semester and participated in the seminar *"Metaphysische und wissenschaftstheoretische Übung über Natur und Geist"* (Shchedrina 2015, p. 61).

In light of Shpet's class attendance and given the deep-seated reluctance on the part of many among Husserl's Göttingen students to embrace Husserl's newly emerging idealist turn, a natural question to ask is to what extent Shpet mingled with them personally and was influenced in his understanding of Husserl's teachings and writings by them. Unfortunately, relying solely on the written record, there is little evidence of any such interaction. Quite possibly owing to the age difference between Shpet and many of Husserl's much younger students, he may not have mingled comfortably with them. The caveat here is that Shpet appears to have made friends by this time with both Alexandre Koyré and Jean Hering, since upon his departure from Göttingen for Edinburgh in late July 1913 they both saw Shpet off, presumably at the train station. Hering was 11 years younger, and Koyré 13 years younger than Shpet (Shchedrina 2015, p. 61).[8] Additionally, none of the names of the most prominent members of the Göttingen students (Stein, Ingarden, Reinach, Hering) appear at all in Shpet's extant correspondence, leading us to conclude that his approach to phenomenology was influenced little, if any, by the student circle around Husserl in 1912/13 (Shpet 2012).

We do know, though, that Husserl and Shpet developed a warm personal relationship by mid-1913 that included not only long conversations, correspondence and an extended repeat visit by Shpet with Husserl in July 1914. Husserl's *Ideas I* was published already in April 1913, and Shpet clearly must have soon acquired a copy, read it, and conceived the idea of writing in 1913 what became *Appearance and Sense* rather quickly. Given his travels that summer not just to Scotland but also back to London and then to Switzerland, Shpet worked quite rapidly reading Husserl's work quickly and completed writing, for the most part, his own book, finishing it by mid-October.[9] It remains Shpet's principal commentary on Husserl's transcendental turn.

---

evidence of a philosophical influence from Chelpanov's rather amorphous but realist Neo-Kantianism. See Nemeth 2017: 268–272. If anything, the influence was later in the reverse direction – from Shpet to Chelpanov. See Chelpanov 1917, in which he focused on the phenomenological method. Given his debt to Shpet, we see that he viewed the goal of that method to be the intuition of essences as against factual determinations by empirical methods.

[8] A reasonable conjecture is that Shpet or Koyré sought out the other owing to their shared origin in Imperial Russia.

[9] Shchedrina writes that Shpet finished work on *Appearance and Sense* on 16 October 1913, since "this date is written in pencil at the end of his personal copy." The same date appears also in Shpet's diary (Shchedrina 2014, p. 142).

3   Phenomenological Idealism in *Appearance and Sense*

Already in his first chapter, Shpet acknowledged the Husserlian quest for a fundamental philosophy, a first philosophy of beginnings and principles. He understood this to be, however, a quest for the foundations of being itself, including that of the cognizing subject, to which Plato, one of the first genuine philosophers in Shpet's estimation, afforded insufficient attention. This, in his mind, stood in contrast to what he termed the "negative" quest merely for cognitive forms. Kant, for example, sought not cognition itself, i.e., the being of cognition, but merely some allegedly universal forms in the hope of learning what and where there is cognition.[10] Despite his shortcoming and oversight with respect to the cognizing subject, Plato importantly recognized the distinction between ideal being and actual being. The latter is concerned with facts, i.e., that which is in a definite time and place. Facts are contingent as against ideal beings, essences, which are necessary. In this way, we can speak of factual sciences, sciences of facts, in contrast to ideal sciences, sciences of essences. As mentioned above, Husserl called phenomenology a science of essences. Shpet, likewise, wrote, "phenomenology can only be a science of essences" (Shpet 1991, p. 11). Husserl's specific contribution to the line of philosophy extending from Plato – a line that Shpet called "positive philosophy" – is his recognition of the being of cognizing reason. The nature of this "being" needs to be philosophically explicated, coupled with then establishing the relation of cognizing reason to other beings.[11] This, however, was, for Shpet, Husserl's problem. Its recognition is also what Shpet saw as Husserl's ultimate contribution to philosophy.

Cognizing reason is manifested in the being of consciousness, and phenomenology, in establishing the nature of this being, characterizes it as intentionality. Thus, consciousness through intentionality grasps or seizes essences. What is this procedure, this grasping or seizing? How is it accomplished? For Shpet, as for Husserl, it could not be a matter of abstraction, for "any abstraction from actuality always remains either a 'part' of actuality, or it is simply a fiction" (Shpet 1991, pp. 12, 47).[12] One thing we can quickly realize is that this grasping of essences requires from us another attitude than the one we have in everyday life, an attitude different

---

[10] In his thesis, Shpet even more explicitly wrote, "Kant's critique can have only a negative, destructive significance, and a philosophy that wishes to be erected on it alone will have to be a negative philosophy" (Shpet 2002, p. 43). Shpet interpreted Husserl's early proclamation of a "return to the things themselves" as a rejection of Kantian and Marburg Neo-Kantian epistemology (Shpet 2002, p. 549).

[11] Strictly speaking, then, Husserl was not, for Shpet, a Platonist, but a representative of an ancient line of thought extending back at least as far as Plato, who was another representative, albeit the most outstanding, of that line. For a contemporary claim that Shpet saw Husserl as a Platonist, see Shijan (2005, p. 286).

[12] Also see Husserl (Hua III/I, p. 108/115), where we find, "One must see, however, that by such an 'abstracting' from Nature, only something natural can be acquired and not transcendentally pure consciousness." That is, the process of abstraction is a distillation or filtering of empirical Nature, but, as such, the remainder is still "natural."

even from that of the natural scientist, who is still concerned with factually given, albeit general, laws and principles. To attain this different attitude, the phenomeno-logical attitude, we need to exclude or make no use of the natural world, of spatio-temporal factual being. Both Husserl and Shpet stressed that this exclusion, this phenomenological epoché, does not signify a doubt, let alone a negation, in the facticity of the natural world either in general or in particulars (Hua III/I, p. 65/61; Shpet 1991, p. 27). What it does mean is that our concern is with the world as eidos, in particular essences in their intimate relation to consciousness, where conscious-ness itself is taken not as does the natural science of psychology, but as an eidos with essential structures of its own. Insofar as we speak of Plato's idealism owing to his theory of forms – in which non-spatiotemporal forms or ideas have a certain reality and "ground" the natural world – so too can we speak of Husserl's *and*, up to this point, of Shpet's phenomenological idealism already in 1913.

Of course, there is more to Husserlian "phenomenological idealism," to inten-tionality and sense-constitution, than this essentialism, regardless of the importance we ascribe to a science of essences. We should emphasize here, however, that Shpet, unlike others around Husserl at the time, seemingly did not object to the *factual* exclusion of the natural world and did not see it as an abandonement of realism for some sort of Cartesian or, worse yet, Berkeleyan idealism. Shpet simply saw the phenomenological epoché as the appropriate further extension of the eidetic reduction.

Whatever we may focus on within the science of essences, the question before us is *how* we attain these essences if it is not through a process of abstraction. Shpet, for an answer, appeals directly to Husserl. To each individually given, there is a necessarily or essentially given. As Husserl wrote, "*it belongs to the sense of any-thing contingent to have an essence*" (Hua III/I, p. 12/7). Just as the individual mat-ter of fact is given through an empirical intuition, an essence is given through eidetic intuition (Hua III/I, p. 14/9; Shpet 1991, p. 14). In other words, for Shpet we can see empirical facts, and we can correlatively also see ideal essences. In eidetic intuition, we can then describe the object of the respective intuiting, viz., essences. The result is, for him, a phenomenological description.

Shpet viewed phenomenology in 1913/14 as contributing to Platonic "positive philosophy" by a determination of the essential being of consciousness. He wrote, "Consequently, the first problem of phenomenology, precisely defined, is: What is the being of pure consciousness, how can it be studied as such, and what is its con-tent?" (Shpet 1991, p. 36). To accomplish this, Shpet viewed Husserl as proposing to clarify, via the eidetic "reduction," the interrelation between consciousness and the transcendent object of consciousness. An essential elucidation of such an inter-relation reveals that there are two types of being: consciousness and reality. For Shpet, as well as in his reading of Husserl, the former is given immanently and as something absolute, whereas "real," physical things are given through adumbrations in appearances (Shpet 1991, pp. 30–31; Hua III/I, pp. 91–94/94–98). Shpet specifi-cally stated that from this distinction and its corollaries Husserl drew conclusions that in his view agree with the preceding (Shpet 1991, p. 31).[13] Unproblematically, the existence of an object of an immanent perception is necessary. I cannot doubt the existence of my consciousness conceived as that very reflection on itself. On the other hand, the existence of a physical thing, say, this book in front of me, is not necessary just because it is given to my perception. Its existence is contingent, i.e., there is nothing countersensical in the doubt that the book is not "really" there. We are not engaging in a Cartesian doubt concerning whether the world truly exists. All Shpet – and Husserl, for that matter[14] – is saying is that there is nothing in the *sense* of an expression of the world's existence that its existence is absolute in the same way that an immanent perception's existence is necessary. Shpet also concluded from this, from the essential necessity of consciousness, that phenomenology always studies whatever it takes as its object in terms of the correlative relationship between consciousness and that object. It can investigate both immanent and transcendent objects, but in either case it is with the "determinate coefficient" of consciousness (Shpet 1991: 35). That is, all philosophical investigations should be undertaken keeping in mind the intentionality of consciousness.

Thus far, then, Shpet followed Husserl's lead in maintaining that the fundamental science of philosophy is an eidetic description of potentially everything, provided, that is, that we never lose sight of consciousness *also taken eidetically*. Since Husserl called this pure or transcendental phenomenology, there is no reason why we cannot label Shpet's program up to this point also as transcendental phenomenology. A transcendental phenomenological investigation keeps in mind throughout the correlative connection between the *cogito* and the *cogitatum* in its essential structures. In other words, it requires the investigator adopt a particular attitude toward the subject matter, the phenomenological attitude. Not to do so is characteristic of the dogmatic sciences and of everyday life. In the phenomenological attitude, our main concern is pure consciousness (i.e., consciousness taken eidetically), the being of which is intentionality. Consciousness always intends, i.e., is directed, toward something. That we exclude all transcendent being does not mean that we strip consciousness of objects. That would be impossible, for it would mean that we eliminate intentionality itself from consciousness. Instead, we make no use of transcendencies as such; we put all positings of something transcendent "out of action." We make no use of transcendent actualities (Hua III/I, p. 106/113; Shpet 1991, p. 37).

For a further clarification of the subject matter or content of phenomenology, we can make use of the fact–essence dichotomy. Each member of that division has an associated intuition, viz., experiential intuition and essential intuition. The former

---

[13] Shpet's wording is, we must admit, somewhat ambiguous. He could have meant that he simply agreed with Husserl's logic. That is, from the distinction mentioned, Husserl provided a logically valid set of conclusions, independent of the cogency of the distinction. However, Shpet could also have meant that he accepted Husserl's distinction as correct as well as the logic leading to the conclusions. Only if we proceed with the latter interpretation, do we have a philosophically interesting claim.

[14] Husserl writes, "Anything physical which is given 'in person' can be non-existent; no mental process which is given 'in person' can be non-existent." Hua III/I, p. 98/102.

gives facts; the latter essences. For every fact or individual thing there is an essence, and every essence has possible corresponding individuals. Nevertheless, phenomenology is not simply concerned with essences, but with what we could call a subset – even though neither Husserl nor Shpet used that term – of the set of essences. For both Husserl and Shpet, the formalism of logic, for example, and mathematical sciences in general are excluded from pure or transcendental phenomenology. The former concern themselves with transcendencies, though these are transcendent in another sense than are the facts of the actual world (Hua III/I, p. 158/170; Shpet 1991, p. 150)[15] In this regard, Shpet quoted Husserl to the effect that transcendental phenomenology, although an eidetic science, belongs to a totally different class than does mathematics (Shpet 1991, p. 87).

Thus, the tool that phenomenology employs, in Shpet's eyes, is essential or ideal intuition in complete disregard of experiential intuition. This follows, he held, from the very spirit of the reduction. We also see that by restricting itself to a description of the immediately given in ideal intuition phenomenology is a pre-theoretical discipline. Shpet – and in this case Husserl too – recognized the possibility of objections against phenomenological description particularly as it approaches ever more concrete levels of individuation, with the here and now. The general issue is how do we engage in description? Employing language to describe anything involves conceptual terminology. Does not this very fact involve theory and thereby jeopardize our very enterprise? When dealing with an eidetic concretum, phenomenology rescinds the individuation and elevates the essential content. Shpet remarked that he did not fully concur with the details of Husserl's treatment, but he wished to proceed to another matter, one that we shall see sharply separates him from Husserl.

Let me stress again that up to this point Shpet shared Husserl's general outlook. *If* what we have discussed thus far amounts to transcendental idealism, then Shpet was such an idealist, *malgré* his silence in the matter. Both Shpet and Husserl could accurately say that philosophically they were idealists, while in everyday life, i.e., in the natural attitude, they were realists. However, Shpet did not share Husserl's belief that the fact-essence dichotomy is exhaustive of all species of being, and therefore that the distinction between experiential intuition and eidetic intuition is exhaustive. Shpet believed that Husserl's dichotomy omits a peculiar species of empirical being, viz., social being. Taking his cue from Husserl's own words that each species of being essentially has a corresponding mode of givenness and along with it a mode of cognition, social being must, therefore, also have its own peculiar cognitive method. (Hua III/I, p. 176/187; Shpet 1991, p. 100). Empathy, Shpet

---

[15]After discussing the possibility of excluding the objects of the material-eidetic sciences from transcendental phenomenology, Shpet added that Husserl's position is "fundamentally correct." They are to be excluded despite their ideality, since they are not taken in their necessary relation to consciousness (Shpet 1991, pp. 53–54). This serves as further testimony at this point to Shpet's adherence to phenomenological idealism, via the phenomenological reduction. Savin writes that Shpet never even once mentions the expression "transcendental reduction" in his third chapter entitled "The Phenomenological Reduction." Although literally true, Shpet does mention in that chapter the phenomenological reduction, which he took to be the same as the transcendental reduction (Savin 1997, p. 25; see Shpet 1991, p. 59).

believed, plays a fundamental role in this mode. Admittedly, Husserl himself recognized a role for empathy, but from the perspective of *Ideas I* did not see it as a fundamental role.[16] This oversight led him, according to Shpet, to overlook social being as a distinctive species of being. Shpet recognized that such an acceptance of social being would entail a significant modification of phenomenology, but he failed to expound on this here in 1913/14. Clearly, in one sense it need not entail a rejection of the essence of phenomenology itself, a description of cognition within the phenomenological attitude, since social being is a species of *empirical* being, which is "put out of play" within that attitude. One could, therefore, accept social being and yet be a transcendental idealist. Yet just as there is a one-to-one correlation between each empirically given something and an essence, i.e., each particular being has a unique individual essence, so there should be an eidetic reduction of social being and then a further phenomenological reduction of the social.[17] In this way, another immense and fundamental field opens up for phenomenological analysis.

Instead of pursuing a phenomenology of the social in *Appearance and Sense*, a topic that he acknowledged would prove long and arduous, Shpet turned instead to details in Husserl's *Ideas I*. One issue to which Shpet attached particular importance is the necessary correlation mentioned above between fact and essence and correspondingly that between experiential intuition and eidetic intuition. We can use both species of intuition to obtain knowledge owing to a third thing that serves as a representation for both. Shpet was aware that this sought-for third thing bears a certain resemblance to Kant's introduction of the schematism in the first *Critique*, but he dismissed the charge rather abruptly for its superficiality.[18] This "third thing" is a concept, and with it the issue looming over our investigation is how a concept can express an intuition. The sense data, *hyle*, of a mental process (*Erlebnis*) lacks anything pertaining to intentionality. These are overlaid by a stratum that bestows sense on them and introduces intentionality to them. Apparently, then, for Husserl such sense-bestowal is as much the essence of consciousness as is intentionality. Indeed, for consciousness to intend something *means* to impart a sense to it. The notion of sense here is wider than the linguistic sphere. It is a moment within all conscious acts whether they are verbally expressed or not.

If, up to this point, Shpet has followed Husserl's lead into a phenomenological idealism, his next move threatens such an accompaniment. Husserl's conception of

---

[16] Elena Gurko has grounds for writing – at least from the vantage point of 1913/14 – that, "A deduction to the mental processes of the other is, for Shpet, possible by means of empathy, and revealed by Husserl but not valued by him in its fundamental significance" (Gurko 1999, pp. 10–11).

[17] Shpet could justifiably be faulted for not carefully distinguishing the eidetic reduction from the phenomenological. On my reading here, he did recognize the distinction, but his failure to be clear has led others mistakenly, I believe, to charge him with departing from Husserl in this regard. One contemporary scholar writes, "It is noteworthy that Shpet, as against Husserl, in fact made no distinction between the phenomenological reduction, properly speaking, and the eidetic reduction" (Evstropov 2014, p. 62).

[18] Shpet calls Kant's schematism "a powerless outburst to fill in the abyss he himself created with his dilemma" (Shpet 1991, p. 102).

the pure Ego is that it is present in all conscious acts. Indeed, Husserl characterized a large role for the pure Ego, saying that it "lives" in the position-taking act (Hua III/I, p. 214/225; Shpet 1991, p. 109). Shpet could not abide such a large sphere of activity for the pure Ego. Although Husserl's depiction of the Ego's "life" has merit, Shpet found it to be exaggerated. Senses are not "created" by the pure Ego, as though those senses were subjective or arbitrary. Although Shpet is quite guarded here, he feared such a move is decidedly a step toward a reductionism – what we may term a "transcendental psychologism," although Shpet did not introduce such an expression. For him, an object can retain its sense throughout changes in the Ego's attentional acts. An enduring intentional object, being the bearer of senses, itself possesses an "inner" sense. Shpet remained unconvinced that Husserl had provided the final word on sense-bestowal. Despite his detailed analysis of the noematic-noetic correlation, Husserl's notion of "sense" remains an abstract form, in the same way that mathematics is an abstraction. For Shpet, on the other hand, there is a distinction between the noematic "Object in the How," of which Husserl spoke, and an object's authentic sense, its intimate something, that which is inherent in the object itself (Shpet 1991, p. 116; cf. Hua III/I, p. 304/316). It makes the object an integral thing. That is, a concrete object has in addition to the Husserlian senses and the bearer of those senses, something else that can be phenomenologically described leading to its actuality.

Admittedly, there is much here that needs a great deal of clarification. Whether Shpet's emendation of Husserl is warranted and whether, even more importantly, it is correct, is not our concern here. What is our concern is whether Shpet, with his talk of an "intimate something," had ultimately abandoned his earlier understanding of the phenomenological reduction, of the exclusion of actual existence from phenomenology, and thereby of its commitment to a form of idealism. Particularly troubling is Shpet's talk of obtaining an object's sense in its actuality by knowing how to reach actuality (Shpet 1991, pp. 117, 123.). Was Shpet inquiring how cognition *reaches* actuality *or* how consciousness *constitutes* "actuality," i.e., the sense of an actual object as a member of a distinct region of being? Husserl partially titled §55 of *Ideas I* "All Reality Existent By Virtue of 'Sense-bestowal'." He wrote there, "Let us note in conclusion that the universality with which, in the deliberations carried out above, we have spoken about the constitution of the natural world in absolute consciousness, should not be found objectionable" (Hua III/I, p. 121/130). Statements such as this lead us to think Husserl identifies "constitution" with sense-bestowal.[19] Shpet, perhaps fearing a lapse into psychologism, rejected such an identification and asked for the source of sense, writing that such a question "is quite legitimate even if it should turn out – which we do not think will happen – that 'constituting' itself is identical with 'sense-bestowal'" (1991, p. 104). If, in light of this, Shpet did not identify the two, what did he see as the concept of constitution?

---

[19] That Husserl did not provide a clear elucidation of his concept of constitution is well known. Moran, undoubtedly, provides the best attempt, writing, "Husserl's notion of constitution should perhaps be thought of as a kind of setting out or 'positing' (*Setzung*), as a giving of sense, 'sense-bestowing' (*Sinngebung*)" (Moran 2000, p. 165).

On the other hand, we have seen that he does recognize that the epoché is an exclusion of the facticity of spatio-temporal being, and even after introducing his talk of attaining, what he calls, authentic actuality, he affirmed that it is thanks to the epoché that this is accomplished. (Shpet 1991, p. 124)

4   From *Eidos* to Comprehension

Already in his "Introduction" to *Appearance and Sense*, Shpet cryptically mentioned that all philosophical problems appear centered around and connected with a single problem, out of which ever new controversies have historically sprung (1991, p. 6). This age-old dispute is that between nominalism and realism, i.e., the problem of universals, although we, in turn, must stress that Shpet was not particularly forthcoming in stating plainly either the general problem, as he saw it, or his particular one. However, by focussing on the question of *how* we "arrive" at something actual, Shpet believed we have before us the path to solving the problem of universals. Husserl's phenomenology, concerned as it is with sense and sense-bestowal, has, he believes, shown the way forward. On the other hand, Kantianism, with its exclusion in principle of a cognition of the thing in itself, has slammed the door shut to actuality and, as such, represents a negation of the essence of philosophy extending from the Greeks. However, the positive answer provided by phenomenology needs to be looked at from a different angle in order to understand its broad, philosophical significance. It has shown through its analysis of the noema-noesis correlation the rationality of actuality. Husserl has accomplished this through the adoption of the phenomenological attitude, which among other things has cleansed our study of psychology. Now, we are faced with taking the next step of penetrating into the actual.

The very nature of Husserl's phenomenology imposed restrictions on its procedure in investigating the problem of pure intentionality. However, Shpet saw his particular concern to be somewhat different than Husserl's, though related to it. The former claimed that the analysis of the noema-noesis correlation pushed him into viewing his problem essentially from the same direction as did Husserl. The latter proceeds from simple experience to a penetration into the essence. Husserl was asking *how* we penetrate into the essence of the actual. The sense of the claim that something "truly exists" is eidetically equivalent to saying that that something is "adequately given." On the other hand, a presentive intuition (*gebende Anschauung*) of something transcendent cannot yield an adequate givenness of this something (Hua III/I, p. 332/343; Shpet 1991, p. 128). But for any object of which we can say that it "truly exists" there must be, on the phenomenological grounds we have seen, the possibility of a consciousness to which that object is given originarily and adequately. Even if we accept this, we can still ask how this object shows its "truth." If we abdicate our responsibility here as philosophers to address this issue, we leave fundamental issues of metaphysics to either dogmatists or those like Kant, for whom both a thesis and an antithesis are equally internally consistent and yet are contradictory.

We started with fact and essence and found their two corresponding species of intuition. Experiencing intuition yields individual objects, the *hic et nunc*, whereas ideal intuition yields pure essences. If we "bracket" everything factual, leaving the essential, how can we deal with the individual, actual thing before us? Is it the case that the essential cannot be individual? How can philosophy return to the things themselves? In viewing essences from within the phenomenological reduction, we have originarily given essences that neither can be reduced nor can change into something else in another attitude. If that were possible, the "essence" in question, would not truly be an essence.

At this point, Shpet could have here turned for a solution to the correlation of the two species of intuition to the problem of expressing what is seen in each. Indeed, he hinted at a recognition of this, a problem that in the twentieth century led to the philosophy of language. In the years ahead, in fact, Shpet did turn to an examination of language. However, here in the final chapter of *Appearance and Sense* Shpet claimed that a deeper examination of the structure of an appearance reveals that it contains more than the two species can show. Although in any object we can find its concrete noema, we cannot locate its "authentic sense" in looking at it in abstraction. A concrete social or cultural object has an "internal something" or "internal sense," i.e., entelechy. True, this can be seen in the natural attitude, but Shpet asserted that in the phenomenological attitude we can see this more clearly. In the latter, we are not distracted by the sheer variety of individual properties given in experiencing intuition. Thus, we find Shpet again affirming the *utility* of phenomenology. Moreover, in the natural attitude we often see or, better, posit entelechy where none exists in a physical thing. In this way, we attribute a "quasi-entelechy" to the object. For example, we can say we see a human face in the clouds or that the human nose was designed as a place to rest one's eyeglasses.

If, in the case of entelechy, we have an originary givenness, we would have to accord a separate species of intuition to it and correspondingly that entelechy would be a given on the same level as the ideally given and the experientially given. Problems arise here, however. Earlier, we saw that for every experientially given there is an ideally given, i.e., an essence. But in a phenomenological description, we find that not all objects have entelechy. If it were otherwise, we would have to admit a third attitude alongside the natural and the phenomenological, and the Husserlian-Shpetian view of phenomenology as the fundamental science would be jeopardized. However, unlike with essences, seeing entelechy does not require a separate attitude or a third originarily giving species or genus of intuition (Shpet 1991, p. 158). Indeed, the seizing of an object's entelechy does require a distinctive act that motivates the positing of belief, but this act that views the noematic sense as a sign of entelechy is hermeneutic. Whereas we can, in a phenomenological description, isolate the various moments of an experience (*Erlebnis*) given in an intuition, the same cannot be done with entelechy, since its recognition is a social act and as such is *essentially* intersubjective. To use Shpet's own example, the entelechy of an axe, viz., to chop wood, was told to me by my father. We certainly appear to be describing the axe from within the natural attitude, but conceivably a phenomenological analysis would yield much the same. Not for a moment did Shpet explicitly denounce the reduction and certainly not its efficacy (see Shpet 1991, pp. 158–159.).

A social or cultural object has an *essential* purpose, one that we add to the physicality of the object. This purpoe is not present "in" the object in the same way as is, say, its color or shape. We know its purpose through a communication from another, but that communication is not itself a property of the object. Whereas we can direct our attention to it, so that it itself becomes an object, communication is not a physical thing as is, say, the axe. For me to make *sense* of the communication, I must comprehend it. This requires reason on my part. Have we, with this turn to comprehension, departed or sundered the phenomenological reduction? Shpet continued to be reticent, though he uses phenomenological terminology throughout his exposition. He reaffirmed that there are only two species of intuition and a single genus, viz., intuition or experience in the broad sense. Comprehension is included here. Phenomenology, sufficiently broadened to include comprehension on the part of the intending consciousness, remains pertinent. We said at the beginning of our study here that transcendental phenomenology requires steadfast attention to the *cogito-cogitatum* nexus within the conscious attitude that excludes any sense of transcendency, all existence apart from that of the *cogito*, the existence of which essentially cannot be excluded. Did Shpet adhere to this?

5   In the Aftermath – Remarks and Affirmations

Although *Appearance and Sense* must remain the definitive expression of Shpet's relation to transcendental phenomenology, Shpet did make a number of corroborative statements in other contexts around the time of the book's publication. After his return to Moscow, Shpet gave a lecture-course on philosophy at the private Shanjavskij University in 1914 and most likely repeated his lectures at the Moscow Higher Women's Courses, a higher educational institution parallel to the public universities, women being barred from attendance at the latter. In such an introductory context, we can hardly expect Shpet to have provided much insight into his own relation to phenomenology. Nevertheless, in the course of the lectures he did offer support for Husserl's positive affirmation of the rationality of reality as against those who simply rejected subjective idealism in the name of the existential reality of the perceptual object.

Of course, we must be careful not to read into Shpet's surviving lecture notes more than glimpses of his position. Nevertheless, he did write, "The correlativity of the contingent and the essence as a necessary relation. *An ideal intuition or the intuition of essence!*" (Shpet 2010a, p. 270). In this way, he at least suggested his reaffirmation of the Husserlian distinction between experiencing intuition and eidetic intuition. He also again stated the intentionality of consciousness and hinted to not only the eidetic reduction, but even the phenomenological reduction: "epoché in relation to the empirical. Pure essence as the remainder. The study of consciousness here – a new science – phenomenology! Intentionality as the object. Ideal laws and relations – in the real itself" (Shpet 2010a, p. 270). Whereas such brief declarations alone can hardly serve as the basis for attributing an elaborated philosophical system to Shpet – or to anyone for that matter – they do lend additional corroboration to his fuller statements in *Appearance and Sense*.

Yet even in these quite reserved remarks Shpet still ventured to express his criticism of Husserl's limited perspective, namely that it failed to discern a particular rational activity in which certain senses are originarily disclosed to the subject. This activity is comprehension, which sees "reason in reality. The significance of interpretation as an answer to the question of the world. [...] Subjectivity does not exclude the possibility of objective interpretation" (Shpet 2010a, p. 271). In this way, Shpet saw reason as not just providing a rational description of what is given, but a rational comprehension. Thus, the world appears not as a house of cards about to collapse in an instant, but as a rationally connected whole. When we say something is real, we express that that thing is stable, that it remains the same despite our different perspectives on it.

Another often overlooked source of information concerning Shpet's views at this time is a lengthy review of a book, *The Problem of Psychic Causality*, by Vasily V. Zenkovsky, who later went on to become a famed émigré historian of Russian philosophy. In his review originally published in 1915, Shpet questioned Zenkovsky's contention that he, Zenkovsky, was actively employing Husserl's phenomenological method in his own psychological research. For Shpet, such a claim made no sense: "The phenomenological method can take place only in phenomenology, as the fundamental philosophical discipline. Psychology, as an empirical science, has its own methods" (2010b, pp. 102–103). Thus, Zenkovsky, in Shpet's eyes, misunderstood the very nature of phenomenology. It, unlike psychology, is not an empirical science, and its subject matter does not include anything empirically given. If we wish to designate the direct object of its concern as the "psychic," then we must bear in mind that an inherent feature of that object is intentionality and the object is given to us eidetically. Charging Zenkovsky with misunderstanding the phenomenological reduction, Shpet wrote that he, Shpet, saw it as "the path from the empirically given in the world surrounding us to pure consciousness as the object of phenomenology (2010b, p. 107). Thus, again we have no reason to think that Shpet disavowed transcendental phenomenology, as he understood it at the time. However, he did add the proviso – which will loom ever larger in the coming years – that phenomenology does not and cannot alone solve every problem. It is the fundamental philosophical discipline, but not the only philosophical discipline. Nor do we need to develop phenomenology to the last iota in order to solve every single problem.

6   Shpet's Ostensibly Mundane Studies

In 1916, Shpet published and defended his huge thesis, *History as a Problem of Logic*. Despite its mammoth size, the work, dealing as it does with historical methodology, displays no overt indication, one way or another, of an allegiance to transcendental idealism. Nonetheless, Shpet did complete a second volume to his study, though it remained unpublished during his lifetime.[20] In this second volume, Shpet allowed himself at times to venture beyond simple scholarship into short meta-historical reflections. Largely abandoning Husserlian terminology, Shpet, neverthe-less, retained his belief in the efficacy of the fact-essence dichotomy. In the introduction to this second volume, he again affirmed that a "scientific" investiga-tion of any object whatsoever can take one of two forms: concrete or abstract. However, even a concrete investigation needs a foundation, a foundation that cannot be a generalized study of the concrete. Shpet wrote, "Of course, there can be no corresponding 'general' concrete fundamental science, but this does not mean that the special concrete sciences are left, so to speak, 'without a foundation'" (2002, p. 564). That foundation is a study of "being in general," which is ontological but, above all, phenomenological. Were it not for Shpet's qualification of the fundamen-tal science as ontological, we could certainly infer that he remained within the orbit of transcendental phenomenology. Thus, it is most disquieting and perplexing when he writes further on that philosophy of history, taken as philosophy, is given the task of cognizing what genuinely exists, relying for this on what is given from the fun-damental philosophical discipline, namely phenomenology, but which Shpet also characterized as "universal ontology" (2002, p. 574). Did Shpet still have in mind here the conception of essences that Husserl wrote of in *Ideas I*?

Clearly, despite the misgivings engendered by some of Shpet's utterances, he remained throughout the period spent composing his *History* text – whenever exactly that was – committed in some sense to phenomenology. As in 1914, he viewed phenomenology as a pre-theoretical investigation and that, as such, serves as the foundation of a theoretical study of any discipline. He remarked, "In this sense, phenomenology is the universal fundamental science" (Shpet 2002, p. 577). It accomplishes its goal through description, non-theoretical description. That is, phe-nomenological description is not interested in constructing a system or a science, but in finding the foundations of the objects themselves being studied. This, in Shpet's eyes, means to separate by way of description what does and does not belong to the investigated object. The result of such an operation, which effectively amounts to the eidetic reduction, is a cognition of the thing in itself.

Shpet returned to the concept of the "social" in the "Conclusion" to the second volume of his *History*. There, he says that it is with the help of pure description that we obtain the meaning of the concept of the social. But where in what is given to the senses do we find "the social"? "Contemporary philosophy," Shpet alleged, in debt to empiricism and rationalism and developed further by Kant, holds that the imme-diately intuited content of a perception is limited to what is presented to our senses.

---

[20] Shchedrina writes that, based on Shpet's letters and diaries, he wrote this second volume in the period 1912–1913. While, certainly the chapters on Dilthey, Wundt, Rickert, et al. may date from early in this period, Shpet's remarks on phenomenology could not have been composed prior to the appearance of *Ideas I*. Yet even such a dating of those remarks leaves open the question why Shpet's terminology in the *History* referring to phenomenological techniques bears a stronger resemblance to that found in his works of a few years later than it does to that found in *Appearance and Sense*. See Shchedrina (2014, p. 143).

The problem of "the social" arises from this artificial and misguided limitation of intuition. Thus, Shpet asked us to seek in intuition, in the immediately given, what allows us to speak of the social and to form a concept of it. What in some intuition of a thing allows us to call it a social object? What is it about this thing, this ashtray, to use Shpet's own example, that allows us to see that it can perform a *social* function? Shpet's further discussion is largely a repetition of what we already observed in his earlier *Appearance and Sense*. However, here in the second volume of his *History*, Shpet saw the social given chiefly in what he now calls "intellectual intuition," although he quickly added the caveat that it would be incorrect to conceive the social as given only in such intuition (2002, p. 1062). Furthermore, he specifically mentioned Husserl as having displayed the presence of essences in intuition.

Granted, then, that during the writing of the *History* Shpet largely retained his position regarding the practical efficacy of the eidetic reduction, did he also maintain an acceptance of the phenomenological reduction – and concomitantly an allegiance to transcendental idealism, even if unacknowledged? Earlier, we found that for Shpet phenomenology is the *fundamental* philosophical discipline, but not the only such discipline. In a particularly pregnant passage, Shpet wrote,

> If we take to examine the sphere of the sense data of intuition, we can say of this entire content that it "'exists" as present to us, that it is an "actual" being. If we, then, state that this being is not "absolute" (in Berkeley's sense), that we establish this only with respect to "consciousness," this does not prevent us from examining it independently of consciousness. In terms of the position laid out here, the "objective" cognition of reality lies in this. The sciences act in this way. Moreover, in strict conformity with this there is a demand: We not only can but we must, if we want objective scientific cognition, examine the given independently of consciousness, as if this dependence did not exist (although, of course, such a dependence is not thereby rejected) (Shpet 2002, p. 1041).

On the face of it, then, Shpet retained his *ultimate* philosophical commitment, in effect, to transcendental idealism. However, that commitment did not preclude other disciplines from undertaking their respective investigations *as though* there were no inextricable nexus between the *cogito* and the *cogitatum*. In the grand scheme of human knowledge, transcendental phenomenology has its role, but so do other disciplines, such as the natural sciences and, for example, history.

Finally, turning to certainly one of, if not the last narrowly focused pieces of *philosophical* reflection from Shpet's pen, namely his essay "Wisdom or Reason?" from early 1917, we find additional corroboration for our above points. This essay, unmistakeably, demonstrates a wide variety of concerns, the most apparent being to trace the kernel of "philosophy as knowledge" – Shpet's euphemism for his conception of phenomenological idealism – back to Parmenides.[21] However, in another distinction, namely, between philosophy and pseudo-philosophy, Shpet remarked

---

[21] The very title of Shpet's essay, though, is an allusion to his dispute with a friend Lev Shestov, who also was on friendly terms with Husserl but who was, one might say, a philosophical antipode of Shpet and Husserl.

that the latter conceives being "not through thought and not in thought, but as if it were in itself and as it would then be" (2019, p. 218). In other words, genuine philosophy – philosophy as knowledge – studies being but always in connection with consciousness, as it is given to and in consciousness. Such, as we saw, is, in part, Shpet's understanding of the phenomenological reduction. The "other" task of philosophy as knowledge, indeed its first task, is "to distinguish what is illusory (*ta phainomena*) from what is real or essential (*ousia*) in given reality itself (*ta onta*)" (Shpet 2019, p. 221). What remains after removing what "fluctuates" is the essential task.

Shpet took particular umbrage with Bertrand Russell's early infatuation with the idea of making philosophy mathematical. Elaborating on remarks we saw in *Appearance and Sense*, Shpet in 1917 viewed mathematics as an *abstraction* from consciousness. Admittedly both yield eidetic knowledge. However, whereas transcendental phenomenology – in Shpet's now preferred locution, philosophy as knowledge – and mathematics deal with essences, the latter is not concerned "with the thought directed toward this object as such" (2019, p. 223). In other words, mathematics deals with essences apart from their direct connection, and thus not in conjunction, with consciousness, itself conceived essentially. As a result, mathematics is, in Shpet's terminology here, ontological. Certainly, mathematics differs from the empirical sciences of facts, the objects of which are contingent, but both concern themselves with a "'dogmatic givenness,' and not a philosophical givenness in the rigorous and precise sense" (Shpet 2019, p. 233).

We can hardly be surprised to find Shpet reaffirming his commitment to the distinction between experiencing and eidetic (or intellectual) intuition. However, we must recognize that they are actually a single intuition, but with different degrees of penetration, or of seeing, owing to a different attitude of consciousness. The transition to philosophy as pure knowledge, the "fundamental science" in principle, is accomplished by divorcing our eidetic judgments of all traces of contingency including their relation to the consciousness of an empirical subject. "For this, we must stop considering experience itself as a 'dogmatically' given thing of the real world" (Shpet 2019, p. 239). And, as we saw above, just as we cease concerning ourselves with experience dogmatically, i.e., in the natural attitude, so in phenomenology we "take consciousness not as an empirical experience of an individual, not as data of 'observation' or of 'self-observation,' but as consciousness given to consciousness, *consciousness in a reflection on itself*" (Shpet 2019, p. 239). Taken essentially, consciousness is not a "thing," and, consequently, causality, a concept from the natural attitude, does not apply to it. It neither acts on mundane objects nor does anything mundane act on it. Consciousness, as an eidos, cannot *belong* to something mundane, just as ideas do not belong to me or to any real being in space and time.

7   A Non-egological Phenomenological Idealism

Shpet, undoubtedly, devoted little attention to the narrowly focussed philosophical problems that haunted his Western contemporaries. However, in arguably his only piece of technical philosophizing, his 1916 essay "Consciousness and Its Owner," Shpet argued against the Marburg (specifically Natorp's) Neo-Kantian and Husserlian conceptions of the ego, or "I." To be sure, I as an individual human being have a consciousness, but, for Shpet, it does not follow from this that within phenomenology, i.e., after the performance of the reduction and thus within phenomenological idealism, we can speak without qualification of a "transcendental ego." We saw above that even for Husserl there is a corresponding essence for everything given contingently. On this basis, we can speak of the essence of a particular human individual. Those, for whom such a claim is self-contradictory, "accept a particular psychological theory, according to which concepts are formed through a process of 'generalization'" (Shpet 2019, p. 162). However, from the phenomenological standpoint, matters stand differently. We can speak of the ideal correlate of an "I." Nonetheless, if we remove all that is contingent from the "I" – thereby conceiving it to be only a "unity of consciousness" – to speak of consciousness as belonging to this essential "I," as its possession, makes no sense (Shpet 2019, p. 178). Apart from all contingency, the "I" is an essence, an essential unity. In support of this position, Shpet mentioned that we can and do speak of a social consciousness, which is conceived as a unity but which does not belong to an "I." Shpet recognized that Husserl said nothing about social consciousness in *Ideas I*, but the former persisted *contra* Husserl concerning the tenability of the positing of a pure "I" logically behind consciousness (see Hua III/I, p. 98/102). Who or what is doing this positing, a positing of an essence? This is what Shpet found to be senseless.

Shpet recognized that Husserl in *Ideas I* introduced the notion of a transcendental I. This, Shpet found to be indefensible. Husserl provided there no evidence, no originary givenness of an I beyond or "behind" the mere unity of consciousness. Husserl had betrayed his own "principle of all principles" and introduced theory where none is needed. (Shpet 2019, p. 190). In excluding the contingency of the given I with the epoché, we obtain an ideal I, i.e., a pure consciousness but only as an object, not as the subject of consciousness. This eidetic I is not the possession of someone; it is no one's. Husserl succumbed to the temptation of subjectivism in positing an "I" as the foundation of consciousness, making it a necessary condition of the unity of consciousness. But *if* we would say that a transcendental I serves as the foundation of a single consciousness, to whom or what would we say is at the foundation of a social or collective or national consciousness? We can say only that the unity of consciousness has no such foundation; it is not a "property" or "possession" (Shpet 2019, p. 198). Husserl, with his transcendental I or ego, has forsaken his own achievement, making phenomenology a hybrid idealism, partially transcendental, but also partially metaphysical.

8 Conclusion

There can be no doubt that the intellectual concerns of Shpet and Husserl sharply diverged after Shpet's return to Russia in 1914. Whereas Husserl increasingly committed himself to viewing his position as an idealism and, concomitantly, to its elaboration as a form of transcendental idealism, Shpet turned to philosophy of language, aesthetics and other studies far removed from Husserl's more narrow purview. We ourselves can only wonder whether Shpet himself ever thought of Husserl's philosophical trajectory during the former's isolation in 1920s Soviet Russia. Husserl's name rarely appeared in Shpet's writings from this period.[22] Thus, it is all the more amazing that Shpet in a 1932 Soviet encyclopedia entry on himself (!) remarked that Husserl provided the correct solution to the problem of cognition through his introduction of the concept of "ideation." Furthermore, "with the help of reflection and the method of the reduction, we can, actually, come to a philosophical analysis and critique of consciousness, taking immediate experience as our starting point" (Shpet 2019, p. 297). In this way, we see that even as manacing storm clouds swirled around him, when it would have been expedious for him at least to have invoked the hallowed names of Marx and Lenin and express unbounded allegiance to them, Shpet instead invoked the name of a German bourgeois professor.

Most importantly for us here, Shpet remained committed to an acceptance of the phenomenological reduction, understood as a reflection on the processes of consciousness in which the *cogito* and *cogitatum* are taken essentially, and therefore without regard to matters of fact, i.e., to contingent existences. This adherence to the reduction as "first philosophy" entailed, at least tacitly, a commitment in turn to transcendental idealism, although Shpet refrained from characterizing his own position so.

Still, the philosophical trajectories of Husserl and Shpet sharply diverged. Husserl probed ever deeper into the explication of sense that he saw as intrinsic to transcendental idealism. Shpet too saw the sheer importance of the explication of sense, but he also would have thought that Husserl's battle with solipsism, based on the works published during his lifetime, was of his own making. From Shpet's viewpoint, Husserl's error lay in his refusal to recognize that such explication is not merely a matter of the consciousness of a single individual, but also includes communal or social consciousness, albeit taken eidetically. As a result, the Husserlian characterization of transcendental idealism stands in need of an appropriate supplementation and also does not preclude mundane higher-order investigations.

---

[22]That, however, some information regarding the philosophical climate in Freiburg reached Moscow during this period is clear from N. Volkov's "Letters from Freiburg." See Volkov (2000). Still in his 1918 *Hermeneutics and Its Problems*, Husserl's name appears only in the last pages, and then only curtly.

References

Chelpanov, Georgij. (1917). Ob analiticheskom metode v psikhologii. *Psikhologicheskogo oboz-renija*, 3–4, 451–468.
Evstropov, M. N. (2014). Gustav Shpet: teorija smysla kak ontologija social'nosti. *Vestnik Tomskogo gosudarstvennogo universiteta*, 379, 61–68.
Gurko, E. (1999). Fenomenologicheskaja redukcija v interpretacii G. G. Shpeta i Ja. Patochki. In *Shpet G. G./Comprehensio. Tret'i Shpetovskie chtenija* (pp. 8–11). Tomsk: Izd. Vodolej.
Hua III/1. Husserl, E. (1976). *Ideen zu einer reinen Phänomenologie und phänomenologischen Philosophie. Erstes Buch.* K. Schuhmann (Ed.), The Hague: Nijhoff; *Ideas pertaining to a pure phenomenology and to a phenomenological philosophy.* F. Kersten (Trans.). The Hague: Martinus Nijhoff, 1982.
Luft, S. (2012). Husserl's method of reduction. In S. Luft & S. Overgaard (Eds.), *The Routledge companion to phenomenology* (pp. 243–253). New York: Routledge.
Moran, Dermot. (2000). *Introduction to phenomenology.* New York: Routledge.
Nemeth, Thomas. (2009). Shpet's departure from Husserl. In G. Tihanov (Ed.), *Gustav Shpet's contribution to philosophy and cultural theory* (pp. 125–139). West Lafayette: Purdue University Press.
Nemeth, Thomas. (2017). *Kant in Imperial Russia.* Cham: Springer.
Parker, Rodney K. B. (2018). Gerda Walther (1897–1977): A Sketch of a Life. In A. Calcagno (Ed.), *Gerda Walther's phenomenology of sociality, psychology, and Religion* (pp. 3–9). Cham: Springer.
Savin, A. E. (1997). Interpretacija i kritika G. G. Shpetom filosofii Ed. Gusserlja. In *Shpet G. G./ Comprehensio. Vtorye Shpetovskie chtenija* (pp. 24–27). Tomsk: Izd. Volodej.
Shchedrina, T. (2014). Fenomenologicheskie shtudii Gustava Shpeta: «Javlenie i smysl» v kontek-ste «Archiva epokhi». *Gumanitarnye issledovanija v vostochnoj Siberi i na dal'nem vostoke*, 1, 142–147.
Shchedrina, T. (2015). The chronicles of the life and works of Gustav Shpet. *Kronos*, 4, 53–90.
Shijan, A. (2005). Shpet kak Platonik. *Doksa, zbirnyk naukovykh prats' z filosofiyi ta filolohiyi*, 8, 286–294.
Shpet, Gustav. (1912). Odin put' psikhologii i kuda on vedet. In *Filosofskij sbornik L'vu Mikhajlovichu Lopatinu* (pp. 245–264). Moscow: Tip. Kushnerev.
Shpet, Gustav. (1991). *Appearance and Sense: Phenomenology as the fundamental science.* Th. Nemeth (Trans.). Dordrecht: Kluwer.
Shpet, Gustav. (2002). *Istorija kak problema logiki. Kriticheskie i metodologicheskie issledo-vanija. Materialy.* V. Mjasnikov (ed.). Moscow: Pamjatniki istoricheskoj mysli.
Shpet, Gustav. (2010a). *Filosofija i nauka. Lekcionnye kursy.* T. Shchedrina (Ed.). Moscow: ROSSPEN.
Shpet, Gustav. (2010b). *Filosofskaja kritika: otzyvy, recenzii, obzory.* T. Shchedrina (Ed.). Moscow: ROSSPEN.
Shpet, Gustav. (2012). *Filosof v kul'ture. Dokumenty i pis'ma.* T. Shchedrina (Ed.). Moscow: ROSSPEN.
Shpet, Gustav (2019). *Hermeneutics and its problems. With selected essays in phenomenology.* Nemeth (Ed./Trans.). Cham: Springer.
Stein, Edith. (1986). *Life in a jewish family.* J. Koeppel (Trans.). Washington, D.C.: ICS Publications.
Volkov, N. (2000). Tri pis'ma iz Frejburga. In I. Chubarov (Ed.)., *Antologija fenomenologicheskoj filosofii v Rossii*, tom 2. Moscow: Izd. Logos.
Walther, Gerda. (1960). *Zum anderen Ufer: vom Marxismus und Atheismus zum Christentum.* Remagen: Otto Reichl.

Edith Stein on a Different Motive that Led Husserl to Transcendental Idealism

Daniele De Santis

Abstract In the following paper we will attempt to analyze and reconstruct Edith Stein's interpretation of Husserl's "transcendental idealism," notably, the reason why, in her opinion, the latter ended up embracing that specific philosophical position. As will soon become apparent, according to Stein, Husserl misunderstands the peculiar ontological structure of individual essences and, in particular, the specific *connection with reality* that they carry within themselves. Without raising the question of whether Stein's own understanding of transcendental idealism perfectly corresponds with Husserl's, we will confine ourselves to discussing, first, the wider context within which she tackles it and, second, the relation between Husserl's idealism and the formal-ontological issue of how to characterize the internal content of individual essences. No matter what we think of Stein's critical assessment, her approach has the great and undeniable merit of forcing the "interpreter" to face the problem of the tight connection between the transcendental dimension and the eidetic dimension of Husserl's thought.

Keywords Phenomenology · Transcendental philosophy · Idealism · Realism · Essence · Intentionality · Edmund Husserl · Edith Stein

1 Positio Quaestionis: *What Question, Exactly?*

When speaking of *reactions* to Husserl's turn to a transcendental-phenomenological idealism, there are two different—although not unrelated—lines of argument one can refer to. (a) On the one hand—in a straightforward *opposition* to Husserl's new (transcendental) agenda—, the *reactions* present themselves as systematic attempts to stick with, and thereby develop further, the idea of phenomenology that was considered faithful to the original spirit of the first edition of the *Logical Investigations*. (b) On the other hand—this second meaning overlaps with the first, but should not in any way be confused with it—, these *reactions* consist in proposing

D. De Santis (✉)
Charles University, Prague, Czechia
e-mail: daniele.desantis@ff.cuni.cz

© Springer Nature Switzerland AG 2021
R. K. B. Parker (ed.), *The Idealism-Realism Debate Among Edmund Husserl's Early Followers and Critics*, Contributions to Phenomenology 112,
https://doi.org/10.1007/978-3-030-62159-9_12

diagnoses of *why* Husserl imposed this new framework on his thought (the most famous case being Roman Ingarden's *On the Motives which led Husserl to Transcendental Idealism*).[1] In other words, they aim at identifying and bringing to the fore (so as to eventually dismiss) those "motives" that (implicitly or explicitly) led Husserl to take that pernicious path and thus fall back into what would be considered an outdated and problematic form of philosophy.

Were we to make use of some Aristotelian expressions in this context, we would say that the difference between (a) and (b) corresponds to what Aristotle refers to as "the fact that a thing is so" (τὸ ὅτι) and "the reason why it is so" (τὸ διότι) respectively. In either case—whether we aim to endorse or recast the phenomenology of the *Logical Investigations*, to take a position against Husserl's turn or to reveal its (more or less) hidden motive, which might turn out to be a false starting point (πρῶτον ψεῦδος)—everything rests on the way we understand Husserl's phenomenology as it is presented in the *Logical Investigations*.

For the sake of brevity, we will distinguish four main interpretations of the phenomenology presented in the *Logical Investigations* (τὸ ὅτι):

  (i) If we designate the phenomenology of the *Logical Investigations* as a "realist" one, then the opposition is between a vague form of *realism* and an equally nebulous *idealism*. For, Husserl himself resorts to the term *idealism* in the *Introduction* to the *Second Logical Investigation* in order to characterize not phenomenology itself, but that theory of knowledge "which recognizes the ideal as the condition for the possibility of objective knowledge in general" (Husserl 1984: p. 112; see De Santis 2016a).

 (ii) If, on the contrary, we label it "idealist," then the opposition is with the *transcendental variety of idealism*: this seems to correspond to Paul Natorp's position in his review of the *Prolegomena*, where he accuses Husserl of simply stating the separation or split between "reality" and "ideality" without actually being able to overcome the separation between them. (Natorp 1901)

(iii) If we maintain that Husserl's "early phenomenology" is committed to an object-oriented description, then the opposition is between *objectivism* and *subjectivism*[2]—the latter meaning:
      (a) Either an analysis of the transcendental subject (be it the so-called pure consciousness or the monad) that aims at working out the subjective (namely, intentional and transcendental) constitution of everything that is;

---

[1] See Ingarden 1976.

[2] For Dietrich von Hildebrand, for example, there is no substantial distinction between (i) and (iii). "[Phenomenology] signifies in fact the most outspoken objectivism and realism. It is this meaning of phenomenology which we find in the writings of Adolf Reinach, Alexander Pfänder, myself, and several others, and which we, at least, identified with the meaning of phenomenology in the first edition of Husserl's *Logische Untersuchungen*" (Hildebrand 1991, p. 273)

(b) Or the mere turn to a different field of investigation ("consciousness" as a new field of inquiry), which does not alter its original assumptions and basic ("objective") methodology.[3]

(iv) There is also a fourth option, held by Hedwig Conrad-Martius (1959) and by Edith Stein (2014) herself in passing, according to which no substantial turn took place, for the *Logical Investigations* were already committed to that subjective (iii.a) form of phenomenology that Husserl explicitly advocated later in his career.[4]

Depending on which of these four interpretations of the *Logical Investigations* we accept, the reason Husserl whole heartedly embraced transcendental idealism will differ as well. With this representing our introductory backdrop, let us see how Edith Stein describes the early *reactions* to *Ideas I* in Göttingen.

Immediately after *Ideas I* was published, Husserl announced to his students that he would meet with them in his home once a week to discuss their questions and concerns about the book. As Stein recalls, she was the first to stop by Husserl's house to express her "concerns," "doubts" and even "objections" [*Bedenken*] to "the Master." As she goes on to point out: "Soon others arrived. All of us had the same question on our mind."[5] Now, what precisely this *question* was about is not perspicuous, for Stein never elaborates on it.[6] Then comes "the fact" (τὸ ὅτι) with regard to the *Logical Investigations*: "The *Logische Untersuchungen* had caused a sensation primarily because they appeared to be a radical departure from critical idealism which had a Kantian and a neo-Kantian character."[7] Two points immediately deserve our attention: First, Stein does not explicitly assert that the *Logical Investigations* accomplished or "meant" to accomplish a *turning away*, but rather *that they appeared* or *seemed to do so* [*erschienen*]. Moreover, one should add that both the meaning and reference of the *appearance* could be construed in a twofold way: the *appearance* can either refer to the departure itself ("they seemed to

---

[3] This seems to be Jean Hering's interpretation in *Phénoménologie et philosophie religieuse* (Hering 1926). Moritz Geiger distinguishes between the turn to the object [*Wendung zum Objekt*] and the turn to the subject [*Wendung ins Subjektive*]. And yet he remarks that: "From the beginning this meant a 'turn to the subjective', which, of course, did not abrogate (rather, it presupposed) the turn to the object, nor must it have been interpreted from the outset in an idealistic way." (Geiger 1933, p. 15)

[4] Stein (2014, p. 164) argues that there is no "absolute break" (*Bruch*) between *Ideas I* and the *Logical Investigations*.

[5] "*Bald fanden sich andere dazu. Alle hatten dieselbe Frage auf dem Herzen.*" (Stein 2010, p. 200)

[6] An indirect reference to this *question* can be found in *Husserl's Phenomenology and the Philosophy of St. Thomas Aquinas*. "In fact, in the years following the publication of *Ideas I*, in which Husserl first spoke of <his 'idealism'>, the main arguments against this point, against this much discussed 'idealism', were addressed. *Again and again, this question was discussed in conversation with eager disciples*, without it coming to a conclusion. In such conversations, the trains of thought which were crucial for Husserl proved ineffective to convince his opponents. And if one of them declared victory in the moment, he would sooner or later come back with his old objections or with new ones." (Stein 1929, pp. 327–328. Emphasis added.)

[7] Stein 2010, p. 200.

accomplish a turning away…") or exclusively to the specific starting point (*terminus a quo*) of the *turning away* ("they seemed to accomplish a turning away *from critical idealism*…"). If in the latter case it is only the *terminus a quo* that is at stake (perhaps the *Logical Investigations* actually meant to accomplish a turning away, yet not from critical idealism), in the former, on the contrary, it is the idea itself of a departure to be called into question (although they seemed or appeared to do so, the *Logical Investigations* meant to accomplish no turning away). Second, if, as mentioned, the departure is *from* a very specific variety of idealism, i.e., the critical one (this being the *terminus a quo* of the turning away), nothing is said about its goal or aim (*terminus ad quem*).[8]

Let us then consider the way Stein goes on to explain the effects of Husserl's first masterpiece and the surprise caused by the release of the 1913 book:

> [The *Logische Untersuchungen*] was considered a "new scholasticism" because it turned attention away from the subject and toward the things themselves. Knowledge appeared again as a receiving, deriving its laws from the things, and not—as claimed by criticism— from a determining which imposes its laws on the things. All the young phenomenologists were resolute realists. However, the *Ideas* included some phrases [*Wendungen*] that sounded very much like as though their Master [*ihr Meister*] wanted to return to idealism. […] It was the beginning of that development which led Husserl, more and more, to what he called "transcendental idealism" […]. (Stein 2010, p. 200)

Here, too, a series of remarks is necessary. First, the *Logical Investigations* are never said to be realist, nor is *Ideas I* designated as "idealist." Only the "young phenomenologists" are described as "resolute realists." It is not even easy to tell whether Stein counts herself among them.[9] Indeed, it is interesting to note that in this passage Stein refers to Husserl as "their [i.e., 'the young phenomenologists'] Master" (our hypothesis here being that Stein might be referring exclusively to the way the *young phenomenologists perceived Husserl and the so-called "turn,"* but not to her own perspective on the matter).[10] Second, the emphasis is not on the definition of "phenomenology" in the *Logical Investigations*, but on the conception of "knowledge" as receiving as opposed to knowledge as determining (the issue at stake being not just gnoseological, but ontological, i.e., bearing on "what" knowledge really "is").[11] Third, although the above excerpt claims that *Ideas I* contain some "inflections" and "phrases" [*Wendungen*] that would lead Husserl to embrace "transcendental idealism," nothing is really said regarding what they amount to. In

---

[8] See Stein 2014, pp. 119–142, and pp. 159–162, where she writes that the *Logical Investigations* accomplished a return, not to "realism," but to the traditional idea of a *philosophia perennis et universalis*.

[9] For a brief historical discussion of Stein's position in the phenomenological movement, see Sepp 1998.

[10] "I have turned over a new leaf when it comes to idealism and believe it can be understood in such a way that is metaphysically satisfying. But it seems to me that much of what is in *Ideas* has to be comprehended differently, though in Husserl's sense, if only he brings together what he has, and in a decisive moment does not leave out of consideration something that necessarily belongs to the subject matter at stake." (Stein 2003, p. 87.)

[11] For an analysis of Stein's theory of knowledge, see Volk 2003.

other words, and to resort to Aristotle's terminology once again, Stein does not question "why Husserl turned to idealism" here.

The goal of the present paper is to analyze and clarify an argument that Stein advances in a long footnote to her *opus magnum*, i.e., *Finite and Eternal Being*, where she fleshes out the motive (τὸ διότι) that, by revolving around the notion of "essence" (*Wesen*), can make understandable the fact (τὸ ὅτι) that Husserl arrived at an "idealist conception of reality" (*idealistische Deutung der Wirklichkeit*). To this end, our analysis will be divided into four main sections: §2 will address Stein's own construal of Husserl's "transcendental idealism"; §3 will present "the footnote," and also discuss the wider context within which Stein comes up with that "hermeneutical hypothesis." This will be followed by a conclusion (§4) in which we attempt to sum up the outcomes of our investigation.

2 Excursus on Stein on Transcendental Idealism

The only systematic analysis Stein explicitly dedicates to Husserl's "transcendental idealism" is in her "habilitation," *Potency and Act*: the famous *Excursus on Transcendental Idealism*, added as a quasi-appendix to the end of §23d. Before getting into our commentary, it is important to say a few words on the specific context in which the *Excursus* appears (Chapter VI, §23) and, more generally, on the overall project of the *Habilitationsschrift*: although *Potency and Act* underwent several revisions over the course of four years (1931–1935), and also provided the basis of *Finite and Eternal Being*,[12] the latter does not in fact offer anything comparable to the *Excursus*. If *Finite and Eternal Being* strives to answer the question as to "the reason" without first elaborating on "the fact" the situation is exactly the opposite with the *Excursus*.

In a nutshell, the goal of *Potency and Act* is to lay the foundation for a "general ontology"—"formal" as well as "material"—so as to provide the groundwork for two specific material regions: the region "nature" (see Chapter IV), and the region "spirit" (Chapter V). Without getting into Stein's ambitious strategy—consisting in a combination of phenomenological methods (e.g., eidetic analysis) and concepts (formal, material, and regional ontology, intentionality), with Aquinas' Aristotelian ontology (the pair potency-act) and metaphysics (different levels of being or reality)—what follows will suffice.[13] Chapter V is dedicated to developing a "spiritual" ontology capable of clarifying what Stein dubs the "core of the person" (*Kern der Person*) by means of a phenomenological account of notions like "habit," "will," "appetition," and "intellect."[14] Now, if the examination of the spiritual being

---

[12] See the "Einführung des Bearbeiters" in Stein 2005 (pp. xi-xxxvii). See also Fritz Kaufmann, who speaks indeed of "a monumental metaphysical system." (Kaufmann 1952, p. 572)

[13] For an important presentation and discussion of this topic, see Tommasi 2003.

[14] For an overall presentation, see Fetz 1993.

(*geistiges Sein*) has to be "eidetic" in the Husserlian sense of the term, and hence able to cover and include any and every possible spiritual entity, then Aquinas' distinction between wanderers or *viatores* ("finite and material-spiritual beings"), *angels* ("purely spiritual, yet finite beings") and *God* ("infinite spiritual being") will also have to fall within its domain. It will be the task of Chapter VI, notably §23, to elaborate upon that "spiritual" and "material" finite being called "human being."

The *Excursus* appears at the end of §23 (d), after the account of the relation between *species sensibiles* and *intelligibiles*, and before that of the understanding and its general relation to sensibility: it addresses a specific problem arisen *from within the intentional analysis of perception*, that is, the relation between "sense-data," or "material of sensation" and the "animating apprehension" (*beseelende Auffassung*). Let us dwell for a moment on the last lines of §23d:

> All perception of sensible things is built upon "material of sensation." We can think of these sense data in terms of what Aquinas calls "phantasma." Insofar as the pure sense data of sensation initiate a movement of the spirit that "animates" them or puts them to use in knowledge, we may call them "motives" (in the widest sense of the word). We should call them "*stimuli*" in order to distinguish them from *those* motives that determine the forward movement as something grasped objectively within the network of spiritual acts. *Before* it enters into an intuitive network, the *phantasma* is still not a *species sensibilis*; it *becomes* one through "the animating apprehension." (Stein 2005, p. 235.)

This excerpt lays out the basic coordinates of Stein's assessment of transcendental idealism, i.e., the problem that Husserl would designate as constitution of material things *via* the intentional analysis of perception. As she remarks at the beginning of the *Excursus*: "It is of the utmost philosophical importance to understand this transformation [i.e., of a *phantasma* into a *species sensibilis*], for this is the point where 'idealism' and 'realism' part company" (Stein 2005, p. 235). Let us stress what has just been remarked:

(I) The *Excursus on Transcendental Idealism*, therefore the problem itself of what such "idealism" amounts to, is introduced within the framework of a spiritual and, more specifically, "personalistic" ontology (i.e., general material ontology of the spirit);

(II) It addresses a problem characterizing the intentional structure of the perception of material things, and hence derived from the specific ontological makeup of the *wanderer* (or *viator*): indeed, human beings are spiritual and, at the same time, "material" finite beings whose experience of "material things" is necessarily mediated by the presence of sense data or stimuli.

Let us focus on the *Excursus* now.[15] Stein intends to make several points here. The first consists in emphasizing the difference between the Kantian and the Husserlian variety of idealism: "The 'throng of sensation' is taken into the forms of the sensibility and the understanding, and in this manner the spirit constructs the world that appears. Such is Kant's interpretation of the 'animating apprehension.' And while Kant clings to a 'thing in itself' as the (real, yet in itself unknown) basis

---

[15] For an interpretation of the *Excursus* that also includes Kant see Ales Bello 2005, pp. 82–87.

of transcendental forming and of the world of appearance, the idealist interpretation that Husserl gives his own teaching on the transcendental constitution of the objective world seems to radically dismiss this last vestige of 'naïve realism'" (Stein 2005, p. 235). Second, after pointing out that Husserl's transcendental idealism consists in working out specific "noetic-noematic" correlations between subjective *Erlebnisse* and *objectual* correlates ("For Husserl, 'thing' and 'thing-like world' (*dingliche Welt*) are nothing else than a label for connections of acts") Stein's main concern is with categorizing the different species of *Erlebnis*, and therefore of constitution, according to the different degree of "freedom" (*Freiheit*) and "binding" (*Bindung*) that characterize them.[16] As we will see, her investigation can be described as a bottom-up approach, starting from the intentional constitution of the perception of material things, *via* recollection, up to that specific form of presentification called phantasy.

For the sake of brevity, we will present Stein's account as a series of theses, which will then be followed by some remarks on our part.

Perception

> When a stimulus of light makes me glance up and I notice that a street lamp has just come on outside, the first thing we find upon reflection when we analyze the inner sequence is the stimulus. [...] The sense-datum occurs as something claiming and fulfilling the actuality of my life [...]. It comes unbidden, enters into the context of my life, [and] I lack the freedom to evoke or expel it by means of my purely spiritual activity. (Stein 2005, p. 236)

As Stein puts it, the "occurrence" or "emergence" (*auftreten*) of the material of *sensation* is not to be understood as a passive reception of mere "dead" matter on the part of the spiritual subject. The material of sensation is indeed said to occur as "something claiming" (*Anspruch Nehmendes*): the material of sensation imposes itself on the subject as a *demand*, and thereby as *limiting its freedom* (*Ich habe nicht die Freiheit, es hervorzurufen oder zu vertreiben*—as she underlines). The notion of "intentionality"—meaning the spiritual subject's openness to a "world of objects" (Stein 2005, p. 238)—stands for the different kinds of demands imposed on us by the different categories of sense-data, which thereby determine a fixed system of laws that rules over our entire spiritual life: "It is the nature of the material itself, its clarity, definiteness, its inner structure, that motivates one apprehension and the relevant sequence of acts without allowing for any choice, whereas material of another kind will admit of more than one apprehension." The phrase "*immanent Transzendentes,*" used to characterize the hybrid nature of the material of sensation, is meant to refer to such *fixed system of laws* to which the spiritual activity of the subject is submitted without exception: *immanent* because it determines and regulates the immanent structure of our intentional life; *transcendent* because it is received as an imposition from the "outside" (or, to put it better, as an *imposed claim* or *imposed demand*).

---

[16] Sepp (2003, p. 21) talks of a "genealogy of a possible encounter between the two ontological spheres of the objectual world and consciousness" (*einer möglichen Begegnung der beiden Seinssphäre von Gegenstandswelt und Bewußtsein.*)

Recollection

As Stein immediately points out, in opposition to this world of perception, there stands "another world of objects that I control with much greater freedom. In *remembrance* I can to a large extent 'presentify' things at will" (Stein 2005, pp. 238–239). For, we have "greater freedom toward our memory world (*Erinnerungswelt*) than toward the 'real world' (*wirkliche Welt*)" (Stein 2005, p. 240); yet, as she hastens to write, even in this other world "we are not completely free." First, our voluntary act of remembrance requires a "motive"[17]; second, what is "intuitive" (*anschaulich*) in the object does not depend on my "free or arbitrary choice."[18] It is worth noting that in both the case of perception and memory (or recollection) Stein speaks of *Welt*, "world": "world of perception," or *real world*, as well as "world of memory." It can be assumed that the designation "*Welt*" stands for the relevant *binding* that the two worlds impose onto the spiritual activity of the subject respectively. Now, if the "world of perception" is said to be actual or real (*wirklich*), it is because such reality expresses its peculiarity, that is, the specific *demands* and *fixed lawfulness* imposed upon us by the material of sensation. (The latter point is not to be underestimated: indeed, as we shall see in the next section, Stein's account of τò διότι revolves around the notions of *real* and *reality* (*wirklich* and *Wirklichkeit*), and, to be more precise, on Husserl's alleged misunderstanding of them.)

Phantasy

The "domain of freedom" is "broader" in the realm of *phantasy*: "I freely 'create' things, events, situations in phantasy. I am not bound to what I once perceived and experienced; in other words, my intentions do not seek fulfillment in something definite and particular that I once experienced nor in the manner that I experienced it" (Stein 2005, p. 241). Yet, in this case, too, my freedom in not "complete":

> [The act of] phantasy is not oriented to the things of experience as remembering is. It is not its purpose to recall some single thing that was once experienced. Phantasy can contrive a world where the sky is green and trees are blue, where things fall up instead of down, rivers run backwards, etc. I mean that phantasy may alter not only the concrete subsistence of individual things, but also the general types of experience and the laws of nature. This free variation, however, has its limits. I can give a thing any color I wish, but it must have *some* color or other. I can constantly vary its shape but I cannot think it without any shape whatsoever; otherwise it would no longer be a "thing." Nor can I think of a lion that is "unlion-like" (*unlöwenmäßig*), without it ceasing to be a lion.
>
> The essence of things (*das Wesen der Dinge*), what they are in themselves and what follows therefrom, sets limits for phantasy [...]. Thus, all intentional life, as long as it forms a thing-like world (*eine dingliche Welt*), turns out to be objectively bound. (Stein 2005, pp. 241–242)

As was already the case with the former two types of *Erlebnis* (perception and recollection), here too the term *Welt* stands for relevant bindings—"thing-like

---

[17] Stein 2005, pp. 240–241.
[18] Stein 2005, p. 241.

world" expressing the specific limit or "laws" imposed onto the spiritual activity of the subject by the "essence" of things. If there is such thing as a *Welt*—be it that of material things directly experienced through perception, or indirectly *via* memory, or the one contrived by our imaginative activity—there will be a set of "laws" binding, and thereby regulating, our intentional life (Stein 2005, p. 242). "World" and "law" seem to be coextensive notions. As Stein concludes this section, "The existence of laws regulating the life of consciousness is *objective being*, i.e., independent of the subject, and because it is presupposed by consciousness, it is *a priori*. The fact that an objectual world arises for the subject through its intentional life is grounded in the laws of consciousness" (Stein 2005, p. 242).

Before moving on to the next section, two observations are in order. As we shall recall, in her *Life in a Jewish Family* Stein points out with great clarity that *Ideas I* contained some "inflections" and "phrases" that would lead Husserl to embrace "transcendental idealism," yet she never asserts that such "idealism" can be found in the 1913 book. In fact—and in perfect compliance with what was stated in the autobiographical text—the *Excursus* refers to the *Cartesian Meditations*,[19] not to *Ideas I*. Without laying too much emphasis on this distinction, it is reasonable to assert that the *thematic* difference between τὸ διότι and τὸ ὅτι *textually* corresponds to that between *Ideas I* and the *Cartesian Meditations*.

Let us now move on to our second observation. Since what we have elaborated upon so far is simply Stein's description of different kinds of noetic-noematic correlations, the question naturally arises as to the specific *idealist* nature of Husserl's transcendentalism: how does Stein understand it? Let us consider the following:

> Admittedly, transcendental idealism does not say (as solipsism does) that the world of things (*dingliche Welt*) is dependent on a particular individual subject; it only claims that such a world is relative to individuals having a certain structure through whose intentional life this world can be constituted. [...] A material thing [...] cannot prove its existence by itself but needs something else for this, a spiritual subject (perhaps several subjects interacting).
>
> Does this impossibility of evincing itself mean that it is impossible for the thing to exist? It is surely absurd to be speaking of being that cannot be experienced in principle: but it is absurd not because "being" means no more than being experienced or at least being able to be experienced but because what is not spiritual cannot be from itself (as our earlier investigations have shown), but can be only as created. [...]
>
> For this reason, it may be correct to say that the world as it appears to us depends upon subjects of our own kind in order to evince itself in such courses of appearance. But it is not absurd to say that the world's being is not identical in meaning to such appearing, nor that another way to apprehend the world is conceivable as well as the existence of the material world in God's sight before there were living creatures on whose senses the world could fall. Being created means being set outside God and having being other than being in the divine spirit. (Stein 2005, pp. 245–246)

---

[19] Though without any specific textual reference, the German title of the book is explicitly mentioned in Stein 2005, page 243.

The way Stein presents the Husserlian "transcendental *idealism*" rests on a series of hermeneutical operations that need to be carefully distinguished and unpacked. In the first place, Stein seems to be proposing what might be called an "anthropologization" of Husserl's idealism: the latter being the thesis that "the world of things is relative to individuals having *a certain structure*," that "the world, as it appears *to us*, depends upon *subjects of our own kind*." This complies with the necessity of discussing Husserl's idealism within the framework of an analysis of the ontological makeup of the "wanderers," and of the mode of knowledge of the world derived from their being spiritual and material finite creatures. If, then, such "idealism" simply mirrors and expresses the ontological structure of a specific kind of beings and their specific relation to the world,[20] it is possible to imagine other beings (for example, "angels" and "God"), as well as "another way to apprehend the world" to which such "idealism" does not apply. This is what allows Stein to break once and for all the equivalence *Sein = Erscheinen*: the "being" of the world cannot be reduced to its appearance to the *wanderers* (therefore accounted for in terms of noetic-noematic correlations) precisely because "another way to apprehend the world is conceivable." It follows that the "objectivity" of the world, and its ontological independence from "us," is secured by its "being created" by God.

To put it more concisely: there exists just one, objective and independent world created by God, and different kinds of being ("finite and material beings," "finite and purely spiritual beings," and one "infinite spiritual being") with their peculiar mode of access to the "one" world. What we call "transcendental idealism" bears exclusively on one of these kinds of being, i.e., the *wanderer*.[21] Even if Stein does not explicitly say so, it is important to emphasize that she is endorsing a version of Husserl's "transcendental idealism" the extent of whose application has been previously reduced to the ontological structure of the *wanderers*: as if such idealism could be accepted only on condition of being limited to a "specific" ontological structure with a "specific" mode of access to the one world.

To summarize, according to the manner in which Stein presents it, "transcendental idealism" boils down to working out different kinds of noetic-noematic correlations, which can be categorized according to the degree of "freedom" that characterizes the process of "constitution" (this corresponding to the *transcendental* side of Husserl's transcendental idealism). In the course of her analysis, Stein makes it clear how the constitution of a relevant "world" of objects is determined by a specific *fixed lawfulness* imposed upon the spiritual intentional life of the subject (this characterizing the *constitutive* activity of the *spirit*, according to the main distinctions between perception, memory, and phantasy). According to the way she endorses it, the *idealist* side of Husserl's transcendental approach is understood as bearing exclusively on the specific mode of being, and hence access to the world, that pertains to that finite, spiritual, and at the same time material being that Aquinas

---

[20] In other words, the relation between the human subject and the world as it is *for us*.

[21] This critical position had already been made explicit in Stein 2014, p. 96.

calls the "wanderer" (*viator*): this also explains the peculiar position that the *Excursus* occupies in *Potency and Act*.

Now, the question as to the sense in which Stein's interpretation and restriction of such idealism also entails an implicit criticism of the Master needs to be held in abeyance. Indeed, it is now time to turn to *Finite and Eternal Being*, and to the footnote mentioned above.

3 Stein and the Motive that Led Husserl to "Transcendental Idealism"

3.1 The Footnote

The footnote in question appears in Chap. III, §6, right after the remark that a "twofold being" (*ein doppeltes Sein*) belongs to the essence of individual things (*Dinge*): this is what Stein designates a "being-in-the-objects, which is a 'becoming' and 'passing away' and, secondly—distinct from the being-in-the-objects—a being as a pure what (*rein Was*) which as such is free from the change of becoming and passing away." Here is the footnote:

> In his *Ideas* (pp. 8ff.) Husserl speaks of the possibility of bringing to the fore the *what* (*Was*) of an individual thing of experience by means of *intuition of essence* or *ideation*. This peculiar kind of intuition, which is distinct from all experience, extracts from the matter of fact of experience its content without performing its *positing* (i.e., the apprehension of the thing as something *real* (*als eines wirklichen*)), and posits such a content as something which could just as well have been realized (*verwirklicht*) elsewhere, that is to say, apart from the context or connection in which it was experienced. [...] The possibility of such a kind of apprehension clearly rests on the aforementioned "twofold essence" of the essence (*Doppel-Wesen des Wesens*). It takes into account only one side, namely, the *essential being* (*wesenhaftes Sein*) and thereby cuts the connection with reality (*Verbindung zur Wirklichkeit*), which belongs to the essence not just externally but intrinsically. On the basis of this initial cut which separates matters of fact and essence, it becomes understandable that Husserl arrived at an idealist conception of reality, whereas his associates and disciples (Max Scheler, Alexander Pfänder, Adolf Reinach, Hedwig Conrad-Martius, Jean Hering, and others), guided by the full sense of the essence (*Vollsinn des Wesens*), became even more confirmed in their realist [conception of reality]. (Stein 1962, p. 82)

Let us unpack Stein's argument:

(1) The fact (τὸ ὅτι) is "that Husserl arrived at an idealist conception, or understanding, of reality": the opposition being between Husserl's *idealist* and his associates' *realist* conception of *reality*. The issue at stake bears on the notion of *reality* or *actuality* (*Wirklichkeit*); yet, Stein does not tell us what this *idealist conception* consists in, and in what sense it is opposed to the *realist* conception;

(2) The "motive" (τὸ διότι) is, in a nutshell, the separation between matters of fact (*Tatsache*) and essence (*Wesen*) and entails two sub-theses:

(2') *Stein's ontological claim*, so to say, to the effect that there is a twofold essence of the essence, or that the essence itself displays a "two-layer structure," including an *essential* and a *real being*;

(2″) Stein's critique of *Husserl's methodological claim*, according to which the "eidetic intuition," or "ideation" is able to disentangle the former from the latter;

(3) Accordingly, such an opposition between *idealism* and *realism*, hence the nature itself of "the motive," is to be understood in a *meta-ontological* way (*sit venia verbo!*): if Husserl disregards the *twofold essence of the essence*, and is thereby led to fully embrace transcendental idealism, his "associates" are guided on the contrary by the "full sense of the essence."

By disregarding the "twofold essence of the essence," Husserl does not acknowledge "the connection with reality" that belongs to the essence as one of its components, and thereby reduces it to the mere "matters of fact" of the essence's factual realization. The duality within the essence between *essential* and *real being* is thus made into the duality between the essence itself and its factual or external realization.[22]

3.2   Stufenreich: *Remarks on the Structure of Essence*

Since everything seems to rest on Husserl's own misunderstanding of the "inner" structure of the "essence" (*Wesen*), it is necessary to explain what an essence is by exploring its internal structure and ontological articulation. As we will see, the main distinction is between two different, yet related, notions of essence, to which Stein refers as essence (*das Wesen*) and "the full what" (*das volle Was*) respectively. It is important to immediately point out (as already mentioned at the beginning of 3.1) that the entire argument addresses only the essence of "things," that is, those objects whose being "extends over some duration" and hence "undergoes some alterations in the course of this duration" (Stein 1962, p. 73.) Now, this is the case with the so-called "world of objects of sense" (*die gesamte Welt der sinnenfälligen Dinge*), also called "nature" (*Natur*). (Although one can already perceive a strong thematic affinity between this problem and the context in which *Potency and Act* discusses transcendental idealism, we will have to wait until the conclusion of this paper to raise the question as to their relation.)

Let us first say a few words on the general meaning that Stein attaches to the concept of essence (*Wesen*). In § 3 of Sect. III (*Wesenhaftes und wirkliches Sein*), Stein introduces the notion of essence with an explicit reference to both Hering (1921) and Husserl: "When Hering's 'principle of the essence' stated that every object has an essence, he had in mind not only objects in the narrower sense of the term. [...] Every thing has *its* essence (*Jedes Ding hat* sein *Wesen*). If it is an

---

[22] For an analysis of the practical dimension of the essence see Lebech 2019, pp. 31–33.

individual thing (*individuum*) [...], then also its essence is individual."[23] The essence is always the essence of something individual, and hence is always an individual essence; as Hering still maintains, "Two (individual) objects which are absolutely alike have two absolutely alike essences, but not one and the same essence. Each of two like flowers, each of two congruent triangles has *its* own essence" (Hering 1921, p. 498). Yet Stein does not fail to recognize that "The essence does not include everything that can be predicated of an object. There are in fact *essential* and *non-essential* properties; and to the determination of *what* and *how* the object is must be added what happens to it: its *fate* (*Schicksal*), that is to say, its activity and passivity (ποιεῖν καὶ πάσχειν), its relation to other objects, its spatial and temporal determinations" (Stein 1962, pp. 70–71).

According to the last passage, the notion of essence includes only what and how (*Was und Wie*) the object is (*Was ist der Gegenstand? Und wie ist er?*), and excludes the "ποιεῖν καὶ πάσχειν" (what Boethius would designate *actio et passio* or *facere et pati*), which is contingent and thus has no place whatsoever in the realm of essence.[24] Stein also accounts for *the essence*: "To the essence of an object, in other words, belongs only what must be preserved, so that 'this object' will remain the same" (Stein 1962, p. 72). Of course, such a notion of essence (i.e., the idea of a set of properties that do not change so that the object remains the same as itself) makes sense only if applied to "the world of becoming and passing away," in which we can distinguish between "some elements that are constant and others that are changing" (Stein 1962, p. 73.) In other words, what in this passage Stein labels *essence* is what comprises the "stable set" (*fester Bestand*) of properties characterizing any changing individual object ("essence in the narrow sense").

Next to this notion of essence, Stein discusses a second concept of essence which she refers to as *das volle Was*. Indeed, if the notion of essence includes only the *stable set* (or "what must be preserved, so that 'this object' will remain the same"), then what is needed is a broader concept of essence, including the alterations, of the object (what she refers to as the "flowing set" (*fließender Bestand*) of properties)— this being precisely what the full what (*das volle Was*) is meant to cover and express. Now, since this new notion of *essence* includes both the *flowing* (with its "becoming and passing away") and *stable set*,[25] we can dub it the "broad, or broader, notion of essence."

All these preliminary conceptual distinctions can be represented as follows[26]:

---

[23] This is what Hering labels the "principle of the essence". For a critical discussion of Hering's principle, see De Santis 2016b.

[24] Aristotle would not agree with this construal of the ποιεῖν καὶ πάσχειν, since they are both considered as "figures of categories" (σχήματα τῆς κατηγορίας) of "being in itself" (καθ᾽αὐτό) and not κατὰ συμβεβηκός (see *Metaphysics*, Δ, 1017a 22–23). We cannot forget that Stein's reading rests on Hering's interpretation of the ποιεῖν καὶ πάσχειν (Hering 1921, pp. 499–500,) which he translates with the German word *Schicksal* ("Schicksale belong not to the domain of the ποῖον εἶναι, but rather to that of the ποιεῖν καὶ πάσχειν").

[25] Stein 1962, p. 73.

[26] Three elements have been intentionally left out of the analysis and thus of the diagram: the notion of "essential core" (*Wesenskern,*) the ποιεῖν καὶ πάσχειν, and the distinction between what

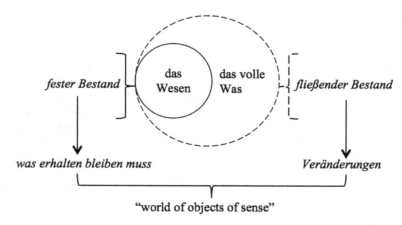

Fig. 1 A broad notion of essence

It is important to keep in mind that by "essence" Stein means two different, yet related, objectivities [*Gegenstaendlichkeiten*] formations: on the one hand, the more technical meaning of the "essence" refers to what we have dubbed the "narrow notion of essence," the stable set of properties determining the object as always the same; on the other hand, by essence Stein means the "individual essence" (*das individuelle Wesen,*) that is to say, the essence of the individual object as a whole, including *the essence* in the narrow sense and the full what (*das volle Was*) or essence in the broad sense (this second meaning fully corresponds to Fig. 1).

It is at this point that Stein explicitly speaks of "a twofold being" (*ein doppeltes Sein*) of the individual essence, in order to characterize *the individual essence*'s intermediate position between the mutable and ever-changing realm of reality and the eternal domain of the essentialities. As she points out in a revealing passage, which immediately precedes the paragraph including the footnote:

> We have previously employed the term *essential being* (wesenhaftes Sein) to designate the being of *essentialities* (Wesenheiten). If at this juncture this same term suggests itself for the designation of that being that is comprised in the essence (*Wesen*), it seems necessary to examine whether it is used in both instances in an identical sense. I am indeed convinced that it is characteristic of the peculiar relationship that holds between essence and essentiality and their respective mode of being (*Seinsweisen*). According to what we have learnt so far about essentialities, it appears certain that their essential being is the only kind of being they possess. By contrast, essences can posses an additional actuality (*Wirklichkeit*) in their respective objects, and a relationship to the objects, whose what (*Was*) they determine, is already implied in their pre-actual being (*vorwirklichen Sein*). Such duality in the being of essences corresponds to the mediating function that they exercise with respect to the essentialities, on the one hand, and the "real o actual world" (*wirkliche Welt*), on the other. The world of essential being is to be thought of as a hierarchical order. (Stein 1962, pp. 81–82)

"belongs to the essence" and what, even without belonging to it, "necessarily follows from the essence." For these latter problems, see De Santis 2015.

As we should recall, it is precisely such an ontologically intermediate position of the essence, and its twofold being, that Husserl is said to disregard. Now, without getting into an analysis of the notion of "essentiality"[27] (which goes far beyond our present concern), let us simply remark that by this quite abstruse term (εἶδος[28]) Stein means those non-individual formations whose realization brings about the "content" or *Was* of the individual essence (i.e., the "stable set"): "The *realization* of the essentiality does not mean that *it* becomes real, but that *something* that corresponds to it becomes real (*wirklich*). The possibility of real being has its ground in the being of the essentiality" (Stein 1962, p. 66).

This is why "individual essences" are said to posses a twofold being, an essential being derived from their being the realization of εἴδη, and a real being due to their being individual essences or, better, essences of individual objects that become and pass away over the course of time. Now, to better clarify the situation, and shed light on what Stein takes Husserl's position to be, a second diagram might be helpful here.

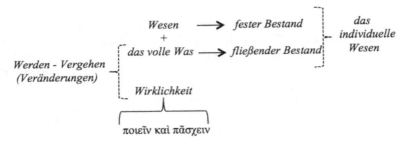

Fig. 2 A twofold being

This diagram could benefit from a brief explanation; the main point to be clarified being the distinction between the full what (including the flowing set proper to the essence as an essence of an individual and real being) and *reality* itself. On the one hand, the full what covers, as already mentioned, the flowing set of the individual essence, and thus makes it possible for the essence itself to undergo alternations. On the other hand—and despite such a connection with reality by means of

---

[27] For a detailed analysis of this notion and its significance in early phenomenology, see De Santis 2014.

[28] See the entire analysis developed in Chapter III, §2, of Stein 1962, pp. 61–67: "Here we encounter one of those formations which Plato had in mind when he discussed the nature of *Ideas* (ἰδεα, εἶδος)." As Kaufmann (1952, p. 572) puts it, "In the wake of Jean Hering's essay in the fourth volume of Husserl's *Jahrbuch*, she attempts at an integration of Plato's self-subsistent ideas (*Wesenheiten*) with Aristotle's immanent substantial forms (*Wesensformen*) which, ultimately individual themselves (Duns Scotus), unfold in the growth of individual and real things. This conformity of the ideal and sensory worlds is accounted for by the Neo-Platonic conception of the ideas in God."

the full what—the individual essence itself is not to be identified with the notion of reality. In fact, the latter includes not only the alterations characterizing the essence and its flowing set, but also the "contingent" "fate" (ποιεῖν καὶ πάσχειν.)

As we can see from the diagram below, it is the understanding of the essence as the full what that secures what Husserl, according to Stein, would disregard: the essence's connection with reality.

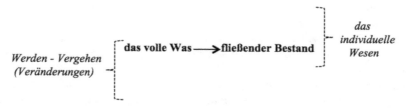

Fig. 3 What Husserl disregards

As we have repeatedly stressed, Stein speaks of a "twofold being of the essence," including an essential and a real being: whereas the essence as *Wesen* means exclusively the former, the essence as *the full what* embraces both. If the full what, notably the essence's *real being* is what Husserl would "disregard" (in the sense of the Latin *ab aliquo abstractio*), then the question is: to what does Husserl focus his attention (in the sense of the Latin *aliquid abstrahere*)?

In fact, Stein's general talk of *essential being* is not at all sufficient to capture what Husserl is really after, but as our footnote adds and explains, "In his *Ideas* [...] Husserl speaks of the possibility of bringing to the fore the *what* (sein Was) of an individual thing." By *the what*, or pure what (*reines Was*) (not to be confused with the above *full what*), Stein means one of the two components of the essence as *Wesen* with its *stable set*, i.e., what Aristotle designates τί εἶναι, the other one being the ποῖον εἶναι[29]: "It is evident that the τί εἶναι reveals the essence in its unity and totality. [...] The τί and ποῖον, τί εἶναι and ποῖον εἶναι, are connected, and with the discovery of this connection we gain access to the structure itself of the essence" (Stein 1962, p. 66).

Before concluding this section we will offer one more diagram to clarify the state of affairs:

---

[29] "to the essence of a particular thing belongs not only its being red, its being soft, its being fragrant, but also its being a rose or its being a bud, which provides the answer to the question: *What is it?*" "It pertains to the rose as a physical object to have form, size, color, and a number of other qualities, etc. We say, 'The rose is red,' and 'red' thus belongs to the ποῖον of the rose. We may also say, 'The color of the rose is red' (or some shade of red, for red is not an ultimate determination). In speaking of color, red does not designate the ποῖον of the rose, but rather relates its τί." (Stein 1962, p. 84)

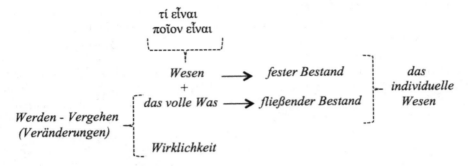

Fig. 4 The two components of *Wesen*

As Stein claims, Husserl "takes into account only one side, i.e., the essential being, and thereby cuts the connection with reality." According to the reconstruction proposed here, this means that—by disentangling the essence as *Wesen* (its τί εἶναι) from the essence as the full what (and its real being, including the stable set)—Husserl ends up overlooking the full-sense of the essence, and thereby *the individual essence* itself. In sum: such would be the motive (τὸ διότι) that led "the Master" to turn to "transcendental idealism."

3.3 Remarks on Husserl's **Tatsache und Wesen** *and Stein's Argument*

Before moving on to the actual conclusion of our investigation, three aspects involved in Stein's argument need to be recalled:

(α) According to what she presents in *Life in a Jewish Family*, *Ideas I* are not said to be committed to any sort of idealism. Indeed, she confines herself to stating that *Ideas I* "contain some phrases" which represent the "beginning" of that "development" that led Husserl to transcendental idealism (in other words, it seems that in *Ideas I* we can find the "bad seeds" of an idealism which is to be looked for only elsewhere);

(β) Likewise, our "footnote" does not assert that *Ideas I* are idealistically committed, but only that the *Matters of fact/Essence* argument makes "understandable that Husserl arrived [later on then, and not in that very same book] at an idealist conception, or understanding, of reality";

(γ) The footnote points to the pages in which the *argumentum ad essentiam et realitatem* (*sit venia verbo!*) unfolds: "In his *Ideas* (pp. 8ff.) Husserl speaks of the possibility of bringing to the fore the *what* (sein Was) of an individual thing of experience by means of *intuition of essence* or *ideation*."

At this juncture we will check where the arguments in Stein's and Husserl's text converge. As we already know, Stein holds that:

(1) "In his *Ideas* (pp. 8ff.) Husserl speaks of the possibility of bringing to the fore the *what (*sein Was*)* of an individual thing"; and Husserl explains that "*At first* 'essence' (*Wesen*) designated what is to be found in the very being of an individual as its *what (sein* Was)" (Husserl 1950, §3).

(2) Such a possibility, as Stein explains, is due to an "*intuition of essence* or *ideation*," and Husserl in fact points out: "Any such *what* can, however, be '*put into an Idea*'. *Experiential* or *individual intuition* can be turned into an *intuition of essence (ideation)*" (§3) (Husserl 1950, p. 13).

(3) Stein blames Husserl for focusing on the *essential being*, the essence construed of as the what or the pure what (*das Was* or *reines Was;*) and Husserl in turn speaks of "pure essence" (*reines Wesen*) as what is given in the intuition of essence or ideation (Husserl 1950, §§3, 4).

(4) This kind of "intuition," according to Stein, "extracts from the matter of fact of experience its content without performing its *positing*"; and Husserl explains that "the intuitive apprehension of the essence [...] *implies not the slightest positing of any individual factual existence*" (Husserl 1950, p. 17).

(5) As a consequence, according to Stein, it "posits such a content as something which could just as well have been realized elsewhere"; and, as Husserl stresses, what is posited is in fact "posited as something that is at this place [but that] could just as well be at any other place" (Husserl 1950, p.12).

A question naturally arises: how are we to understand Stein's *reaction* to Husserl, her *diagnosis* of the motive that led him to transcendental idealism? How are we to explain that a "meta-ontological" problem led Husserl to embrace transcendental idealism?

For the sake of hermeneutical honesty (which should prompt us to *subtract interpretations* rather than to *over-interpret* the text by piling hermeneutical layers upon one another), the interpreter has to confess that "the footnote" does not offer us any hint whatsoever as to how that question might be answered. Indeed, as we already know, the only text in which Stein explicitly tackles the issue is the *Excursus*: it is thus time to go back to where we started so as to see whether the relation between the two texts can help shed some light on this rather obscure matter.

4 Conclusion

Our attempt has not been, nor will it be in this conclusion, to evaluate Stein's argument, let alone to find out whether her claims bearing on the "motive" are really legitimate and well grounded, or if her overall account of Husserl's transcendental idealism is consistent and truthful to Husserl's own position and understanding of that doctrine. Our only concern has been to explore the manner in which she understands Husserl's idealism, and to reconstruct the wider backdrop against which she comes up with a specific hermeneutical hypothesis concerning the reason that—*volens nolens*—led Husserl to transcendental idealism. Accordingly, our analysis has been focusing on two texts, the *Excursus* and a footnote from *Finite and Eternal Being*. Now, faced with the difficulty of connecting the different arguments unfolded in these two works, the interpreter has to make a choice: either embrace a form of hermeneutical agnosticism and thus conclude that the two writings under scrutiny deal with two different, and to a certain extent "heterogeneous," topics or advance some interpretative hypothesis in order to make sense of the possible relation linking two books that, although quite different, are intimately connected.

We have decided to take the second route. Nevertheless, a new and serious interpretative problem arises and needs to be recognized. As we have already observed, the way *Potency and Act* presents and defends the doctrine of transcendental idealism betrays (at least "implicitly") a critical stance on the part of Stein herself: transcendental idealism, and the correlative idea of "constitution," seems to be acceptable only as long as it is limited to the ontological makeup of the *wanderer*, and to the specific access to the world that characterizes the latter. In other words, it sounds acceptable (and *de facto* accepted by Stein in that text) only on condition that its application is limited to a specific form of the "spiritual" and "personal" region: we could refer to these as "Husserl's *universal idealism*" and "Stein's *anthropological idealism*" respectively. Now—as a matter of fact—it is impossible to tell whether the version of transcendental idealism implied (and never "made explicit") by the footnote corresponds to the one endorsed in the *Habilitationsschrift*. Either answer seems plausible: (i) Stein could have radicalized her position and decided to reject transcendental idealism as such; or (ii) "the motive" could be taken now as critically accounting only and exclusively for "universal idealism." In this latter case, Stein would be playing (her own) *idealism* against (Husserl's own) *idealism*.

Here, too, we will go for the second hypothesis: the link between the two writings being represented by the notion of *reality* and the different, yet complementary, ways it is used in those two texts. The projects are undeniably different: if *Finite and Eternal Being*, or at least the chapters under analysis are exclusively concerned with the "formal-ontological" problem of the structure of individual essence, *Potency and Act* is by contrast interested in propounding a "personalistic" ontology. Yet the notion of *reality* itself is employed, as already mentioned, in a complementary manner: while in *Finite and Eternal Being* it characterizes, or contributes to characterizing, the essence of individual things, namely, of all those things that become and change over the course of time, in *Potency and Act* it characterizes, or contributes to characterizing, the specific act (i.e., perception) by which the *wanderers* have access to those very same individual and mutable things (in perfect compliance with Husserl's co-relative constitution, the ontological formation is assumed as a transcendental clue referring back to specific subjective *Erlebnisse*).

At this point the *commentary* (as we have tried to develop it so far) needs to be led, if not even replaced, by an explicit *interpretation* that will unavoidably step beyond the boundaries of the texts (as they are offered to us) without going against them. As we will recall, in *Potency and Act* the world of perception is said to be *real* because its *reality* mirrors its peculiarity, that is, the specific demands and fixed lawfulness imposed on us (i.e., our finite, and spiritual being) by the material of sensation. As a consequence, the following can be reasonably "assumed": if, as Stein remarks, Husserl can be blamed for taking "into account only one side, i.e., the essential being, and thereby cuts the connection with reality" that characterizes and makes up the ontological *structure* of the essence of individual things, then (*correlatively* and from the point of view of the "anthropological idealism" of *Potency and Act*) one can argue that it is *perception itself* that is stripped of what phenomenologically differentiates it, for example, from phantasy (as a specifically distinct act). If this were really the case, Stein would also be criticizing Husserl for not recognizing, or maybe for overlooking, the specific difference between two fixed systems of law (i.e., the one characterizing perception and phantasy respectively). Hence "universal idealism," which does not accept being a mere doctrine mirroring the "metaphysically" peculiar makeup of the *wanderer*, and of its specific gnoseology and access to the one world created by God. Are we facing a sort of πρῶτον ψεῦδος on the part of Husserl? Regardless of what we might think, Stein's *reaction to Husserl's transcendental idealism* has the great merit of addressing the issue in its inner unity, and of forcing us to raise the question as to the relation between the two hemispheres of Husserl's phenomenology: the *eidetic* and the *transcendental*.

Acknowledgements This work was supported by the Czech Science Foundation, financing the project "Intentionality and Person in Medieval Philosophy and Phenomenology" (GAČR 21-08256S).

References

Ales Bello, Angela. 2005. *The Sense of Things. Towards a Phenomenological Realism*. Trans. A. Calcagno. Dordrecht: Springer

Conrad-Martius, Hedwig. 1959. Die transzendentale und die ontologische Phänomenologie. In *Edmund Husserl. Recueil commémoratif publié à l'occasion du centenaire de la naissance du philosophe*, 175–184. La Haye: M. Nijhoff.

De Santis, Daniele. 2014. L'idea della fenomenologia come fenomenologia delle Idee. Su di un *peri ideon* tra Gottinga e Monaco. In *Di Idee ed essenze. Un dibattito su fenomenologia e ontologia (1921–1930)*, ed. D. De Santis. Milan: Mimesis: 7–136.

De Santis, Daniele. 2015. Wesen, Eidos, Idea. Remarks on the "Platonism" of Jean Hering and Roman Ingarden. *Studia Phaenomenologica* 15: 133–158.

De Santis, Daniele. 2016a. Notes on Husserl's *Idealismus* in the *Logische Untersuchungen* (*Via* Lotze's Interpretation of Plato). *Research in Phenomenology* 46 (2): 221–256.

De Santis, Daniele. 2016b. Jean Hering on *Eidos*, *Gegenstand* and *Methexis*. Phenomenological Adventures and Misadventures of "Participation." *Discipline Filosofiche* 26 (1): 145–170.

Fetz, Reto Luzius. 1993. Ich, Seele, Selbst. Edith Steins Theorie personaler Identität. In *Studien zur Philosophie von Edith Stein*, ed. M. Rath, P. Schultz, 286–319. Freiburg, München: Karl Alber.

Geiger, Moritz. 1933. Alexander Pfänders methodische Stellung. In *Neue Münchner Abhandlungen. Festschrift für Alexander Pfänder*, ed. E. Heller, F. Löw, 1–16. Leipzig: Barth.

Hering, Jean. 1921. Bemerkungen über das Wesen, die Wesenheit und die Idee. *Jahrbuch für Philosophie und phänomenologische Forschung* 4: 495–543.

Hering, Jean. 1926. *Phénoménologie et philosophie religieuse*. Paris: Alcan.

Hildebrand, Dietrich von. 1991. *What is Philosophy?* London-New York: Routledge.

Husserl, Edmund. 1950. *Ideen zu einer reinen Phänomenologie und phänomenologischen Philosophie. Erstes Buch. Allgemeine Einführung in die reine Phänomenologie*. Husserliana 3. Den Haag: M. Nijhoff.

Husserl, Edmund. 1984. *Logische Untersuchungen. Zweiter Band. Erster Teil*. Husserliana 19.1. Den Haag: M. Nijhoff.

Ingarden, Roman. 1976. *On the Motives which led Husserl to Transcendental Idealism*. Den Haag: M. Nijhoff.

Kaufmann, Fritz. 1952. Endliches und ewiges Sein. Versuch eines Aufstiegs zum Sinn des Seins by Edith Stein; Teresia Benedicta. *Philosophy and Phenomenological Research* 12 (4): 572–577.

Lebech, Mette. 2019. Essence, *eidos*, and Dialogue in Stein's "Husserl and Aquinas. A Comparison". *The New Yearbook for Phenomenology and Phenomenological Research*, XVII: 22–36.

Natorp, Paul. 1901. Zur Frage der logischen Methode. Mit Beziehung auf E. Husserls 'Prolegomena zur reinen Logik. *Kant Studien* 6: 270–283.

Sepp, Hans-Reiner. 1998. La postura de Edith Stein dentro del movimiento fenomenológico. *Anuario Filosófico* 1: 709–729.

Sepp, Hans-Reiner. 2003. Edith Steins Position in der Idealismus-Realismus-Debatte. In *Edith Stein. Themen—Bezüge—Dokumente*, ed. B. Beckmann, H.-B. Gerl-Falkovitz, 13–21. Würzburg: Königshausen & Neumann

Stein, Edith. 1929. Husserls Phänomenologie und die Philosophie des hl. Thomas von Aquino, *Jahrbuch für Philosophie und phänomenologische Forschung. E. Husserl zum 70. Geburtstag gewidmet* 10 (Special Issue): 315–338.

Stein, Edith. 1962. *Endliches und ewiges Sein. Versuch eines Aufstieges zum Sinn des Seins*. ESGA 11/12. Freiburg: Herder.

Stein, Edith. 2003. *Briefe an Roman Ingarden*. ESGA 4. Freiburg, Basel, Wien: Herder.

Stein, Edith. 2005. *Potenz und Akt. Studien zu einer Philosophie des Seins*. ESGA 10. Freiburg: Herder.

Stein, Edith. 2010. *Aus dem Leben einer jüdischen Familie und weitere autobiographische Beiträge*. ESGA 1. Freiburg: Herder.

Stein, Edith. 2014. *Freiheit und Gnade und weitere Beiträge zu Phänomenologie und Ontologie*. ESGA 9. Freiburg, Basel, Wien: Herder.

Tommasi, Francesco Valerio. 2003. "…verschiedene Sprachen redeten…" Ein Dialog zwischen Phänomenologie und mittelalterlichen Scholastik im Werk Edith Steins. In *Edith Stein. Themen—Bezüge—Dokumente*, ed. B. Beckmann, H.-B. Gerl-Falkovitz, 107–133. Würzburg: Königshausen & Neumann.

Volk, Peter. 2003. Erkenntnistheorie bei Edith Stein. In *Edith Stein. Themen—Bezüge—Dokumente*, ed. B. Beckmann, H.-B. Gerl-Falkovitz, 81–95. Würzburg: Königshausen & Neumann.

Senses of Being and Implications of Idealism: Heidegger's Appropriation of Husserl's Decisive Discoveries

Daniel O. Dahlstrom

Abstract This paper attempts to shed light on Heidegger's critical appropriation of Husserl's phenomenology. It begins by reviewing Heidegger's basic criticisms of Husserl's philosophical approach as well as his ambivalence towards it, an ambivalence that raises the question of whether Heidegger shares Husserl's idealist trajectory. The paper then examines how Heidegger appropriates what he regards as two of Husserl's "decisive discoveries," namely, Husserl's accounts of intentionality and categorial intuitions. Regarding the first discovery, the paper demonstrates how Heidegger tweaks the method of phenomenological reduction for the purpose of describing intentional experience in terms of being-in-the-world. As for the second discovery, the paper shows how Heidegger adapts the basic sense of categorial intuitions, both pre-thematically and thematically, into his existential analysis. In conclusion, the paper discusses how the role of horizons in Heidegger's analysis of temporality provides him with firm reasons to resist an idealist interpretation of phenomenology.

Keywords Intentionality · Categorial intuition · Being-in-the-world · Horizon · Reduction · Noesis · Noema · Essence

D. O. Dahlstrom (✉)
Boston University, Boston, MA, USA
e-mail: dahlstro@bu.edu

© Springer Nature Switzerland AG 2021
R. K. B. Parker (ed.), *The Idealism-Realism Debate Among Edmund Husserl's Early Followers and Critics*, Contributions to Phenomenology 112,
https://doi.org/10.1007/978-3-030-62159-9_13

1   Introduction

In the spring of 1923 Heidegger tells students that the young Luther and the paragon Aristotle guided him in his searching, and that Kierkegaard provided powerful impulses. But it was Husserl, he adds, "who gave me my eyes."[1] From the fall of 1921 to the spring of 1924, not a single semester goes by when Heidegger is not holding a seminar on either Husserl's *Logical Investigations* or *Ideas I*.[2] In the summer of 1925 he acknowledges before his students that, opposite the founder of phenomenology, he still considers himself a novice and the following semester he extols the author of the *Logical Investigations* for bringing the great tradition of Western philosophical thought to completion.[3] After stating that the investigations in *Being and Time* were "only possible on the foundation laid by Husserl," especially in the *Logical Investigations*, Heidegger publicly expresses his gratitude to Husserl for helping him in his early teaching stint at Freiburg (1916–23) become adept "in the most diverse regions of phenomenological research," help that took the form of "intense personal direction" and "the freest access to unpublished manuscripts." Not surprisingly, it would seem, *Being and Time* is dedicated to Edmund Husserl "in reverence and friendship."[4]

Yet, in those same lectures during the summer of 1925, Heidegger provides his students with a critical review of Husserl's thought, leaving no mistake that in the mid-1920s he is bent on giving phenomenology a quite different meaning and direction. Two years earlier, in his first Marburg lectures, after reviewing the fundamental differences between Husserl and Descartes, he takes Husserl to task for falling in line with Descartes' fraught concern for certainty and the formation of a theoretical science at the expense of phenomenological findings regarding the being of consciousness.[5] In the summer of 1925 lectures, utilizing some of the unpublished manuscripts that Husserl had so generously made available to him, Heidegger presents his students with an "immanent critique of the progression of phenomenological research itself," as a means of freeing up the question of being, a question never raised *expressis verbis* by phenomenology's founder.[6] A few weeks before the start of these lectures Heidegger tells an audience in Kassel that "Husserl misunderstood his own work," taking his bearings all too narrowly from theoretical experience. A

---

[1] Heidegger GA63, 5. I am grateful to Andrew Butler for helpful suggestions and astute criticisms of an earlier version of this paper.
[2] Kisiel 1985, 196.
[3] Heidegger GA20, 168; GA21, 88.
[4] Heidegger SZ, V, 38, and 38 Anm. 2; GA14, 93–99; GA15, 373–76.
[5] Heidegger GA17, 266–75.
[6] Heidegger GA20, 124. Heidegger also criticizes Husserl's epistemic construal of the basic structure of all intentionality (GA20, 169).

year later (1926) Heidegger confides to Jaspers that if *Being and Time* is written against anyone, then it is Husserl.[7]

These conflicting signals about Husserl's phenomenology are consonant with Heidegger's complex appropriation of phenomenology itself.[8] Late in life he pays homage to phenomenology in his 1963 retrospective "My Way into Phenomenology." Heidegger recounts how, as a seminarian, he first turned to Husserl's *Logical Investigations* in the hopes that Husserl, as Brentano's student, would shed some light on the issues that continued to trouble Heidegger after reading Brentano's dissertation on Aristotle's account of the manifold senses of 'being.' Those hopes were initially dashed but only because, as Heidegger himself puts it, he was not searching in the right way. Yet even after study of Emil Lask's works provided new impetus to examine the *Logical Investigations*, he still puzzled over the meaning of phenomenology. The turning point came, as Heidegger recalls it, with the publication of *Ideas I* in 1913 and, more decisively, with Husserl's arrival in Freiburg in 1916, affording Heidegger the opportunity "to meet with Husserl personally in his workshop."[9] Yet, even as he attests to the importance of phenomenology for his early development, he tempers his enthusiasm by observing that Aristotle and the Greeks, with their understanding of *aletheia*, conceived the basic insights of phenomenology "more originally."[10] Even the words of praise at the end of the 1963 retrospective are riddled with qualifications. After noting that "phenomenological philosophy" is today an historical designation for one movement among others, he insists that what is most proper to phenomenology is not a movement and not a thing of the past, but an enduring possibility of thinking what needs to be thought. But he then concludes that if phenomenology is experienced in this way, then the label can disappear "in favor of the matter of thinking."[11]

---

[7] Heidegger and Jaspers 1990, 71. Although these last two paragraphs paraphrase remarks made in the opening paragraphs of Dahlstrom 2001, Ch. 2, the following paper significantly departs from that earlier treatment of Heidegger's critical appropriation of Husserl's thought.

[8] See Dahlstrom 2018a, 211–228.

[9] Heidegger GA14, 97.

[10] Specifically, what passes in phenomenology for the purported self-announcement of phenomena in acts of consciousness was conceived more originally. Thus, phenomenology re-discovered the fundamental feature of Greek thinking, "if not philosophy as such." The more this insight became clear to Heidegger, the more the question weighed upon him: whence and how does the thing itself, what phenomenology demands be experienced as such, determine itself? "Is it consciousness and the objectivity of what is an object for consciousness or is it the 'to be' of the particular entity in its unhiddenness and hiddenness?" The question is obviously rhetorical and yet Heidegger's follows it with a repeated invocation of phenomenology's role: "Thus I was brought again to the question of being, illuminated by the phenomenological stance, and troubled in a manner different from the way I was before by the questions that proceeded from Brentano's dissertation" (Heidegger GA14, 99).

[11] Heidegger GA14, 101. Phenomenology is not distinguished, as other philosophical disciplines are, by a subject-matter but as a way of doing things or a 'how of research' (see Heidegger SZ 27f, GA20, 105). The context of "My Way into Phenomenology" should not be overlooked. The essay's purpose is, in part, to tout Hermann Niemeyer, the head of the publishing house so closely linked to the phenomenological movement throughout the twentieth century. For this purpose, Heidegger

2   Heidegger's Basic Criticisms, His Ambivalence, and the Question of Incrimination

The idea that the name can go as long as a certain experience of phenomenology persists probably reflects Heidegger's own moves away from phenomenology, at least as a methodological self-description, after 1930.[12] But even before he dissociated his own thinking from transcendental phenomenology, indeed, before he completed the final draft of *Being and Time*, he had mounted strident criticisms of specific aspects of Husserl's phenomenology. These criticisms deserve a separate study as does the question of their import in the light of Husserl's subsequently published and unpublished writings.[13] However, two criticisms, criticisms of the method and the motivation of Husserl's phenomenology, deserve more than passing mention.

The *first* criticism takes aim at Husserl's "ontological myopia." Heidegger charges Husserl with failing to raise the critical question of what 'to be' means specifically in regard to intentionality, the central theme of phenomenology.[14] Heidegger perhaps makes the point most clearly in a passage from a letter to Husserl. After indicating his agreement with Husserl about the irreducibility of the world's "transcendental constitution" to beings as they are typically understood, Heidegger notes that determining "the sort of being of the entity in which 'world' is constituted" remains a problem. He then adds:

> That is the central problem of *Being and Time*, that is to say, a fundamental ontology of being-here. It is necessary to show that the sort of being of humanly being-here is completely different from that of every other being and that it is the very sort of being that it is precisely by containing in itself the possibility of the transcendental constitution. [...]The constituting is not nothing, thus something and something that is [*seiend*] – albeit not in the sense of the positive. The question of the sort of being of the constituting [entity] itself is not to be gotten around.[15]

For the rest of the1920s, after the publication of *Being and Time*, this issue of the transcendence peculiar to being-here (*Da-sein*) repeatedly takes center stage for Heidegger.[16]

---

draws attention to Niemeyer's publication of major works on phenomenology by Husserl, Scheler, and himself. Not to praise, but to bury phenomenology in such a setting would be unseemly and this must be taken into account in evaluating the complimentary tone of Heidegger's remarks about phenomenology.

[12] See Heidegger 1959, 414; Heidegger 1954, 95–99.

[13] For some steps in this regard, see Dahlstrom 2001, Ch.2; Crowell 2013, 74–77; Engelland 2017, 213–222.

[14] Heidegger GA21, 98f; Husserl Hua III/1, 191: "Der Begriff der Intentionalität, in der unbestimmten Weite umfaßt, wie wir ihn gefaßt haben, ist ein zu Anfang der Phänomenologie ganz unentbehrlicher Ausgangs- und Grundbegriff."

[15] Husserl Hua IX, 601–602. For a valuable discussion of a Husserlian response to these remarks, see Luft 2002, 18–22.

[16] See, for example, Heidegger GA9, 123–175.

But Husserl also fails to raise the question of the meaning of 'being' in general. Instead, he tends to equate the meaning of 'being' with "being an object of or being true for theoretical, scientific knowing."[17] In this regard, Heidegger contends, Husserl is in step with the Western philosophical tradition of presupposing that the being of "things" in general – whether they be entities divine, numerical, or natural – is equivalent to their presence. Hence, it is no coincidence, as Heidegger sees it, that the characterizations of intentionality both before and after the phenomenological reductions – the putatively "natural attitude," on the one hand, and the so-called "absolute being of pure consciousness," on the other – have all the trappings of theoretical, "naturalistic" constructions utterly removed from the world in which human beings actually work and live.[18] Nor, in Heidegger's eyes, is this basic difficulty removed by Husserl's attempts – in lectures later published as *Phenomenological Psychology* and in *Ideas II* (personally communicated to him by Husserl in the winter of 1924–25) – to elaborate a personalist account of the subject in whose acts the sense of nature is disclosed.[19] Thus, despite taking pains to show that Husserl rather than Brentano deserves the credit of discovering the genuine significance of intentionality,[20] Heidegger contends that, precisely because Husserl construes subjectivity as the counterpart of nature (*der Gegenwurf von Natur*), his analysis remains in the ambit of the very naturalism he is trying to combat.[21] In this connection, reminding Husserl of a conversation the two had in Todtnauberg regarding the distinctiveness of "being-in-the-world," Heidegger writes to his erstwhile mentor: "Doesn't a world belong to the pure ego at all, as part of its very essence?"[22]

A *second* criticism is directed at what motivates Husserl to pursue philosophy in the way that he does. In his first Marburg lectures, Heidegger argues that Husserl's brand of phenomenology is primarily concerned with securing "known knowledge" and that the singular motivation for this concern is an *Angst* in the face of existence

---

[17] Heidegger GA20, 165: "Diese Frage, was erforschen wir am Bewußtsein als seinem Sein, formuliert Husserl auch so: Was können wir an ihm fassen, bestimmen, als objektive Einheiten fixieren? Sein heißt für ihn nichts anderes als wahres Sein, Objektivität, wahr für ein theoretisches, wissenschaftliches Erkennen. Es wird hier nicht nach dem spezifischen Sein des Bewußtseins, der Erlebnisse gefragt, sondern nach einem ausgezeichneten Gegenstandsein für eine objektive Wissenschaft vom Bewußtsein."

[18] Heidegger GA20, 145–149; 155. The term 'naturalistic,' as Heidegger applies it to the character of the natural attitude, is not equivalent to 'physicalistic,' but instead designates an extension of ontological categories paradigmatically appropriate for natural objects; see Heidegger GA17, 273f, 303. Heidegger's criticism no doubt overreaches, particularly given some of the analyses undertaken by Husserl in *Ideas II*.

[19] Heidegger GA20, 165–171.

[20] Heidegger GA20, 34–46.

[21] Heidegger GA20, 165: "Gegenüber dem Transzendenten, dem Physischen der Natur, ist das Psychische das immanente Gegebene, es ist, wie Husserl hier sagt, 'der Gegenwurf von Natur.'" Heidegger is referring to Husserl's essay, "Philosophie als strenge Wissenschaft" (Husserl 1910, 314).

[22] Husserl Hua IX, 274 Anm. 1.: "Gehört nicht eine Welt überhaupt zum Wesen des reinen ego? Vgl. unser Todtnauberger Gespräch <1926> über das 'In-der-Welt-sein' (*Sein und Zeit*, I, § 12. 69) und den wesenhaften Unterschied zum Vorhandenen 'innerhalb' einer solchen Welt."

(or, less dramatically, the fear of being-here).[23] It is unclear whether Heidegger is using *Angst* here in precisely the sense elaborated a few years later in *Being and Time*. Nevertheless, he is suggesting at the very least that something like anxiety or fear for existence is responsible for Husserl's Cartesian penchant of modeling philosophy's endgame on theoretical sciences like mathematics and physics – as though the anxiety could be removed or the corresponding threat mitigated by adequate computation and management of the physical world. In contrast to the innovative, forward-looking, "productive logic" of the ancients,[24] Husserl is bent on the reactionary project of securing the unchanging conditions of the possibility of knowledge already possessed.

These criticisms, whatever their ultimate merit, underscore the scope of Heidegger's departure from Husserl's phenomenology. When combined with Heidegger's subsequent efforts to distance his thinking from transcendental phenomenology and its idealism, they can have the effect of blinding us to the lasting impact of Husserl's phenomenology on Heidegger. Yet Heidegger's attitude towards Husserl's work is clearly ambivalent. The indictment of Husserl's ontological prejudices is joined by enthusiasm for a philosophical breakthrough that Heidegger intends to make his own.

This ambivalence raises questions concerning the nature – and specifically, given his own criticisms, the incriminating nature – of his appropriation of Husserl's phenomenological method into his own thinking. The import of these questions for Heidegger's conception of philosophy at the time he was drafting *Being and Time* is particularly patent. Can Heidegger be sure or, better, is there sufficient reason to think that his appropriation of phenomenology does not in some way involve commitments of the very sort that he criticizes? Does not, for example, the very project of analyzing the sense and essence of Dasein's distinctive being betray (for good or for ill) its Husserlian patrimony? How can this project even get off the ground without principles of selection and differentiation (e.g., the differentiation of beings from being) that mimic a phenomenological reduction and the idealism that, by Husserl's lights, it entails? How different are Heidegger's investigations of essences in *Being and Time*, at least structurally, from Husserl's eidetic phenomenological inquiries? In other words, is not the existential analysis in *Being and Time*, like any formal study, committed to understanding essential features and does not this understanding entail a commitment to an ideality of some sort? Does not Heidegger's phenomenological project in *Being and Time* – like Husserl's idea of a phenomenological science – presuppose the persisting presence of what it unpacks, even if what

---

[23] Heidegger GA17, 97–99. With its *ad hominem* character, this criticism of Husserl's motivation is interesting because it was delivered two years prior to the criticism of Husserl's phenomenological method and content (the criticism of his "ontological myopia" mentioned earlier) and because it forms a substantial part of the first Marburg lectures given by Heidegger, after leaving Freiburg and getting out from under Husserl's shadow.

[24] Heidegger SZ, 10.

the analysis turns up is the timely character of Dasein? And to this extent, at least, does not *Being and Time* lie in the orbit of a phenomenological idealism?[25]

3   Heidegger's Appropriation of the Decisive Discoveries of Husserl's Phenomenology

With these questions in mind, the rest of this paper sets aside Heidegger's criticisms of Husserl and single-mindedly pursues certain themes and methods of Husserl's phenomenology taken up by Heidegger into *Being and Time* (and in lectures and writings shortly before and after its publication). For this purpose, I focus principally on Heidegger's account of what, in the spring of 1925, he takes to be the two "decisive discoveries" of Husserl's phenomenology: intentionality and categorial intuitions.[26] These are, to be sure, by no means the only aspects of Husserl's thought that have a decisive influence on Heidegger's efforts to refashion the significance of "phenomenology." Husserl's published and unpublished reflections on time, for example, are enormously important to that endeavor.[27] Heidegger's appropriation of Husserl's phenomenology, moreover, is as much methodological as thematic. As Heidegger himself puts it: "The expression 'phenomenology' primarily signifies a concept of method."[28] Though the reductions and other methodological moves elaborated by Husserl as the *sine qua non* of phenomenological inquiry are often thought to be missing from Heidegger's early philosophy, they in fact figure decisively in his attempts, throughout the 1920s, to fashion a distinctive sort of phenomenology.

Accordingly, the discussion on the following pages focuses on what Heidegger deems Husserl's "decisive" discoveries, but with an eye, too, to Heidegger's appropriation of these other crucial aspects of Husserl's phenomenology in the mid-1920s. Heidegger's appropriation of phenomenology in some sense is, it scarcely bears noting, undeniable. Nor is it up for debate that he appropriates it to his own self-styled project of fundamental ontology. Phenomenology supplies, in his words, the only "way of treating" the ontological subject matter of *Being and Time*.[29] As he puts it in the lectures of the summer of 1925: "There is no ontology alongside a

---

[25] Or is the entire effort of *Being and Time* a youthful misadventure, a mistaken detour (*Abweg*) taken by Heidegger under the spell of his erstwhile mentor? See, among others, Van Buren 1994, 136, 365–367.

[26] Heidegger 1992/3, 159–160. A few months after this April 1925 address, Heidegger adds a third such discovery – "the original sense of the a priori"; Heidegger GA20, 34–122.

[27] Within the confines of this paper, I do not elaborate on this temporal aspect. Suffice to say, however, that although both thinkers regard temporality as foundational, the differences between their analyses are profound. While Husserl analyzes it as internal to and co-constitutive of sensory consciousness, Heidegger analyzes it, by contrast, as structurally co-constitutive of being-in-the-world.

[28] Heidegger SZ, 27.

[29] Heidegger SZ, 37f.

phenomenology but rather scientific ontology is nothing else but phenomenology."[30] By 'fundamental ontology,' Heidegger means the study of or propaedeutic to the disclosure of the senses of 'being' based upon the analysis of the allegedly paradigmatic sense of 'being-here' (*Da-sein*). The next two sections attempt to demonstrate how profoundly Heidegger draws on Husserl's phenomenology for this analysis, initiated in the published parts of *Being and Time*. To the extent that the demonstration is successful, it helps explain (a) why Heidegger was ultimately unable to "kick away the ladder" of phenomenology that he used to mount to a fundamental ontology and, accordingly, (b) why he considered it necessary to "turn" away from that transcendental phenomenological method that dominated his thinking in the 1920s.

3.1   Intentionality, Phenomenological Reduction, and Being-in-the-World

Heidegger's claim that Husserl discovered intentionality is, as he is quite aware, at odds with the standard view of many of his contemporaries, especially of neo-Kantian stripe, that Husserl merely took over the notion from Brentano. Heidegger does not dispute the fact that the currency of the term 'intentionality' at the turn of the century must be traced to Brentano's psychology. For Brentano what is distinctively characteristic of "psychic phenomena" is their intentionality, the fact that, in various distinctive ways, they are directed at or intend something (indeed, as Brentano would eventually maintain, whether it otherwise exists or not).[31] However, while fully subscribing to this much of Brentano's doctrine, Husserl adds an essential modification and it is on the basis of this essential modification that Heidegger insists that responsibility for the breakthrough in understanding intentionality has to be laid at Husserl's doorstep, not Brentano's.[32]

Husserl's breakthrough is to have appreciated that, corresponding to the various sorts of intentional experiences or acts directed at objects (for example, thinking x, imagining x, perceiving x, and so on), allowance must be made for the various ways in which those objects are intended (for example, x as it is thought, the imagined x, the perceived x, and so on), ways which, like the intentional acts to which they essentially and respectively correspond, are to be distinguished from the objects themselves. There is, accordingly, a basic unity to the concrete intentional experience, a unity such that, to every intentional act (or aspect of the same), there is a

---

[30] Heidegger GA20, 98.

[31] Brentano 1925, 133f; see Husserl Hua XIX/1, 385–87 and Tugendhat 1970, 27 Anm. 17; cf. also Bell 1991, 234 n. 18 for the difference between the inexistence of a mental content (according to Brentano's early theory of intentionality) and its nonexistence, a possibility which he later builds into the criterion of an intentional relation.

[32] Heidegger GA20, 35–63.

specifically corresponding intentional content (or aspect of the same).[33] In Husserl's terminology, the full intentional content (noema) of an intentional act (noesis) is comprised of not simply its object, but also and, indeed, primarily its "sense."[34] Moreover, that sense is typically not a mental image or representation of the object. Neither in the case of perceiving a tree nor in the case of registering (for Husserl, "perceiving") the fact that the tree is an oak, do I typically form an image of the oak tree. Rather the tree itself or that fact about the tree is perceived through its sense. Indeed, even imagining a tree requires a sense of the tree.

Though drafted after the analysis of truth in the *Logical Investigations*, the noesis-noema structure of intentionality brings to relief the sort of identity in difference presupposed by that analysis. Thus, the affirmation of the truth of an assertion, that is to say, the acknowledgment that what is asserted about something obtains or is present in some manner, is only meaningful because what is asserted can be entertained as possibly true or false (that is to say, it can be entertained in its absence and thus in the absence of evidence of it). On this account, truth consists in the coincidence of two different ways or, as explained above, two different "senses" in which something, indeed, the same thing is "intended" (or, what is the same, two different ways in which the same thing presents itself or is given relative to different conscious acts). The sense of the tree in the thought of it when absent from my line of sight is "empty," "merely meant"; the sense of the tree in the perception of it when present in my line of sight is "fulfilled," "given.") As noted earlier, truth is thus initially defined by Husserl as the correlate of an identification, the identity of two senses: "the complete agreement between the meant and the given as such."[35]

The noesis-noema distinction has other implications as well. By means of it, according to Husserl, phenomenology ranges over the entire natural world as well as all ideal worlds, encompassing them as the "sense of the world" and doing so by means of essential laws which combine the sense of the object and the noema in general with the closed system of noeses. These connections conform to rational laws and their correlate is the "actual object" which, for its part, respectively presents an index for completely determinate systems of teleologically unified formations of consciousness. The *telos* involved is the truth of things, the givenness or evidence of the senses of them, within a global, rational system.[36]

---

[33] Bell 1991, 115; Bernet et al. 1993, 91f; cf. Heidegger GA20, 61: "Wenn wir diese Bestimmung gegenüber der Brentanoschen abgrenzen, so ist zu sagen: Brentano sah an der Intentionalität die Intentio, Noesis, und die Verschiedenheit ihrer Weisen, aber er sah nicht das Noema, das Intentum."

[34] Husserl Hua III/1, 297: "Jedes Noema hat einen 'Inhalt', nämlich seinen 'Sinn', und bezieht sich durch ihn auf 'seinen' Gegenstand"; see, too, Husserl Hua III/1, 302–03. Or in the terminology of the *Logical Investigations*, corresponding to the specific "quality" of each intentional act, there is a specific "content" or "matter"; cf. Husserl Hua XIX/1, 425–31. For Heidegger's characterization of noesis and noema as well as the respective sorts of phenomenological investigations they entail, see Heidegger GA20, 129.

[35] Husserl Hua XIX/2, 65-52; Hua III/1, 324: "Der 'Satz' 'bewährt' oder auch 'bestätigt' sich, die unvollkommene Gegebenheitsweise verwandelt sich in die vollkommene."

[36] Husserl Hua III/1, 336–37: "So umspannt die Phänomenologie wirklich die ganze natürliche Welt und alle die idealen Welten, die sie ausschaltet: sie umspannt sie als 'Weltsinn' durch die

Access to this "phenomenological field" requires bracketing the "entire natural world" in which we normally, in our natural attitude, find ourselves as well as any appeal to sciences which presuppose this world. Among the latter are the empirical disciplines of psychology and physiology and even the humanities (*Geisteswissenschaften*) insofar as they examine conscious acts as events in the natural order in their relation to other such events. As phenomenologists, Husserl emphasizes, "we may not assume or claim anything that we cannot make essentially transparent to ourselves in pure immanence."[37] Since, to this end, it is necessary to refrain from any appeal to whatever is said to "transcend" pure consciousness, the claims of purely eidetic disciplines, both formal and material (for example, algebra and theoretical physics, respectively), must also be suspended. In addition to these phenomenological reductions, as they are sometimes called, it is necessary finally to attend solely to the essential features of the experiences as they present themselves in the wake of the reductions.[38]

In the wake of the reductions, it bears emphasizing, the phenomenologist works with the same phenomena that were at hand before they were "bracketed." The reductions, in other words, are by no means to be understood as a canceling or denial of what presents itself in the natural attitude or to the scientist who pursues his research on the basis of the natural attitude. As Husserl puts it, what is bracketed is not "wiped away," but rather "re-evaluated" in view of the status it possesses within the "pure experiences" making up the domains of phenomenological research.[39]

While no less important than the bracketing of the "natural world" and the sciences of it, all of the refinements of the phenomenological reduction discussed above are, Husserl notes, premised on that initial reduction. The latter is what first makes it possible to shift one's focus to the "phenomenological field" and grasp what presents itself within it.[40] If all that the general thesis of the natural attitude encompasses "in an ontic respect" is thus put "out of play," as Husserl phrases it,

---

Wesensgesetzlichkeiten, welche Gegenstandssinn und Noema überhaupt mit dem geschlossenen System der Noesen verknüpfen, und speziell durch die vernunftgesetzlichen Wesenszusammenhänge, deren Korrelat 'wirklicher Gegenstand' ist, welcher also seinerseits jeweils einen Index für ganz bestimmte Systeme teleologisch einheitlicher Bewußtseinsgestaltungen darstellt."

[37] Husserl Hua III/1, 127; see, too, Hua III/1, 51: "Das Prinzip aller Prinzipien" and Hua III/1, 314–317: "Die erste Grundform des Vernunftbewußtseins: das originär gebende >>Sehen<<."

[38] Husserl Hua III/1, 157: "Nur die Individuation läßt die Phänomenologie fallen, den ganzen Wesensgehalt aber in der Fülle seiner Konkretion erhebt sie ins eidetische Bewußtsein und nimmt ihn als ideal-identisches Wesen, das sich, wie jedes Wesen, nicht nur hic et nunc, sondern in unzähligen Exemplaren vereinzeln könnte."

[39] Husserl Hua III/1, 159; Hua XIX/2, 686–87. Thus, the reductions are to be understood, not so much as a means of taking leave of ordinary experience, but rather as a means of recovering key overlooked aspects of it.

[40] Husserl Hua III/1, 129–30.

"there remains a region of being, in principle unique, which can, indeed, become the field of a new science - that of phenomenology."[41]

The description of phenomenology and its method in the preceding paragraphs could, without the slightest alteration, be just as well applied to the phenomenology that Heidegger regards as the methodological counterpart to ontology in *Being and Time*. As noted earlier, the point is often made that the phenomenological bracketing is not to be found in Heidegger's work.[42] But Heidegger, too, insists that ontic considerations of human existence, specifically in the sciences of anthropology, psychology, and biology, be set aside in an effort to unpack its ontological *sense*.[43] Indeed, Heidegger's phenomenological project, like Husserl's, requires the exclusion of any attempt to understand what 'to be' means by referring it to some being, be it God or nature, as though it were explicable in a way analogous to the way in which one being within the world is said to be explained or caused by another.[44] By the same token, in the effort to understand being-in-the-world as such, all otherwise legitimate efforts to comprehend human beings as transcendent objects, on hand within the world, must be put out of play. "This particular being does not have and never has the sort of being of something only on hand within the world."[45]

Heidegger even adds two distinctive twists to the method of reduction as he takes it up into his phenomenology.[46] His aim is to pose the question of the sense of being (*Sinn des Seins*) and, accordingly, as a means of exposing and thereby bracketing "the fatal prejudice" that prevents the question from being raised, he builds into his phenomenological project the task of dismantling the history of ontology.[47] In addition, the first section of *Being and Time* is nothing less than an attempt to elaborate and then bracket the inauthentic (though nonetheless telling) ways in which human beings project (intend, are related to) themselves, others, and things within the world, ways in which what "being" means for them in each case is constituted and

---

[41] Husserl Hua III/1, 65–69; 158–59: "Durch die phänomenologische Reduktion hatte sich uns das Reich des transzendentalen Bewußtseins als des in einem bestimmten Sinn >>absoluten<< Seins ergeben."

[42] See, for example, Tugendhat 1970, 263; for a review of differing views on this topic, see Dahlstrom 2001, 113n72.

[43] Heidegger SZ, 45: "Die existenziale Analytik des Daseins liegt vor jeder Psychologie, Anthropologie und erst recht Biologie." See also Heidegger SZ, 51 where Heidegger notes that, in relation to "positive sciences," the investigation pursued in *Being and Time* is carried out "not as 'progress,' but rather as a retrieval and ontologically more transparent purification of what has been ontically discovered."

[44] Heidegger SZ, 6.

[45] Heidegger SZ, 43.

[46] In his lectures Heidegger's attitude toward the phenomenological reduction is ambivalent. In the summer of 1925 he charges that the phenomenological reduction – at least in the hands of Husserl – is "fundamentally unfit to determine positively the being of consciousness" (Heidegger GA20, 150); in the summer of 1927 he describes how the phenomenological reduction figures in his own determination of the project of phenomenology as fundamental ontology; see Heidegger GA24, 29.

[47] Heidegger SZ 3-4, 21, 25. For Heidegger's insistence on the quite positive dimensions of this project of "destruction" with respect to the history of philosophy, see SZ 20 and 22–23.

disclosed. Only by virtue of this "existential" version of the phenomenological reduction can there be any assurance of disclosing what it means for humans, in the authentic sense of the term, "to be." Just as the entire natural world remains before and after Husserl's phenomenological reductions, so the ontic world remains fully intact as commitments within it are suspended in the pursuit of fundamental ontology. The aim of the phenomenological reductions is to grasp the essence of the intentional experience as it intuitively presents itself. So, too, the aim of Heidegger's versions of the methodological epoché is to grasp the essence of being-in-the-world as well as the essential manners of being disclosed within the phenomenon of being-in-the-world.[48]

To be sure, in *Being and Time* "being-in-the-world" replaces "intentionality" but the noetic-noematic structure of the latter as "a region of being, in principle unique" continues to inform the existential analysis of "being-in-the-world." In lectures Heidegger is even more explicit, construing intentionality as the *ratio cognoscendi* of transcendence, transcendence as the *ratio essendi* of intentionality, and arguing that both are grounded in "being-in-the-world."[49] Yet with this difference, there remains an unmistakable parallel between Husserl's account of intentionality and Heidegger's concept of being-in-the-world. The parallel begins with their common dismissal of representationalist attempts to elaborate the structure of intentionality or being-in-the-world in terms of analogies with pictures.[50] In a similar vein, according to both accounts, what originally presents itself in perception is not sense-data, but constituted objects.[51]

More substantially, Heidegger's insistence that being-in-the-world be understood as a "unified phenomenon" iterates Husserl's emphasis on the basic unity of the intentional experience. Just as to each noesis there is a distinctively corresponding noema according to Husserl's account of intentional experience, so the expression "being-in-the-world" is meant to signify – among other things – that there is no human existence without a world and no world without human existence (where, of course, world and nature are not identical). Correspondingly, Heidegger urges that the terms "being-in" in the expression "being-in-the-world" not be understood in the sense of the enclosure of one spatial object within another where each could conceivably remain its basic way of being if separated. Instead, Heidegger's use of "being-in" in "being-in-the-world" is cognate with the use of such expressions as

---

[48] Just as the Husserlian reduction supposes a natural attitude, so Heidegger's ontological-existential analysis supposes an ontic-existential comportment.

[49] Heidegger GA24: 89–92, 230–31, 249.

[50] Husserl Hua III/1, 89–91; Heidegger SZ 217–218.

[51] Husserl Hua III/1, 207–08: "Das Ding, das Naturobjekt nehme ich wahr, den Baum dort im Garten; das und nichts anderes ist das wirkliche Objekt der wahrnehmenden 'Intention'. Ein zweiter immanenter Baum oder auch ein 'inneres Bild' des wirklichen, dort draußen vor mir stehenden Baumes ist doch in keiner Weise gegeben, und dergleichen hypothetisch zu supponieren, führt nur auf Widersinn." Cf. Heidegger SZ 163–164; also Husserl Hua III/1, 225–29.

"being in love," "being in fear of," "being in the mood for," "being in the process of," "being in the habit of," or "being involved with."[52]

Yet the parallel between Husserl's account of intentionality and Heidegger's existential analysis of being-in-the-world runs even deeper. Heidegger's unraveling of the various senses of being disclosed in being-in-the-world seems to be a successful adaptation of Husserl's account of the centrality of sense within the structure of intentional experience. Husserl, it may be recalled, distinguished between the object and the sense of the intentional experience, that is to say, between what is observed, perceived, judged, felt, remembered, or imagined (as the case may be) and how it is respectively observed, perceived, judged, felt, remembered, or imagined. So, too, Heidegger's analysis of the manners of being disclosed in my being-in-the-world (or, more broadly, my being-here, my *da-sein*) supposes a distinction between the particular being (*Seiendes*) encountered by Dasein in being-in-the-world as well as what that particular being might be and the sense in which it is (*Seinssinn*), a sense disclosed in the way that is encountered. "When a particular being within the world [...] is understood, we say, it has sense. Strictly speaking, however, what is understood is not the sense, but rather the particular being (*Seiendes*) or the being (*Sein*), as the case may be. Sense is that within which the understandability of something is maintained. What is able to be articulated in the course of the sort of disclosure of things that is said to understand them is what we call 'sense'."[53] Building upon the difference between something and its sense (what is intended and how), Heidegger also differentiates between ontic and ontological senses (corresponding to different deployments of 'as'). For example, when I use a hammer as a hammer, e.g., for hammering nails into a wall, hammering is the ontic sense, i.e., how I concretely relate to the hammer. At the same time, however, I use it as something handy or ready-to-hand, and therein lies its ontological sense, a sense relative to my being-in-the-world.

---

[52] Heidegger SZ 53–54.

[53] Heidegger SZ 151; cf. also SZ 54. In this connection, a basic similarity to the use of 'sense' in both phenomenologies should not go unmentioned, namely, the common effort to elucidate sense as the condition of meaning. For Husserl, sense is presupposed by meaning, the latter applying to linguistic constructions such as words and sentences (cf. Husserl Hua III/1, 284–85; cf. also Heidegger SZ, 166 Anm.1 for Heidegger's reference to this account; see also Husserl Hua XIX/1, 56–57 and Tugendhat 1970, 36 Anm. 44). An analogous constellation is elaborated by Heidegger in two respects. First, understanding is a condition for interpretation (*Auslegung*) and not vice versa, that is to say, understanding, here conceived as a practical wherewithal and know-how, need not be ex-pounded (*ausgelegt*) and take the form of assertions (*Aussagen*). Second, discourse (*Rede*), precisely as a way of communicating with one another, is the condition for language (*Sprache*) and linguistic entities - and not vice versa (cf. Heidegger SZ 160–167, esp. 161). On the differences between Husserl and Heidegger in this regard, see Taminiaux 1991, 59–61.

3.2   Categorial Intuitions, Reflection, and the Disclosiveness
of Being-Here

According to Husserl, the phenomenologist avails himself of the region of pure consciousness through reflection, not introspection.[54] Most experiences are "lived through (Jedes Ich erlebt seine Erlebnisse)"[55] without themselves being focused upon. Nevertheless, Husserl contends, precisely because they are "lived through," experiences *and what is contained in them* can become the objects of reflection (a reflection which in turn, as itself an experience, can be objectified or nominalized and thereby the object of further and further reflections).[56] The capacity to reflect extends, it bears iterating, to all the components of the experience (that are also not directly the focus of the experience). The stream of experiences (together with all the intentional features of them) "can be grasped in an evident way and analyzed" through reflection.[57] Unlike introspection that merely registers a sentiment or state of mind, reflection discloses what presented itself and how it did so as well as the way in which it was attended to or entertained in the original experience. Acts of reflection, performed in the context of the phenomenological reductions, and their analysis are accordingly the "fundamental" and "indispensable" staples of phenomenology.[58]

Reflection also enables the phenomenologist to specify what are initially unreflected experiences or parts of experiences. Determining the essential character of such experiences is based, as Husserl puts it, on "the reflective intuition of the essence" of the experience and what is contained in it.[59] The quoted phrase importantly suggests something like a "pre-reflective" intuition of essence. In his account of categorial intuitions in the *Logical Investigations* Husserl had, indeed, already sketched the way in which categorial forms, states of affairs, logical and empirical truths, as well as universals are intuited unthematically (or as parts of wholes) before being subsequently nominalized and thereby grasped thematically (on their own).[60]

Husserl contrasts categorial intuitions with straightforward, sensory intuitions or perceptions (*schlichte, sinnliche Wahrnehmungen*). More precisely, he construes categorial intuitions as acts "founded" upon straightforward, sensory intuitions.

---

[54] Husserl Hua III/1, 162: "die phänomenologische Methode bewegt sich durchaus in Akten der Reflexion."

[55] Husserl Hua III/1, 162–63; 95: "Die Seinsart des Erlebnisses ist es, in der Weise der Reflexion prinzipiell wahrnehmbar zu sein."

[56] Husserl Hua III/1, 77: "Im cogito lebend, haben wir die cogitatio selbst nicht bewußt als intentionales Objekt; aber jederzeit kann sie dazu werden, zu ihrem Wesen gehört die prinzipielle Möglichkeit einer *'reflektiven' Blickwendung* und natürlich in Form einer neueren cogitatio, die sich in der Weise einer schlichterfassenden auf sie richtet."

[57] Husserl Hua III/1, 165.

[58] Husserl Hua III/1, 162–65.

[59] Husserl Hua III/1, 172.

[60] Husserl Hua XIX/2, 657–93; see, too, Heidegger GA20, 89.

While the latter paradigmatically confirm and correspond to names ("Cologne") or terms for individual "real" objects ("this white paper"), categorial intuitions provide the evidence for what corresponds to entire assertions ("Cologne is larger than Bonn") as well as to terms for categorial forms or "ideal" objects and cognates of such terms ("this sky's being blue," "Fred *and* Ginger").[61]

While a categorial act must be performed by the individual who registers either the fact that the paper is white or what is expressed by the conjunction of 'Fred' and 'Ginger,' neither that fact nor what is expressed by that conjunction is a mere product of that act. Herein lies the reason for the use of the time-honored metaphor 'intuition' (or, more literally, 'looking at': *Anschauung*) in this connection, a use insisted upon by Husserl who rejects the notion of an intellectual intuition. Once again, Husserl emphasizes that reflection is necessary in order to focus on (thematize) the categorial intuition and what is contained in it, thereby rendering objective (*vergegenständlich machen*) what corresponds to terms such as 'is,' 'and,' 'or,' and the like. However, that reflection is dependent upon initially unthematic intuitions of what such terms mean or, more precisely, unthematic intuitions of wholes in the composition of which the significances of those terms play an integral role. [62] The blue of the sky is not fabricated but given, given in a sensory intuition; so, too, in an analogous way, the state of affairs (*Sach-verhalt*) – the sky's being blue, its relation to that property – is not fabricated but given in a categorial intuition.[63]

Heidegger's enthusiasm for Husserl's account of categorial intuitions is understandable, given the way in which it is mirrored in his own account of existentials.[64] To be sure, in *Being and Time* Heidegger sets up an explicit contrast between the meanings of the terms 'existential' and 'category,' depending upon whether the manner of being peculiar to "being-here" or to something else is meant respectively.[65] However, even shortly before adopting this terminology, Heidegger did not shy away from employing the term 'phenomenological category' in the same way that he would later use the term 'existential.' Moreover, in the very last seminar that Heidegger held, he acknowledged the crucial role played by the notion of categorial

---

[61] Husserl Hua XIX/2, 657–61, 665–76. As the last example suggests, categorial intuitions are often intuitions of the relation of parts within a whole or of parts to a whole. In 1919, as he became more adept at phenomenological seeing and worked on a new interpretation of Aristotle, Heidegger's interest returned once again to the *Logical Investigations*. In particular, he came to see, as he puts it, the import of the difference between sensory and categorial intuitions (developed in the Sixth Logical Investigation) for determining the multiple senses of 'being.'

[62] Husserl Hua XIX/1, 484–95; Hua XIX/2, 685–87; Sokolowski 1974, 33f: "'Is,' 'and,' and 'next to,' as syncategorematic components of categorial wholes, are the deposit left by various categorial, 'intellectual' acts of consciousness. They are not read off things as attributes but originate in the acts by which consciousness articulates discrete parts within what it intends, and simultaneously composes a whole out of these parts."

[63] As these glosses suggest, Husserl does not appear to thematize existence as such, something akin to the meaning of the existential quantifier. Indeed, he seems to concentrate solely on being white, expressed in the proposition 'this paper is white' that corresponds to that very state of affairs.

[64] Heidegger GA20, 34.

[65] Heidegger SZ, 44, 54.

intuition in his development of the project of fundamental ontology.[66] Nor should Heidegger's early use of "hermeneutic intuition" and "intuition by way of under-standing" be overlooked in this connection.[67]

There are salient structural parallels between Heidegger's use of 'existential' in *Being and Time* and Husserl's use of 'categorial intuition.' In both cases, what 'to be' means in any instance can be identified neither with a straightforward, sensory perception nor with a theoretical construction. Instead, it is given in a specific act of consciousness (Husserl) or in a way of being that is disclosive (Heidegger). Thus, in the case of both the categorial intuition and the existential, the meaning of 'to be' is given-and-realized in an unthematic, pre-reflective way that can, nonetheless, be adequately unpacked by philosophical reflection or, as Heidegger also puts it, retrieved through existential analysis.[68] Just as categorial intuition is found both in experience and in phenomenological reflection upon the experience, so existential understanding is found in existence and in existential analysis.

To be sure, in Heidegger's account, Husserlian "intuition" gives way to the more basic unity of existentials comprising – equiprimordially – the emotional state or disposition one finds oneself in (*Befindlichkeit*), one's projections or understanding (*Verstehen*), and one's ways of identifying this-or-that and communicating it (*Rede*). But the insight into this primordiality is, at least in some respects, itself a holdover from his interpretation of Husserl's phenomenological investigations. In his gloss on categorial intuition (in lectures given around the time of the final composition of *Being and Time*), he lauds Husserl's investigations for drawing attention to how thoroughly our ways of behaving are pervaded by assertions.

> Factically, it is even the case that our most straightforward perceptions and graspings are already *expressed*, still more, *interpreted* in a definite way. As far as what is primary and most basic, we do not so much see objects and things but instead speak about them; more precisely we do not express what we see but the reverse, we see what one says about the matter.[69]

"Even the phenomenological intuition of essence is," as Heidegger puts it, "grounded in the existential understanding."[70] Thus, Heidegger is by no means rejecting the phenomenological intuition of essence; instead he is grounding it within an existen-tial unity that defines one's way of being-in-the-world.[71] Moreover, in the ground itself Heidegger identifies something with a kinship to intuition, namely, a way of looking at things (*Sicht*) or seeing one's way around a workplace (*Umsicht*), that is

---

[66] See Heidegger GA21, 410 and GA15, 377f. In different ways, each thinker maintains the prece-dence of possibility over actuality; see Husserl Hua III/1, 178.

[67] Heidegger GA56/57, 65, 109, 117, 219; GA58, 138.

[68] Heidegger SZ, 194, 197.

[69] Heidegger GA20, 75.

[70] Heidegger SZ, 147.

[71] Heidegger GA20, 75. Still, if Husserl overemphasizes the role of perception in his account of intentionality, Heidegger's initial presentation of being-in-the-world overstates the extent to which the latter is shaped by praxical involvement (if I may be allowed the phrase).

grounded in the understanding's projections.[72] In the same context, to be sure, he also takes pains to distinguish his concept of "understanding" from "taking up something on hand in its on-handness in a purely non-sentient way."[73] Husserl, as Heidegger was perfectly aware, completely rejected the notion of an intellectual intuition. Yet Heidegger criticizes him for taking perception or, more precisely, a certain scientific attitude towards perception, as the *basic* orientation for the analysis of the modes of intentionality. That orientation brings with it the ontological prejudice that the on-handness of the object of perception (the 'to be' of that sort of being) provides the global determination of being.

Nevertheless, despite the implicit criticism of Husserl and the different center of gravity of Heidegger's analysis, the profound structural parallel alluded to above persists. Such a parallel exists, moreover, not only between Heidegger's account of existential disclosure and the account of categorial intuition in the *Logical Investigations* but also between the former and the account of eidetic intuition in *Ideas I*. Thus, for example, when Heidegger distinguishes handiness (*Zuhandensein*) and on-handness (*Vorhandensein*) as senses of being proper to tools and theoretical objects respectively, he claims to be relating, in his own words, how these various entities "in an essential way" disclose themselves within a "preontological" understanding.[74]

Finally, Husserl is emphatic that phenomenology's aim is to determine in a rigorous way the essences of experiences and what is contained in them.[75] In analogous fashion, Heidegger characterizes the subject of the existential analysis in terms of the self-disclosure of its essence. The designation 'Dasein,' he notes, is selected precisely to indicate that the "essence" of the entity in question consists in having to be its own being.[76] Or, as he frequently also puts it, "the essence of this particular being is its existence."[77] Similarly, Heidegger explains that it is of the very "essence" of Dasein to have an understanding of being, to be precisely as a possibility (*Seinkönnen*), to have its death before it as a defining possibility, to have a conscience, and to be capable of being authentic or not.[78] In a cognate vein he remarks that "there is a constant unresolvedness in the essence of the basic constitution of

---

[72] After all, Husserl gave him his eyes; see Heidegger SZ, 146: "Das Verstehen macht in seinem Entwurfcharakter existenzial das aus, was wir die Sicht des Daseins nennen." Taminiaux interprets this passage as an indication that "the traditional privilege of intuition (Anschauung), the privileged status of seeing remains" (cf. Taminiaux 1991, 65). But such an interpretation must be reconciled with Heidegger's further remarks in the same context, grounding "all sight primarily in understanding" (Heidegger SZ, 147).

[73] Heidegger SZ, 147.

[74] Heidegger SZ, 200f.

[75] Husserl Hua III/1, 156-58.

[76] Heidegger SZ, 12, 42.

[77] Heidegger SZ, 298, 231, 133.

[78] See, respectively, Heidegger SZ, 231, 233, 248, 262, 278, 42f, 323.

Dasein."[79] Not surprisingly, he also speaks of the essences of the respective existentials as well as the essence of truth.

Such instances could be multiplied, but the examples cited suffice to illustrate that a reflection on essences is very much a part of the project of fundamental ontology in *Being and Time*.[80] To be sure, Heidegger is trying to elaborate the essences (*Wesen*) of various senses of being and shortly after the publication of *Being and Time* he undertakes to reconstrue *Wesen* verbally as a kind of "prevailing," i.e., with a kind of valence prior to the bi-valence of assertions.[81] Nevertheless, much as in the Husserlian phenomenological reflection, Heidegger's existential analysis of these essential/prevailing structures of being is based upon the original disclosure of them within or as modes of Dasein's being-in-the-world.[82]

The way in which phenomenological reduction and reflection are together operative in Heidegger's analysis can be illustrated in terms of the "as-structure" so central to his analysis. Taking a fork in hand and using it *as* a fork is an example of what Heidegger deems the "hermeneutical as-structure," a structure which renders perspicuous the basic meaning of 'understanding' as a kind of self-disclosive projecting in the use of things. When someone takes (uses) something as a fork, she also takes (understands, projects) it as "handy" (*zuhanden*). Taking something as a fork exemplifies the existentiell hermeneutical as-structure (or understanding), while taking it as handy exemplifies the existential hermeneutical as-structure (or understanding).[83] In the example cited, handiness is the essential sense of what it means for it to be, its *Seinssinn*. In order to attend to that sense of being, it is obviously necessary to bracket the existentiell understanding and reflect upon the essential structure of being-in-the-world (or what Husserl calls the "phenomenological residuum" that remains as a result of the reduction). According to Heidegger, the "as-structure" is always relative to some foregoing projection by the understanding and, hence, in the last analysis must be grounded in an account of temporality.[84]

---

[79] Heidegger SZ, 236.

[80] Thus, Heidegger speaks of the essences of *Befindlichkeit* (Heidegger SZ, 190), *Rede* (SZ, 296), *Verstehen* (SZ, 214), and *Wahrheit* (SZ, 222), but also of the essences of *Sorge* (SZ, 285), *Negation* (SZ, 285), *Entschlossenheit* (SZ, 298), *Zeitlichkeit* (SZ, 329, 348), and *Geschichte* (SZ, 378).

[81] Heidegger 1949; see Dahlstrom 2010, 185–207.

[82] Several of Heidegger's subsequent essays and lectures take the form of essentialist analyses, each with a common structure; see Dahlstrom 2018b, 39–56.

[83] The origin of the "apophantic as-structure" of assertions ("it is a fork") is, Heidegger contends, the hermeneutical as-structure; cf. Heidegger SZ, 158f; GA21, 156.

[84] Heidegger SZ, 148–151, 360; see note 27 above.

4 Concluding Remark: The Unconstituted World

As mentioned in the second section above, Heidegger's question to Husserl "Doesn't a world belong to the pure ego at all, as part of its very essence?" crystallizes a basic difference between the two phenomenologists. Still, one might contend that Heidegger's conception of worldhood as an existential and his incorporation of the world into the basic phenomenon of being-here testify to the legacy of the sort of idealism championed by Husserl's phenomenology. The issue is fraught, to be sure, not least given Heidegger's reticence to couch his phenomenology in terms of idealism or realism.[85] Further complicating matters is an interpretation of the world in *Being and Time* that is open to different readings in this connection. By way of conclusion, I would like to suggest briefly how that interpretation lies, as it were, at the center of this storm, while also conveying what I take to be Heidegger's confidence that his interpretation should not be construed in idealist terms. Whether that confidence is justified is a topic for another time.

A crucial text in this regard is Heidegger's interpretation of the world in relation to timeliness (*Zeitlichkeit*). He explains timeliness as the unity of the ways of being outside oneself in terms of the future, having been, and present. (Thus, futurally, I stand out towards something coming *at* me; by way of having been, I go back *to* something else.) But each of these respective ways of standing out towards something requires a horizon into which it stands. Yet, while neither on hand nor handy, the world is nonetheless, Heidegger contends, something that unfolds or has its time (*zeitigt sich*) in this timeliness.

> It [the world] *is*, along with the outside-itself character of the ecstasies, *here*. If no being-here [*Dasein*] exists, there is also no world *here* [...].[86]

This passage provides an unmistakable opening for interpreting Heidegger's analysis in idealist terms, i.e., in terms that suggest the world's immanence to being-here. Yet the issue is by no means straightforward, given the fact that he is speaking, not of the world's existence or reality as such, but of its *being here*, a set of terms that he has restricted to the disclosiveness of the entity for whom being is at issue. [87] From this perspective, the claim is innocuous or at least neutral on questions of idealism or realism. Insofar as 'being-in-the-world' is a metonym for 'being-here' for whom it is essential to be and, indeed, to be in a way that discloses its manner of being, it is impossible for it to be without disclosing its world. But this disclosure of

---

[85] This reticence is evident even when he broaches the topics of realism and idealism; see Heidegger SZ §33.

[86] Heidegger SZ, 365

[87] So, too, it might be argued that any footing for the charge of idealism is removed, given that the sense of 'world' here is not that of the totality of entities but the system of possibilities grounded in Dasein's being 'for-the-sake-of-itself'; the world in that sense trivially depends on Dasein, but that fact is indifferent to the question of whether any entities exist without Dasein. My thanks to Andrew Butler for this observation.

the world no more renders the world immanent to being-here than seeing the sky makes it immanent (confined to) my consciousness of seeing it.

The experience of the future, of having been, and of the present is, in each case, an experience of being outside ourselves, where there is something that we experience ourselves doing (standing out, the ecstatic character) and something that we experience as complementary to what we do (the horizon). While we have no experience of horizons without ecstasies, they must be distinguished from the projections themselves that make up the ecstasies.[88] To put the point more baldly (if less carefully), there is something about the horizons that is not of our making. As in Husserl's use of the term, Heidegger's use of 'horizon' to capture a temporal dimension strains the metaphor, in one respect. But it also points to the need for broadening the dimension to include spatiality (as in Heidegger's later use of 'time-space'). Precisely by tying the existential conception of the world to the unity of horizons so construed, Heidegger removes the possibility (at least in his own mind) of conflating the world with Dasein's projections. For Heidegger, in short, what militates against interpreting his existential phenomenology in idealist terms is his insistence on the transcendent character of the timely horizons and, thereby, of the world itself. "With a grounding in the horizonal unity of the ecstatic timeliness, the world is transcendent."[89]

References

Bell, David. 1991. *Husserl*. London: Routledge.

Bernet, R., Kern, I., and Marbach, E. 1993. *An Introduction to Husserlian Phenomenology*. Evanston, Illinois: Northwestern University Press

Brentano, Franz. 1925. *Psychologie vom empirischen Standpunkt*. Edited by O. Kraus. Leipzig: Meiner.

Crowell, Steven. 2013. *Normativity and Phenomenology in Husserl and Heidegger*. Cambridge: Cambridge University Press.

Dahlstrom, Daniel O. 2001. *Heidegger's Concept of Truth*. Cambridge: Cambridge University Press.

———. 2010. "The Prevalence of Truth" in *Truth*. Edited by Kurt Pritzl. Washington, D.C.: Catholic University of America Press, 185–207.

———. 2018a. "The Early Heidegger's Phenomenology" in *The Oxford Handbook of the History of Phenomenology*. Edited by Dan Zahavi. Oxford: Oxford University Press, 211–228.

———. 2018b. "Im-position: Heidegger's Analysis of the Essence of Modern Technology" in *Heidegger on Technology*, Edited by Aaron Wendland, Christos Hadjioannou, Christopher Merwin. New York: Routledge, 39–56.

Engelland, Chad. 2017. *Heidegger's Shadow: Kant, Husserl, and the Transcendental Turn*. New York: Routledge.

Heidegger, Martin. 1992/3. "Diltheys Forschungsarbeit und historische Weltanschauung," *Dilthey-Jahrbuch* 8: 143–180.

———. GA17; 1994. *Einführung in die phänomenologische Forschung*, Gesamtausgabe, Bd 17. Herausgegeben von Friedrich-Wilhelm von Herrmann. Frankfurt am Main: Klostermann.

---

[88] They also may point to a place or, better, a time-space, within which the ecstasies figure.

[89] Heidegger SZ, 366.

_____. GA58; 1993. *Grundprobleme der Phänomenologie*, Gesamtausgabe, Bd 58. Herausgegeben von Hans-Helmuth Gander. Frankfurt am Main: Klostermann.

_____. GA24; 1975. *Grundprobleme der Phänomenologie*, Gesamtausgabe, Bd 24. Herausgegeben von Friedrich-Wilhelm von Herrmann. Frankfurt am Main: Klostermann.

_____. GA21; 1976. *Logik. Die Frage nach der Wahrheit*, Gesamtausgabe, Bd 21. Herausgegeben von Walter Biemel. Frankfurt am Main: Klostermann.

———; 1959. *Nietzsche II*. Pfullingen: Neske.

_____. GA63; 1988. *Ontologie (Hermeneutik der Faktizität)*, Gesamtausgabe, Bd 63. Herausgegeben von Käte Bröcker-Oltmanns. Frankfurt am Main: Klostermann.

_____. GA20; 1988. *Prolegomena zur Geschichte des Zeitbegriffs*, Gesamtausgabe, Bd 20. Herausgegeben von Petra Jaeger. Frankfurt am Main: Klostermann.

_____. SZ; 1972. *Sein und Zeit*. Tübingen: Niemeyer.

_____. GA15; 1986. *Seminare*, Gesamtausgabe, Bd 15. Herausgegeben von Curd Ochwadt. Frankfurt am Main: Klostermann.

———; 1954. *Unterwegs zur Sprache*. Pfullingen: Neske.

———; 1949. *Vom Wesen der Wahrheit*. Frankfurt am Main: Klostermann.

_____. GA9; 1976. *Wegmarken*, Gesamtausgabe, Bd 9. Herausgegeben von Friedrich-Wilhelm von Herrmann. Frankfurt am Main: Klostermann.

_____. GA56/57; 1999. *Zur Bestimmung der Philosophie*, Gesamtausgabe, Bd 56/57. Herausgegeben von Bernd Heimbüchel. Frankfurt am Main: Klostermann.

_____. GA14; 2007. *Zur Sache des Denkens*, Gesamtausgabe, Bd 14. Herausgegeben von hrsg. Friedrich-Wilhelm von Herrmann. Frankfurt am Main: Klostermann.

Heidegger, Martin und Jaspers, Karl. 1990. *Briefwechsel 1920–1963*. Edited by Walter Biemel and Hans Saner. Frankfurt am Main: Klostermann.

Husserl, Edmund. Hua III/1; 1976. *Ideen zu einer reinen Phänomenologie und phänomenologischen Philosophie, Erstes Buch: Allgemeine Einführung in die reine Phänomenologie*, Husserliana Bd III/1. Herausgegeben von Karl Schuhmann. Hague: Nijhoff.

_____. Hua XIX/1; 1984. *Logische Untersuchungen*, Zweiter Band, Erster Teil, Husserliana, Bd XIX/1. Herausgegeben von Ursula Panzer. Hague: Nijhoff.

_____. Hua XIX/2; 1984. *Logische Untersuchungen*, Zweiter Band, Zweiter Teil, Husserliana, Bd XIX/2. Herausgegeben von Ursula Panzer. Hague: Nijhoff.

_____. Hua IX; 1962. *Phänomenologische Psychologie*, Husserliana Bd IX. Herausgegeben von Walter Biemel. Hague: Nijhoff.

———; 1910. "Philosophie als strenge Wissenschaft," *Logos*, Bd. I, Heft 3: 289–341.

Kisiel, Theodore. 1985. "On the Way to *Being and Time*: Introduction to the Translation of Heidegger's *Prolegomena zur Geschichte des Zeitbegriffs*." *Research in Phenomenology* 15: 193–226.

Luft, Sebastian. 2002. *Phänomenologie der Phänomenologie*. Dordrecht/Boston: Kluwer.

Sokolowski, Robert. 1974. *Husserlian Meditations*. Evanston, Illinois: Northwestern University Press.

Taminiaux, Jacques. 1991. *Heidegger and the Project of Fundamental Ontology*. Albany, New York: SUNY Press.

Tugendhat, Ernst. 1970. *Der Wahrheitsbegriff bei Husserl und Heidegger*. Berlin: de Gruyter.

Van Buren, John. 1994. *The Young Heidegger: Rumour of the Hidden King*. Bloomington/Indianapolis: Indiana University Press.

Not Idealist Enough. Satomi Takahashi and Tomoo Otaka on Husserl's Idealism

Genki Uemura

Abstract The present paper aims at reconstructing the reactions to Husserl's idealism in the writings of two of his Japanese students: Satomi Takahashi (1886–1964) and Tomoo Otaka (1899–1956). While both Takahashi and Otaka hold that Husserl's phenomenological "idealism" is ultimately not idealism at all, they argue for this claim in quite different ways. Takahashi argues that Husserl's position is not idealist enough to establish subjective idealism, which he takes to be the Master's intended position and which Takahashi himself favors. In contrast, Otaka finds a possibility of realism in Husserl's position.

Keywords Edmund Husserl · Satomi Takahashi · Tomoo Otaka · Idealism · Realism · Phenomenological reduction · Intersubjectivity · Meaning · Noema

1 Introduction

From the 1920s to the early 1930s, many scholars from Japan studied philosophy in Freiburg with Husserl and Heidegger.[1] Some published articles or books on phenomenology, discussing ideas that were accessible only to those who had direct access to Husserl and Heidegger at the time. For instance, Hajime Tanabe, who was in Freiburg from 1922 to 1923, appreciated the view of Heidegger *before* the publication of *Being and Time* as a *Lebensphilosophie* alternative to Husserl's constitutive phenomenology (cf. Tanabe 1924). The situation was different, however, when

---

[1] See Nitta, Tatematsu, and Shimomisse (1978, 11) and Tani (2013, 20) for some information on these scholars. Note, however, that they do not provide a complete list of the Japanese students of Husserl and Heidegger in Freiburg. Some of those students, including Takahashi and Otaka, published memoirs of their days in Freiburg. See Otaka (1938), Takahashi (1929c), Mutai (1964), Usui (1984), and Haga (1988). It remains largely unexplored why phenomenology gained such popularity among Japanese scholars. For a somewhat speculative explanation, see Altobrando & Taguchi (2019, 3–4).

G. Uemura (✉)
Okayama University, Okayama, Japan
e-mail: uemurag@okayama-u.ac.jp

© Springer Nature Switzerland AG 2021
R. K. B. Parker (ed.), *The Idealism-Realism Debate Among Edmund Husserl's Early Followers and Critics*, Contributions to Phenomenology 112,
https://doi.org/10.1007/978-3-030-62159-9_14

283

it came to Husserl's idealism, which he had developed further in lectures and publications during his Freiburg years.[2] While Husserl's Japanese students characterized his philosophy as *transcendental* phenomenology, most of them, consciously or unconsciously, were relatively silent about one of its most controversial consequences, namely, the idealism that Husserl believed was entailed by his phenomenology.[3] Two exceptions, however, were Satomi Takahashi (1886–1964) and Tomoo Otaka (1899–1956).[4]

Let us begin by briefly discussing the backgrounds of Takahashi and Otaka. Born in Yamagata, Takahashi studied philosophy from 1907 to 1915 at Tokyo Imperial University (now the University of Tokyo). In his first year as a graduate student, Takahashi published his first article "Ishiki-Gensho no Jijitsu to sono Imi [Facts of Conscious Phenomena and their Meaning]" (Takahashi 1912), in which he criticized Kitaro Nishida's *An Inquiry into the Good* [*Zen no Kenkyu*] (Nishida 1992). This was followed by several survey articles on German philosophy and the first Japanese translation of Bergson's *Matter and Memory*. After six years as a high school German teacher, in 1921 Takahashi became an associate professor in the Faculty of Sciences at Tohoku Imperial University (now Tohoku University). In 1924, he obtained a position in the Faculty of Letters and Law at the same university, from which he retired in 1947. From 1925 to 1928, under an order from the Japanese Ministry of Education, Takahashi studied for two years in Germany. He first visited Heidelberg where he attended lectures of Heinrich Rickert, followed by Freiburg from the autumn of 1926 to the summer of 1927, attending Husserl's *Einfühlung in die Phänomenologie* (WS1926/27) and *Natur und Geist* (SS1927) lectures (cf. Takahashi 1931, 240–241).[5]

Tomoo Otaka was born in Busan, Korea, and studied law at Tokyo Imperial University. After finishing his undergraduate study, he started working on sociology and philosophy under Shôtarô Yoneda and, after Yoneda's retirement, Nishida in

---

[2] See, for instance, Husserl's *Nachwort* §5 (Hua V, 149–155).

[3] A typical example is Tokuryu Yamauchi (1890–1982), who was in Freiburg in 1920. According to Yamauchi, there is no significant development of Husserl's thought from the *Logical Investigations* to *Ideas I* and that his position is already established, and even better developed, in the former (cf. Yamauchi 1929, 1–2).

[4] Another Japanese student whose work is potentially within the scope of the present essay is Gôichi Miyake (1895–1982). As Cairns (1976, 17–18) reports, Miyake presented the paper "Die Intersubjektivität und die Konstitution der objektiven Welt" at a private seminar with Husserl on 13 August 1931. Both Cairns and Eugen Fink attended the seminar as well. Unfortunately, Miyake did not publish the paper and no manuscript of it has been discovered (I owe thanks to Kiyoshi Sakai and Rie Wakami for this information).

[5] Large parts of *Einfühlung in die Phänomenologie* in 1926/27 (Ms. F I 33) are published in a scattered manner across Hua IX and Hua XIV (see: https://hiw.kuleuven.be/apps/hua/details. php?cmd=search&words=F%20I%2033 last accessed on 21 August 2018). The *Natur und Geist* lectures from 1927 are published as Hua XXXII. Takahashi also attended *Phänomenologische Übungen für Vorgeschrittene (über Humes Treatise)* and *Phänomenologische Übungen für Vorgeschrittene (über Kant)* (cf. Schumann 1977, 313, 322). According to Risaku Mutai (1964, 175), during the winter semester 1926/27, every week Husserl invited Takahashi and Mutai to his home for discussion.

Kyoto.[6] In 1928, he took a position as a professor of philosophy of law at Keijo Imperial University, which had been established in 1924 in the city now called Seoul as part of the Japanese colonial policy. Like Takahashi, Otaka also had an occasion to study abroad in an early stage of his career. After studying under Hans Kelsen in Vienna, he arrived in Freiburg in 1930. At that time, Husserl had already retired from the university. Instead of attending lectures, he had personal seminars with Husserl on a regular basis (cf. Usui 1984, 612).

The present essay is structured as follows. The two main sections deal with Takahashi's and Otaka's reactions to Husserl's idealism respectively. As indicated by the title, these two Japanese philosophers both hold that Husserl's idealism is not idealist. However, they take this claim in quite different ways. Takahashi argues that Husserl's position is not idealist enough to establish *subjective idealism*, which he takes to be the Master's aim and which he himself favors. In contrast, Otaka finds a possibility of *realism* in Husserl's position. Interestingly, the reasons for their opposing claims partially overlap. Both Takahashi and Otaka hold that Husserl's alleged idealism does not immanentize transcendent objects in nature.

2 Husserl's Failed Attempt at Subjective Idealism – Satomi Takahashi

To put it crudely, Takahashi's reaction to Husserl's idealism consists of two steps. First, he understands Husserl's *intended* position as subjective idealism. Even though he does not explicitly define subjective idealism, the position Takahashi has in mind could roughly be understood as the idea that there is everything is *in* consciousness. Second, he argues that the *real* position of his teacher in Freiburg does not amount to subjective idealism. Thus, he writes: "In Husserl, the thought that every objectivity is constituted and grounded by pure subjectivity seems to be an *a priori* conviction, as it were, or a fundamental assumption" (Takahashi 1930, 76). In this section, we reconstruct how Takahashi arrives at this conclusion circa 1930.

2.1 Egological and Intersubjective Reductions

A key to Takahashi's interpretation and assessment of Husserl is the method of phenomenological reduction. This is already suggested by the titles of two of his articles: "Husserl's Phenomenology. On his Phenomenological Reduction in Particular [*Husseru no Genshôgaku. Toku ni sono Genshôgaku-teki Kangen ni tsuite*]"

---

[6]For more on Otaka's biography, see Uemura and Yaegashi 2016, 350–352. Note that Otaka's surname is sometimes transliterated as "Odaka," which is closer to the Japanese pronunciation of his name than "Otaka." However, considering the fact that Otaka called himself "Otaka" in his German writings, I have used this same spelling, which is probably better known outside of Japan.

(Takahashi 1929b) and "The Possibility of Phenomenological Reduction [*Genshôgaku-teki Kangen no Kanôsei*]" (Takahashi 1930). As he writes in the latter, the phenomenological reduction is something "only by means of which the object of phenomenology, namely the realm of phenomena shows itself and thus what Husserl calls phenomenology is made possible" (Takahashi 1930, 45). Consequently, the phenomenological reduction plays an important role in both steps of Takahashi's reaction to Husserl.

It is remarkable that Takahashi, referring to the lectures by Husserl that he attended, distinguishes two types of phenomenological reduction: (i) egological and (ii) intersubjective. "By those reductions," he writes, "all the objects (natural and social ones) are exhaustively reduced in subjectivity and made into the so-called 'phenomena' for phenomenology" (Takahashi 1929b, 8). In a similar vein, he characterizes the phenomenological reduction as the *immanentization* of transcendent beings (cf. Takahashi 1929b, 30). This is, in short, exactly why he considers Husserl to be an idealist. It might be disputable whether Takahashi's understanding of the phenomenological reduction is true to Husserl. Takahashi's reformulation seems to be in tension with Husserl's insistence that nothing would be lost by performing the phenomenological reduction.[7] Setting aside this issue, one might also wonder whether Husserl's intended position is *subjective* idealism. Husserl would be an idealist of a certain sort if he, as Takahashi holds, attempts to immanentize transcendence by means of the phenomenological reduction. However, the very notion of an *inter*subjective reduction seems to show that Husserl's idealism is not confined to a single subject. To see how Takahashi would reply to this potential objection, let us look at his discussion of the two types of phenomenological reduction and their relationship.

Let us begin with the egological reduction. Even though Takahashi distinguishes the egological and intersubjective reductions, he emphasizes the former and even conflates it with phenomenological reduction *in general*. In his paper on the possibility of phenomenological reduction, he confines his discussion to the egological reduction and characterizes it provisionally as a reduction of the thesis of natural attitude (cf. Takahashi 1930, 47). He then draws on §§31–32 of *Ideas I* and explains the reduction as follows (cf. Takahashi 1930, 50–51): There is a similarity between the phenomenological reduction and Descartes' method of doubt, even though their aims are different. In the phenomenological reduction, as well as Cartesian doubt, we set our presuppositions and convictions "out of action" or we "parenthesize" and "suspend [*ausschalten*]" them; but we thereby do not deny nor cancel them. Such a standard recapitulation of Husserl's idea also appears in "Husserl's Phenomenology," where Takahashi has not differentiated the egological and intersubjective reductions (cf. Takahashi 1929b, 7–8).

---

[7] See, for instance, *Cartesian Meditations* §§ 14–15 (Hua I, 70–75, especially 72–73 and 75).

2.2   Intersubjective Reduction

To locate the intersubjective reduction in Takahashi's reconstruction of Husserl, we must take into consideration two further points he ascribes to the Master in "Husserl's Phenomenology." First, according to Takahashi, the egological reduction consists in what he calls *thematic abstraction* (cf. Takahashi 1929b, 26–27). Thematic abstraction is an operation through which the natural sciences obtain their field of research, namely *nature [Natur]*, from the world of naïve, everyday experience. Unfortunately, Takahashi does not further explain what this abstraction amounts to. Given that he mentions Galileo in this context, we could understand it as a process of excluding so-called secondary qualities from nature, which do not figure in laws of physics and thus are often regarded as merely subjective.[8] It is not Takahashi's aim, nor ours, to examine such a procedure as it manifests itself in modern natural sciences. What matters for Takahashi is that the abstraction from the world of everyday experience is a precondition for transcendental phenomenology. Accordingly, it is by abstracting subjective or "egoic [*ichlich*]" elements from the everyday world that phenomenologists attain their theme, namely pure consciousness.

One might ask how such a thematic abstraction of the subjective is possible. Takahashi answers in the following manner:

> Even if it is anonymous [i.e., not thematic], a perceiving ego always stays with a perceived object. And, generally speaking, the world exists only for an ego who experiences it; a relation to an ego essentially belongs to the world. Therefore, the world, which may not actually be experienced, must be able to be experienced as a matter of possibility. Since an experiencing ego has the relation to the experienced world, it is always possible for us to direct our gaze of thematization from the objective to the subjective. (Takahashi 1929b, 28)

Takahashi's move hardly seems convincing. In this passage, the essential relationship between the world and ego is merely taken for granted. Is this not, one may ask, nothing other than a main thread of Husserl's idealism that needs justification?[9] To the best of our knowledge, however, nowhere does Takahashi provide an argument for this presupposition. This might possibly be due to his aforementioned view according to which Husserl's idealism remains a mere conviction. Since our present aim is not to examine Husserl's position as such but to reconstruct Takahashi's reaction to it, we will not go further into this issue.

Instead, we shall focus on an important remark that Takahashi makes just after the passage quoted above:

> However, we still live in the world. We have the world and, surprisingly, we are at the same time had by the world. We find the world in front of us and yet find ourselves in the world.

---

[8] Even though Takahashi only mentions the name of the father of modern sciences in this context, it is almost certain that he has in mind Galileo's discussion of secondary qualities in *The Assayer* (Galileo 2008, 185–189).

[9] This is how Husserl himself conceives the situation in *Cartesian Meditations* §41 (Hua I, 116–121).

> Since we belong to the world in this way, we have two gazes of thematization—one towards
> the world and the other towards the subjective—intertwining in us, and this makes it more
> difficult to perform thematic abstraction thoroughly in phenomenology than in the natural
> sciences. (Takahashi 1929b, 28)

Takahashi's contention, in short, is that our being in the world makes it difficult for
us to abstract the subjective from our everyday experience. It is at this point that he
refers to Husserl's claim concerning the radical change of attitude involved in the
phenomenological reduction (cf. Takahashi 1929b, 29–30). A phenomenologist,
who is, as a "child of the world [*Weltkind*]," interested in things in the world, should
stop engaging with them and become a non-engaged, impartial bystander. Such a
phenomenological attitude is characterized as a habit that contrasts with the natural
attitude. If we succeed in changing our attitude in this way, we then undergo a
"splitting of the I [*Ich-spaltung*]," namely splitting of the ego into a thematized ego
on the one hand and an ego that reflects on the thematized ego on the other. Thematic
abstraction is operated by the latter, higher-order ego, whereas the former, first-
order ego belongs to pure consciousness as the theme of phenomenology. It should
be noted that Takahashi does *not* claim that the first-order thematized ego is the only
element of pure consciousness. Rather, an object of consciousness, for instance a
table that I am perceiving, is also included in the sphere of phenomenological investigations, insofar as it is perceived by my thematized ego. In this way, thematic
abstraction, in which the phenomenological reduction consists, involves the immanentization of transcendent being.

It would be beyond our present aim to discuss further how Takahashi understands Husserl's phenomenological reduction. However, a remark on the (potential)
source for his interpretation is worth making. By incorporating thematization into
phenomenological reduction, Takahashi conceives this method as *reflection* of a
certain sort. However, as Takahashi himself reports in his "Possibility of
Phenomenological Reduction," Husserl did not immediately agree with him that
phenomenological reduction is a sort of act of reflection.[10] Takahashi further writes:

> Since I wanted to prove my idea that phenomenological reduction is an act of reflection, I
> asked Professor Husserl about it, but he did not seem to have paid much attention on that
> point. Later in his lectures, however, he gradually came to connect the two things [=phe-
> nomenological reduction and an act of reflection] together. This made me feel delighted
> because I had the impression that he proved my idea. However, I cannot say anything defi-
> nite about Professor's idea. For I did not asked again about that. (Takahashi 1930, 62n2)

Takahashi is probably taking about Husserl's *Einführung in die Phänomenologie*
lectures in 1926/27, in which phenomenological reduction is discussed with reference to the notions of reflection and theme (cf. Hua IX, 443–444).[11] At the same

---

[10] In the same article, Takahashi develops this interpretation by arguing that the phenomenological
reduction is an act of reflection that has neutrality modification as one of its partial acts. See
Takahashi (1930, especially, 59–62).

[11] Husserl expresses a similar view even more explicitly in his *Phänomenologische Psychologie*
lectures in 1925: "Ich ändere also hinterher mein *thematisches* Interesse und sehe mir jetzt diesen
ganzen subjektiven Prozeß an. Diesen mache ich ausschließlich zum Thema: nur die ihn als seiend

time, Takahashi's use of the term *Weltkind* suggests that he might know something about the following idea presented in Husserl's *Erste Philosophie* lectures in 1924, even though he did not attend them: "One who wants to be a phenomenologist must free oneself from the natural childhood of the world [*Weltkindschaft*] and apply phenomenological reduction to all the types of world-childly experiencing, presenting, thinking, and living in general and to all correlational types of worldly-natural existence [*Dasein*]" (Hua VIII, 123).

Second, having delineated the field of phenomenology, Takahashi emphasizes the difference between the Husserlian pure consciousness and the Kantian consciousness in general or transcendental apperception (cf. Takahashi 1929b, 31). While the latter is thought to be something super-individual that serves as the condition of possibility of experience, the former is a stream of lived-experience (*Erlebnisstrom*) with concrete content. Accordingly, Takahashi claims that even the pure ego, which Husserl accepts under influence of Paul Natorp, "is not separated from the stream of lived-experience and therefore it is *individual* just as that stream" (Takahashi 1929b, 31, my italics).

Against this background, Takahashi gives two roles to the intersubjective reduction, namely "to rehabilitate phenomenologically the objectivity of nature that is abandoned by egology and to reduce and ground phenomenologically the socio-historical-cultural world, to which egology never pays attention" (Takahashi 1929b, 32–33). Since the world is objective only in so far as it is intersubjective, egological phenomenology, which confines itself to experiences of a single ego, could not help but immanentize the world *without objectivity*. This would cause trouble for a phenomenology of the socio-historical-cultural world. Society, history, and culture presuppose not only a plurality of subjects and their interaction but also an objective nature. They are, in other words, built on one and the same world of material things (cf. Takahashi 1929b, 36–37).[12] The question then is how to accommodate the plurality of subjects phenomenologically.

Even though Takahashi does not put much emphasis on this, it is at this juncture that *the individuality of pure consciousness* matters for two reasons. First, if pure consciousness is not individual, i.e., if it is the super-individual condition of possibility of experience, it would not make any sense in the first place to talk about two or more subjects of pure consciousness. Second, Husserl's phenomenology of empathy (*Einfühlung*), only by means of which one can attain transcendental intersubjectivity, would be feasible only if pure consciousness is individual. Empathy, which Takahashi rephrases as "perception of the mind of an alter ego," is in need of the body of the other as a medium (cf. Takahashi 1929b, 33). It is only with the help of the analogy between my body and the body of the other that I come to know the

---

habende reflektive Erfahrung sei in Geltung. Nur diese reine *Reflexion* soll mir den Boden geben, auf dem ich sicher stehe und denke, den Boden der reinen Subjektivität. Hier finde ich den Strom reiner Erlebnisse mit ihren reellen und ideellen [=intentionalen] Gehalten" (Hua IX, 192, emphasis added).

[12] The same idea plays an important role in Otaka (see section 3 below).

other mind by way of interpretation (Takahashi 1929b, 35).[13] If pure consciousness is not individual, it would be nonsensical to say that its subject is embodied and thus analogous to an alter, embodied ego.

2.3   How Husserl's Idealism Fails

According to Takahashi, it is thanks to the idea of intersubjectivity that Husserl's phenomenology is closer to Leibniz's monadology than Kant's subjectivism (cf. Takahashi 1929b, 38). In Husserl, the role played by Kantian conscious in general is assigned to the "open multitude [*offene Vielheit*]" of subjectivity (cf. Takahashi 1929b, 39). According to Takahashi, Husserl holds that Kant entirely misses this point.[14]

Despite this, however, Takahashi concludes that Husserl's position is even closer to Descartes.

> With regard to its immediacy and fundamentality, alter ego is not on the same footing as ego. In short, it is nothing more than a modification of ego. Even if all the objective nature and all the other humans are negated, ego would still remain. On this point, we must say, Husserl's phenomenology ultimately coincides to the greatest extent with Descartes. Here lies the reason why phenomenological reduction has to be initiated with egological reduction, no matter how the latter is abstract (Takahashi 1929b, 39).

A similar remark is found also in the beginning of Takahashi's discussion of the intersubjective reduction.

> [A]ccording to Husserl, what is immediately perceivable with evidence is one's individual subjectivity, which is exactly the source of the truly critical and scientific foundation. That

---

[13] It may be disputable whether Takahashi represents Husserl's position correctly, especially when it comes to the tension between his characterizations of empathy as perception and as interpretation. It should be noted, however, that Takahashi relies only on Husserl's lectures he has attended and that, at this moment, he has not read the fifth *Cartesian Meditation* (cf. Takahashi 1931).

[14] Here Takahashi refers to a script or scripts (*hikki*) of Husserl's *Natur und Geist* lectures in 1919 (cf. Takahashi 1929b, 43n16). It remains a mystery how Takahashi obtained the script(s), but this should not be so surprising given that notes from the same lectures, taken by Erna Halle, were circulated in Munich (cf. Briefwechsel III/2, 257) and that Alexander Pfänder made an excerpt of them (cf. Hua Mat IV, XII–XIII). Anyway, thanks to the publication of the lectures in question, now we can confirm that Takahashi gets Husserl's point right. "Es ist klar, dass, was wir Welt nennen, seinen vollen Sinn erst erhält durch Beziehung auf eine unbestimmt offene Vielheit mit uns kommunizierender Subjekte, aus welcher Vielheit jedes beliebige Gegensubjekt austreten, aber auch beliebige neue eintreten können (wofern sie nur Subjekte sind, die in Einfühlungszusammenhänge mit uns treten, deren Leiber als Leiber wir verstehen und die unsere Leiber als solche und als Ausdrücke unserer Erlebnisse verstehen können). *Kant hat merkwürdigerweise das Problem der Intersubjektivität völlig übersehen.* Schon für die transzendentale Ästhetik bedeutet Intersubjektivität eine konstitutive höhere Schicht, ohne deren Berücksichtigung die Konstitution einer Natur als vortheoretische Erfahrungseinheit nicht geleistet werden kann" (Hua Mat IV, 195, emphases added).

is why phenomenological reduction must first and foremost be egological reduction. (Takahashi 1929b, 31).

In this way, the interpretation of Husserl that Takahashi ends up endorsing is controversial and unfavored by today's standard. As recent scholars have emphasized, it is both exegetically and philosophically more plausible that Husserl conceives transcendental subjectivity as *intrinsically intersubjective*; an ego is nothing other than *an ego among alter egos*. According to this reading, the primacy Husserl gives to the egological reduction should be understood as reflecting the fact that intersubjectivity is phenomenologically attainable only as *my* being among others.[15]

It would be uncharitable and unimportant, however, to disparage Takahashi on this point. Uncharitable, because even though he had some privileged access to Husserl's thought by the standards of his time, it was still very limited from our current perspective. He did not read any of the manuscripts form Husserl's *Nachlass* on which the recent scholarship draws. Unimportant, because, as we will see soon, Takahashi's claim that Husserl's real position is not subjective idealism would hold independently of the issue under discussion.

In favor of his interpretation of Husserl as a failed subjective idealist, Takahashi argues that the neutralization of positing a transcendent object does not really amount to the immanentization of that object. There are two reasons for this. First, the alleged immanentization of transcendent objects is incoherent with the very idea of phenomenological reduction (cf. Takahashi 1930, 68). If, as Husserl maintains, phenomenological reflection does not deny anything of our natural attitude, we should be able to reflect on objects of consciousness as something transcendent. Otherwise, our everyday conviction that they are transcendent would be false. Second, the phenomenological reduction does not immanentize transcendent objects but thematically abstracts noemata as their *copies* (cf. Takahashi 1930, 70–73). Takahashi's argument for this claim runs as follows. A phenomenologist deals with objects of pure consciousness as noemata, which are indeed immanent to pure consciousness in so far as they are correlated with noeses. However, since noemata are characterized as meanings, they make up a *sui generis* realm (just like Bolzano's realm of presentations in themselves [*Vorstellungen an sich*] or Rickert's realm of validating values [*Wertgeltung*]). Therefore, noemata are not transcendent objects in the world but abstractions thereof; just as natural sciences abstract nature from the world of everyday experience, phenomenology abstracts meanings from the same world. To put it differently, transcendental phenomenology, contrary to its promise, stops short of genuine transcendence. This is exactly why Takahashi find it unsuccessful for Husserl to defend subjective idealism.

Takahashi further argues that intersubjectivity does not help to achieve Husserl's intended aim, namely, the immanentization of transcendent objects (cf. Takahashi 1930, 74). Since the transcendence of objects has already been shut down by the egological reduction, the intersubjective reduction could not rehabilitate it. "What can be grounded by the latter would just be the objectivity in the sense of commonality or generality, but not transcendence as such" (Takahashi 1930, 74).

---

[15] Further on this line of interpretation, see, for instance, Zahavi (2003, 120–125).

2.4 Assessing Takahashi's Interpretation

Takahashi's interpretation of Husserl seems to be highly controversial for us today. Let us briefly overview two potential objections to his reading. First, Takahashi's interpretation of noema is quite similar to the so-called *Fregean* or *West-Coast* interpretation, against which so many objections have been raised.[16] Both Takahashi and proponents of the West-Coast interpretation are indeed correct in that Husserl characterizes noema as meaning or sense. As some commentators point out, however, this does not mean that Husserl conceives noemata as numerically distinct from worldly, transcendent objects.[17] It must be noted here that Takahashi might agree with such an objection if the issue is about the interpretation of the position that *Husserl wants* to establish. Takahashi would probably not dispute this point. For what he attempts in this context is rather to show how *we should* understand the relevant claims of Husserl (cf. Takahashi 1930, 72). If the problem is framed in this way, the exegetical inadequateness would not be fatal for Takahashi's interpretation of noema (even though it would be a bit misleading to call it an *interpretation*).

Second, Takahashi's discussion of intersubjectivity in this context might also be disputable. For, as we have pointed out, the primacy that Takahashi gives to the egological reduction is questionable. However, even if we follow the current interpretation and admit that Husserl's transcendental subjectivity is intrinsically intersubjective, a question Takahashi raises in this context would remain crucial: Is the transcendence of an object the same as the commonality of it for us? If transcendence implies mind-independence, the answer to this question might be *no*. Indeed, one could further object to Takahashi by saying that Husserl is not operating with such a strong conception of transcendence. His aim, the objection continues, is rather to suggest that transcendence should be understood in terms of the commonality for us (where the range of *us* may be ideally maximized). Such a reply, however, would face another problem pointed out by Takahashi. Would that suggestion, then, conflict with Husserl's insistence that nothing of the natural attitude is denied by phenomenological reduction?

If, as the above consideration suggests, Husserl does not hold a coherent set of ideas when he is discussing his idealism, Takahashi's interpretation of Husserl would gain some support. It would then be a suggestion for what Husserl *should have said* in order to avoid inconsistency. Needless to say, it is another thing whether the suggested position would be *the best*. Be that as it may, Takahashi's reading, according to which Husserl's idealism is fraught with a certain tension or possibly incoherence, certainly touches upon an important issue.

---

[16] For the West-Coast interpretation of noema, see Føllesdal (1968). A more recent version of this interpretation can be found in Smith (2013, 245–273). For objections against this interpretation, see, for instance, Drummond (1990, chap. 5) and Zahavi (2004). Note that we *do not* mean that Takahashi's interpretation of noema is the same as the West-Coast interpretation. There are some important differences between them. For instance, proponents of the latter would not agree with Takahashi's claim that noemata are copies and that they are abstracted from the world.

[17] For an overview of this interpretation, see Zahavi (2003, 59–60; 2004, 48–50).

Before closing the section on Takahashi, it must be noted that, contrary to what one might expect, he is *not* happy about Husserl's failure to immanentize transcendent objects. In the concluding section of "The Possibility of Phenomenological Reduction," he writes:

> I do not only reject the subjective standpoint that Husserl's phenomenology seems to promise, but also radicalize such a subjectivism and maintain that all objectivities lie in the subjective and that noesis encompasses noema. That is, I hold the standpoint of experience-monism [*taiken ichigen no tachiba*]. In my opinion, therefore, every transcendence does not only get grounded by experiences; it also obtains in them. Thus, intentional experiences are not the ultimate experiences but an abstraction from even more original experiences in which they exist. (Takahashi 1930, 78)

It is not our present concern to discuss Takahashi's own version of subjective idealism called "the standpoint of experience as a whole [*taiken zentai no tachiba*]" or "the standpoint of wholeness [*zentaisei no tachiba*]" (cf. Takahashi 1930, 78–84, see also Takahashi 1929a). We mention it only because it makes visible an interesting contrast between Takahashi and the other Japanese student of Husserl under discussion here: Tomoo Otaka.

3   Discovering the World of Meaning With Husserl – Tomoo Otaka

Like Takahashi, Otaka holds that Husserl's position is not really idealist because it deals with noemata or meanings rather than objects themselves. Unlike Takahashi, however, Otaka is happy about this consequence. According to him, Husserl's idealism is in fact a defensible version of *realism*.

3.1   *Otaka's Limited Use of Husserl's Idealism in the 1930s*

The first instance of Otaka expressing his realist interpretation of Husserl with reference to the term *idealism* appears to be in his 1936 *A Theory of the Structure of States* [*Kokka Kozo-Ron*].

> Husserl's phenomenology, in order to ask about the ultimate meaning of the actuality of the world and various objects in it, reduces the transcendent relation between subject and object to the immanent relation in pure consciousness. After the detailed analysis of the structure of pure consciousness, it then dares to understand the obtainment of those objects as an achievement of the collective act of constitution by [the plurality of] interacting transcendental subjectivity. That is, every object, which is first constituted by a single ego as a unity in the manifolds of intentional acts of consciousness, is then gradually brought to objective actuality by being posited as a convergent point for acts of consciousness of many egos. In this way, Husserl's phenomenology takes an idealistic point of view in so far as it finds the grounds of actuality in the constitutive act of transcendental subjectivity. However, such an idealism does not end up with a mere idealism. It has a strong tendency to start off from

actuality and return back to it and thus it aims at synthesizing idealism and realism on a wider scale. (Otaka 1936, 32)

As this passage shows, Otaka shares, to some extent, a view of Husserl similar to that of Takahashi.[18] There are two points of agreement. First, Otaka holds that the phenomenological reduction consists in the immanentization of transcendence.[19] Second, he gives primacy to the egological reduction over the intersubjective reduction.[20]

These similarities notwithstanding, there is also an important point of disagreement between the two Japanese philosophers. As we have briefly mentioned, Otaka, unlike Takahashi, takes it that Husserl's idealism is a sort of realism. Such an idea is stated in more detail in the note appended to the passage quoted above.

Husserl's phenomenology is indeed an idealism in so far as it attempts to solve all philosophical problems with the help of the reduction to pure subjectivity. Nevertheless, unlike previous versions of idealism, it is not opposed to realism. For, while common idealism considers the world of phenomena to be an illusion and finds actuality somewhere beyond it, phenomenology stays with common sense and the empirical sciences, attempting to admit the actuality they ascribe to the world of phenomena. Unlike common sense and the empirical sciences, however, phenomenology does not presuppose the actuality of the world from the beginning. Instead, it attempts to elucidate the grounds for why the actuality of the objective world, about which common sense and the empirical sciences never doubt, can be acknowledged as certain so that they never need doubt it. (Otaka 1936, 35n7)

Takahashi would probably object to Otaka's idea here. If, as Takahashi claims, the phenomenological reduction is merely the replacement of transcendent objects with noemata, phenomenology would, at best, be able to ascertain the actuality of the latter, which are nothing but *copies* of the former. Would this not fall short of the realism of common sense and empirical science? We will come back to this problem in the end of this section.

As far as *A Theory of the Structure of States* is concerned, Otaka himself seems to find it disputable whether the idealist claims he ascribes to Husserl really holds universally: "Now we do not want to decide whether purely actual objects, such as [material] things in nature, or purely ideal objects, such as logical and mathematical

---

[18] We do not mean to claim that Otaka was influenced by Takahashi on this point. Even though Otaka's library includes a copy of Takahashi's *Husserl's Phenomenology* [*Husserl no Genshôgaku*] (Takahashi 1931), in which the two aforementioned articles are collected, there is no trace of reading in it. Given the fact that Otaka was a heavy annotator, we have no good evidence for the claim that he read Takahashi's book closely.

[19] Otaka is committed to this view even more explicitly in his introduction to philosophy of law from 1935. There he holds that, after transcendental (i.e., phenomenological) reduction, which give rise to the immanentization of objects, one finds the correlational opposition between noesis and noema in consciousness (cf. Otaka 1935, 184–186). Essentially the same idea is found also in Okata (1948, 98–99).

[20] In *A Theory of the Structure of States*, Otaka is skeptical about whether *the individual subjectivity first view*, as it were, he draws from Husserl is plausible, claiming that intersubjectivity should rather be put first (cf. Otaka 1936, 36n10; Uemura & Yaegashi 2016, 358–359). As we have pointed out in section 2, however, such an interpretation of Husserl is dismissed by many contemporary commentators.

laws, are achievements of the collective constitution of subjectivity, namely transcendental subjectivity" (Otaka 1936, 33). The problem of the existence of genuine transcendencies, however, does not seriously matter for Otaka here. His main topic in *A Theory of the Structure of States*—the constitutive analysis of actually existing states such as Japan and France—would remain neutral with regard to it. The idea that an actually existing object is just a unity of the manifold of intentional acts, even if it does not hold for things in nature and logical/mathematical laws, would be plausible when its scope is limited to socio-historical objects such as states (cf. Otaka 1936, 33–34). Thus, in the period before the end of World War II, Otaka makes use of Husserl's alleged idealism only for this specific purpose.[21]

3.2   A World of Meaning

It is in the period after WWII that Otaka comes to subscribe to a more comprehensive version of (what he understands as) Husserl's idealism. In his "Metaphysics and Empiricism in Philosophy of Law [*Hô-Tetsugaku ni okeru Keijijô-gaku to Keiken-ron*]" in 1948, Otaka claims that, from a phenomenological point of view, the world is correlated with the *possibility* of experience. His argument for this claim starts from elaborating Husserl's notion of noema (cf. Otaka 1948, 99). When I am perceiving a table in front of me, my perception is under incessant change; it varies depending on my position, angle, and so on. In contrast to such noeses of consciousness, the table I am perceiving remains one and the same. "To put it differently, various noeses of the perception of the table 'intend' the one table as their 'noema'" (Otaka 1948, 99). From this, Otaka concludes that "the table as the noema of consciousness, unlike the acts of noeses, 'actually' *does not appear in consciousness. The table as a whole*, which is the polar point of intentional experiences, is *not visually perceivable*" (Otaka 1948, 99, emphasis added). Here we shall focus on how Otaka sketches his interpretation of Husserl's idealism. His discussion consists of four steps.

First, Otaka points out that we lay "noetic light" only on a limited range of objects. The example he uses runs as follows (cf. Otaka 1948, 100). As I am writing this paper in a barrack in Hongô (the town where the University of Tokyo is located) which is in ruin, what I can see right now are a piece of writing paper, a pen, a table, a tiny room, and some other stuff. Those objects do not appear in their totality in my perception. Rather, "I take them to be there by virtue of my intentional experience of perception. In other words, even an object that is immediately given in our perceptual noeses exists only as a 'noematic core', which is intended by various noeses" (Otaka 1948, 100). That is, since our perceptual experience transcends what is actually given in it, it makes accessible to us things *as wholes*; this is exactly how intentionality functions.

---

[21] For a more detailed reconstruction Otaka's phenomenology of the social in this period, see Uemura & Yaegashi (2016) and Yaegashi &. Uemura (2019, §3).

It is in the second step that Otaka reaches the core idea of Husserl's idealism. Drawing on the insight he has gained in the first step, Otaka writes:

> [E]very object that we think exists objectively is given as a noema. This holds even for objects on which we are shedding light by perceptual noesis right now. Furthermore, needless to say, all the other objects exist only noematically for us. At the same time, this shows that a noema would remain what it is if the noesis that illuminates it disappears. I go out of my house to my office at the university. I know what my office looks like, what it is equipped with, and how books are arranged in it. I always know these things merely noematically. Now, as I arrive at the office, unlock the door, and enter into the room, those objects, the actuality of which I have known only noematically, are taken into my noetic immediate experience. Then, however, the tiny room of my small house and the table in it, which were in front of my eyes 30 minutes before, exist only noematically for me. In this way, *the world in which we live is a world of noematic objects*. (Otaka 1948, 100, our italics)

Since one and the same noema can be intended by many noetic experiences, its existence is not exhausted by its being correlated with *one* (or some) of them. Otaka calls the range of such a single, actual experience "horizon". Therefore, according to him, the world of noematic objects exists regardless of whether it is in the horizon of experience or not. To many readers of Husserl, Otaka's use of the term "horizon" will sound odd.[22] What matters now, however, is not his choice of words but the idea he means to express with them: We know that some objects exist even when we are not actually experiencing them. This is not only plausible but also attributable to Husserl without disputation.

In the third step, Otaka elaborates the idea sketched in the second step into a principle concerning how we know what exists in the world: "What assures us that an object exists is nothing other than the circumstance that this object, which is considered to exist noematically, *can be* taken into our noetic horizon" (Otaka 1948, 101, emphasis added). It is thanks to such a possibility that I usually never doubt whether things I think exist really exist. As he quickly qualifies, this epistemological principle is expanded to the community of subjects.

> Thanks to 'words', we can learn something that others know about the noematic world. Having heard some facts on which they shed noetic light, we can trust them. However, whether I take existent objects into the noetic horizon by myself or I trust the result of the noetic illumination of others, the more often the noetic immediate experiences are performed, the more certain they are. Furthermore, the more people jointly shed light on the same object, the more certain the result of that gets. [...] In this way, we have a common world of noematic objects and, to confirm the actuality of those objects, we always jointly take part in the task of shedding light on them by means of noetic, immediate experiences. Husserl calls the commonality of this noetic-noematic world "phenomenological intersubjectivity". (Otaka 1948, 101–102)

What is remarkable here is that Otaka emphasizes the importance of actual or occurrent (*aktuell*) experiences. Even though our everyday belief in the actuality (*Wirklichkeit*) of things is ascertained by the *possibility* of experiencing them, the

---

[22] According to Husserl himself, to the horizon of an actual given experience, non-actual, potential experiences also belong (cf. Hua I, 81–83). Thus, he famously speaks about the world as horizon or *Welthorizont* (cf. Hua VI, 145–146).

source of such certainty lies in, and is maintained by, experiences that we have *here and now*. This idea plays an important role when Otaka argues that his epistemological principle holds also for scientific knowledge (cf. Otaka 1948, 102). According to him, a scientific claim is true and thus a piece of knowledge only after scientists have confirmed it through experience, and it remains so only while it is confirmed, that is, as long as it has not disconfirmed by some other experiences.

In the final fourth step, Otaka combines the epistemological principle just introduced with the following claim about the intersubjective structure of the world: "Phenomenology takes it that actuality is such a thing [i.e. something that is shown intersubjectively]" (Otaka 1948, 103). The world in which we live, as well as our knowledge of it, is something on which we can (but may fail to in actuality) shed light in experience. Thus, it is within the bounds of the possibility of experience. This is what Otaka has in mind when he is talking about the world of noematic objects. Such an idea, which he draws from Husserl's phenomenology, is certainly idealist in so far as it confines itself to the realm of possible experience.[23] At the same time, it has some realist features in that it *does not* lead to the claim that everything is *in* consciousness. For, as pointed out in the first step, noematic objects, which are objects as wholes, *never* appear in their totality in our experience.

To determine more precisely how Otaka conceives of the synthesis of idealism and realism in Husserl, we must clarify the status of noematic objects. In his 1948 paper, Otaka deals with the world of noematic objects exclusively as the *cultural* or spiritual world as opposed to the natural world. According to him, the cultural world is *a world of meaning* (cf. Otaka 1948, 104–106). His discussion in this context is dense and elliptic, but we can reconstruct its main line as follows, in so far as it is necessary for our present purpose.[24] According to Otaka, we bring things in nature into the cultural world by giving meaning to them. For instance, when we take Polaris as a guidepost, we give the meaning *guidepost* to it and, thanks to this, it is no longer a mere object in nature without meaning. In this way, some things in the cultural world are objects that are made up of natural stuff *plus* meanings. To bring about cultural objects of this sort, we often process things in nature so that we can give them the relevant meanings, as when we are making tools out of some natural materials. Being objects *with meaning*, cultural objects remain longer than individuals who have created them and become sharable for a wider range of people as "noematic 'common goods'" (cf. Otaka 1948, 106). Therefore,

> the world of spirit or culture, in which we live, is a world of "meaning" that is thus created by the joint work of endlessly many individual spirits [i.e., human subjects] and that is thus objectified as noematic common goods. In this way, phenomenology has presented the actual world as a "world filled with meanings". (Otaka 1948, 106).

---

[23] As far as this point is concerned, Otaka captures Husserl's idea very well. See, for instance, *Ideas I* §48 (Hua III/1, 102–103).

[24] The aspect of Otaka's thought presented here is also found in his writings from the 1930s. See Uemura & Yaegashi 2016.

As it should now be clear, for Otaka the world of noema as unities of meaning is a creation of our experiential activity (this amounts to idealism); and its objectivity is exhausted by its intersubjective shareability or commonality (this amounts to realism).

3.3 (Potential) Objections and Replies

In response to Otaka's Husserl-inspired position, two skeptical questions could be raised. First, how can Otaka account for things in nature in his framework? He is not exempt from this question simply by limiting the scope of his claim to cultural objects. For he now holds that "*every* object that we think exists objectively is given as a noema" (Otaka 1948, 100, our italics). Second, even if he manages to deal with things in nature in accordance with his idea, would he thereby really present a version of realism? In the 1948 paper, as well as in earlier works, Otaka holds that Husserl's phenomenology, from which his own position draws, is committed to the realism of common sense and of the empirical sciences.[25] However, that our common sense, naïve belief in the existence of the world, if it is considered from a phenomenological point of view, would amount to the belief that the meanings we have created are sharable by all human subjects, sounds implausible.

To the best of our knowledge, Otaka does not address these questions explicitly. However, the second chapter of his *On Liberty* [*Jiyû-Ron*] (1952), in which he expands on the views presented in 1948, provides us with some notions that could be developed into responses to them. Let us start with reconstructing the response to the *first* skeptical question. Having argued that things in nature are noemata which, as unities in noetic manifolds, do not appear in experience in their totality (cf. Otaka 1952, 62–63), Otaka further explains where this claim ultimately leads.

> Objects that make up the world lie in the realm of noemata, which is apart from the direct noetic illumination. Such a mode of being can be called "being-*qua*-meaning [*imi-teki son-zaisei*]". Objects as noemata are neither visible nor hearable; they are not in memory. Rather, they exist as "meanings". The fact that the being of those objects is being-*qua*-meaning is inseparably connected with the fact that they have their "names". Objects as known by humans are named. [...] We call various things that exists in the world by "common noun", and eventually give them "proper names" if necessary. Without seeing an existing object, one can "understand" it by hearing someone else naming it and explaining its figure, color, size, and other characteristics. *It is nothing other than a meaning, because it can be named and understood through spoken or written language, even though it cannot be captured by senses. All the things that have to do with humans have senses and thus exist meaning-wise for them.* (Otaka 1952, 64–65, our italics)

---

[25] For the realism of common sense, see the following passage: "Phenomenology raises the questions of whether objects we are seeing exist as we see them and whether the world we live in exists as we live in it; and it attempts to give positive answers to them. In this sense, the standpoint is phenomenology is quite obviously 'realism'" (Otaka 1948, 98).

What we have been considering is mainly the structure of the material or physical world. Through this consideration, we know that even objects in the material world do not directly appear to the senses in their noematic objectivity and that every object that is not taken into the horizon of noetic immediate experience is a being-*qua*-meaning, which is named, spoken of with words, and understood through explanation. It is a great achievement of Husserl's phenomenology to have elucidated the fact that even *the material world, which is usually thought to be apprehended by the senses, has the structure as the world of "invisible" meaning* in this way. (Otaka 1952, 68–69, our italics)

It may seem that, in these passages, Otaka brings objects in nature into his framework by regarding them as members of *the world of meaning*, accessible to us by means of language. This is, however, a misleading way of putting his idea. Otaka is *not* claiming that the world of meaning includes the material world or nature *as such*. While the world of meaning is created by humans, the objects themselves that make up the material world exist independent of such creation (cf. Otaka 1952, 70–71).

What is, then, the relationship between things in nature and the world of meaning? One answer that we can certainly ascribe to Otaka is the following. As he points out, humans tend to receive the natural world in a *value-laden* way (cf. Otaka 1952, 71). For them, things in nature present themselves as useful, benefitable, dangerous, harmful, and so on. Humans sometimes worship those objects and even see something supernatural and divine in them. Thus they "take things in nature as stuff, acknowledge human meanings in those things *qua* stuff, and make those material objects into value-objects [*kachi keishô*] beyond the material" (Otaka 1952, 72). In this way, Otaka holds that things in nature belong to the world of meaning in so far as we build certain meanings upon them by conferring values to them.

Such an answer, however, is insufficient if we take into consideration the full picture of Otaka we have been considering so far. It could not account for his claim that objects in nature *as wholes*, which do not appear in perceptual experience, are located in the world of meaning. Arguably, a material object remains one and the same in perceptual experience *not* by virtue of the value humans confer to it.

Even though Otaka does not seem to be aware of this difficulty, we can develop a way out from it for him. As we have seen, when Otaka is discussing objects-*as-wholes*, he talks about language as a door (if not *the* door) to the world of meaning. According to him, those objects-as-wholes are meanings by virtue of their *expressibility*. It is because we can name, speak of, and explain some of the details of, say, a mountain over there, by using words that the mountain-*as-a-whole* has meaning. Taking this idea alone, however, does not lead to a solution to the present problem. The expressibility of the mountain does not seem to explicate how it remains one and the same in manifolds of *perceptual* experience. To save Otaka from the difficulty, therefore, we must resort to a somewhat speculative interpretation. That is, we must ascribe to him the idea that I see an object as something that remained/remains/will remain one and the same before/during/after this particular episode of seeing, because I can *name* it. Given this idea, it would be more appropriate to say that, according to Otaka, in seeing things-as-wholes in nature, we *map* them *onto* the world of meaning; when I am seeing the mountain as a whole in nature, I locate it in the world of meaning.

Without considering whether and to what extent the idea at stake is correct, we shall try to in order to square with the *second* skeptical question. According to our interpretation, Otaka would leave nature as such totally intact, because his reconstructed position has only to do with the world of meaning, which is built on, but distinct from, nature. Then, Otaka's Husserl-inspired idealist claim would stop short of making material objects themselves mind-dependent. This may seem to secure his realist claim as well. However, the situation is not that simple. For, according to our interpretation, Otaka could not talk about the intersubjectivity of material objects themselves but only of the meanings onto which they are mapped. Therefore, *if* Otaka's aim is to defend realism concerning mind-independent material objects, we would have to say that he *fails*. Otaka could not respond to the second skeptical worry properly.

To escape such a conclusion, we must resort to a somewhat speculative interpretation again: Otaka's project, at least as it is presented in *On Liberty*, does *not* aim at defending *phenomenologically* the kind realism that the second skeptical question presupposes, namely realism about nature as a *mind-independent* world of material objects. Then the skeptical concern would not be appropriate when assessing Otaka's *phenomenological* claim; what he is trying to clarify in this context would only be how the world of meaning, which is created by us, is *structured*. On this reading, defending realism phenomenologically would be nothing over and above explicating how things in nature are located in the world of meaning so that they are intersubjectively accessible for us. As far as *On Liberty* is concerned, this interpretation is not so far-fetched. In the second chapter, Otaka begins his discussion by referring to Heidegger's notion of being-in-the-world, and characterizes humans as "world-creating-being [*sekai o tsukuritsutsu aru sonzai/Welt-erzeugend-sein*]" (cf. Otaka 1952, 56–57). We are humans, he would say, only in so far as we are living in the world of meaning that we create. Therefore, it would be no wonder and even natural if his *phenomenological* analysis in that chapter is confined to our human life in the world of meaning, leaving the mind-independent nature out of the scope of phenomenology.[26] Nothing would be wrong with such a limitation, given that phenomenology is an investigation from within our perspective.

To make our interpretation more faithful to Otaka, we must deal with his commitment to the reality of nature *as such* in *On Liberty*. As he repeatedly points out, the world of meaning is something built by humans *on nature* (cf. Otaka 1952, 72–76, 77, 91–92, 96–97, 231). He also remarks that *nature places certain limitations* on the creation of meanings (cf. Otaka 1952, 131–132). Those claims would be unintelligible without a mind-independent nature, which is, however, beyond the scope of phenomenology. Here we should bear in mind that this would lead to an incoherence only on the assumption that every philosophical claim can and must be

---

[26] Here we can take into consideration Crowell's (2015) claim that phenomenology as transcendental philosophy focuses on meaning. But we should not understand Otaka's position solely in accordance with such a picture, because Otaka's conception of meaning does not coincide with Crowell's. Whereas Crowell conceives meanings as the *modes of givenness* of objects, Otaka maintains that meanings are something we create in the cultural world of meaning.

made *within* the limits of phenomenology. If this assumption is dropped, it would be possible to hold the realism in question for some *non*-phenomenological reasons while retaining the Husserlian phenomenological idealism when it comes to the world of meaning. Now, since Otaka often expresses his commitment to the reality of a mind-independent nature, it is plausible that we should drop the above assumption in interpreting him. If this is true, Otaka would have to claim that Husserl fails to pursue his original project of transcendental phenomenology, which encompass *all* the philosophical problems within its field (cf. Hua V, 141).

4   Conclusion

Herein we have reconstructed how Takahashi and Otaka react to Husserl's idealism. In closing, let us summarize the outcomes of our discussion with a short remark on a problem that their reactions have in common.

According to Takahashi, Husserl's idealism fails to be subjective idealism, because it fails to immanentize transcendent objects. Rather, he claims, what Husserl could achieve is only a substitution of transcendent objects with noemata as their copies. Otaka would agree to a certain, limited extent, with Takahashi. Otaka also claims that noemata do not belong to the world of material objects. But the agreement between Takahashi and Otaka is only partial. There are at least two important differences. First, for Otaka, noemata are not copies of material objects in nature; they are meanings that humans build on the world of material or physical objects. Second and even more importantly, Otaka would not talk about Husserl's failure to establish subjective idealism. Given our discussion above, we can conclude that what Otaka understands as Husserl's idealism is *not idealist at all*. For Otaka, Husserl's position is compatible with realism concerning a mind-independent nature.

We have not focused on whether and to what extent Takahashi's and Otaka's interpretations of Husserl are correct. It seems difficult to defend Takahashi's interpretation in its entirety because it rests on the often-criticized idea that noemata are numerically distinct from worldly objects. Precisely for the same reason, Otaka's interpretation of Husserl also faces a serious exegetical problem. One might wonder why they share this problematic view on noema. Most likely, this is because they both understand Husserl's characterization of noemata as *meanings* under the assumption that meanings make up a *sui generis* realm. As we discussed, Takahashi mentions Bolzano's presentations in themselves and Rickert's validating values in discussing Husserl's noemata.[27] Likewise, when Otaka is dealing with noemata as meanings, he seems to draw on the conception of culture or spirit [*Geist*] as a realm

---

[27] In this respect, Takahashi's interpretation could be regarded as a variation of the early reception of Husserl that situates the founder of phenomenology in the context of Hermann Lotze and Bolzano (cf. Varga 2018, 109).

of meanings, which is opposed to nature.[28] It seems natural for the two Japanese philosophers to adopt such an assumption against the background of the then contemporary philosophy: Bolzano's semantic objectivism, South-West Neo-Kantianism, and *Lebensphilosophie*. Against such a backdrop, it would not be surprising that they interpret Husserl's noemata as something numerically distinct from objects in nature. In other words, *if* Takahashi's and Otaka's interpretation is flawed, that would show how Husserl's conception of noema was novel and, perhaps, revolutionary in his time.[29]

References

Altobrando, A. & Taguchi, S. (2019). "Introduction. On the Originality and Fruitfulness of the Encounter between Phenomenology and Japanese Philosophy." In S. Taguchi & A. Altobrando (Eds.), *Phenomenology and Japanese Philosophy*, Cham: Springer.

Cairns, D. (1976). *Conversations with Husserl and Fink*, Den Haag: Nijhoff.

Crowell, S. (2015). Phenomenology and Transcendental Philosophy. Making Meaning Thematic. In S. Gardner & M. Grist (Eds.), *The Transcendental Turn* (pp. 244–263). Oxford: Oxford University Press.

De Warren, N. (2015). Concepts without Pedigree. The Noema and Neutrality Modification. In A. Staiti (Ed.), *Commentaries on Husserl's Ideas I* (pp. 225–255). Berlin/Boston: De Greyter.

Føllesdal, D. (1968). Husserl's Notion of Noema. *Journal of Philosophy* 66/20, 680–687.

Galileo (2008). *The Essential Galileo*. Edited and Translated by M. Finocchiaro. Indianapolis: Hackett.

Haga, M. (1988). Kleine Begegnung. In H. R. Sepp (Ed.), *Edmund Husserl und die Phänomenologische Bewegung. Zeugnisse in Text und Bild*, (pp. 17–19). Freiburg/München: Alber.

Husserl, E. (Hua I; 1950). *Cartesianische Meditationen und Pariser Vorträge*. S. Strasser (ed.). The Hague: Martinus Nijhoff.

Husserl, E. (Hua III/1; 1976). *Ideen zu einer reinen Phänomenologie undphänomenologischen Philosophie. Erstes Buch. Allgemeine Einfuhrung in die reine Phänomenologie*. K. Schuhmann (ed.). The Hague: Martinus Nijhoff.

Husserl, E. (Hua IV; 1952a). *Ideen zu einer reinen Phänomenologie und phänomenologischen Philosophie. Zweites Buch. Phänomenologische Untersuchungen zur Konstitution*. M. Biemel (ed.). The Hague: Martinus Nijhoff.

Husserl, E. (Hua V; 1952b). *Ideen zu einer reinen Phänomenologie und phänomenologischen Philosophie. Drittes Buch: Die Phänomenologie und die Fundamente der Wissenschaften*. M. Biemel (ed.). The Hague: Martinus Nijhoff.

Husserl, E. (Hua VIII; 1959). *Erste Philosophie (1923/24). Zweiter Teil. Theorie der phänomenolo- gischen Reduktion*. R. Boehm (ed.). The Hague: Martinus Nijhoff.

---

[28] In *A Theory of the Structure of States*, Otaka appeals to such a split between nature and spirit, which he ascribes to Dilthey (cf. Otaka 1938, 103). Note, however, that he does not mention Husserl's noemata in this book.

[29] As De Warren observes, being introduced for an entirely new science called transcendental phenomenology, "the noema is an experimental concept in the making over which Husserl never gained complete mastery" (De Warren 2015, 230). This is why our remarks here are only provisional, leaving intact so many controversial issues concerning noema.

Husserl, E. (Hua IX; 1962). *Phänomenologische Psychologie. Vorlesungen Sommersemester 1925.* W. Biemel (ed.). The Hague: Martinus Nijhoff.

Husserl, E. (Hua XIV; 1973). *Zur Phänomenologie der Intersubjektivität. Texte aus dem Nachlass. Zweiter Teil: 1921–1928.* I. Kern (ed.). The Hague: Martinus Nijhoff.

Husserl, E. (Hua XXXII; 2001). *Natur und Geist. Vorlesungen Sommersemester 1927.* M. Weiler. Dordrecht: Kluwer.

Husserl, E. (Hua Mat IV; 2002). *Natur und Geist. Vorlesungen Sommersemester 1919.* Michael Weiler (ed.), Dordrecht: Kluwer.

Nitta, Y., Tatematsu, H. & Shimomisse, E. (1978). Phenomenology and Philosophy in Japan. In Y. Nitta & H. Tatematsu (Eds.), *Japanese Phenomenology. Phenomenology as the Transcultural Philosophical Approach*, (pp. 3–17). Dordrecht/Boston/London: Reidel.

Mutai, R. (1964). Ryugaku Jidai no Takahashi Satomi-san [Mr. Satomi Takahashi in his Studying Abroad]. In R. Mutai, *Shisaku to Kansatsu*, Tokyo: Keisô Shobô,1968.

Nishida, K. (1992). *An Inquiry into the Good.* M. Abe & C. Ives (trs.), Yale University Press.

Otaka, T. (1935). *Hô-Tetsugaku* [Philosophy of Law]. Tokyo: Nihon Hyôron Sha.

Otaka, T. (1936). *Kokka Kozo-Ron* [A Theory of the Structure of States]. Tokyo: Iwanami Shoten.

Otaka, T. (1938). Husserl-sensei no Eisei [The Passing-away of Professor Husserl]. *Hôristu-Jihô* 10 (8), 29–3

Otaka, T. (1948). Hô-Tetsugaku ni okeru Keijijô-gaku to Keiken-ron [Metaphysics and Empiricism in Philosophy of Law]. *Hô-Tetsugaku Shiki-hô* 1, 90–113.

Otaka, T. (1952). *Jiyû-Ron* [On Liberty]. Tokyo: Keisô Shobô.

Takahashi, S. (1912). Ishiki-Gensho no Jijitsu to sono Imi [Facts of Conscious Phenomena and their Meaning]. Reprinted in *Takahashi Satomi Zenshû*, vol. 4 (pp. 153–182), Tokyo: Fukumura Shuppan, 1973.

Takahashi, S. (1929a). Taiken Zentai no Tachiba [The Standpoint of the Experience as a whole]. Reprinted in *Takahashi Satomi Zenshû*, vol. 1 (pp. 84–96). Tokyo: Fukumura Shuppan, 1973.

Takahashi, S. (1929b). Husseru no Genshôgaku. Toku ni sono Genshôgaku-teki Kangen ni tsuite [Husserl's Phenomenology. On his Phenomenological Reduction in Particular]. Reprinted in *Takahashi Satomi Zenshû*, vol. 4 (pp. 5–44), Tokyo: Fukumura Shuppan, 1973.

Takahashi, S. (1929c). Husserl no Koto [On Husserl]. Reprinted in *Takahashi Satomi Zenshû*, vol. 4 (pp. 139–150). Tokyo: Fukumura Shuppan, 1973.

Takahashi, S. (1930). Genshôgaku-teki Kangen no Kanôsei [The Possibility of Phenomenological Reduction]. Reprinted in *Takahashi Satomi Zenshû*, vol. 4 (pp. 45–84), Tokyo: Fukumura Shuppan, 1973.

Takahashi, S. (1931). *Husserl no Genshôgaku no Jo* [Preface to *Husserl's Phenomenology*]. Reprinted in *Takahashi Satomi Zenshû*, vol. 7 (pp. 241–243). Tokyo: Fukumura Shuppan, 1973.

Takahashi, S. (1932) *Husserl no Genshôgaku* [Husserl's Phenomenology], Tokyo: Daiichi Shobô.

Takahashi, S. (1962). Gakusha o Okoraseta Hanasi [A Story about How I Made Some Scholars Angry]. Reprinted in *Takahashi Satomi Zenshû*, vol. 7 (pp. 209–223). Tokyo: Fukumura Shuppan, 1973.

Tanabe, H. (1924). Genshôgaku ni okeru Atarakishi Dôkô [A New Movement in Phenomenology]. Reprinted in *Tanabe Hajime Zenshû*, vol. 4, Tokyo: Chikuma Shobô, 1962.

Tani, T. (2013). Reading and Rereading the *Ideen* in Japan. In *Husserl's* Ideen. eds. L. Embree & Th. Nenon (pp. 19–34). Dordrecht/Heidelberg/New York/London: Springer.

Usui, J. (1984). Ryûgaku Jidai no Omoide [A Memoir of My Study Abroad]. *Tetsugaku Kenkyû* 550: 609–617.

Schuhmann, K. (1977). *Husserl Chronik. Denk- und Lebensweg Edmund Husserls.* The Hague: Nijhoff.

Smith, D. W. (2013). *Husserl*, London: Routledge.

Uemura, G. & Yaegashi, T. (2016). The Actuality of States and Other Social Groups. Tomoo Otaka's Transcendental Project? In H. B. Schmid & A. Salice (Eds.), *The Phenomenological Approach to Social Reality* (pp. 349–379). Dordrecht: Springer.

Varga, P. A. (2018). Husserl's Early Period. Juvenilia and the *Logical Investigations*. In D. Zahavi (Ed.), *The Oxford Handbook of History of Phenomenology*, (pp. 107–134). Oxford: Oxford University Press.

Yaegashi, T. & Uemura, G. (2019). Otaka Tomoo's Conception of Sovereignty as Nomos. A Phenomenological Interpretation. In S. Taguchi & A. Altobrando (Eds.), *Phenomenology and Japanese Philosophy*, Cham: Springer.

Zahavi, D. (2003). *Husserl's Phenomenology*, Stanford: Stanford University Press.

Zahavi, D. (2004). Husserl's Noema and the Internalism-Externalism Debate. *Inquiry* 47/1: 42–66.

Author Index

© Springer Nature Switzerland AG 2021
R. K. B. Parker (ed.), *The Idealism-Realism Debate Among Edmund Husserl's
Early Followers and Critics*, Contributions to Phenomenology 112,
https://doi.org/10.1007/978-3-030-62159-9

Subject Index

A
Absolute existence, 14, 16, 17, 137,
    177–179
Abyss (*Abgrund*), 43, 199, 210, 211, 213
Anthropology, 104–105, 109, 113, 271

B
Being-in-the-world, 14, 112, 145, 146,
    265, 268–273, 276, 278, 279,
    288, 300
Being-*qua*-meaning, 298, 299

C
Cartesian doubt/skepticism, 17, 225, 286
Categorial intuitions, 18, 267, 274–278
Certainties, 146, 165, 167, 262, 297
Cognitions, 75, 79, 80, 83, 85, 90, 96, 102,
    103, 106, 109, 111, 139, 144, 155,
    162–164, 181, 199, 201, 211, 223,
    226–229, 233, 234, 237
Consciousness of reality
    (*Wirklichkeitsbewusstsein*), 15, 136,
    141, 142, 145–147
Constitution, 19, 57, 68, 69, 85, 86, 169, 208,
    210, 211, 228, 240, 244, 245, 248, 257,
    264, 277, 293, 295
Constructions, 102, 103, 105, 111, 114, 154,
    179, 265, 276
Correlationism, 5, 6

D
Descriptive psychology, 2, 29
Dialectics, 78, 100, 104, 105, 111, 114, 179, 197
Drives, 82, 213

E
Egological reduction, 286, 287, 290–292, 294
Egology, 289
Eidetic description, 225
Eidetic intuition, 58, 61, 100, 220, 224, 226,
    227, 231, 250, 277
Empathy, 147, 226, 227, 289
Essences, 2, 17, 18, 56, 58, 64, 76–79, 81–85,
    88, 91, 92, 94–96, 105, 107–110, 113,
    144, 146, 154–157, 159–166, 168, 177,
    178, 185, 195, 196, 204–206, 208–210,
    213, 220, 223–227, 229–231, 233–236,
    243, 246, 247, 249–258, 265, 266, 272,
    274, 276–279
Essential intuition (*Wesensanschauung*), 76,
    160, 185, 225
Evidence (*Evidenz*), 8, 15, 75, 137, 145, 160,
    165, 169, 174, 181, 183, 184, 186, 189,
    190, 211, 221, 222, 236, 269, 275, 290
Existences, 2, 4, 6–9, 13, 18, 56, 58, 59, 64,
    82, 86, 89, 100, 103, 112, 137, 146,
    161, 178, 179, 181, 183, 184, 186, 188,
    194, 200, 202–211, 225, 228, 231, 237,
    247, 256, 265, 266, 271, 272, 276, 277,
    279, 289, 295, 296, 298

© Springer Nature Switzerland AG 2021
R. K. B. Parker (ed.), *The Idealism-Realism Debate Among Edmund Husserl's
Early Followers and Critics*, Contributions to Phenomenology 112,
https://doi.org/10.1007/978-3-030-62159-9

CPSIA information can be obtained
at www.ICGtesting.com
Printed in the USA
LVHW081529030922
727559LV00003B/72